Marketing

3rd edition

David Stokes

conti
LONDON •

Continuum

The Tower Building	370 Lexington Avenue
11 York Road	New York
London SE1 7NX	NY 10017-6503

www.continuumbooks.com

First edition published 1994
Second edition published 1997

000602

British Library Cataloguing-in-Publication Data
A catalogue record for this book is available from the British Library.

ISBN: 0-8264-5680-4 (paperback) 0-8264-5858-0 (hardback)

Typeset by YHT Ltd, London
Printed and bound in Great Britain by Martins the Printers, Berwick upon Tweed

Also available in the series:

Fundamentals of Hospitality Marketing: Steve Mawson
Marketing for Schools – 3rd edition: David Evans
Marketing: Principles and Practice: Tom Cannon
Small Business Marketing Handbook: Iain Maitland
Tourism Marketing: Eric Laws

658.8/STO

Dedicated to Sue, Andrea, Bryony, Kim and Kit

CONTENTS

Dr DAVID STOKES

Dr David Stokes is a Principal Lecturer and Assistant Director of the Small Business Research Centre at Kingston Business School, Kingston University. Educated at Oriel College, Oxford and the City University Business School, he has had wide experience of marketing in both the private and public sectors in a career involved in the management of both large and small enterprises. The subject of his PhD thesis was the development of marketing practices in public sector primary schools during the 1990s. As well as teaching marketing at a popular business school, he is actively engaged in developing marketing strategies for a number of medium-sized companies. Currently, he is chairman of the Academy of Marketing's special interest group in marketing and entrepreneurship. He is also author of *Small Business Management* published by Continuum.

PREFACE

PURPOSE OF THIS BOOK

The purpose of this book is to provide a course of study that engages the reader in both the practice and the theory of marketing. It aims to enable the reader to discover marketing principles through both their own experiences and their reflections on what happens around them, supported by information on the main theories of the subject.

As an introductory text, it can be used in the classroom by students following full- or part-time business and management courses at university or college. It is also suited to those studying at home as part of a distance learning programme or for their own interest and self-development. The material in the book has been developed from the teaching of, and feedback from, marketing components in HND, BA (Business Studies), Certificate in Management, Diploma in Management Studies and MBA courses as well as workshops and seminars for practising managers.

'NOT ANOTHER MARKETING BOOK?'

There are many publications that cover the same theoretical ground as this book. *Marketing 3rd edition* aims to fill a need by being different in three main ways:

❑ The reader is encouraged to actively learn from a series of short case studies before theories of marketing are presented. In this way, practical examples aim to stimulate the reader's comprehension, rather than rely on a passive absorption of information.

❑ The book presents material which applies established marketing principles to a wide variety of contexts. The text draws on cases and examples from the non-profit as well as the private sector, from small as well as large enterprises, and from services and industrial markets as well as the traditional areas of consumer marketing.

❑ Principles of marketing are presented concisely, recognising that many readers wish to gain an overview of the subject as quickly as possible, before studying particular aspects in more detail, or because their business management specialisation lies in other fields.

APPROACH

The book is structured around an active learning approach. Although a considerable amount of information is presented in the text, the aim is to impart skills and knowledge by engaging the reader in interesting activities and exercises which build on existing experiences and understanding. Marketing is ideally suited to this approach because we experience and witness it consciously or unknowingly most days of our lives. The primary focus of marketing is on customers and their needs, and we are all customers with needs. Therefore we can draw on our own experiences as consumers in a wide range of contexts to develop and check our understanding of marketing theory and see how it is applied in practice. We can use our experiences as a shopper to develop a better understanding of retail marketing. We can reflect on our own use of education and health services to understand better the marketing of services in the public sector. We are all exposed to advertising and packaging messages and can think of those that influence us and those that have less impact. If we have access to the Internet, we can make our own judgments on the implications of this latest development on marketing. Marketing activities are going on around us all the time from market surveys in the high street to mail shots received at home, and they all offer an opportunity to learn about marketing.

STRUCTURE OF THE BOOK

The book is divided into chapters with the following structure:

❑ *Case study*: each chapter begins with a short case to provoke consideration of the topics of the unit. Activities at the end of each case study are designed to develop understanding of specific sections of the chapter and help lines direct the reader to these sections.

❑ *Text and examples*: the main text of each chapter explains marketing theory by a summary of the key principles followed by examples of how they can be seen working in practice. These examples are drawn from a wide context to reflect the penetration of marketing activities well beyond its original base in fast moving consumer goods.

❑ *Key points*: a summary of the main topics covered is given towards the end of each chapter.

❑ *Developing marketing skills*: the reader is invited to use their own personal experiences in a series of exercises which reflect on the subject matter of the unit. One exercise – 'Developing a marketing plan' – follows the sequence of creating a marketing plan for a product or service chosen by the reader. Recommendations are also given for further reading on the topic of the chapter.

Chapters 1 to 12 cover the basic principles of marketing, from market research to marketing communications and selling. Chapter 13 considers the implementation of marketing in different contexts including small businesses, the non-profit sector and the Internet. Chapter 14 contains further case studies that illustrate the various contexts of marketing decisions.

An appendix at the end of the book gives some self-test questions and examples of possible examination questions so that the reader can confirm their understanding of the chapters.

HOW TO USE THIS BOOK

This book can be used as a work book with the help of a teacher or lecturer in the classroom, or as the basis of unsupervised work at home, or a mixture of both.

However used, the cases, activities and exercises are the basis for the learning process. It is recommended that the book is used in the following way:

❑ First read the short case at the beginning of each unit. These describe a particular scenario and ask the reader to draw conclusions about marketing principles from it.

❑ Attempt the activities at the end of each case. If necessary use the help line to sections in the text to complete the activities, but first try to develop answers independently of the text. If you can discover marketing principles for yourself by observing them in practice you are more likely to fully understand and appreciate the theory.

❑ Complete your reading of the text and the examples.

❑ Undertake the exercises at the end of each unit. These exercises are designed to develop and confirm your understanding of theory by personal experimentation and practice. Although it may be tempting to move on to the next chapter, it is important to attempt some of the exercises in the 'Developing marketing skills' sections. Preferably, undertake the ongoing exercise of developing a marketing plan in stages at the end of each unit. (This is summarised below.)

❑ When you have completed working through the units, test your understanding by using the appendix of self-test and examination questions at the end of the book.

DEVELOPING A MARKETING PLAN

A regular exercise at the end of each unit is headed 'Developing a marketing plan'. This ongoing activity is designed to build into a marketing plan around a product or service of your choice. The first activity asks you to choose a product or service as the subject of the plan, the second activity designs the structure of the plan, and so on. The titles of the activities are as follows:

1. Preparing for marketing

2. Planning for marketing

3. An internal audit

4. An external audit

5. A SWOT analysis

6. The research plan and implementation

7. The marketing strategy

8. The product strategy

9. Pricing strategy

10. Planning the marketing communications

11. An advertising, sales promotion and PR strategy

12. The distribution strategy

13. Forecasting and controlling the marketing plan

As each of these activities relates to the topic of the chapter, it provides a useful ongoing exercise to underpin your work through the book.

ACTION LEARNING

In summary, to get the most out of this book follow an action learning cycle:

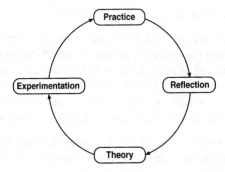

- ❏ *Practise* marketing as an outside observer by considering first the case at the beginning of each unit which describes an aspect of marketing in action.

- ❏ *Reflect* on what this reveals about marketing through the activities at the end of the case.

- ❏ *Theorise* about the principles of marketing as described in the main text and the examples given of marketing in practice.

- ❏ *Experiment* through your own personal experiences in the exercises at the end of each unit.

- ❏ *Practise* what you have learned through the ongoing exercise of developing a marketing plan. (You can also practise your understanding of the book through the self-test and examination questions in the appendix.)

CHAPTER 1

What is Marketing?

Marketing is an elusive term. It describes both a management strategy focusing on customer satisfaction, and a series of functions such as advertising, product development, selling and market research. This chapter introduces the concept of marketing by exploring basic marketing principles, and comparing them to alternative approaches. It looks at the development of marketing, its adoption by various sectors of our economy and the impact of the Internet. It concludes by examining some of the concerns expressed about the effectiveness of some marketing strategies and their potential social effects.

1   CASE STUDY: METROPOL ZOO

Note to reader: case studies such as this are designed to help you 'discover marketing' by giving you the opportunity to observe and consider principles in practice through a specific scenario, before reading about them in the more generalised context of the sections which follow. It is recommended that you read the case study, and consider the issues that it raises as you read the appropriate sections of the chapter.

Metropol Zoo had reached a crisis point in its long history as one of the world's leading zoological gardens. Despite a growth in the number of people making visits to other attractions, the city-centre zoo had seen a steady decline in the number of its visitors in recent years. In 1991 the zoo attracted over 1 million of the estimated 15 million visitors to the city through its gates; ten years later, this had fallen to under 800,000 of 20 million city tourists. Traditional attractions such as the Metropol Museum had revamped their image with innovative, inter-active exhibits whilst new, purpose-built, themed attractions added to the visitor's choice. Competition for the family day-out had intensified with the development of many exciting adventure parks within an hour's travel time of the city. The image of the zoo was tainted by environmental concerns stimulated by animal rights activists who continued to protest about the captivity and exploitation of wild animals. Falling attendance had coincided with a reduction in the amount of public funds available to the Zoo as both central and local government had reduced their grants and subsidies.

A new strategy was needed to deal with the deteriorating financial position that now threatened the very existence of the zoo. Some out-of-town zoological gardens had successfully developed fun parks alongside their animal enclosures but Metropol Zoo's position in the heart of an already overcrowded city ruled out this option. Now a radical new proposal had been put forward for consideration by the directors of the zoo which used virtual-reality technology to create exciting wild life scenes and adventures within the space limitations. The removal of the stock of large caged animals would make room for a series of simulators and interactive exhibits. These showed animals in their natural environment in ways which the zoo could not normally re-create, and even more importantly, put the visitor in the role of participator and not just observer. Virtual-reality expeditions simulated not only animal habitats but also exciting experiences such as white water rafting or ballooning as the visitor explored the great outdoors. Computer games allowed participants to choose survival strategies in a variety of hostile environments from deserts to jungles whilst lion attacks could be experienced from the perspective of the herd of deer.

The proposals had split the Directors of Metropol Zoo into two opposing camps. One group led by the Finance Director, Alan Grover, argued that the changes would transform the commercial viability of the zoo because they met customer needs more closely. The opposing lobby led by the Director of Conservation, Jane Rose, claimed they would be selling out to short-term market forces when the public would support the long-term conservation work of the zoo if it was properly publicised.

'I hope my presentation has illustrated some of the excitement as well as educational value which our latest equipment can now offer to your visitors. For this is certainly what customers want in a world where fantasy adventures are increasingly dominating the entertainment market whether in books, films, television programmes, computer games or simulated events.' Robin Jollop, the salesman from 'Visionary', a company marketing virtual-reality equipment, sat down at the end of his presentation to the Directors of Metropol Zoo. Despite their divided opinions on the proposals, the Directors were all clearly impressed by the capabilities of computerised graphics and sensory effects.

'Your technology is very impressive – congratulations.' It was the chairman, Sir Ralph Daines, who spoke first. 'But our expertise lies in conservation not computerisation. Zoological gardens have always been a sanctuary for the natural world, an escape from the latest developments of society. These new products do not seem to play to our strengths at all.'

'No, but they complement them,' replied Jollop. 'You have the knowledge and understanding of the animal kingdom. These machines can help you demonstrate it to people who are confined to concrete jungles for 90 per cent of their lives. With these new technologies we can go on safari for the day and experience other worlds without leaving our own. It's what the customer needs – a convenient and inexpensive way of experiencing nature.'

'But it's not the real thing at all. People are not experiencing nature through your products. They are experiencing another man-made imitation of it.' Jane Rose couldn't contain her disagreement any longer. 'And imitations are not what people want any more. We have moved away from artificial ingredients and additives in many of our products – in food and body care products for example – and we are increasingly demanding natural products and ingredients. It's the same with animals. Our customer surveys tell us that over 60 per cent of people still want to see the big cats and elephants in zoos before they disappear altogether.'

'Yes, but people never know what they want until it is presented to them,' said Grover. 'This marketing idea of asking people what they need just doesn't work in practice. If you had asked a Victorian what they wanted to travel around in during the day and entertain them at home in the evening, they would not have mentioned a car or a television set. Very few people know the possibilities of the technology we have just seen. So what's the point in trying to find out what people want when they don't know what is possible?'

'If you are saying that we should ignore public opinion which we believe is ill informed I would agree with you. That's exactly why we haven't given in to pressures from these so-called environmentalists who claim to stand for animal rights. Without us some of these animals wouldn't have an existence at all.' The chairman re-entered the fray on a favourite theme.

'But opinion, however ill informed, is on their side. Look at our falling gate receipts as the proof. We have no choice but to adapt to the times,' said Grover. 'This new technology is not going to disappear. I visited one American national park where you can watch wildlife films on giant wrap-around screens at the entrance.'

'And how long is this particular fad going to last?' asked Rose. 'Just because computer graphics and a few gimmicks have awakened people's imaginations, it doesn't mean we have to jump on this particular bandwagon. We are being asked to change our entire policy on breeding and keeping animals in captivity. This is not something we can turn off and on like a tap just because fashions in entertainment shift temporarily. We are a public service, not a product that can be sold like a Hollywood movie. I am sure we can put our case as conservationists, not exploiters of animals and attract our visitors back again with some positive publicity.'

Jollop, the salesman from Visionary, listened unmoved as the debate intensified around him. He knew that, whatever they decided, the customer was always right.

Points to consider

1. Give the directors your advice on their future marketing strategy. Which approach best represents the marketing concept of identifying and satisfying customer needs?

See sections 2 and 3.

2. There are alternative approaches, or 'business orientations' to customer orientation. What alternative orientations are illustrated here?

See section 4.

3. Do you think Jane Rose is right in saying that marketing a zoo is not the same as selling a Hollywood movie?

See section 5.

4. What criticisms of the marketing concept are illustrated in this case? How would you answer them?

See section 6.

5. The directors are considering new attractions made possible by advances in technology. In what ways could other technological developments, such as the Internet, help?

See section 6.

2.	THE MARKETING CONCEPT

If a cross-section of the public were asked to give an instant definition of the word 'marketing', their responses would vary. Some associate it with 'advertising', 'selling' or 'research', others with 'making profits' or 'finding out what people want'. A few might have less favourable images seeing it as 'getting people to buy something they don't really want'. Marketing can be all these things except, hopefully, the last.

The reason for this diversity of meaning is that marketing is both a management philosophy and a function in an organisation. As a philosophy it insists that an organisation is focused on the needs of customers. As a function it includes activities which affect customers such as pricing, advertising, selling and market research. In this sense it can represent both the *strategy* and the *tactics* of an organisation.

❑ As a *strategy* which gives an overall direction to an organisation, marketing ensures that the concept of satisfying customers is a common theme throughout all policies and activities.

This is sometimes referred to as the *'marketing concept'* which, if adopted, means that an organisation sees the customer as central to everything it does. All activities are driven by what the customer needs. It is based upon the premise that no company or institution can exist for very long without customers. A business does not survive unless someone regularly purchases what it has to offer. Even a non-profit organisation, such as a public service or a charity, cannot justify its existence without its equivalent of 'customers'; a college needs students and a hospital exists to help patients, for example. Accepting that organisations cannot exist without customers, the marketing concept gives them the key role in determining strategy. Customers are consulted on what their needs really are, and products or services developed to meet those needs.

❑ As a *tactic* that can be employed on a day to day basis by an organisation, marketing includes functions that directly affect customers such as research, product development, distribution, pricing, selling and advertising. These functions are referred to as the *marketing mix*, a group of interrelated management techniques and activities aimed at understanding and influencing customers.

● *Marketing has been defined as: 'the management process responsible for identifying, anticipating and satisfying customer requirements profitably' (UK Institute of Marketing). This definition of marketing as a management process revolving around customer requirements can be illustrated by the changes in fortunes of many well-known companies. For example, Marks and Spencer became one of the UK's most successful retailers by continually adapting to changes in customer needs, but ran into trouble when they ignored this basic principle. The original concept of meeting the need for a wide range of products offering exceptional value for money was developed in the late nineteenth century by Michael Marks who sold a range of low priced goods on market stalls with the advertising slogan: 'Don't ask the price, it's a penny'. His son Simon Marks with partner Israel Sieff continued the same theme of value for money when they took over the business from 1915 but they developed new ways of fulfilling it. The low overheads of the market stall were exchanged for the buying advantages of bulk purchases as they rapidly expanded into a large company of many stores. Perceiving that their customers' main requirement at that time was for a wider range of affordable clothing, M & S adopted a price limit of 5 shillings per item in the late 1920s. However Simon Marks recognised that customer needs were never static when in the 1930s he described successful retailing as involving 'constant alertness and study of the changing habits, desires and tastes of the consumer'.*

By the 1960s, Marks & Spencer had used this understanding to shift their appeal away from a reliance on low price to an additional insistence on offering only goods of the highest quality. They implemented this policy through rigorous quality control methods and demonstrated their faith in what they sold by offering immediate refunds or exchanges for any faulty items. In 1993, as other retailers began to deliver equivalent levels of quality, the new chairman Sir Richard Greenbury stated a need for improved service levels to complement their quality and value for money philosophy: 'Providing friendly and efficient service for an increasingly discerning and demanding customer is a top priority.' The numbers and knowledge of shop floor staff were increased to implement this latest interpretation of customer needs.

But expansion into overseas markets and internal power struggles over who was to run the company distracted directors' attention away from the market place. The company began to lose touch with key customer groups. By the late 1990s, M&S's mainstream customers, women over 35 years old, expected fashion as well as value-for-money and quality. The company's own brand, St. Michael, began to lose its appeal as newer, designer labels became widely available. As sales growth slowed and profits dropped, the board announced its intentions to 'refocus the company towards the customers'. They set up a 'Customer Insight Unit' to understand the shopping habits and demographics of their customers. In 2000, the new chairman, Luc Vandervelde overturned M&S's traditional policy of selling only under the St. Michael trademark and introduced new ranges such as Autograph designer collections, Salon Rose lingerie and Count on Us reduced fat foods, reflecting the company's perceptions of how consumer needs had changed. Their web-site offered the option of ordering products directly over the Internet. Appointments of high profile designers to key posts was further evidence of a new emphasis on fashion. In 2001, they sub-contracted not only the manufacture but also the design of a new range of women's clothes to George Davies, the founder of the Next chain of stores. Consumers' verdicts on these changes are still uncertain, but M&S's past success story and recent need for drastic action illustrate both the benefits of focusing on customer needs and the dangers of complacency in interpreting them.

3.	THREE PRINCIPLES OF MARKETING

Three ideas are fundamental to the marketing concept:

❑ Customer orientation

❑ Organisational integration

❑ Mutually beneficial exchange.

Customer orientation

If an organisation focuses itself first and foremost on the needs of customers then it is *customer-oriented*. There are alternative orientations which companies can adopt as we will explore later. Customer-oriented organisations centre their strategies and activities on the needs of the marketplace as expressed by actual and potential customers. Such companies strive not just for more sales but *customer satisfaction* in all that they do. They want 'customers who come back and products that don't'.

There are usually several stages to achieving this aim:

❑ *Finding out what customers want or anticipating what they will want.* This is normally done by regular communications with consumers in the marketplace by a variety of means ranging from formal market research to informal conversations and contacts.

❑ *Fulfilling the perceived needs of customers.* The identification of customer requirements is followed by the mobilisation of resources to fulfil those needs. The perceived needs of the marketplace are translated into products or services.

❑ *Monitoring progress towards satisfying customers.* By encouraging a continuous flow of reactions from the marketplace, organisations can check the extent to which they are satisfying customers.

❑ *Improving customer satisfaction.* Customer orientation implies a continuous effort to improve existing levels of satisfaction and the flexibility to change in line with shifts in customer needs.

These stages represent a management process that continuously identifies customers' needs, translates them into products, evaluates satisfaction with those products and improves them as necessary. It is this evolutionary aspect of marketing which has lead companies like Marks & Spencer to shift their interpretation of customer needs over the years and pay the price if they fail to do so. Figure 1.1 illustrates this process of customer satisfaction.

• *The start-up of a new business can illustrate this process in action. For example, some customer-oriented entrepreneurs decided to open a restaurant. They found there was a need for a fast-food style restaurant (there were none in their local area despite the popularity of such restaurants in other geographic markets with a similar population profile). They fulfilled this need by equipping premises, employing staff, buying supplies and opening the restaurant. They*

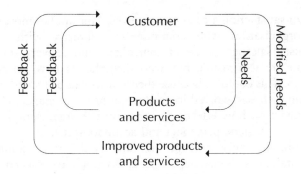

Figure 1.1: *The process of customer satisfaction*

monitored the response of the marketplace by talking to customers and placing a suggestions-box in the restaurant. In reaction to comments made, they improved the standards of customer service in the restaurant and modified their menu. They evaluated satisfaction with these changes and made further modifications as necessary. As marketing entrepreneurs, they had learned the principle of adapting their plans according to the changing needs of their customers.

Long-term customer relationships

Customer orientation usually implies establishing and maintaining *long-term* customer relationships. One-off sales from a large number of buyers are usually less beneficial than developing the loyalty of a smaller group of customers over a period of time. The advantages of keeping customers so satisfied that they remain loyal include:

❑ It costs more to attract new customers than to retain existing ones.

❑ A satisfied customer recruits new ones by making recommendations to their friends and acquaintances.

❑ A satisfied customer is less likely to shop around when considering a repeat purchase.

❑ Customers are more likely to buy other products or services from a company they have already bought from.

Organisational integration

Marketing is an overall business philosophy, a way of doing things as well as a set of management techniques. So it has to permeate the entire organisation. Everyone in the organisation has to understand the marketing concept if it is to be a guiding principle behind all activities. The marketing department cannot implement the concept of customer satisfaction alone. It has to be integrated into all levels and all functions of an organisation from the chief executive to the receptionist, and from the sales department to service delivery or production areas.

The reason for this is straightforward. Everybody in an organisation can affect the level of satisfaction a customer receives. This applies most obviously to anyone in the organisation who communicates directly with customers, such as receptionists, salespeople, credit controllers, and delivery staff. It also applies to those who are less visible but who nevertheless have an impact on customer satisfaction. This could be because their efforts can be judged directly by customers (for example, those involved in production or maintenance) or because their work has an impact on how effectively others in the organisation can serve customers (for example, trainers, personnel and accounts staff).

In Figure 1.2 this principle is illustrated for a company organised on departmental lines. Some departments do not have the customer as a natural focus for their day to day activities, because they have little direct communication with the marketplace. Nevertheless, they are an integral part of customer satisfaction, like a spoke in a wheel revolving around the hub of customer needs. If they fail to function in line with customer needs, they can have the effect of a broken spoke, causing the wheel to buckle and not run true.

- *Imagine yourself as a customer of the restaurant described in our previous example. What will influence your level of personal satisfaction from a visit? It is likely to be a combination of factors including the service of the waiting staff, the quality and variety of food prepared by the kitchen staff, and your impression of the environment as influenced by the cleaning and maintenance staff. If there are problems behind the scenes then you are likely to feel the impact without necessarily understanding the cause. For example you could be irritated because your favourite menu item is not available and complain to the waiter. You would not be aware that the problem was caused by a bookkeeper*

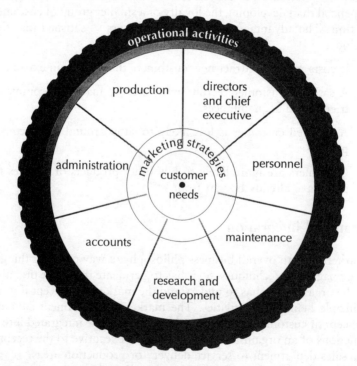

Figure 1.2: *The organisational marketing 'wheel'*

who overlooked some payments to suppliers who in turn refused to deliver some vital ingredients. It is not just the entrepreneurs who established the restaurant who need to be customer oriented.

New information and communication technologies are influencing the development of marketing in many ways, as we will discuss later. One of the less obvious ways is through improvements to the internal communications of an organisation. Employees now have instant access to each other and customer information via email and intranets (internally linked computer systems). Customer enquiries and contacts can be handled efficiently through computerised systems providing instant access to relevant information.

Mutually beneficial exchange

The marketing concept cannot be a one-sided process in which the customer is the only winner. The organisation that serves the customer has to gain too.

It seems only logical to ask customers what they want and then provide it for them. However this 'customer is king' approach has to be balanced to make sure that the king does not turn into a tyrant. Customer needs cannot be met at any price. An organisation has needs too, varying from the need to suitably reward its employees and shareholders to requirements to reinvest in new products or equipment and to conform to the law of the land. These place constraints of two main types on an organisation's ability to deliver what customers want.

❑ *External constraints* can limit an organisation's power to serve its customers. For example, we all want goods at lower prices but inflation or high rates of interest may force businesses to continue to raise prices to survive. Public services may be unable to meet all the demands of their users because of financial or political constraints. Society may justifiably impose constraints on how far organisations can go to satisfy individual customers (for example, restrictions on buying alcoholic drinks for certain age groups).

❑ *Internal constraints* also influence an organisation's ability to meet customer preferences. The aims and objectives of a business may preclude it from certain markets. The strengths and weaknesses of an organisation indicate which customers the organisation is capable of satisfying and those that it is not. Successful companies in fact tend to target their activities towards what they know they are good at, avoiding markets where they have less to offer.

• *Marks and Spencer have always regarded their strengths to lie in retailing. From the beginning they avoided any direct involvement in manufacturing even though this was a function which vitally affected their customers' levels of satisfaction. However their philosophy has been to influence how items are made rather than manufacture them for themselves, leaving the actual production to specialist organisations.*

In this way, marketing acts as a *link* between suppliers and consumers. A supplier has certain abilities and potential to provide goods and services; consumers have certain desires and needs. Marketing is the process that brings the two together by matching the capability of a company or organisation with the needs of customers.

The result is an *exchange* that should benefit both parties. In the commercial world this means:

❏ the company receives payment and some profit to meet future customer needs;

❏ customers receive benefits that satisfy their wants.

This represents a balancing act between the needs of the customer and the goals of an organisation as represented in Figure 1.3.

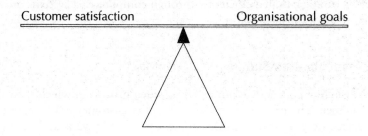

Customer satisfaction   Organisational goals

Figure 1.3: *The balancing act*

- *The aims of the entrepreneurs who set up the restaurant were to make money and enjoy the task of running their business. Customers were happy and came back for more. However although the restaurant satisfactorily filled a need, it did not meet the objectives of the entrepreneurs. Its location in a very small town meant that the number of potential customers was relatively small. Recession in the economy and high, local unemployment caused a drop in custom that could not be countered by service improvements and marketing tactics. As the business began to lose money most of the pleasure for the owners was replaced by worry. With their personal goals no longer being met, the entrepreneurs decided to close the business and turn away even their satisfied customers. Customer satisfaction and organisational goals were not in balance.*

4. ALTERNATIVE CONCEPTS

Organisations do not always focus primarily on the needs of the customer. There are alternative concepts or 'orientations' that have been called:

❏ *The production concept* (or production orientation) in which emphasis is placed on the efficiency of production before consumer choice.

❏ *The product concept* (or product orientation) which focuses on the quality of the product or the possibilities of technology as a first priority.

❏ *The service concept* (or service orientation) which emphasises the specialist nature (and sometimes the jargon) of the particular service on offer.

❏ *The sales concept* (or sales orientation) which emphasises the techniques of marketing, particularly selling techniques, rather than the overall philosophy.

These concepts are discussed below.

The production concept

In his book, *Wealth of Nations*, Adam Smith looked at the economic systems of his era (the late eighteenth century) and wrote:

> 'Consumption is the sole end and purpose of all production; and the interest of producer ought to be attended to, only so far as it may be necessary for promoting that of the consumer ... But in the mercantile system, the interest of the consumer is sacrificed to that of the producer; and it seems to consider production and not consumption as the ultimate end and object of all industry and commerce.'

Adam Smith recognised the key role that the consumer ought to play. But he also saw that at a time when the industrial revolution was just beginning, industry was more concerned with improving production efficiencies than with making what customers wanted. Producers were 'production oriented' rather than consumer oriented, adopting the 'production concept' as their basic philosophy.

The *production concept* assumes that markets need products to be made available in large quantities at the lowest possible price. Producers should therefore standardise products as much as possible in order to increase production and benefit from the economies of scale made possible by higher throughput.

Such a concept is useful if demand for a product is greater than supply. Availability through increased production then becomes the first priority. This was the case for many goods in Europe immediately after the Second World War and in the former communist 'Eastern Bloc' countries, where shortages were common. It can also be beneficial when the costs of manufacturing and distributing a product put it beyond most pockets.

In this case the rationale might run as follows:

❑ This new process means that we can speed up our production and produce much more of this product.

❑ At the moment this is a luxury item as it is expensive and only a few people can afford to buy it.

❑ If we produce more, we can cut the costs of each item produced.

❑ This means we can reduce prices so much that many more people can afford it and we can sell our extra production.

❑ However it will only be cheaper if we don't interrupt the production process which means we must have one standard product.

❑ This will reduce customers' choice ... but if we don't do it this way they couldn't afford it and then they would have no choice at all.

This was the logic behind many aspects of commerce during the industrial revolution. New automated looms reduced the price of cloth and made more of it available to wider markets. But standardisation of production meant that less types of weave and colour were produced than had been made previously by small-scale craft workers. Later on, the development of the automobile began as an expensive hobby for the rich because of the high costs of producing each car individually. Henry Ford amongst others changed all that by concentrating on less choice and the higher production efficiencies of standardised products. Their philosophy, epitomised by Ford's famous comment that customers could have any colour providing it was black, made sure that the car rapidly became available to more and more people.

This philosophy has also been the justification for the creation of large monopolies. If production or the provision of services is concentrated, then economies of scale will operate to produce lower prices. In many markets it can now be seen that competition provides even greater stimulus to lower prices with the added benefit of greater consumer choice and influence. However there have been many examples where concentration of resources has initially favoured consumers. For example, the introduction of a uniform postal system in Britain in 1840 meant that for the first time a letter could be sent anywhere in the country for a standard price (one penny for a 'Penny Black'). Previously postal services had been fragmented and much more expensive with the receiver of a letter paying the charge calculated on a per-mile basis.

Production orientation may have originally made possible the widespread availability of some products and services, but, increasingly, customers now demand products that are more tailored to their individual needs.

The product concept

'Product oriented' organisations focus their efforts primarily on producing better products of higher quality and with more features. It is assumed that customers always want improvements to the specification and features of the products they buy before other considerations.

The logic of the argument might be as follows:

❑ Customers are always looking for better products with higher performance and quality.

❑ Technological developments make it possible to improve our product if we devote the resources to it.

❑ This will give us a competitive advantage as customers want improved products.

❑ We should therefore direct all our resources towards producing a better product as we will automatically sell more.

Organisations based on a philosophy of product orientation thus devote their energies to continuous improvements to existing products or the design of the 'ultimate' advanced product. Such organisations are sometimes successful because there is sufficient demand for their product developments.

However there can be problems in this approach:

❑ Product improvements may be desirable but not at the expense of other ingredients in the marketing mix such as pricing or reliability. Better performance may increase prices to a level at which many customers are not prepared to pay. Concorde was a technological breakthrough in passenger flying. Unfortunately the operating costs made it a service which only a very few could afford and the social costs of noise pollution to the environment restricted it to a small number of routes. Other improvements to product specifications may be at the expense of reliability.

- *The history of the British motor car industry contains many examples of vehicles with higher specifications than their rivals, but which were outsold in world markets because the increased performance was at the expense of reliability. In the 1970s, the Triumph Stag's design and specification were heralded as breakthroughs for high performance saloons. Unfortunately its unreliability, compared to cars like BMW with adequate but less advanced engineering, made it less popular. BMW went on to become market leader in the performance saloon category, whilst Triumph has all but disappeared.*

❑ Immediate demand for new products or features is not guaranteed just because they become technologically possible.

- *Many advanced features have been incorporated into video recorders such as the facility to programme recording requirements up to a year in advance. However, research has shown that consumers rarely use these functions and do not know how to carry out many of the operations of which their equipment is capable. In response to the problems of this product-led development, some manufacturers have introduced products that are simpler to use, including all-in-one television/recorders.*

❑ Focus on improving one particular way of doing things may blind a producer to possible substitute products which may fulfil the same need in a different way. Organisations can develop 'tunnel vision' by assuming customers need developments to existing products when really they need a better way of performing the same job, regardless of the product.

- *Typewriters were the standard way of reproducing one-off documents such as letters on paper. Many large companies including IBM and Remmington continuously invested in developments to give their customers better products such as the introduction of electric typewriters and later the 'golfball' typing head. Their efforts were concentrated on improving the typewriter and they overlooked a better way of achieving the same end. Newcomers to the market transformed 'typewriting' into 'word-processing', particularly after the introduction of personal computers.*

Whilst product improvements may seem desirable, they are not always the best method of meeting customer needs.

The service concept

The 'product' of some organisations is not a physical object but an intangible service that may involve specialised knowledge or skills. The delivery of some services involves a very specialised understanding of disciplines such as accountancy, law and medicine, or of trades such as carpentry, plumbing and typesetting. As professions are based on a high degree of specialisation it follows that those outside of the profession have less knowledge and depend on those within the profession to specify and deliver the appropriate service. This can lead to misinterpretations of demand by the professionals whose in-depth knowledge may blind them to what is really required.

The logic of the service-oriented argument may run as follows.

❑ My fellow professionals and I are the specialists in this field with many years of detailed experience behind us. It is our responsibility to deliver a service of the highest possible quality.

❑ It is up to us to define the quality and type of service which we provide as those that use our services do not understand it as well as we do.

❑ Criticisms of what we do are usually based on ignorance. After all we are trying to deliver the best possible service and only we know how best to do it.

❑ Customers should therefore trust us to do the best possible for them, and stop complaining.

Whilst in most instances, professionals identify correctly the type of service a particular customer requires, in some cases they may be blinded to real needs by their specialist knowledge. This orientation around the service may for example lead accountants to produce complex and detailed reports full of accurate information that unfortunately is meaningless to managers who are meant to be guided by them.

Lawyers produce legal agreements which may seem faultless to fellow lawyers but which are incomprehensible to those who have to implement them. For example, a company may have an agreement (or licence) to manufacture another company's patented product. The terms of the agreement may be understood by the solicitors who drafted it, but not necessarily by the managers responsible for implementing the production process.

Monopolies may encourage services to focus inwardly rather than outwardly towards the customer. In the public sector, services such as education and the health service are delivered to customers who may have little choice in what they receive. Whilst the professionals who deliver such services may believe they always act in the best interests of their users, customers can have other views which tend to be suppressed in deference to the specialist knowledge of the professional. As a result, opportunities to improve services may be missed because of the lack of proper consultation between deliverers and users. Recognition of this problem has lead to attempts to address it such as the appointment of more parents as school governors and the use of surveys of patients' satisfaction in hospitals.

The sales concept

Some organisations concentrate on selling and promoting, using some of the techniques of marketing, without adopting the overall philosophy of responding to real customer needs. The focus of sales oriented companies is on how to sell their existing products or services, rather than on finding out what they should offer in order to meet customer requirements more closely. The sales concept assumes that the existing products or services of the organisation meet most customer needs and that sales or promotional techniques are all that is required to increase acceptance and demand.

The reasoning behind this philosophy might be as follows:

❑ The product we are offering does fulfil a need. It's just that the customer doesn't realise it yet.

❑ Customers are naturally resistant to purchasing, especially when it involves changing to different products.

❑ Our job is to overcome this resistance by 'educating' the customer in the benefits of our products.

❑ It is justifiable to use the latest sales and promotional techniques as these help the customer to make a decision that we know is in their best interests.

Problems in this approach include:

❑ The product or service on offer does not meet customer needs. The producer has misread the market place and is now selling something that is out of step with demand.

- *This approach is not limited to physical products. It can often be seen at work in politics, for example when a political party decides what it thinks is best and then attributes widespread opposition to 'presentation' problems. This in turn justifies the use of sophisticated public relations exercises attempting to 'sell' the policies to an unwilling public. Both Conservative and Labour governments have run into problems using such tactics to sell unpopular taxation changes. In the early 1990s, Margaret Thatcher's government introduced the now notorious 'poll tax'. Opposition was put down to a lack of understanding that would disappear when the benefits of the new tax over the old system of rates were felt in practice. The answer was an intensive campaign to sell the new system that was only finally scrapped when it became obvious that this approach was not working. Tony Blair's government had similar problems in 2000 when mounting discontent over increases in the price of fuel culminated in a blockade of petrol depots. Although the disruptions were officially put down to the activities of a vocal minority, the government recognised more widespread discontent by reducing duties on some fuels.*

❑ The real usefulness of a product is well below the expectations (or claims) of the organisation selling it. The limited acceptance of the product or service only encourages the seller to convince wider markets of the 'necessity' of their offering. This is a particular problem when the sale is of a 'one-off' product (one that is unlikely to be repurchased). As the seller does not depend on repeat purchases, they can be less concerned with how their product lives up to the claims made for it, and spend more time finding the next sale.

- *Sellers of one-off products (e.g. time-share holiday apartments) can be particularly tempted into using high pressure sales techniques to overcome what they believe to be 'natural' resistance but which in reality represents a more fundamental objection to purchasing. This has lead to government intervention to insist that contracts for the purchase of certain goods and services such as insurance policies contain clauses enabling customers to cancel their agreement within a certain period of time.*

❑ When individuals or organisations do not have access to the most suitable products they adopt a sales orientation to sell what they have available. Sales people may be tempted to pose as 'consultants' offering 'solutions' to fit customer needs when, in reality, they have only one product or range to sell.

Organisations are sometimes forced to adopt this position because superior products or services are not available to them.

- *The Xerox Corporation of America and their UK partners Rank Xerox successfully excluded other companies from selling plain paper office copiers for many years because of their protective patents. Competitors were forced to sell copiers using coated paper, often overcoming resistance to this inferior product by using hard sell techniques. These companies acknowledged the inferiority of what they were selling by switching to plain paper copiers as soon as the Xerox patents expired.*

Whilst a sales orientation may overcome short-term problems caused by surplus or obsolete stocks it does not provide long-term solutions to customer needs. It therefore tips the balance towards meeting organisational objectives at the expense of the customer.

A summary of the marketing concept and alternative orientations

The marketing concept, oriented around customers, and alternative orientations that organisations can adopt are summarised in Figure 1.4.

It is interesting to note that an organisation's aims do not necessarily change with its orientation. These are alternative strategies for achieving the same objectives. The growing popularity of the marketing concept has come about because it has worked. More and more successful companies have adopted a marketing orientation, particularly as competition has increased. Large and small organisations in diverse sectors including the not-for-profit and public sectors are also recognising the benefits of this approach.

Orientation	Focus	Methods	AIMS
Production	Production efficiency	Higher volumes and lower costs through standardisation and centralisation	
Product	Product improvement	Customer benefits through advanced products and features	**Increase profits (private sector)**
Service	Service delivery	Develop specialist skills and knowledge	**Improved provision of services (public sector**
Sales	Sales volume	Use promotional techniques to sell more existing products and services	
Marketing	Market needs	Fulfill customer needs, aligned to own strengths for mutually profitable exchange	

Figure 1.4: *Alternative orientations*

5. THE DEVELOPMENT OF MARKETING

The need for marketing strategies

The concept of marketing is as old as commerce itself. Exchanges of goods and services between different members of society were made easier by the development of a marketplace – literally a place where people could meet and trade their surpluses for items they needed. As the numbers of transactions increased, merchants arrived to simplify the exchange process by providing a centralised buying and selling point. They provided a service that helped those with a surplus – something to sell – trade with those who had a shortage – a need to buy.

These merchants, whether they operated in the ancient bazaars of the Middle East, the medieval cities of the Mediterranean or the shops of Victorian England, based their trade on understanding what the buyers in the marketplace wanted and knowing where to get it at the right price. To fulfil their role in society, they had to be 'customer oriented'.

Why do modern organisations need marketing strategies and specialist managers to implement this basic principle which earlier traders instinctively understood?

❑ *Companies and other organisations have become more remote from the customer because of their size.* Economies of scale made possible by the industrial revolution meant that businesses became bigger. As organisations grew they developed layers of management to run them. This removed key decision-makers at the top of the management structure from direct contact with the marketplace and the customer. The merchant's intuitive understanding of demand, arising from regular customer contact, could not be gained from a remote boardroom. Marketing has developed techniques such as market research to overcome this deficiency.

❑ *The complexity of modern business may distract attention away from the customer.* Modern managers work in an environment subject to a complicated mixture of forces and influences. Employees, suppliers, government, financial institutions, unions, competitors, potential competitors, not to mention bosses, all compete with the customer for management time and attention. The customer is often forgotten in the urgency of dealing with immediate problems.

❑ *Systems and policies can create inflexible organisations unable to respond quickly to changes in customer needs.* Organisations need policies and systems to deal with their increasingly complex environment. Efficient work needs order not chaos around it. Unfortunately order can also create inflexibility. Established ways of doing things are often difficult to change. However, customer preferences are constantly changing and require adaptable organisations to keep up with them.

❑ *Many more products and services are now possible than are needed.* The development of technology and information has created endless possibilities for new products and services. Translating these possibilities into products with a viable demand is an increasingly difficult task. As there is a surplus of invention, modern marketing techniques are needed to predict and support the winners in the marketplace.

These influences represent forces that increase the chances of customer needs being ignored or misread. The increased number of potential products and services that can be made available to customers has increased the possibility of errors in making those choices. The development of large organisations working in complex environments has increased the chances of customers being disregarded or misunderstood by those aiming to serve them. The discipline of marketing has developed in order to counter these influences which lessen the chances of correctly interpreting customer preferences.

The historical development of marketing

Although marketing can be said to have originated with the development of surpluses within an economic system and therefore with the beginnings of trade itself, it has only developed into a formalised management concept in relatively modern times. The adoption of the concept has been gradual, its influence not being felt equally in all parts of our economy. Some sectors have embraced its principles before others.

Since the 1950s the sequence of adopting marketing principles in the UK has approximately followed the pattern outlined below:

❑ *Consumer packaged goods* were the first to be marketed using modern techniques. Unilever, Proctor and Gamble, and Mars were amongst the earliest companies to see the benefit of marketing their fast moving consumer goods (fmcg) such as cereals, soap powders and confectionery.

❑ *Consumer durables* such as washing machines, record players, cameras and television sets soon followed, marketed by companies like Hoover, Electrolux and Philips.

❑ *Industrial products*, particularly in office equipment and supplies became more widely marketed in the 1960s as companies such as Rank Xerox and Letraset followed the example of the consumer marketeers by developing differentiated, branded products in business-to-business markets.

❑ *Industrial commodities* felt the influence of marketing later as organisations such as British Steel and British Coal fought for survival in highly competitive markets by using marketing strategies to target their production.

❑ *Consumer services*, such as financial services, adopted marketing principles as their role in the economy grew and competition increased. For example, banks and building societies have fundamentally changed their services to be more in line with consumer demand. However, marketing approaches had to be adapted to suit the context of intangible products. Services marketing focuses more on the development of longer-term relationships with customers, rather than immediate transactions (relationship marketing is discussed further later in this section).

❑ *Small businesses* became an increasingly significant part of developed economies from the 1970s and 1980s. Whilst understanding the need for customer focus, many owners of smaller firms have neither the inclination nor the resources for formalised, mass marketing campaigns. Instead, they have developed an entrepreneurial-style of marketing in which personal contact and word-of-mouth recommendations play an important part.

❑ *Professional services* are now marketing their organisations more actively. Professions such as accountancy and law have been opened up to more competition, and partners have begun to recognise that marketing has a role to play not only in attracting new business but also in helping to ensure the satisfaction of existing clients.

❑ *The not-for-profit sector* has also adopted marketing strategies. Charitable organisations have long been recognised as leading exponents of direct marketing in their appeals for funds. Political parties use market research and advertising agencies to guide their election planning.

❑ *Public sector* managers have become influenced by marketing principles. The decentralisation of resources and authority in public services such as hospitals and schools has enabled them to become more responsive to the needs of individuals as 'customers'. Headteachers have to consider the marketing of their schools in order to maintain or increase the flow of funds which are now allocated on a per student basis.

❑ *The Internet* has created new opportunities for marketing in all industries and market sectors. It has spawned a new sector of companies that trade on-line. It has given existing businesses fresh ways of communicating with customers via web-sites or email. In an age of large, global markets, it has enabled organisations to become more accessible to individual customers. Whilst much of the publicity surrounding the Internet has involved consumer marketing organisations such as Amazon and lastminute.com, the most rapid development of Internet applications has been in business-to-business markets. It is estimated that 85 per cent of e-commerce transactions are currently between businesses, whilst only 15 per cent involve domestic consumers.

Over the last half-century or so, marketing has developed away from its roots in large companies selling fast moving consumer goods. Small businesses increasingly recognise the benefits of marketing in their struggle to survive and prosper. Political parties are now presented to us like many of the products we buy. Towns market themselves to attract tourists, industry and events such as the Olympic Games. The increasing competition for jobs has brought marketing to the level of the individual as applicants market their services to employers. Entrepreneurs can market goods and services immediately and inexpensively to an international audience via the Internet.

6. THE MARKETING DEBATE

In this way, managers in diverse sectors of the economy have adopted marketing practices. But the spread of marketing has raised some concerns. The development of the marketing concept has generated a debate in two key areas:

❑ Are traditional marketing principles still effective in the newer contexts in which they are being applied?

❑ Are there potentially harmful social effects in marketing activities, especially when applied to sensitive areas such as education and health?

Is marketing effective in all contexts?

Management critics have raised important questions about the development of marketing:

Does the concept apply in all market conditions?

Is it appropriate to use the marketing concept in all markets – for example, in industries where technology is changing so rapidly that customers cannot keep sufficiently up-to-date to express informed preferences? New products such as personal computers were not developed because market research indicated a strong need but because innovators made them possible. In other markets the specialist is always going to be better informed than their customers; how far should accountants, solicitors and teachers go in meeting their customers' requirements if they believe they are misinformed or misguided, for example?

- *For example, in some markets customer preferences can change rapidly, but the lead-time for new product development is much longer. Consumer preferences for wine have shown many fluctuations in recent years as the pre-eminence of the traditional European growers has been challenged by newer tastes from California, Australia and South America. Unfortunately for established vineyard owners who may wish to respond to the competition with new products of their own, a new vine can take five years from planting to producing a drinkable crop. In that time consumer tastes may have moved on again. How can suppliers meet customer needs in these circumstances?*

Does customer-orientation discourage longer-term investment and originality?

Market research among potential consumers is unlikely to have come up with many of the key modern inventions (e.g. electricity, telephones, radio, television and the world wide web) because they were unimaginable before they were invented. Research and development based only on customer preferences is likely to be risk-free and lead to modifications to existing products rather than radically different concepts. Most people are more able to visualise improvements to products with which they are familiar than to visualise totally new ones. Breakthrough concepts and products are the province of the dreamer or innovator who is prepared to step into the unknown. Marketing on the Internet has been driven largely by new companies, not established ones. The leading dot.com consumer marketing companies, Yahoo!, eBay and Amazon are new ventures.

Concerns such as these imply criticism for a *market*-oriented, rather than a customer-oriented, approach. As we have seen, the marketing concept recognises that the strengths and needs of an organisation have to be taken into account as well as the requirements of customers. A traditional vineyard may have to rely on its long established reputation for quality rather than make changes to accommodate every new whim of the market. Managers may be tempted to ignore organisational expertise and needs in an effort to meet short-term customer requirements at all costs. But the marketing philosophy looks for solutions that will be of long-term benefit to the consumer. This includes encouraging innovations that are too advanced for most consumers to visualise but still meet a known need. However it is true that existing organisations do become over-focused on the way things are, rather than on the way things could be. It is sometimes left to visionary entrepreneurs to create the innovations that meet customer needs more closely than existing products and services. Manufacturers of traditional vacuum cleaners refused to accept James Dyson's concept of the bag-less machine. He had to prove that his new product met customer needs more closely, by successfully selling his breakthrough product himself.

Does traditional marketing place too much emphasis on the transactions of buying and selling products rather than building relationships with existing and potential customers?

Modern marketing had its origins in fast moving consumer goods where the emphasis was on moving tangible products rapidly through the distribution chain to targeted, yet anonymous, groups of consumers. The shift in our economy towards services, rather than manufactured products, means that longer-term relationships between sellers and buyers have become more significant than the actual moment in which a transaction takes place. The marketing of consumer services tends to rely more on the building of goodwill between the parties involved than the promotion of specific products. In industrial, or business-to-business markets, the building of long-term relationships through personal contacts is often more important than taking a specific order. Hairdressers, accountants and directors of advertising agencies often take their clients with them if they change company because the relationship is more important than the organisation. Several influential marketing commentators have criticised traditional 'transactional marketing' and expressed a need for a different type of *relationship marketing*. One of them summed up this emphasis as follows:

> *'Marketing can be seen as relationship management: creating, developing and maintaining a network in which the firm thrives. A new approach to marketing stresses the building of relationships rather than the promotion of products.'*
> (Gummesson, 1987)

The concept of 'customer relationship management' (CRM) adopts this relationship focus in order to provide products and services tailor-made to individual preferences. Electronic commerce can provide organisations with a wealth of data on individual customers through computerised transactions, loyalty schemes and tracking devices on the Internet. This information can be used to customise products and services more closely to customers' specific needs. For example, buyers can specify the exact configuration and features of the computer they require and order it directly from manufacturers such as Dell Computers who assemble made-to-order PCs.

What are the social effects of marketing?

Marketing has been seen as symptomatic of some of the problems in a modern capitalist society. It has been accused of:

❑ encouraging consumption at the expense of the environment;

❑ stimulating individual desires and greed and disregarding the need to be of service to others;

❑ brainwashing gullible consumers into buying products and services which they do not really need or want;

❑ facilitating the sale of shoddy or otherwise undesirable goods;

❑ inflating prices because of excessive expenditure on advertising and promotion;

❑ encouraging competition at the expense of the common good.

These concerns have been partly responsible for the emergence of consumerist and environmental movements attempting to prevent the exploitation of both people and the planet.

The supporters of marketing point out that it has lead to a number of benefits to society:

❑ a wider choice of affordable goods;

❑ efficiencies and lower prices through economies of scale and competition in the market place;

❑ effectively communicating what is on offer from suppliers;

❑ developing the notion of serving others through the concept of serving customers.

'Societal' marketing

The criticism remains that by following the notion of consumer sovereignty, marketing can disregard the wider needs of society. Marketing may bring together suppliers and customers whose needs are both met but sometimes at the expense of other members of society. For example, oil companies have met customer requirements for a range of energy products but at the expense of environmental damage to even those societies who have not directly benefited from the cheap, accessible energy sources.

For this reason, the concept of *societal marketing* places a third element into the balance between supplier and customer needs – the longer-term needs of society. The concepts of conventional marketing have been expanded to include these three elements:

❑ customers' short-term wants and long-term needs;

❑ organisational needs in the long as well as the short term;

❑ world society's interests and welfare.

Although there are still many pressures and temptations to make short-term profits from short-term consumer requirements, there is evidence that organisations are

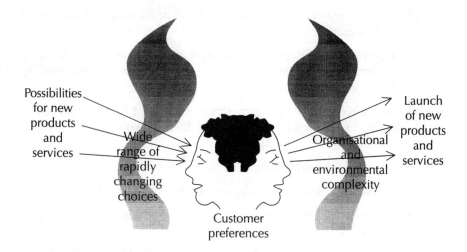

Possibilities for new products and services

Wide range of rapidly changing choices

Customer preferences

Organisational and environmental complexity

Launch of new products and services

Figure 1.5: *The balancing act of societal marketing*

increasingly developing strategies which include longer-term considerations of the needs of their customers and the welfare of society in general.

The development of the concept of 'relationship marketing' emphasises long-term relationships in the business environment aimed at developing goodwill even at the expense of short-term transactions that acquire customers.

- *The Body Shop, one of the UK's most innovative retailers, based its customer appeal on a concern for the environment. Its body care products are developed from 'natural' substances, packaged in environmentally friendly, recyclable containers. Employees are encouraged to take time off for voluntary service in the community. Founder Anita Roddick uses company resources to support endangered societies in South America, and research into sustainable business activities. As well as the usual Annual Report to shareholders, the Body Shop reported on its non-commercial achievements in a 'Values Report' which judged its performance against social and environmental criteria. Since its first shop opened in Brighton in 1976, the company has heavily influenced the development of the body care market by appealing not only to customers' cosmetic needs but also their social needs to express concerns for the environment.*

7. KEY POINTS

❑ Marketing is both a management *philosophy* which determines the strategic orientation of an organisation, and a *function* involving a series of techniques such as advertising, selling and research.

❑ As a management philosophy, the marketing concept represents a strategy involving three basic propositions:

- ❑ *customer orientation* – the primary focus of the organisation is on the needs of the customer;

- ❑ *organisational integration* – everyone in the organisation accepts and implements a customer orientation. It is not just the responsibility of the marketing department;

- ❑ *mutually beneficial exchange* – there has to be a balance between the needs of the customer and the strengths of an organisation so that both customer and organisational needs are met.

❑ Alternative orientations which can be adopted include:

- ❑ *production orientation* – focusing on the efficiency of supply;

- ❑ *product orientation* – stressing the highest possible product specification and quality;

- ❑ *service orientation* – emphasising the expertise of the service deliverer;

- ❑ *sales orientation* – using sales techniques to sell what is available.

❑ Although the basic principles of marketing are as old as trade itself, it has developed rapidly as a body of knowledge since the 1950s, with successive industry types and economic sectors adopting a more customer-oriented approach.

❑ *The Internet* has created new opportunities for marketing and enabled organisations to become more accessible to individual customers. The most rapid development of Internet applications has been in business-to-business, rather than business-to-consumer, markets.

❑ The marketing concept has been criticised in two main areas:

- ❑ *its effectiveness as a management strategy* in some market conditions or circumstances;

- ❑ *its effects on society*. This has lead to the notion of 'societal' marketing that puts the welfare of society into the balance alongside customer and organisational needs.

8. DEVELOPING MARKETING SKILLS

Exercises

1. From your own personal experiences as a customer, think of an organisation that you consider to be 'customer-oriented'. Think also of one that is not. What lead you to these conclusions? What were the essential differences in the way you were treated in each case?

2. You are the owner of a vineyard producing mainly sweet desert wines. Over the last decade the demand for your wines has declined as consumers' tastes have changed. As it will take at least five years to grow new productive vines, you now have to make some decisions on your marketing approach. How will you

match your particular strengths to consumer demand to ensure a 'mutually profitable exchange'?

3. As a Minister in Her Majesty's Government, you have been asked to introduce legislation which curbs some of the excesses of organisations which seek to over-exploit consumers through sophisticated marketing techniques whilst retaining the benefits which marketing can give to society. What do you suggest?

Developing a marketing plan

At the end of each Unit you will find activities like this one under the heading of 'Developing a marketing plan'. These are designed to build into a marketing plan around a product or service of your choice. A fuller overview is given in the Preface.

Activity 1 Preparing for marketing

The first step is to choose a subject for your marketing plan. This should be a product or service that you can find out about in terms of its potential market and customers, and make recommendations about marketing strategy and tactics. Bear in mind the following points when making your decision:

❑ Choose a product or service that interests you. You are much more likely to be motivated to do the required research and analysis about something that you personally find interesting. If you have an interest in the topic you could have a head start in understanding the market as you may yourself be a customer or potential customer. Consider products related to your hobbies or sports, special interests, where you live, your family background, and where you work or study.

❑ Your product or service can exist now, or it can be a fictional new development provided this does not stray beyond the realms of what is currently possible (a spinning wheel that converts corn into gold will not do!).

❑ It will probably be more manageable to choose a particular product or service rather than a generic range of products or an industry, for example a specific car rather than 'saloon cars' or the 'motor car industry'. A study that is limited in scope but represents a detailed evaluation of the marketing possibilities of one product or service is more beneficial than broad generalisations about a wider area.

❑ Your choice does not have to be in the private business sector. It can be in the non-profit sector such as a charity or club. It can be a public service such as a course of studies, a library, a hospital (or related medical service) or local leisure facilities.

❑ You will need access to information about your chosen topic so make sure it is freely available. Avoid areas where there could be security problems (for example, military developments or 'sensitive' business areas because of competitive intelligence).

FURTHER READING AND REFERENCES

General texts

Brassington, F. and Pettit, S. (2000) *Principles of Marketing*, 2nd edition, FT/Prentice Hall, chapter 1.

Kotler, P. (2000) *Marketing Management*, 10th edition, Prentice Hall, chapters 1 and 2.

Customer orientation

Greenley, G.E. (1995) Market orientation and company performance, empirical evidence from UK companies, *British Journal of Management*, **12**, pages 1–13.

Kohli, A. and Jaworski, B. (1990) Market orientation: the construct, research propositions and managerial implications, *Journal of Marketing*, April, **54**(2), pages 1–18.

Narver, J. and Slater, S. (1990) The effect of marketing orientation on business profitability, *Journal of Marketing*, October, **54**(4), pages 20–35.

Relationship marketing

Gronroos, C. (1994) From marketing mix to relationship marketing: towards a paradigm shift in marketing, *Management Decision*, **32**(2), pages 4–20.

Gummesson, E. (1987) The new marketing – developing long-term interactive relationships, *Long Range Planning*, **20**(4), pages 10–20.

Internet development

Chaffey, D., Mayer, R., Johnston, K. and Ellis-Chadwick, F. (2000) *Internet Marketing*, Pearson Education, chapter 1.

Chaston, I. (2001) *E-Marketing Strategy*, McGraw Hill, chapter 1.

Keynote Report (2000) *Internet Usage in Business*, 4th edition, Keynote Ltd.

CHAPTER 2

Planning for Marketing

This chapter looks at marketing as a formal or informal process that identifies needs and organises resources to satisfy them. It examines how marketing plans are produced, identifying the four stages of analysis, objectives, methods and evaluation, reviewing each stage in some detail. It outlines the benefits of planning, stressing the need for integrated, specific plans which look behind the current situation to assess opportunities and threats in the market place.

1. CASE STUDY: LINKLINE ELECTRONICS

Peter Blair founded LinkLine Electronics in 1993, when governments around the globe were looking to entrepreneurs to create new economic growth. Although he had no formal management training or qualifications, Blair found it relatively easy to obtain the £150,000 required for working capital, equipment and machinery. In return for the loan, the bank manager did ask for a business plan which was duly written by a firm of accountants and gathered dust in Blair's filing cabinet thereafter. 'I don't have time to write or read plans. I'm too busy putting them into practice,' he argued.

His energetic selling and opportunistic approach to the market paid off. Although the pattern of trading was typical of a new start up with first year losses, LinkLine was making profits by its second year and achieved a turnover of £500,000 by year three. Sales continued to climb and exceeded £600,000 in 1996 when LinkLine recorded profits of £60,000.

Blair had carved out a viable niche in a very competitive market by designing electronic circuits for specialised applications, tailor-made to individual customer needs. His customers were other larger electronic companies who had a problem; they were developing products which could not use conventional circuits because they were unsuited to the environment in which they would be operating.

'Some of my early customers wanted ultra-lightweight circuits for space probes,' Blair explained. 'Others needed electronics which were unaffected by temperature extremes, for example in ignition modules for engines which had to start even whilst very cold but continue to run when the engine had become much hotter. I had the technology to cope with many of these specialised applications, but I had to adapt to suit each customer. It was not something you could easily predict or write up as a standard marketing approach or sales plan.'

Then came problems. Sales fell in 1997 for the first time and the trend continued the following year when turnover was only two thirds of the 1997 peak. Many of LinkLine's customers were in the military, space or automotive sectors – markets which were hit by both falling prices and external events. Blair responded in typical entrepreneurial style by redoubling his selling efforts and looking for new markets.

'I went to companies making spare parts for cars for instance,' Blair explained. 'I figured that if people were not buying new cars, they would be needing more repairs which means more spare parts. So I found a new market designing circuits for replacement ignition modules.'

Unfortunately this did not immediately help LinkLine's profits. Blair had to cut his prices because of the longer distribution chains of the new business, and his profit margins fell. Nevertheless he survived when many other small businesses did not. The bank had become increasingly nervous about LinkLine's finances and when a major customer went bankrupt leaving Blair with a large unpaid debt, they threatened to call in their overdraft which had grown to £100,000 by 2000. Blair was furious, claiming his business had now turned the corner as his recent trading record showed:

Year (£000s)	1996	1997	1998	1999	2000
Sales:	610	920	790	620	680
Gross profit:	300	440	400	250	270
Overheads:	240	350	360	310	260
Net profit:	60	90	40	(60)	10

Reluctantly, Blair agreed to the bank's proposal that an advisor should help him draft a marketing plan.

'I suggest you focus your marketing plan on providing sales leads, new ways in to potential customers,' he said to the advisor. 'If I don't sell more, I don't survive so my number one priority is sales and promotions. And as I am the one who does most of the marketing, I don't have time to write up elaborate plans which no-one else but me would need to read.'

Points to consider

1. What would you include as the main stages in a marketing plan for LinkLine?

See section 2.

2. If you were the marketing advisor to LinkLine, what further information would you require to complete the plan? Group the information into the stages you identified above.

See sections 3–7.

3. Which environmental factors are likely to have impacted on LinkLine's fortunes and which will influence its future?

See section 3.

4. How would you persuade Blair of the need for marketing planning? What advantages could his business gain from such an exercise?

See section 8.

5. What problems or potential disadvantages of marketing planning does this case illustrate?

See section 9.

2. THE PROCESS OF MARKETING PLANNING

The marketing process

If the marketing concept is to be implemented, a process is required which identifies or anticipates customer needs and fulfils them in a way which meets organisational needs for profit or other objectives. As we have seen in Chapter 1, this is a circular process of several stages:

❑ identification of customer needs;

❑ identification of the strengths and needs of the supplying organisation;

❑ organisation of resources to satisfy customer needs in line with organisational objectives;

❑ monitoring and evaluation of the results of these activities;

❑ identification of new or modified customer needs;

❑ implementation of new or modified ways of meeting customer needs.

Some organisations follow this pattern formally. Others use more informal planning methods.

- *Alan Sugar founded Amstrad on the demand for the new electrical audio goods such as transistor radios, tape recorders, amplifiers, tuners, turntables and car radios which boomed in the mid-1960s. Initially he did not develop any products himself; he identified the need for a more efficient distribution of the new products from the manufacturers or importers to the retailers and consumers and organised resources to do it. In doing so he was able to monitor the market place and found some consumer needs that were not being met by the existing manufacturers. At the time the acrylic, or perspex, dust covers and plinths for record players were very expensive because of the high costs of the raw materials. Sugar decided to develop his own product using a lower cost, injection moulding process provided by a sub-contractor. He was soon selling dust covers at a fraction of the previous price, the success of which gave him the resources to look for more new products in the electrical and electronic markets. Like many successful entrepreneurs, Sugar did not go through the stages of the marketing process in a formalised, planned way. But he nevertheless followed the process of identifying and satisfying a need, evaluating the results, modifying his approach, observing the results and beginning the process all over again as new opportunities came along.*

Other organisations operate a more formal system to achieve the same end. This is particularly necessary as organisations grow in size and the variables affecting the matching process between supplier and consumer become more numerous and complex.

- *For example, the Royal Dutch Shell Group operates in several major industrial sectors, including energy, chemicals, metals and forestry, in more than a hundred countries. Identification and satisfaction of customer needs cannot be left to chance in this complex environment. The management structure is*

29

decentralised through a series of operating companies each of which produce an annual business plan covering the next five years. An integral part of these plans is a statement of marketing strategy and details of marketing activities that are developed through a process of marketing planning.

The marketing planning process

Marketing planning is a structured way of looking at the match between what an organisation has to *offer* and what the market *needs*. It can be used to investigate the marketing options of an entire organisation with multiple products, or it can be used to plan the marketing of a single product or service, or a group of products.

The process has four basic stages which are similar to other planning models in that they ask the following questions in sequence:

❑ *Where are we now?* This can only be answered by an *analysis* of the existing position both inside and outside of the organisation.

❑ *Where are we going?* This requires an examination of where we are currently headed and where we should be headed through the setting of some precise *objectives*.

❑ *How do we get there?* Detailed activity plans and marketing programmes are needed next, to establish the marketing *methods* that will be used to meet the objectives.

❑ *Are we getting there?* We will need ways of measuring the impact of our activities through some system of *evaluation* so that we know at any time how we are doing.

It is a circular process in that it begins by an analysis of the existing situation and includes an evaluation of the new activities that have taken place. In turn this evaluation will become part of the analysis of the situation in the future so that the

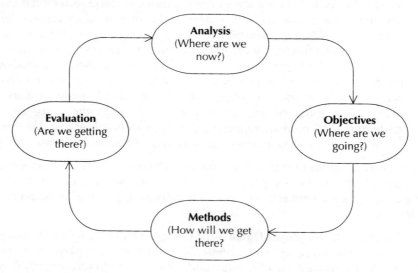

Figure 2.1: *The basic marketing planning process*

planning cycle can begin again. This basic process is illustrated in Figure 2.1.

Each of these four basic stages can be further sub-divided, as we will discuss below.

3. ANALYSIS (WHERE ARE WE NOW?)

The analysis stage includes finding out all the information that currently exists about the internal and external environments of the project and filling any obvious gaps through research. Some of the categories that are considered in the analysis stage are illustrated in Figure 2.2 below.

Corporate objectives

The marketing plan is central to the planning and development of any organisation. It will have a significant influence on a whole range of issues from the cash flow to the scheduling of production or service delivery. It cannot be developed therefore in isolation from the corporate planning process. In particular, a marketing plan will take as its starting point the objectives of the corporation or organisation.

- *Let us suppose we have been asked to put together a marketing plan for a company called Kitchen Care which is launching a new service which provides the detailed design and fitting of commercial kitchens from factory canteens to up-market restaurants. Before considering anything else we need to know how this new service fits into Kitchen Care's overall plans and priorities. We need to know what constraints may apply to its launch and how easily it fits with their existing operations. We need to know their corporate objectives.*

Some organisations formalise their corporate goals into a 'mission statement'. Others have definite objectives which are only communicated informally, and some have no clear objectives at all. A necessary prerequisite for marketing planning, however, is a statement of corporate goals in answer to the question, 'What business are we in?' The answer given should reflect the 'over-arching goals' of an

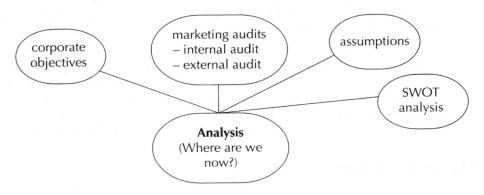

Figure 2.2: *The analysis stage*

organisation – goals which reflect its core purpose, its reason for existing in the first place and its vision for the future. Its relevance lies in establishing a concise summary of the task to be done, not a recital of well-intentioned aims.

Corporate or organisational objectives are stated in many different ways. However, for marketing planning to proceed it is desirable to understand the following general points about the goals of an organisation:

❑ *What business are we in? (mission)*

What needs will be satisfied, or benefits provided by the organisation's existence? In other words, how will its existence be justified in relation to its customers or those it seeks to serve? How will the organisation be different from others – what will distinguish it from others attempting to satisfy the same needs? In summary, how does the organisation define:

❑ customer groups to be served (who?);

❑ customer needs to be filled (what?);

❑ expertise/technologies to be utilised (how?).

❑ *What are the parameters? (beliefs and values)*

What is the scope of the organisation's activities? What are the boundaries that it does not wish to cross, or potential expansion areas that it wishes to avoid? In particular how does the organisation see itself in terms of:

❑ scope of activities;

❑ values of the organisation;

❑ legal and other constraints.

❑ *What are the priorities? (specific objectives)*

What does the organisation want to achieve this year, and over the next three to five years? What are the top priorities in the short term and the longer term.

Organisations differ widely in how they specify their objectives. Many small firms, for example, have no written objectives at all but still have very clear aims and goals, usually inside the head of one or two key people. Other organisations have written mission statements, and some document not only their strategy but specific objectives as well. Some examples taken from the private and public sector are given in Figure 2.3.

● *In the case of Kitchen Care, there are no written statements of mission or corporate objectives like the examples in Figure 2.3. However we know there are clear views on where the company is going and what its market strategy should be, so we decide to interview the managing director and other key executives to try and establish the parameters within which we will have to work.*

The marketing audit

When applied to business management, the term 'audit' means a review and

---

THE BODY SHOP

'To dedicate our business to the pursuit of social and environmental change

To creatively balance the financial and human needs of our stakeholders: employees, franchisees, customers, suppliers and shareholders.

To courageously ensure that our business is ecologically sustainable: meeting the needs of the present without comprising the future.

To meaningfully contribute to local, national and international communities in which we trade, by adopting a code of conduct which ensures care, honesty, fairness and respect.

To passionately campaign for the protection of the environment and civil rights and against animal testing within the cosmetics and toiletries industry.

To tirelessly work to narrow the gap between principle and practice whilst making fun, passion and care part of our daily lives.'

(The Body Shop Plc, Report and Accounts, 2001)

HARD ROCK CAFÉ

'Hard Rock Café will maintain and develop its memorabilia, increase its market share, and continue to be acknowledged as the world's most successful themed Rock Restaurant.'

PIZZAEXPRESS

'PizzaExpress consistently produces delicious foods and drink at value prices served by friendly staff in stylish surroundings.'

(PizzaExpress Annual Report, 2000)

Figure 2.3: *Mission statements and goals – some examples*

appraisal of a specific function or activity. It is most commonly applied to the financial function involving an investigation into the accuracy and adequacy of accounting records over a period of time. When applied to marketing, it has a similar meaning except that it has a more strategic and forward-looking dimension as well. A marketing audit examines and evaluates the marketing operations of an organisation, but it also includes two other important aspects:

❑ A marketing audit does not examine just the activities associated with marketing but also the underlying philosophy and concepts on which the activities were based. In other words, it evaluates whether an organisation is following the marketing concept, as outlined in Chapter 1, or whether it is operating under a different set of principles and policies.

❑ A marketing audit looks at what has happened to date *plus* potential new areas and possibilities. It summarises the marketing environment, highlighting past successes and problems in order to evaluate future opportunities. It evaluates current information but also suggests further research requirements.

- *Our audit of the marketing of Kitchen Care might reveal that the company had hitherto adopted a rather sales-oriented approach with most of its efforts going into selling its existing product range, irrespective of customer types and product applications. Sales staff had been encouraged to sell*

33

kitchen equipment and cleaning materials to whomever they could, with little after-sales follow up or advice. Research into restaurant owners however revealed a lack of knowledge of new hygiene regulations in commercial kitchens and an opportunity to offer a more tailor-made service involving an advisory sales approach.

A marketing audit is concerned with establishing the environmental factors facing the organisation which have marketing implications now and in the future. Such an analysis will need to look internally and externally.

The internal audit

The internal audit examines the marketing areas over which the organisation has control and summarises the choices that have been made to date including such information as:

❑ past marketing objectives and success rates;

❑ sales or revenue – analysed by sector, for example geographic region, customer type, products;

❑ market shares and trends – are shares increasing or decreasing?;

❑ profit margins and pricing strategy;

❑ product range, perceived quality and historic developments;

❑ promotional methods used and success rates;

❑ distribution channels used;

❑ marketing resources available and past allocations – personnel, organisation and budgets;

❑ market research available.

The external audit

The external audit examines factors external to the organisation which can influence the planning and execution of marketing activities. These include:

❑ *Business and economic environment.* This is often considered through a STEP analysis which reviews factors under the headings of:

   ❑ Social and cultural

   ❑ Technological

   ❑ Economic

   ❑ Political

❑ *Market environment.* This examines trends in the total market such as:

   ❑ its size, growth and trends in volume and value;

   ❑ benefits sought and offered;

   ❑ standard terms and conditions of sale;

❑ principal distribution methods;

❑ purchasing patterns (e.g. seasonality, prices paid);

❑ usual communication methods (e.g. salesforce, direct mail);

❑ trade associations and their influence.

❑ *Competitive environment*. This examines the competitive forces at play within the market or industry. As well as reviewing the competitive standing of the traditional rivals, competitive forces include other factors:

❑ potential new entrants;

❑ barriers to market entry;

❑ potential substitute products or services;

❑ relative power of buyers;

❑ relative power of suppliers;

❑ existing organisations, their reputation and likely activities.

A summary of information which might be contained in such an analysis is shown in Figure 2.4.

---

1   INTERNAL AUDIT
- Historic marketing – objectives, methods and success
- Sales or revenue – types and sources
- Existing customers – groups, perceptions, behaviour
- Product/service range – perceived quality, developments
- Profit margins and pricing
- Research – available information and gaps
- Resources available – people, budgets

strengths and weaknesses in relation to the external environment
assumptions on which information is based

2   EXTERNAL AUDIT

Environmental factors:
- social and cultural
- technological
- economic
- political

Market information:
- size and growth
- trends
- potential new customers
- benefits sought and offered
- purchasing patterns
- communication methods

Competitive forces:
- existing competitors
- potential new entrants
- barriers to market entry
- substitute products or services
- power of buyers
- power of suppliers

opportunities and threats revealed by the external audit
assumptions on which information is based

Figure 2.4: *Checklist for a marketing audit*

SWOT analysis

A useful way of summarising the internal and external marketing audit is by a SWOT analysis. This focuses on

Strengths
Weaknesses $\Big\}$ These tend to relate to the internal audit

Opportunities
Threats $\Big\}$ These tend to relate to the external audit

This is normally a short summary of the key issues to emerge from the marketing audit. It represents a useful tool for relating the needs of the marketplace to what an organisation believes it is good at. A SWOT analysis helps to show where there is a good fit between an organisation's strengths and market opportunities and where there are threats which may expose areas of weakness.

- *A SWOT analysis of Kitchen Care included the following observations:*

  - *Strengths: Established product range; large database of customers; trained salesforce.*

  - *Weaknesses: Low value per sale (most of their products cost relatively little); many small accounts (customers bought relatively small amounts from them); low sales revenue per sales person (because of the first two weaknesses).*

  - *Opportunities: New EC hygiene and health care regulations; trend to sub-contract to outside firms many health and safety aspects of commercial kitchens, such as cleaning and pest control.*

  - *Threats: Competitors offering complete 'hygiene service' including cleaning; many small commercial caterers ceasing to trade because of need to conform to new regulations.*

  Kitchen Care decided to combine their strengths with the opportunities in the market and offer a complete kitchen design and maintenance service. This would also have the benefit of increasing the value of each account (addressing a weakness) and counter competitive threats. However the audit also revealed that the company had little formal information on customer attitudes to existing and potential new services, so a need for further research was highlighted.

Assumptions

The marketing audit makes certain assumptions over which the organisation has little or no control, particularly when it looks ahead to potential opportunities and threats. These may be about the national economy (e.g. the rate of inflation, rates of exchange), or about competitive activity (e.g. resources available to competitors, strategies adopted by them). Whatever they concern, it is important that these assumptions are made clear in the marketing plan. They can be used in several ways, including:

❑ Evaluation of the plan once activities have begun. It is important to identify correct and incorrect assumptions in any assessment of the outcomes of the plan.

❑ Assessment of the risks involved in adopting the plan. If some assumptions are crucial to the success of the plan, these need to be identified and questions asked, such as:

❑ What is the likelihood of this not being so?

❑ What are the consequences of this not being so?

Figure 2.4 summarises the main points of analysing 'where are we now?'.

| 4. | OBJECTIVES (WHERE ARE WE GOING?) |

Once a thorough analysis of the existing and potential marketing environment has been made, the next step is to establish some objectives.

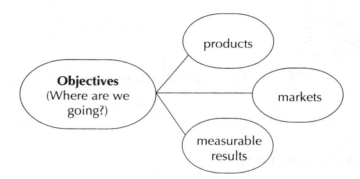

Figure 2.5: *Marketing objectives*

The focal point of a marketing plan is the setting of marketing objectives. Quite simply, these are the results wanted from the planned marketing activities. However they should not be so general that they are confused with the overall objectives of the business of which they are a part. Nor should they be too specific about individual aspects (of, for example, pricing or distribution targets), which are part of the methods used to achieve the marketing objectives. They represent *what* is to be achieved in measurable terms, but not *how*.

Guidelines for setting marketing objectives involve relating products or services to markets with measurable results.

Products and markets

Marketing objectives are primarily concerned with *products or services* and *markets*. Setting marketing objectives involves matching products and services to their markets. However we have already stressed that planning is not just about what already exists but also what may potentially exist. Marketing objectives

37

therefore look at *new* as well as *existing products* and *new* as well as *existing markets*. Objectives can therefore specify targets in terms of:

❑ existing products in existing markets – a market penetration objective;

❑ existing products in new markets – a market extension objective;

❑ new products in existing markets – a product development objective;

❑ new products in new markets – a diversification objective.

This produces the matrix structure shown in Figure 2.6.

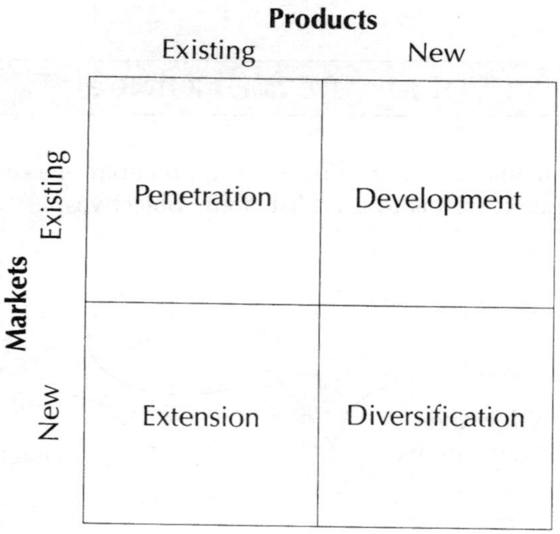

Figure 2.6: *Products and markets*

Measurable results

Marketing objectives are *measurable* and *time specific*. In order to know when an objective has been achieved it has to be measurable. A key question to ask about objectives therefore is: 'how will we know if we have been successful in reaching our objectives?'

- *The objectives specified in Kitchen Care's marketing plan were: 'To increase market share and profitability by launching a new commercial kitchen design and maintenance service'.*

This could be criticised on several counts:

- *There are no objectives which can be specifically measured. What level of increase in market share or profits makes a satisfactory result?*

- *There is no time period specified. How soon do we expect results – this year, next year?*

- *The market is not specified. To which market are we launching this new service? In which market are we expecting to increase our share?*

> To overcome such criticisms, more measurable objectives were agreed as follows: 'To launch a kitchen design and maintenance service, targeted at owner-managed restaurants, testing the concept in the first year in Lancashire, Yorkshire and Derbyshire with a sales budget of £500,000, and launching the service nationally with sales in excess of £2 million by year 3'.

Quantifiable objectives which can be used to measure progress in specified time periods are essential for meaningful feedback and monitoring of the plan.

In summary, marketing objectives are concerned with what products or services are to be sold in which markets, in what quantities or values, and when.

5. | MARKETING METHODS (HOW WILL WE GET THERE?)

Marketing methods specify how marketing objectives are to be achieved in the context of the organisation's environment. Once marketing objectives have been set, the next stage of the planning process is to work out and specify the strategies and activities that help the organisation meet those objectives.

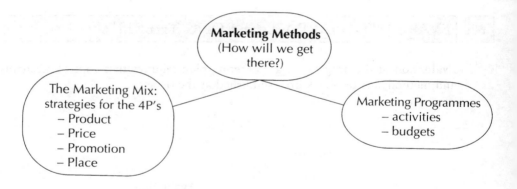

Figure 2.7: *Marketing methods*

The marketing mix

Whilst there are influences in the marketing environment which are not within the direct control of any one organisation (state of the economy, changes to the law, developments in taste and lifestyle, etc.), there are other variables which can be controlled and used to meet objectives. These controllable variables are usually summarised as the 4 Ps of the marketing mix:

❑ Product

❑ Price

❑ Promotion

❑ Place (including distribution methods)

- The marketing mix and each of the 4 Ps will be discussed in later chapters. It is sufficient to note here that decisions about which product to sell at what price, in what place, supported by what promotion are the key elements in most marketing strategies.

Marketing programmes

Detailed action plans or marketing programmes can be specified from the overall strategies for each of the variables in the marketing mix. At this stage the resource implications of the programmes can be calculated and budgets drawn up.

- *Kitchen Care decided on the product specification of their proposed new service, drew up a pricing schedule, and decided on the place (in this case the geographic area) where it would be sold. A promotional programme was scheduled involving a mailing to prospective customers, training in the new service for the sales team, and an action plan of selling activity. These activities were costed and the resource implications quantified into a budget for the product launch.*

6. EVALUATION (ARE WE GETTING THERE?)

Evaluation of the progress of a marketing plan requires that control mechanisms and methods for feedback are established at the outset.

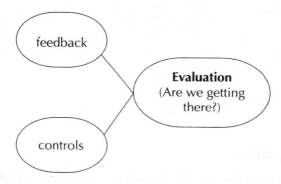

Figure 2.8: *Evaluation*

Controls

Once the marketing plan is being implemented, how can its progress be monitored and controlled? This calls for standards against which results can be measured, and contingency plans for modifying marketing programmes if results do not match expectations.

❏ *Standards of performance* stem from the objectives set for the marketing plan. This is why it is important to make these objectives as specific as possible stating both quantities and a timescale.

- *Kitchen Care's objective was to achieve sales of their new service of £500,000 in the first year. This provided an obvious standard against which the progress of the plan could be judged.*

❏ *Measurement of results* may not be as simple as this however. What if our marketing objective is to take a 10 per cent market share in the first year? We will need to set up a method to measure market share during the year. This involves making assumptions about the size of the total market and its likely growth rate during the period of the plan so that we can estimate our share to the whole.

❏ *Contingency plans* are needed to cope with significant variances from the plan. If results are a long way short of the standards anticipated, how long do we wait before making changes and what kind of changes are envisaged?

- *Kitchen Care's plan involved testing the market by limiting its launch in the first year to Lancashire, Yorkshire and Derbyshire. If sales were insufficient to avoid loosing money in the first year (which was calculated at 80 per cent of the first year's sales target, or £400,000), then the new service would not be offered to other geographic areas at that stage, but would be modified and re-tested for a further year.*

Feedback

Although it is important to look at quantifiable results to control the implementation of a marketing plan, it is also necessary to look behind the figures to find out why results are what they are. How is the customer reacting to our plan? Is their perception of what we are offering, and how we are offering it, as we expected? There are many sources for the feedback necessary to answer such questions, including:

❏ *Internal sources of information.* Anyone within an organisation who has contact with the marketplace receives feedback from customers and potential customers.

- *Kitchen Care held weekly meetings with their sales people to specifically ask for feedback on the launch of the new service. Others in the company were also able to contribute to feedback, from the telephonist who received inquiries to the maintenance engineers and cleaners who carried out the service.*

❏ *External sources of feedback.* There are also formal and informal ways of obtaining feedback outside of an organisation. One important indicator will be any new activity of competitors in reaction to a marketing programme. Formal market research may also be necessary to test customer reaction to part of a marketing plan.

- *Promotions can be followed up in this way with surveys carried out to probe people's reaction to advertising approaches. Kitchen Care tested their mailshot to potential customers by interviewing a sample of those who had received the mailing and asking for their reactions to it.*

7. THE COMPLETED PLANNING PROCESS

The evaluation stage is not only the final stage of a marketing planning cycle. It is also the beginning of the next. Information provided by the evaluation of one plan provides further data for the analysis stage of another plan or an update of the original plan. Figure 2.9 shows the completed process.

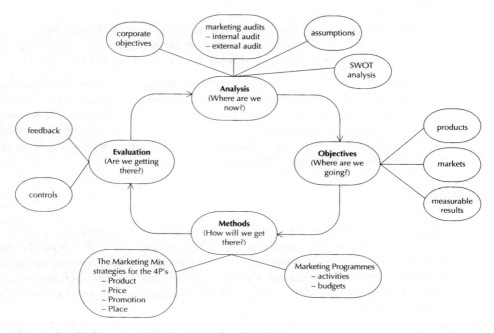

Figure 2.9: *The completed marketing planning process*

8. THE BENEFITS OF PLANNING

Planning the organisational journey

Research has shown that most organisations do not produce marketing plans. Ninety per cent of companies involved in one study did not undertake the necessary procedures to produce co-ordinated plans for their marketing activities (McDonald, 1992).

This seems a strange state of affairs considering some of the more obvious problems that a lack of planning brings to any management situation. An organisation without a plan can be compared to a ship which has been inadequately prepared for its journey. Without a clear idea of which port they are ultimately headed for, the captain and crew are in danger of drifting aimlessly, going nowhere, (*no direction*). If they have not done their homework on the likely climatic conditions that may be encountered en route, then they will be less prepared to cope with the dangers of the passage, (*inadequate information*). If they have not calculated and acquired the provisions needed, they are in danger of running out before completing the journey, (*insufficient resources*). If some officers on board have made plans and preparations independently without full discussion with one another, then conflict and confusion is likely to pull the ship in different directions, (*lack of teamwork*).

Commercial enterprises and public sector organisations have their equivalent of a journey to make towards their objectives and can experience similar problems through a lack of planning.

The benefits of planning

The benefits to an organisation which carefully plans where it is going, and how it is to get there, help avoid some of the following potential pitfalls:

❑ *Direction to activities through agreed, specific objectives.* A common purpose helps motivate those involved to achieve their shared vision.

❑ *Information on the environment to help an organisation adapt quickly to changes.* Up to date information on what is happening inside and outside of an organisation not only helps foresee new circumstances but can also speed up responses to changes.

❑ *Resources allocated in line with the demands of the objectives and the likely environment.* Once objectives have been set and the environment examined, an assessment of the resources needed (people, money, equipment, premises, etc.) can be made to ensure the practicality of the tasks ahead.

❑ *Teamwork to build individual roles into the overall objectives.* People who know what is expected of them and how their roles interact with others are in a better position to make a co-ordinated effort towards the common goals.

The benefits of marketing planning

Many activities and functions within an organisation can benefit from planning as outlined above. There are particular reasons why it is important to plan the marketing function.

Direction

Marketing planning strongly influences the direction and objectives of the entire organisation as marketing objectives relate products or services to markets.

● *For example, a manufacturer of jeans may decide on the marketing objective of gaining 10 per cent of the UK teenage market for leisure jeans.*

● *A school may have the marketing objective of increasing their intake of pupils by improving their image among parents living in areas geographically further from the school.*

Such objectives form a significant input into the overall objectives of the organisation. As organisations exist to satisfy customers with their products or services, any objective which relates markets and customers to products will have an impact on the whole organisation. Other functions can be crucially affected by marketing objectives.

- *The production department of the jeans manufacturer will be affected by the marketing objective in terms of the quantity and type of jeans it will be expected to produce.*

- *A marketing objective involving an increase in the numbers of pupils accepted into a school has a crucial impact on the organisation of every aspect of school life from the timetabling of lessons to the arrangements for school dinners.*

As marketing objectives form a crucial input into the overall objectives of an organisation, some commentators have argued that marketing planning and corporate planning are inseparable and should be the same process. Here we have adopted the view that marketing planning can be undertaken as a separate exercise, provided that an assessment of the overall corporate or organisational objectives and constraints has already been made. We need to know the general direction in which we are headed before we can plan the detail of the marketing activities.

Information

The marketing planning process begins with an analysis of the market environment and possible developments within it. It looks at the marketing strengths and weaknesses of an organisation in relation to its market place. It tries to assess the trends and likely changes that may affect customer requirements. This marketing information can often be crucial to an organisation's ability to survive in today's rapidly changing environments.

In the private sector it is increasingly those companies that adapt fastest to movements in customer demand that survive and thrive. This speed of response depends on an awareness of the trends in consumer demand which comes from the analysis stage of marketing planning. Our manufacturer of jeans will need to be aware of the fickleness of teenage fashion and stay very close to their consumers if they are to last long in this market, for example.

The public sector is also undergoing rapid change. Many developments have increased the effects of market forces so that public services now have to be increasingly aware of their marketplace and adapt to changes within it. The amount of money made available to a state school, for example, now very largely depends on the number of pupils it can attract. Schools that accurately assess the requirements of parents and pupils, through an analysis of their marketplace, can use this information to increase their pupil intake and therefore their total funds.

Marketing planning can keep organisations in touch with their marketplace and help them adapt more rapidly to changes.

Resources

An important part of marketing planning is forecasting demand. A marketing plan normally contains a sales forecast or a budget of income or funds that will be generated. This information is important in deciding the allocation of resources not just for marketing but for other functions as well.

- *The production department of the jeans manufacturer may decide that new equipment will be needed to cope with the increased sales predicted in the marketing plan. The distribution department may also need additional resources to deliver a larger output.*

- *A plan which foresees more pupils at a school will have important effects on the total level and allocation of resources in many ways including the numbers and duties of staff and the availability of classrooms.*

Thorough marketing planning assists the accuracy of these forecasts and therefore helps appropriate decisions to be made in many other areas.

Teamwork

We stressed in Chapter 1 that marketing is not just the responsibility of a marketing department or an advertising agency. Marketing specialists may be required to apply some of the *techniques* of marketing, but marketing as a *philosophy*, which relates the strengths of an organisation to the needs of its customers, is the responsibility of everyone. If marketing is to be a 'whole organisation' activity in this way then everyone needs to understand the marketing objectives of the organisation.

This understanding will be made more difficult without a formalised marketing planning process. If marketing plans develop informally, and often in reaction to events rather than ahead of them, then those not directly involved in making marketing decisions may feel no real commitment to them. The process of marketing planning is a good opportunity to gain the commitment of others to marketing objectives by:

- ❑ *Involvement in the process.* In particular, the analysis stage of developing a marketing plan can benefit from input from many sources. In drawing up the marketing plan for the school in our previous example, the school caretaker was asked to provide information on some of the physical limitations to pupil numbers (size of classrooms, number of toilets, etc.) and as a result was better informed about future plans.

- ❑ *Communication of the results.* Plans developed only in the heads of those directly involved are largely invisible to others. A written marketing plan provides a method of informing others about future intentions. A summary of the marketing plan provided to the production manager of the jeans manufacturer helped this department foresee some peaks in demand following a planned advertising campaign and increased their motivation to cope with it.

9. | PROBLEMS IN MARKETING PLANNING

Lack of planning

Despite these benefits, only a small minority of organisations undertake an integrated process of marketing planning.

The reasons for this include:

❑ *Insufficient understanding of the process or benefits of planning.* Many organisations believe they do not have the necessary skills to produce a plan without help. In a recent survey, over 40 per cent of businesses identified marketing planning as a priority area for training in their company. Other enterprises may be less than convinced of the benefits that marketing planning can bring.

❑ *Pressure on 'doing' rather than planning.* Whilst many managers recognise the need for more planning, they cannot escape from short-term, daily activities to devote sufficient time to analysing and planning the longer term. Today's problems always seem to command higher priority than tomorrow's issues.

❑ *Emphasis on unstructured opportunist activities rather than planning and control.* At the macro-economic level, recent governments have rejected collectivist, centralised planning in favour of encouraging a diversity of individual effort. This has been mirrored at the micro-economic level by increased recognition of the value of entrepreneurs who seek opportunities and make things happen. Unfortunately there is a perception that entrepreneurship and planning do not mix well, that entrepreneurial management can only flourish when it is free from the constraints of structured plans. Many commentators have demonstrated the opposite to be the case, that entrepreneurial activity is in fact helped by a structured, planned approach. However, their advice is largely ignored by entrepreneurs, who research show to be reluctant to formally plan their marketing strategies. Smaller businesses, for example, rarely undertake sophisticated and integrated marketing programmes. They rely instead on more random and basic marketing efforts, often in reaction to activity in the marketplace.

Misconceived planning

Some organisations produce what they describe as marketing plans but which in practice do not represent a fully developed marketing strategy:

❑ *Short-term plans based on financial targets.* Some organisations plan and organise their marketing efforts simply by making short-term sales forecasts, cost budgets and schedules of marketing activities.

  • *The managers of 'Personal Financial Services', a company selling investment policies and pension plans, decided at their annual marketing review that they could increase their revenue by 20 per cent if they took on an extra sales person, and sent out more mail shots.*

This is a process which looks only at what already exists and makes short-term plans based on that limited picture. It is often driven by annual financial targets related to increasing profits or minimising costs.

  • *In our example, the managers of Personal Financial Services undertook to increase profits by 30 per cent, which they calculated they could do by limiting their cost increases to 10 per cent whilst their sales grew by the assumed 20 per cent. Halfway through the year the Chancellor of the*

Exchequer announced taxation changes which undermined the attractive-
ness of their major investment product and made them tear up their plan
and start again.

This planning is often limited to accepting the *short-term, internal* requirements
of the company and projecting those forward. It does not take account of the
likely *longer-term* impact of *external* influences in the marketplace, such as
political and other environmental influences, and potential competitive activity.

❑ *Marketing planning developed separately from other organisational functions.*
Some organisations develop marketing plans without fully taking account of
corporate plans and constraints, and the planning of other functions. This can
become a frustrating waste of effort or, worse, a mismatch of aims and
activities.

- *A marketing team at a well-known national charity produced a publicity*
  plan using case histories of clients helped by the organisation. Unfortu-
  nately this overlooked a corporate policy which demanded complete
  confidentiality for clients and the publicity programme was scrapped.

- *Whilst the sales department of an electronics manufacturer were planning*
  on a large increase in units sold, the engineering department were planning
  on cost savings which would have made it impossible for them to provide
  the necessary technical support for a big jump in sales.

❑ *Over-generalised intentions.* Some marketing plans make statements which are
full of good intentions but fail to show how these can be realised in practice.

- *A restaurant chain had the stated marketing objective of 'matching their*
  menu and services to customer requirements'. Unfortunately, this was not
  helpful to the managers as it did not go on to specify which customers were
  to be targeted nor what their requirements were. Different groups require
  different menus and service. Was this restaurant aiming to provide a
  relaxed atmosphere which would appeal to those who wished to linger over
  their meal? Or was it trying to serve those who needed more functional fast
  food? Marketing activities which arise from very general objectives can
  easily become misdirected and confused.

- *Managers at a hospital developed a marketing plan which included the*
  intention of 'informing patients better'. While this may seem a commend-
  able objective, it is not specific enough on its own to represent any real
  progress. A marketing plan would need to detail which patients were to be
  informed about what, by whom and how.

❑ *The least line of resistance.* Most organisations have a natural tendency to sell
products which are easiest to sell, and to sell into those markets where there is
least resistance. Thus some products may be neglected because they require
additional effort even though their potential is great. Likewise, some markets
are ignored because the initial barriers to market entry are high even though the
pickings are rich once the market has been entered.

Some marketing planning effectively encourages this misallocation of resources
because it looks ahead only from the position of what is already happening. If

planning merely forecasts demand for products based on their current acceptance in the marketplace then it could be reinforcing existing inefficiencies and bad practice.

- *Kitchen Care offered several products and services to improve hygiene and cleanliness in commercial kitchens. Some of these were manufactured products such as cleaning materials, insect repellents and mesh screens for windows. Their sales team found these relatively easy to demonstrate and sell. They also offered a contract cleaning service for heavily soiled areas. The sales team tended to avoid selling this service as it was more complex to explain and organise even though the profit margins were higher and potential demand was good. A marketing plan based only on projections of current sales patterns continued to underrate this service by emphasising the products with the least line of resistance to the sales team.*

  Kitchen Care also avoided selling to government departments as specifications for products used in their canteen facilities were very rigorous. Proof of conforming to quality standards were a significant barrier to entry to this market as procedures to obtain them were time consuming and initially expensive. However, this also made the market less competitive and more profitable. Again Kitchen Care's marketing planning overlooked this area as it focused only on existing outlets for their products and services.

The planning and organising of marketing can represent more than just a routine review of annual budgets and activities. It is an opportunity to investigate how an organisation can improve the match between its products or services and the short- and long-term needs of the marketplace.

10. KEY POINTS

- ❑ The marketing concept is implemented through a process which is either informally followed or planned in a more structured way.

- ❑ A structured marketing planning process asks the following questions representing stages in the process:

  - ❑ *Where are we now?* – the *analysis* stage which looks at corporate goals, conducts internal and external marketing audits, makes assumptions and summarises with a SWOT analysis.

  - ❑ *Where are we going?* – setting *objectives* in relation to products and markets by establishing measurable results.

  - ❑ *How do we get there?* – deciding marketing *methods* which include strategies for the 4 Ps of the marketing mix, activity programmes and budgets summarising the resource implications.

  - ❑ *Are we getting there?* – *evaluation* of the results through controls and feedback.

- ❑ The benefits of planning for marketing are that it provides direction, information and resources, and assists teamwork.

❑ The problems in planning marketing are that it is often not done at all, or that it is done in a short-term or non-integrated way.

11. DEVELOPING MARKETING SKILLS

Exercises

1. You have decided to get a new job or apply for a course of study, and wish to market yourself to prospective employers or education establishments. You decide to do this in a structured way by drawing up a marketing plan for yourself. Use the headings of analysis, objectives, methods and evaluation to write a plan to market yourself. As a minimum, produce a personal SWOT analysis and specific objectives with outline methods to achieve them.

2. Does the organisation for whom you work, or the institution where you study, have a mission statement? If it does, do you think it is an appropriate and meaningful statement of objectives? Is it sufficiently publicised? If there are no published objectives, draw up what you would consider to be an appropriate statement of mission and corporate objectives.

3. You are the owner of a fast food restaurant with a limited and rather dated menu of grilled burgers and fried chicken appealing mainly to customers in the 15 to 25 year old range. In order to improve sales you wish to look at either new products or new markets or a combination of the two. Suggest some possible marketing objectives in these categories.

Developing a marketing plan

In the first activity, you chose the subject for a marketing plan. The second activity is to decide the format of your plan, the information you are likely to need and how you are going to get it.

Activity 2 Planning for marketing

❑ Decide the headings for your plan: are the headings discussed in Chapter 2 appropriate or will you require some different ones?

❑ What information do you already have available for the plan?

❑ What further information will you require?

❑ How will you get it?

FURTHER READING AND REFERENCES

General texts

Armstrong, G. and Kotler, P. (2000) *Marketing: an Introduction*, Prentice Hall, chapter 2.

McDonald, M. (1992) *Strategic Marketing Planning*, Kogan Page.

Mudie, P. (1997) *Marketing: an Analytical Perspective*, Prentice Hall, chapters 1–3.

Writing a marketing plan

McDonald, M. and Morris, P. (1989) *The Marketing Plan: a pictorial guide for managers*, Heinemann Professional Publishing.

Westwood, J. (1996) *How to Write a Marketing Plan*, Kogan Page.

Internet marketing planning

Chaffey, D., Mayer, R., Johnston, K. and Ellis-Chadwick, F. (2000) *Internet Marketing*, Pearson Education, chapter 6.

Hardaker, G. and Graham, G. (2001) *Wired Marketing*, John Wiley & Sons, chapter 12.

CHAPTER 3

The Marketing Context

In this chapter we look at the internal and external influences on marketing decisions. Marketing managers cannot directly control the environment in which their organisations operate, but factors such as economic and competitive conditions have a crucial influence on marketing decisions. A continuous appraisal of this environment is therefore an important part of the marketing process. This chapter categorises the types of environmental forces facing marketing management and gives some examples of their effects. It examines the internal aspects of an organisation that affect marketing strategies, the external environmental factors (competitive, social and economic contexts) and the role of marketing management in relation to these forces.

1.	CASE STUDY: ROBOTS AND REFORM IN THE HEALTH MARKET

Max Scallon settled into his airline seat, pulling out the papers he needed to read on his flight from New York to London. He was the marketing director of the Robotic Research Corporation of America and was on his way to a series of meetings to test the viability of launching their latest product 'Georgie', in the UK and the rest of Europe. Following its launch two years earlier, Georgie had become an instant hit in America where each product had produced savings of up to $100,000 a year in hospitals. Georgie was a robot capable of delivering up to 350lbs of materials to pre-determined destinations, or cleaning and polishing floors. In American hospitals, Georgie was loaded in a central materials management department with goods from X-rays to toilet rolls and programmed for delivery destinations. Using its memory map, it calculated the route and set off around the long corridors typical of large hospitals. Sensors guided it round any obstacles whilst it calculated the deviation to ensure it returned to its route. A centralised controller watched progress and in the event of problems, Georgie could use pre-recorded messages such as 'I am lost. Please report my position to the operator', to ask for help from passers-by. Georgie could also clean the floors it travelled over as the flick of a switch changed it from 'carry' to 'clean' mode and activated its brushes and polishers. Georgie was a very efficient worker, available seven days a week, and 23 hours a day (the other hour was for recharging its batteries and undergoing any necessary maintenance). It could do the work of three human workers, allowing more resources to be devoted to patient care.

Max had decided the time was right to launch Georgie into the UK as a springboard into European markets. On the plane, he looked first through his briefing notes on the healthcare market in the UK.

Filenote: UK healthcare market

Market: *75 per cent of UK healthcare is provided by the public sector through the National Health Service. Expenditure on the NHS since its inception in 1948 has quadrupled after taking account of inflation. Actual expenditure has risen from £400 million in 1949 to £40 billion in 2000. The private sector currently has a 25 per cent share of healthcare expenditure and is becoming increasingly important, especially in the care of the elderly.*

Demand for healthcare is growing at the same time as the costs of its provision are escalating. The UK population is ageing as life expectancy has increased to over 70 years for males, and to nearly 80 years for females. Growth in the elderly population has already caused short-term funding problems. The shrinking of young age groups combined with increases in older age bands has longer-term funding implications (16–24 year olds decreased from 9.3 million in 1985, to 7.4 million in 2000. Conversely, 45–59 year olds have increased from 6.2 million in 1985 to 7.5 million in 2000). Technological advances in surgery techniques and drug treatments have increased the costs of some healthcare and mean more illnesses can be treated. Cost-cutting measures include an increase in day surgery for minor operations.

A further major problem is serious staff shortages. The NHS is the largest single employer in Europe with around 1 million employees. Expansion of healthcare services, relatively low pay for medical and support staff, and full employment in the national economy have lead to chronic shortages in the NHS. The government have attempted to improve the position with advertising and other initiatives to recruit and retain staff, but the problem is not likely to be solved easily.

Industry structure: *The NHS was reorganised in the 1980s and 1990s by the Conservative government in line with its themes for changes in other public services. The separation of the role of purchaser from the role of provider – a split of management responsibility between those who specify the quality of a service and those who provide it – created markets or at least 'quasi-markets' in healthcare.*

'Purchasers' are the district health authorities responsible for deciding what services are required in their area, arranging and paying for contracts with providers of the services, and setting and monitoring quality standards. Doctors' practices also control budgets to purchase healthcare for their patients. 'Providers' include hospitals, and community and family health services.

The 'Patients Charter' of 1991 laid down what the UK public could expect from its health service, specifying standards in such areas as waiting lists, complaints and information. The Labour government have attempted to tackle problems with extra funds targeted at specific objectives, such as the reduction of waiting lists.

The private sector is still very dependent on private medical insurance for its income. However it is playing an increasing, complementary role alongside the NHS. Some NHS patients are now treated in private hospitals and some NHS hospitals provide private healthcare facilities. The government's private finance initiative has tried to introduce external funding into the NHS and encourage partnerships with private healthcare organisations.

Max considered how his corporation would cope with supplying this fast changing sector. Their objectives were clear: 'to be the most recommended international supplier of robotic products'. But so far their customers had been confined largely to private sector organisations in North America. His company was young as were most of the managers. The Robotic Research Corporation had grown very rapidly to reach sales of $40 million in 2000, driven on by the innovative ideas and enthusiasm of its youthful directors such as Max who had just celebrated his 29th birthday. Their international strategy was to use 'Georgie' as the spearhead for penetrating the European market. Max's visit was to evaluate not only the potential market for the product, the level of competition and other likely barriers to its acceptance, but also the logistical issues of selling, supplying and servicing a complex technological product at a distance.

To help him with this evaluation, Max had arranged to meet a number of healthcare managers. His first appointment was with Ruth Davies who was the newly appointed director of marketing at Queens Hospital Trust. Ruth had informed Max that she needed to introduce innovations that not only produced efficiencies, but also produced good publicity for the hospital that needed to market itself to patients and to healthcare purchasers alike. As Max looked forward to their meeting, he recalled her words on the telephone: 'The aims of marketing here are the same as any other organisation – more satisfied customers. But the environment is very different to say marketing consumer goods. Healthcare is an emotive subject as it is so often a matter of life and death.'

Points to consider

1. What types of internal influences on marketing decisions face Max Scallon. What illustrations of these does this case provide?

See sections 2 and 3.

2. What are the main influences in the external environment which face Max and the Robotic Research Corporation in marketing their products in the UK healthcare market? What illustrations of these does this case provide?

See sections 4 and 5.

3. What internal and external factors are particularly important for Ruth Davies to consider in marketing Queens Hospital? How would you advise her to manage them?

See sections 3 to 7.

2. THE MARKETING ENVIRONMENT

The ability of an organisation to satisfy the needs of its customers is conditioned by the environment in which it operates. This environment can be classified into three parts:

❑ *The internal environment* such as the objectives, stakeholders, resources, culture and structure of the organisation which determine the scope and conduct of its marketing activities.

❑ *The external, micro-environment* of competitors, customers, suppliers and intermediaries which have a direct influence on marketing decisions.

❑ *The external, macro-environment* of social, technological, economic and political forces which have a more indirect influence on marketing strategies.

These environmental forces are the 'sea' in which an organisation either swims or sinks in its efforts to meet customer needs through its marketing decisions. Figure 3.1 illustrates this environment in which marketing decisions are made.

We will explore each of these influences in more detail, illustrated by some examples.

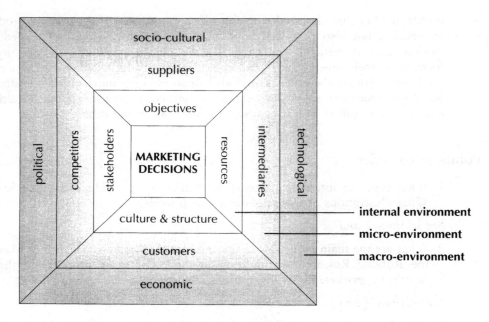

Figure 3.1: *The environment of the marketing process*

3. THE INTERNAL ENVIRONMENT

Some forces are outside of the marketing management function but remain within the internal environment of the organisation as illustrated in Figure 3.2.

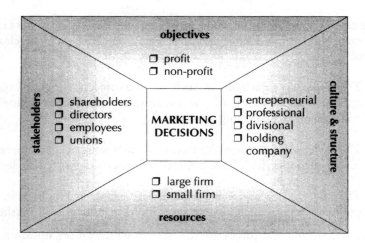

Figure 3.2: *The internal environment*

Organisational objectives

Marketing decisions are made in the context of a specific organisation and its objectives. One organisation may want to grow as quickly as possible, whilst another may not wish to grow at all. These overall objectives are clearly a major influence on marketing plans and decisions. In Chapter 2 we saw that an understanding of corporate objectives is a necessary first stage in the marketing planning process (Chapter 2, 'Corporate objectives').

One basic difference between the objectives of different types of organisation is the role of *profit*:

❑ In the private sector, the profit objective is usually taken for granted and marketing is often seen as a means of maximising the profits of a business.

❑ In the public sector, the role of profit is replaced by other objectives. A state hospital, for example, does not have the objective of maximising profits but of providing high quality patient care. There are other types of organisations such as charities and clubs that also fall into this non-profit sector.

The marketing environment in the public sector

Historically, marketing did not play a significant role in the management functions of public services and the non-profit sector, but (as we saw in Chapter 1, 'The historical development of marketing') it has been adopted increasingly in recent years, spurred on in the UK by increased competition and changes to funding methods. However, the environment of these non-profit organisations still influences their ability to fully adopt marketing principles. There are several factors that potentially inhibit marketing in public services:

❑ Public sector organisations operate in restricted market conditions. Some are effectively monopoly suppliers (e.g. social services). Most exist in heavily regulated markets subject to ongoing direction from one or more source (e.g. the educational 'product' of a school is prescribed by the National Curriculum).

❑ Objectives may be multiple and contradictory (e.g. cut costs and improve services simultaneously). This is often because more than one group of people can lay claim to being the 'customer' of a public service. It may be difficult to regard the users of a service as 'customers' (e.g. inmates of a prison), or it may inappropriate to consider their expressed needs in the same way as traditional consumers (e.g. the desire of school pupils for longer playtime and less homework).

❑ Public services are accountable to a wide audience and ongoing public scrutiny because they are intended for the general good. All activities can be scrutinised by the public in a way that does not exist in the commercial world, especially for smaller enterprises such as private family businesses. For example, schools have governing bodies of typically 12 to 15 governors, in contrast to equivalent-sized private sector enterprises that are generally controlled by one or two owner-managers.

❑ Specific consumer groups are not targeted because services are generally available to all, so there is less specialisation than in the private sector (e.g. most state schools admit both boys and girls of all abilities, whilst private schools are selective in their admissions).

- *A town library provides services funded by ratepayers and controlled by local government. It has constraints in line with those listed above:*

  - *It is a monopoly supplier of free book loans for many of its customers. Many people do not have access to other libraries for the publications they require and they therefore have no choice of supplier for this service.*

  - *It has contradictory objectives. One objective is to provide a loan facility to as many people as possible and a measure used to monitor the success of the library is the number of users taking out books. Another objective, set by the controlling council, is to keep costs to a minimum, restricting expenditure to a tightly defined budget. The more books a library has, the more its services are used, and the more it is judged to be meeting the first objective. The second objective however demands restrictions on book purchases and therefore limitations to the use of the library.*

  - *It has less freedom to determine its own destiny. There are considerable constraints on management initiatives to improve services as all major decisions not only go through an internal hierarchy but are also subject to the scrutiny of an elected body – in this case the County council. This only meets five times a year and any items for consideration first have to pass through a complex structure of sub-committees. As decisions can therefore involve many stages and take a long time, the library is sometimes very slow to respond to changes in customer needs.*

  - *Customers are not targeted and often have imprecise or conflicting needs. As its services are available to the general public, the library does not target one group in particular. Rather it has to accommodate as best it can the needs of many different customer types sometimes with unclear or even conflicting needs. For example, the heaviest users of the library are children, who are stimulated by exciting environments, and senior citizens, who prefer peace and quiet.*

Stakeholders

Every organisation has stakeholders – groups of people or individuals who are affected directly or indirectly by the performance of the organisation. They may have a direct stake in its fortunes as employees or shareholders, or they may be external stakeholders such as suppliers or customers. These stakeholder groups often have different expectations of the organisation; for example, employees expect good pay and job security whilst shareholders expect a high return on their investment. Sometimes these expectations are in conflict and compromise objectives are needed to satisfy the interested parties. Marketing decisions not only have to conform to corporate objectives but also take account of possible conflicts of emphasis among stakeholder groups.

Figure 3.3 shows some examples of internal stakeholder groups for different types of organisations and potentially contentious areas that may have an impact on marketing decisions.

Stakeholders	Conflicting expectations of marketing decisions
LARGE COMPANY Institutional shareholders (e.g. pension schemes, investment trusts) Private shareholders Non-executive directors Senior managers Junior managers Employees Unions	Senior managers and institutional shareholders may wish to invest in longer-term marketing strategies involving corporate advertising. Junior managers and some private shareholders may prefer more visible, shorter-term results from marketing campaigns to gain promotion or maximise capital gain.
SMALL COMPANY Owner-manager Partners Managers Employees Investors	The owner-manager may desire the independence and personal control of a relatively static business and only undertakes marketing activities if existing sales are threatened. Other partners and managers advocate pro-active marketing campaigns to generate more sales growth
PUBLIC SERVICE (A LIBRARY) Local taxpayers Councillors Officers Employees	Councillors, responding to the need to keep down the local taxes of their voters whilst improving services, expect more efficient use of the same level of resources. Officers interpret this into a marketing strategy which promotes greater use of the existing library facilities and book stock by extending the opening hours and shortening the loan period of popular books. Employees object to working the increased number of unsocial hours and users dislike the pressure to return books quicker.

Figure 3.3: *Examples of conflicting expectations of marketing decisions among stakeholders*

Organisational resources

The resources available to an organisation form another important influence on marketing. The differences in marketing approaches between small and large firms in the private business sector illustrate the impact of this.

Smaller firms

In the 1970s and 1980s smaller businesses became a much more significant force in the national economies of Europe and the USA. In the UK, the vast majority of all businesses (99 per cent) employ less than 50 people. These firms account for approximately 50 per cent of total employment, and 40 per cent of total sales turnover.

The owner-managers of small businesses often have a paradoxical attitude to marketing because of their relative shortage of resources. On the one hand, they may dismiss marketing campaigns as something that only larger companies can afford. On the other hand, the same owner-managers adopt marketing-oriented practices because the small size of the business allows them to stay close to the customer and adapt rapidly to new needs. One of the advantages which small firms have demonstrated over larger companies is their ability to respond flexibly to shifts in customer demand.

The resources of small firms do not usually run to specialist marketing departments. Responsibility for marketing is often taken by the owner-manager, who may have little knowledge or experience of specialised aspects. This environment tends to give marketing in the small firm a distinctive style with a number of characteristics:

❑ *Lack of formalised planning of marketing strategies*: marketing in small firms tends to be ad-hoc, often in reaction to competitive activity.

❑ *Restricted in scope*: small firms are unable to incur the same pro-rata level of marketing expenditure as larger companies. Fixed costs (such as salaries or rent) tend to account for a higher proportion of sales revenue than in larger companies, leaving the small firm less to spend on marketing activities.

❑ *Simplistic and haphazard*: small businesses rely more on random, basic marketing efforts than sophisticated, integrated campaigns.

❑ *Evolutionary*: marketing practices in new ventures tend to evolve with the business. An initial phase of marketing activity when the business is first set up is superseded by a more reactive approach in which marketing efforts respond to customer enquiries or competitive threats. More positive marketing approaches may be adopted as the firm grows, leading to the planned, integrated campaigns of larger companies.

Whilst small firms may adopt a customer-oriented strategy to survive and thrive in today's competitive markets, resources and other constraints restrict their use of the tactics and techniques of marketing. These resource limitations often combine to create marketing strategies that are dependent on the personal characteristics of the owner-manager, a small number of existing customers and personal recommendations to acquire new customers, as illustrated by the following case of a start up business.

● *Carolyn Foster set up DuckEgg, with the aim of providing a website design and management service to developing businesses. She knew from experience that owners of fast-growing firms wanted a quick service at low cost. By doing most of the work herself and keeping overheads down, she was able to offer both. Although she had been trained in computer graphics, her experience of marketing was limited to designing promotional material. Her first customers came from personal contacts rather than any planned campaign, but the customer base increased gradually as existing clients recommended others. One customer in particular was expanding very quickly and took up more and more of her time as their Internet applications grew. They demanded personal attention to their problems, and soon she was spending half of her time on their business. Eventually, their continued expansion meant they could employ their own full-time webmaster, and Carolyn's business lost over half of its turnover. However, she had learned much about marketing in these early business dealings and she invested more resources in a marketing campaign aimed at building a wider base of customers.*

Larger firms

Marketing tends to become a specialist function as companies grow. In larger companies a marketing department is given the responsibility of carrying out the various processes of researching, planning, implementing and controlling marketing programmes. The environment of such a department includes other functional areas of the organisation such as production, finance, and human resources.

Because large companies have the resources to employ specialists, marketing programmes tend to be professionally conceived and executed. However there are pitfalls in this particular marketing environment such as:

❑ *Marketing managers become remote from the customer.* Changes in customer needs can be overlooked as each marketing specialist concerns themselves only with their part of the jigsaw without seeing the overall picture.

❑ *Other departments leave marketing to the specialists*, forgetting that it is not just a business function but a concept which has to involve everyone.

❑ *Marketing planning is done in isolation* by the marketing group with insufficient integration into the work of other departments.

Organisational culture and structure

Culture

Marketing decisions are taken within the context of the internal 'culture' of an organisation. This culture consists of the underlying values, attitudes and assumptions that an organisation adopts. It influences the way in which an organisation considers new ideas and options, how it reacts to events around it and how it structures itself. In many organisations, cultural factors work subtly; in others, the culture is such a powerful force that it resembles an ideology. For example, the Body Shop has advocated specific values relating to the environment, animal rights and traditional communities with a missionary vigour and operational style that has been described as 'management by infection'.

Structure

The distribution of responsibility and authority within an organisation is an important part of its culture. The organisational structures that result influence all decision-making including marketing. Some typical structures include:

❑ *The Entrepreneurial Organisation*: the owner-manager or small group of entrepreneurs retain centralised control over all-important decisions including marketing.

❑ *The Professionalised Organisation*: decision making is delegated to specialists usually organised into functional departments such as finance, production and marketing.

❑ *The Divisionalised Organisation*: operating divisions take the day-to-day decisions relating to their designated products or services, within a policy framework laid down by head office.

❑ *The Holding Organisation*: operating units, often in very diverse areas of business, are encouraged to act almost like independent organisations under the umbrella of a holding company.

The structure of the marketing function reflects the overall culture and structure of the organisation. In an 'entrepreneurial' organisation, the owner-managers may make all the important marketing decisions calling in outside specialists such as an advertising agency when needed. In a 'professionalised' organisation, a specialised marketing department may control all the day-to-day marketing decisions. This can be organised in a number of ways. Some of the options are illustrated in Figure 3.4

❑ *Functional specialists*, for example a market research manager, an advertising manager, a new products manager and a sales manager, all report to the marketing director. A common organisational form reflecting the specialist nature of some marketing tasks, this structure becomes less appropriate as an organisation grows and becomes involved in more markets and more products.

❑ *Product managers* have individual responsibility for the marketing of products or brands supported sometimes by specialists such as an advertising and promotions manager. This structure is typical of companies marketing branded consumer products (e.g. soft drinks and cereal producers).

❑ *Market managers* have responsibilities divided according to customer groups and markets rather than products. Service companies are often organised this way; for example, banks and financial institutions appoint separate managers responsible for marketing to businesses and domestic users.

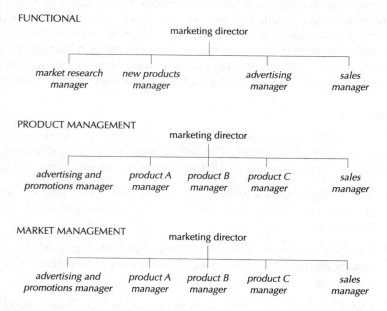

Figure 3.4 *Some options for organising marketing*

<table>
<tr><td>4.</td><td>THE MICRO-ENVIRONMENT</td></tr>
</table>

Marketing decisions may be directly affected by a number of external forces in the immediate market environment. These include suppliers, intermediaries, customers and competitors, as illustrated in Figure 3.5.

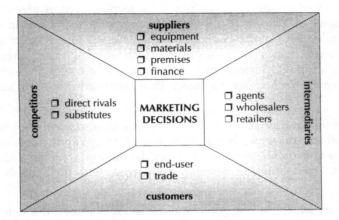

Figure 3.5: *The micro-environment*

Suppliers

The ability of an organisation to acquire the resources it needs to meet its own customers' requirements crucially affects its chances of success. Other businesses, organisations or individuals are the *suppliers* of these resources. The resources needed vary widely and include:

❑ equipment, raw materials, components and supplies bought from other companies;

❑ premises and associated services such as telephones, heating and cleaning supplied by landlords and other companies;

❑ specialised services such as training and advertising offered by agencies and institutions; and

❑ financial resources and services supplied by banks, investors and credit card companies.

Relationships with suppliers may be overlooked because priority is given to dealing with customers. But the ability of an organisation to meet their customers' needs may rely heavily on suppliers.

• *Jaguar Cars was a loss-making subsidiary of British Leyland when John Egan took over as managing director in 1980. A key problem was Jaguar's poor reputation for reliability particularly in the crucial export market of the USA. An analysis of customer complaints found that faulty components from suppliers were to blame for 60 per cent of key failures. Egan decided to involve the suppliers in improving quality to a much higher standard. He re-negotiated*

61

purchasing contracts to include penalty clauses for fault levels above an agreed level. He invited suppliers to join internal groups monitoring quality levels so they understood the problems more fully. By 1984 sales had increased in all major markets, especially the USA, and Jaguar finally shrugged off its unreliable image. Its marketing success hinged on the support of its suppliers.

Theories of relationship marketing reinforce the importance of suppliers and other 'markets', as well as customers (see chapter 4, section 7). Managers today recognise the importance of building partnerships with important suppliers in order to serve the common interests of their organisations. Successful buyers no longer depend on playing 'power games' with suppliers (such as deliberately keeping visiting salespeople waiting). Instead they make use of advances in information and communications technology to make their relationships with suppliers more effective:

❑ Electronic Data Interchange (EDI) allows customers and suppliers to handle transactions electronically via phone lines. Orders and invoices can be sent via computers, avoiding the need to re-key data into accounting and stock control systems. Over a third of businesses now trade with their supply chain in this way.

❑ 'E-procurement' – buying goods and services for business through the Internet – is also growing rapidly. Manufacturers offer products through electronic catalogues. Larger companies are setting up their own 'electronic market-places'. For example, the WorldWide Retail Exchange consists of over 100,000 companies supplying goods and services to about 20 major retail chains such as Boots, Marks & Spencer and Tesco in the UK, Casino in France, and K-Mart and JC Penney in the USA. The advantage for the purchasing retailer is that they can ensure a competitive marketplace of approved suppliers, whilst the suppliers achieve exposure to the largest potential customers.

Intermediaries

Organisations do not always deal directly with the consumer of their product or service (more of this in Chapter 4). Intermediaries help in the processes of selling and physically delivering products to customers. These include:

❑ *sales agents* who represent a number of different organisations in the marketplace by promoting and selling their products and services;

❑ *wholesalers* who provide easier access to retailing outlets, which can be fragmented numerically and geographically; and

❑ *retailers* who provide access to consumer markets by locating themselves in convenient shopping areas.

These intermediaries play an important marketing role in penetrating the market for a particular product and any changes to the way in which they operate can be crucial.

● *Smith's Crisps were the household name for crisps in the 1950s and 60s. Famous for their little blue salt packets, Smith's products sold extensively through many small outlets such as grocers and public houses. By the 1970s distribution of food products was changing rapidly with the growth of multiple retailers and supermarkets. The popularity of out-of-town superstores in the 1980s reinforced the concentration of retailing into fewer, much larger outlets.*

At first Smith's did not change fast enough to cope with this rapidly changing environment. The short shelf life of their crisps was designed for distribution through localised outlets such as the corner shop and pubs and instant or rapid consumption once purchased. The new supermarket chains needed longer-life food products in larger sizes suitable for more leisurely, family consumption. Competitors such as Golden Wonder crisps, ready salted in family-sized, longer-life plastic packs, took an increasing share of a rapidly growing market. By the 1980s, Smith's failure to respond to changes in the distribution environment had reduced its share to 14 per cent of a market it once dominated.

Smiths responded with new marketing strategies more suited to the changed needs of the intermediaries in the marketplace, improving Smith's position in the snacks market (interestingly these strategies included a nostalgic appeal to previous consumption habits by re-launching the blue salt packet).

Customers

If intermediaries come between an organisation and the final consumer or 'end-user' of the product, then these intermediaries may themselves become the customer who buys the product. In the example above, Smith's sells its crisps to its direct customers in the snack trade such as the supermarkets and other retailers rather than the consumer. Marketing strategies can target the end-user, thereby aiming to 'pull' the product through the trade. Alternatively products can be 'pushed' into the distribution trade in the expectation that they will be sold on to the consumer. (The changing role of customers in a supply chain is examined more fully in Chapter 4.)

Competitors

Organisations usually have to compete with other organisations for customers. The success or failure of private sector businesses has depended for some time on their ability to satisfy customer needs better than competitors. In many markets, competition comes not only from *direct rivals* but also *substitutes* that perform the same task in a different way or compete for the same slice of disposable income. For example, a restaurant competes not only with other local restaurants, but also with other methods of eating conveniently (such as take-aways and ready-made meals) and other places of social contact (such as public houses and coffee bars).

Markets have become increasingly competitive in areas that traditionally were not considered subject to competitive forces. The environment of some industries such as gas, electricity and telecommunications has been made more competitive by the removal of state control and monopoly status of suppliers. Public services such as education and the health service have entered a more competitive arena by the introduction of many changes to the way they are structured and operate.

- *State schools at primary and secondary level faced little competition until the education reforms introduced during the 1980s and 1990s. Parents and children had very little say in their choice of school unless they joined the small minority (approximately 7 per cent) of pupils paying fees for education in private schools. The Education Reform Act of 1988 introduced many changes, aimed at making educational provision more competitive, on the assumption that this would improve its quality. The introduction of two key concepts in particular have made the school environment more competitive:*

  - *The idea of 'parental choice' gives parents the right to send their children to whichever state school they choose providing it has enough space to take them. Parents can become active customers in the sense they can exercise some choice based on what different schools have to offer.*

  - *Schools are allocated money mainly on the basis of the numbers of pupils attending a particular school. The more pupils a school admits, the more funds it receives. Moreover a school has considerable freedom over how it uses the money allocated to it. Headteachers can decide whether to spend additional funds on more staff, new books, computers or other facilities. Schools have a real incentive to attract as many pupils as possible by competing with neighbouring schools. Not only do they receive more money by doing so, they can spend it according to their own local priorities.*

  Some schools have adapted to these changes in the educational environment very rapidly, adopting marketing strategies to increase pupil numbers and hence the resources available to their school. Others are more reluctant to fully embrace what they consider to be unnecessary commercial practices. Whatever the rights and wrongs of the moral argument, the management of schools has fundamentally changed.

(The role of competitive forces is considered more fully in Chapter 4.)

5. | THE MACRO-ENVIRONMENT

The marketing environment also includes forces that have a more general impact on organisations. These are sometimes summarised by the acronym STEP or PEST (which we have already used in Chapter 2, section 3, 'The marketing audit'), representing the following influences:

- ❏ Socio-cultural
- ❏ Technological
- ❏ Economic
- ❏ Political

This is shown in Figure 3.6.

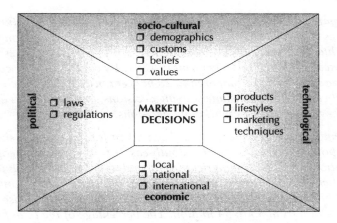

Figure 3.6: *The macro-environment*

Socio-cultural environment

Social and cultural forces condition how individuals translate their needs into the specific products and services which they want. If marketing is to play its full role in matching product benefits to customer needs then an understanding of the social and cultural environment is essential. This environment can be sub-divided into demographic and cultural aspects:

❑ *The demographic structure* of a society describes its human population in terms of size, location, age, ethnic origin, occupation, sex, and other statistical measures.

❑ *The culture* of a society is made up of a complex mixture of many beliefs, values, customs, habits, laws and understandings that are learned from parents and other members of society. Some or these cultural influences (for example, observing traditions such as birthdays and Christmas) are deeply engrained and take many years to evolve. Others are more fickle, presenting constant marketing challenges because of their impact on the buying habits of society (for example, our re-discovered concern for the natural environment with increased emphasis on 'green' issues).

Marketing management constantly needs up-to-date information in both of these areas as changes can present threats to current strategies or offer opportunities for new ones.

• *The Census of the UK population provides many insights into the habits and structure of our society which have considerable marketing significance. A comparison of modern census data with information from a census carried out over a century earlier in 1891 reveals that some of the cultural and demographic trends are not quite as we thought.*

One cultural influence commonly believed to be in decline is the institution of marriage. However, a comparison of recent data with the census of 1891 shows that a higher proportion of people are married today than in Victorian times. 60 per cent of all people over 15 are married according to the 1991 census compared to 41 per cent in 1891. However an important feature of the modern figures is that we are marrying later and couples are living longer compared to one hundred years ago. Only 11 per cent of people aged 20 to 24 are now married compared to 19 per cent in 1891. By contrast 43 per cent of those over 85 are still married, compared to 28 per cent in 1891. As the composition of the family unit affects consumer buying decisions, these and more detailed statistics are key ingredients in marketing decisions.

A demographic change that has been taken for granted is a significant shift of the population towards the South-east of England as people leave areas traditionally reliant on agriculture or industries now in decline. Although the number of people living in the South-east has risen from 9.1 million in 1891 to 16.8 million in 1991, this is mainly a reflection of the increase in the total UK population from 33 to 54 million. The percentage of the total population living in the South-east has gone up from 27.5 per cent to 31 per cent, but this is less than has generally been supposed, with most other areas showing increases in the total number of inhabitants. The population of Scotland declined slightly to 5.1 million in 2001. However, this was due not to population movement, as there has been a net inward migration, but to an increase in the numbers of older people dying, which has exceeded birth rates.

Technological environment

Advances in technology affect the marketing environment in a number of ways:

❑ *The creation of new opportunities for products and services* is the most obvious impact of technological change. Advances in information and communications technology have generated large numbers of new products. Each successful new product presents opportunities for additions and refinements to add to the proliferation. More powerful, smaller computers, advanced mobile phones, and digital television have spun off different products as new applications of the technology emerge.

  • *Computer games have developed into a large, international market for companies such as Nintendo in the United States. Their success has created marketing opportunities for the development of new products. British brothers Richard and David Darling invented 'Game Genie', a device for making computer games more or less difficult for the player. Nintendo were concerned at the effective upgrading of their products with no benefit to themselves and sued on the grounds of copyright infringement. 'Game Genie' survived such legal action, and sales of this complementary device alone were over £100 million per annum.*

❑ *Technological advances can also change the distribution of existing products and services.* For example, the way in which we obtain cash to spend has evolved from bank counters to dispensing machines. Digital products such as music and print can be downloaded via the Internet. Groceries, holidays, pensions, and a whole range of other products can now be ordered via a computer or telephone at home and delivered direct to the consumer.

❑ *Our consumption patterns and life styles evolve* as a result of technological changes. There have been many recent examples. Developments in transportation systems have changed our purchasing habits as the spread of car ownership enabled convenient shopping further from home, culminating in the development of one-stop, out-of-town shopping centres. New technology in the kitchen, from microwaves to mixers, has reduced meal preparation times allowing our eating habits to fit in with busy lifestyles and creating the need for a whole new range of food products.

❑ *Marketing techniques have changed* as a result of technological possibilities. New ways of gathering information have had a particularly significant impact on consumer marketing.

  • *Electronic point of sale (EPOS) data capture allows major retailers to analyse sales, control stocks and evaluate marketing programmes at hitherto unknown levels of speed and accuracy. The laser reading of bar codes on product labels at checkouts provides fast and detailed information about what is sold and when – information that can then be used to improve the turnover and efficiencies of the store. It is used to control and re-order stock and provide statistics that can monitor the sales of individual products by the minute.*

    A marketing tool developed from this technology targets customers with discount coupons based on what they have just purchased. Computerised equipment at the checkout scans customers' purchases and promotes other products by giving them discount vouchers for items they have not bought. This can be used by competitors to tempt customers away from the brand they have just purchased the next time they shop. For example, if a customer's purchases include a tin of Campbells soup they may be given a discount voucher to buy Heinz next time. It can also be used to promote categories of product that the customer has not purchased. If a store wishes to promote, say, its delicatessen lines, then vouchers are given to anyone without delicatessen items in their basket.

Economic environment

The economic environment affects how much we have to spend and how we are likely to spend it. Therefore, it plays a significant role in determining the likely demand for products and services. Marketing is influenced by local, national and international economic factors.

❑ *The local economy* of a region is important particularly when exceptional circumstances create significant variations to national trends. High levels of unemployment created by the decline of the dominant local industry may depress demand for luxury goods in that area, for example.

❑ *National economic factors* such as interest rates, exchange rates, unemployment levels and rates of inflation have obvious implications on products and services in the market place. Marketing planning involves making assumptions about these key statistics and evaluating the impact of any likely changes. As Britain's post-war economy was dominated by 'boom or bust' cycles, successful organisations have had to demonstrate the flexibility to respond quickly to changed economic climates.

❑ *International economic developments* have longer-term significance which are sometimes more difficult to evaluate. Changing growth rates in other national economies affect exports and imports, which in turn influence national and local economies.

- *The Chinese economic area including China, Taiwan, Korea and Hong Kong has become a fourth power to rival North America, Japan and Europe in the world economic hierarchy. This economic area has expanded counter-cyclically to the rest, averaging annual growth rates of between 7 to 8 per cent in times when the more established economies were showing much lower or negative growth rates. China itself has been exporting at record levels, helped by a plentiful supply of cheap skilled labour. For western economies such as the UK this presents a threat and an opportunity: the threat of a further erosion of the manufacturing base, particularly in labour intensive industries, and the opportunity of a fast growing export market for specialised goods and services which are not available in China.*

Political environment

The political environment of laws, regulations and interventions by central and local government, political agencies and pressure groups is an increasing influence on the marketing of any organisation. Recent legislation has had two main aims:

❑ *To protect the consumer*: there are many UK and EC regulations designed to protect the consumer from being harmed by products or misled by suppliers. Products and services, and the environment in which they are sold, have to conform to health and safety standards. Customers are entitled to accurate information about what they are buying and to take back anything that does not do what is claimed. In some circumstances, customers have a legal right to change their minds; after signing a contract for insurance cover or a time-share apartment, for example, customers have an enforced 'cooling-off' period of 30 days in which to reconsider their decision away from any pressure created by the sales environment.

❑ *To ensure full and fair competition*: organisations are also protected from each other. Legislation regulates competition in the private sector in order to prevent one or more suppliers dominating a particular market against the interests of customers. The EC is particularly concerned to see that companies in different member states compete on equal terms, free from artificial subsidies which may distort competition in favour of the less efficient.

In the UK, public sector services have been forced to become more open to competitive forces. Some services such as the maintenance of public places and buildings by local authorities, hospitals, schools, and other government institutions are subject to compulsory competitive tendering which ensures that a number of competing bids are taken into account before contracts to supply a service are awarded.

These political pressures to increase the power of the customer over the supplier affect all aspects of marketing from the design and pricing of a product to how it is promoted and distributed.

- *The marketing of beer came under UK government scrutiny when the Monopolies and Mergers Commission investigated the big breweries. Their report, published in 1989, described the supply of beer in Britain as a complex monopoly. Six large brewers, including well-known names such as Bass, Whitbread and Courage, controlled many of the outlets for their products. 87 per cent of all public houses were either owned by breweries or 'tied' to them in a way that restricted sales to their products only. According to the Commission, the big breweries had used this stranglehold on the distribution system to keep out smaller competitors and increase prices unjustifiably. As a result of the report, brewers that owned more than 2000 pubs were forced to free half of those above this minimum level from any tie to the brewery and allow them to become 'free houses'. Pubs that remained tied to a brewery were forced to sell at least one cask-conditioned beer ('real ale') from an independent brewery. This political intervention changed the scope of marketing activities in the industry. The UK beer market has been static for some time, and demand has shifted away from traditional dark British beers to lagers and premium ales such as the best selling brands Stella Artois, Guinness and Caffreys. This change in the market coupled with the pressures of regulation caused the major UK breweries to re-think their strategies. Bass and Whitbread intensified their efforts to diversify whilst selling off their brewing interests. Scottish and Newcastle, now the largest UK brewer, expanded outside of the UK by acquisitions such as Kronenbourg. Whilst the large breweries have contracted and merged, smaller, independent breweries such as Greene King have survived by offering distinctive real ale products to niche markets.*

6. | MANAGING IN THE ENVIRONMENT

Scanning the environment

All of these factors, from industry-specific influences to general economic trends, form an environment that affects marketing decisions. Information about this environment is therefore a crucial input into the marketing process. The accelerating pace of technological change makes it harder to keep up, whilst the increased competitiveness of markets means that it is even more essential to do so.

Some organisations systematically analyse their environment to formally assess the possible impact of trends and external events. Environmental scanning techniques can help this analysis. QUEST (an acronym for 'Quick Environmental Scanning Technique') is one technique that allows managers of an organisation to pool their views on the future in a systematic way.

Other managers keep in touch with their environment in less formal ways. Successful entrepreneurs often develop informal networks to keep them in touch with what is happening around them. Some seem to have an instinctive understanding of developments in their environment. Alan Sugar, the founder of Amstrad, described one of the reasons for his success as an 'in-built aptitude for scenting the way the wind is blowing'. Research studies among a number of entrepreneurs suggest that those who succeed work hard at developing contacts to give them as much feedback from their environment as possible.

Whatever way it is gained, making judgements about the likely trends and events in the environment is a key part of the marketing process. This is not always easy to get right. Management overreactions to external factors are as frequent as not doing enough.

- *Western economies slowed down in the late 1980s, affecting a number of key sectors. The aircraft industry looked as though it would be particularly affected by downturns in travel and tourism. The leading aircraft maker Boeing acted swiftly by cutting out many of its suppliers and reducing its workforce drastically. When orders picked up again, the company could not cope with the increased demand. Its competitor, European Airbus, gained from Boeing's inability to produce enough jumbo jets.*

  The 1990s provided a decade of unprecedented economic growth. Many organisations flourished in this stable, predictable climate. By 2000/2001, growth slowed – quickly in the USA and more slowly in Europe. Mangers were faced with a situation of uncertainty that many had not faced before. Mistakes were again made by over-hasty reactions to the changing environment. For example, Marks and Spencer decided to close down its French stores in 2001. But the company found it had acted too swiftly without proper consultation with the French unions. Public relations and sales were worsened by the resulting court case.

Changing the environment

Marketing management cannot directly control these factors in the macro, micro and internal environment. For this reason they are sometimes referred to as the 'uncontrollable' elements in the mix of possible marketing decisions.

This does not mean that marketing management always accepts passively what is happening around it. The relationship between marketing and external forces is an interactive one and there are times when marketing influences its environment. Some instances of this include:

❑ *Influencing the internal environment* within an organisation. We described one of the key principles of the marketing concept as 'organisational integration' which means that the entire organisation has to adopt a customer oriented strategy, not just the marketing department (Chapter 1, 'Organisational integration'). The marketing function may need to monitor decision making within other departments of an organisation and influence them towards a customer-based approach.

❑ *Managing the micro-environment.* Organisations may try to actively manage aspects of their immediate micro-environment such as their relationships with suppliers and intermediaries. We have already seen how Jaguar set about regulating their suppliers through contractual arrangements (see 'Suppliers' above).

❑ *Modifying the external environment.* In some instances, organisations use marketing techniques to modify the external forces that particularly affect them. Organisations 'market' their viewpoints on certain issues through direct representations and lobby groups to try and influence decision-makers at local, national and international levels.

- *The large breweries made strong representations to the government and members of parliament following the report of the Monopolies and Mergers Commission on the supply of beer (see 'Political environment'). This pressure forced the government to modify the Commission's initial proposals which recommended more sweeping reforms including the forced sale by the breweries of many of their pubs.*

Whether they are actively managed in this way or simply monitored for their possible effects, environmental influences are an important initial input into the marketing decision-making process.

7. | KEY POINTS

An understanding of the context within which an organisation operates and the environmental influences around it are an essential part of the marketing decision-making process. The marketing context can be classified into three main types:

❏ *The internal environment* of organisational factors such as:

- ❏ *Objectives.* Profit is a common objective in the private sector, although some smaller businesses prefer independence to growth. The public sector have other, sometimes conflicting, objectives such as the provision of a high quality service and meeting spending targets.

- ❏ *Stakeholders.* Many groups from shareholders to employees with a vested interest in an organisation may place different emphasis on marketing strategies.

- ❏ *Resources.* Large and small firms differ in the way they approach marketing because of differences in their human and financial resources.

- ❏ *Culture and structure.* The internal culture, made up of organisational values, beliefs, and assumptions, influences the marketing decisions an organisation makes and how it structures itself for decision making.

❏ *The micro-environment* of external forces specific to an organisation including:

- ❏ *Suppliers* who influence the resources available.

- ❏ *Intermediaries* who come between a business and the final consumer.

- ❏ *Customers* in the trade or end-users.

- ❏ *Competitors* trying to satisfy the same customer.

❏ *The macro-environment* of forces having a more general impact including:

- ❏ *Socio-cultural* changes to the structure and attitudes of society.

- ❏ *Technological* advances in what is possible.

❑ *Economic* factors at local, national and international level.

❑ *Political* and legal constraints.

❑ *Managing marketing* in this environment involves:

    ❑ *scanning* it to understand what is happening and likely trends;

    ❑ *influencing* it when this is possible and appropriate.

8. | DEVELOPING MARKETING SKILLS

Exercises

1. Consider the educational establishment at which you are studying or one with which you are familiar (e.g., a former school or college). Assume that you have been asked to advise them on developing a marketing strategy. Analyse the environmental factors, both internal and external, which would influence your recommendations.

2. Think of an entrepreneur who has rapidly developed a business (such as Alan Sugar of Amstrad, Anita Roddick of Body Shop, or Richard Branson of Virgin). What environmental factors have helped the development of their business? Which internal and external factors may threaten them or provide them opportunities in the future?

3. Which environmental factors will be particularly influential in shaping your chosen career in the next five years?

Developing a marketing plan

Activity 3 An internal audit

Carry out an internal marketing audit of the organisation or product of your choice. This should enable you to summarise its strengths and weaknesses in relation to any future marketing activities. In particular consider the objectives, resources, culture and structure of the organisation. Identify basic information such as product range, sales or income, past marketing objectives, methods and success rates, (see also Chapter 2, 'The marketing audit' for a summary of areas to be covered).

FURTHER READING AND REFERENCES

General texts

Kotler, P. (2000) *Marketing Management*, 10th edition, Prentice Hall, chapter 4.

Public sector marketing

Common, R., Flynn, N. and Mellon, E. (1992) *Managing Public Services: Competition and Decentralisation*, Oxford, Butterworth-Heinnemann.

Hannagan, T. (1992) *Marketing for the Non-profit Sector*, Macmillan Press, chapter 6.

Walsh, K. (1994) Marketing and public sector management, *European Journal of Marketing*, **28**(3), pages 63–71.

Small business marketing

Carson, D., Cromie, S., McGowan, P. and Hill, J. (1995) *Marketing and Entrepreneurship in SMEs*, London, Prentice Hall.

Hall, G. (1995) *Surviving and Prospering in the Small Firm Sector*, London, Routledge.

Stokes, D. (2000) Marketing in small firms, in Carter, S. and Jones-Evans, D. (eds) *Enterprise and Small Business: Principles, Practice and Policy*, Harlow, FT/Prentice Hall.

Impact of the Internet

Chaffey, D., Mayer, R., Johnston, K. and Ellis-Chadwick, F. (2000) *Internet Marketing*, Pearson Education, chapter 4.

Wheatley, M. (2000) Supplies on de-mand, *Supply Management*, **21**, September, pages 11–12.

CHAPTER 4

Customers and Competitors

The common theme of 'customers' and their 'needs' is of such significance in the study of marketing that this chapter looks at the meaning of these words more closely. It seeks to define customer needs compared to wants and examines some of the different types of customers. It looks at how customers are grouped into markets and analyses some of the competitive forces at play.

1. CASE STUDY: KITWELL JEANS

Dominique Saldo was working on a marketing strategy report to the directors of her company, Kitwell Ltd. She had recently been appointed as marketing manager of this clothing manufacturer and wanted to make an impact with her first presentation to the board. The problem was that the way forward was far from clear in her mind.

Kitwell was a long established producer of work clothing and men's and boys' jeans. Originally a manufacturer of work-wear garments, the company had turned to making jeans in the 1950s. This had almost certainly saved the company from the fate of many other British manufacturers in the post-war years that found themselves unable to compete with cheaper imports of textiles and clothing principally from the Far East. The UK clothing industry had become increasingly polarised into a small number of large companies able to generate sufficient economies of scale to survive and a large, fragmented group of smaller manufacturers relying on their rapid, flexible response to demand from specialised markets.

Fortunately for Kitwell, they concentrated on what was to become the most profitable product sector of the clothing market – jeans. The metamorphosis of jeans from the utilitarian working garment of the early century to a symbol of youthful rebellion in the 1950s and 60s continued through the 1970s and 80s as they became a highly branded, fashion garment. Jeans are still an essential item in any young person's wardrobe. Consumers buy 60 million pairs per annum in the UK representing sales of over £1 billion at retail prices. Approximately £10 million of advertising supports well-known brand names that control an estimated 85 per cent of total sales. The brand differentiation of otherwise similar products has allowed prices to become relatively high and manufacturer's margins remain good compared to other sectors of the clothing market.

Kitwell had prospered by developing good relationships with the key outlets for jeans – the multiple chains and specialist jeans retailers. Instead of competing with the top brand names, Kitwell had concentrated on producing own-label garments for the multiples and one-off special products and sale offers for the specialist retailers. They sold direct to the larger retail chains and through wholesale warehouses and cash and carry outlets to smaller retailers. However these relationships were often complex; for example, they sub-contracted some of their larger orders to other overseas manufacturers and some of their wholesale outlets also sold direct to the public.

Dominique reflected on her briefing meeting with the managing director.

'Keep it simple', he had told her. 'We are dealing with an eternal fashion garment, and it's the under 25 year olds who drive fashion in this country. Whatever we do, we must maintain our saleability to that age group.'

But a number of factors made Dominique uncomfortable with the tried and tested approach. Firstly, the age group that they had historically relied upon had decreased in number. In the late 1980s there were nearly 16 million 15 to 24 year olds in the UK, but numbers had fallen to 12 million by the turn of the century. Secondly there were signs that the new generation of that age group would neither want the same clothes, nor buy them through traditional outlets. An increasing demand for 'environmentally friendly' jeans made of organic fibres and natural fabrics was one sign of change. Dominique also recognised that the youth market was the most likely group to adopt new behavioural patterns as a result of advances in information and communications technology. Buyers under 25 already formed a significant percentage of Internet shoppers. Clothing was a fast developing e-commerce purchase category, although it still lagged behind favourite on-line products – CDs, books and computer items. Could jeans manufacturers afford to be driven by this increasingly volatile section of the market when other groups such as children under 14 and the over 45 year olds had become more numerous?

The nature of competition was also changing. Kitwell, like other surviving UK manufacturers had side-stepped the cheaper imports by concentrating on the shorter runs of the latest styles. Now other European producers in the Republic of Ireland, France, Belgium, Italy and Malta were taking an increasing share of this market. The leading brands increasingly adopted a global approach to their marketing, competing in North American and European markets with the same products and promotional strategies. At the same time they multiplied the numbers of products on offer. Jeans are no longer the standard blue denim of the 1960s as colours and finishes have proliferated. Darker shades in looser fits currently prevail over the tighter look of the 1990s. Dominique also noted that one of the leading brands had launched a range of corduroy jeans. Could it be that the market for the basic five-pocket denim jean had peaked? She recalled that earlier in the 1980s the sale of jeans had declined sharply as other types of casual trousers had become more popular until the re-launch of Levi's 501s through the famous 'launderette' advertising campaign had revitalised the whole market.

Kitwell's direct customers in the wholesale and retail trade were also becoming more demanding. For example, the delivery time for supply of new lines to some multiples had become shorter and shorter as the retailers tried to stay on top of the shifts in consumer demand. Dominique recalled the exasperation on the face of Kitwell's manufacturing manager as he had explained to her his difficulty in changing production lines from the 'distressed' look to an 'antique' finish in a matter of days. There was also a trend for manufacturers to become retailers as some of the well-known names had begun to open up their own outlets selling direct to the public.

Dominique knew that she would have to come up with something special if they were to survive in a market in which a declining number of key consumers were being chased by too many competitive products.

Points to consider

1. Consider the needs and wants of customers in the jeans market. What is the underlying customer need that jeans are fulfilling? What do different types of customers want when they buy a pair of jeans?

See sections 2 and 3.

2. Examine the structure of Kitwell's market. Who are their direct customers and what benefits do these customers seek from their suppliers? (It may be useful to draw a diagram of the various types of customers in the chain between manufacturer and consumer.) What business should Kitwell consider themselves to be in?

See sections 4 and 5.

3. Analyse the competitive forces in the jeans market. What is the state of development of the market and what are the trends among existing competitors? How will the relative power between the buyers and suppliers influence developments? How great are the barriers that may deter new entrants? What are the likely threats from substitute products? Are these factors likely to improve or depress the profitability of the industry?

See sections 6 and 7.

4. Suggest some marketing strategies which Dominique could consider.

2. | NEEDS, WANTS AND DEMANDS

We have described marketing as an exchange process that matches the capabilities of suppliers with the needs of customers. If sufficient people *want* a product or service then the role of marketing is to match this *demand* with the supply of a product which meets this *need*. Notice that we have used three different terms in this sentence – want, demand and need – to indicate the rationale for the supply of products and services to customers. Each has a complementary but different significance in the role of marketing.

Needs

What do we *need* to survive and thrive in this life? This fundamental question has perhaps more to do with philosophical debates on the meaning of life than a text on marketing, but its significance here lies in the distinction which can be made between our needs and our wants.

If you were asked to write a list of everything you wanted and a list of everything you needed, which would be the longer list? The chances are that your list of wants is longer than your assessment of your needs. Although we tend to *want* many things, our basic *needs* are relatively few.

The American psychologist Abraham Maslow (1954) narrowed them down to five key needs, arranged as a series of steps, or a 'hierarchy of needs', from the most fundamental to the most difficult to obtain:

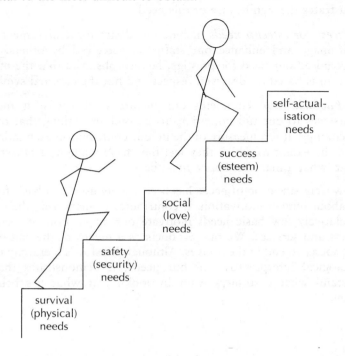

Figure 4.1: *Maslow's hierarchy of needs*

❑ *Survival (or physiological) needs* are the basic biological requirements for the survival of our bodies. As they include such fundamental needs as food, drink and sleep, we cannot consider other desires until these are met. If we are very hungry and tired, our concern for other needs is minimised until we have eaten and slept. We tend to take the fulfilment of these needs for granted in western societies, until the means to gratify them is removed. Threats to survival such as ill-health sweep away our concerns for other needs, as anyone who has suffered serious illness will testify.

Once we have satisfied one level of need, we progress to the next. According to Maslow, 'man is a wanting animal. As one desire is satisfied, another pops up to take its place.' As it does, we tend to lose interest in the fulfilled need and concentrate our energies on the next level of need. Once our physiological needs for survival are met, we tend to take them for granted as we seek to fulfil other needs higher up the ladder.

❑ *Safety (or security) needs* are next in the hierarchy. Included here is the need for some guarantee that our physical needs will be met in the foreseeable future, that we will have shelter and some form of income. We like to have the security of knowing that at least our basic needs can be met for some time to come.

❑ *Social (or love) needs* indicate our desire to belong to a group where we are

77

accepted and receive affection. This may be represented by family, friends, workmates, a sports team or social club. The use of solitary confinement as a punishment that deliberately excludes the possibility of social contact, illustrates the significance of this need.

❑ *Success (or esteem) needs* include our desire for achievement to improve our self-image and enhance our status as perceived by others. Whilst Maslow recognised our need for prestige, he also observed that the most healthy self-esteem is based on deserved respect and not the external symbols of success.

❑ *Self-actualisation* completes our hierarchy of needs. It means developing ourselves to our full potential, 'to become everything that one is capable of becoming'. It is a measure of the unique contribution each individual can make and the extent to which they feel they have made it, a reflection of the belief that 'what a man can be, he *must* be'.

Maslow's classification of needs has been widely used as a basis for understanding more about human motivation. It contributes to marketing theory by illustrating that relatively few basic needs motivate our acquisition of seemingly countless products and services. We buy products as a means to the end of fulfilling these needs, not as an end in themselves. Although Maslow's hierarchy represents only a psychological interpretation of our needs, it demonstrates that we can only understand what customers want by looking at what lies behind a purchase decision.

Wants

'Wants' represent the means of fulfilling needs and can be innumerable. Take a child into a toy store and they will usually express many different wants. The child may be expressing a single need in their social desire for play, but they will see many ways of meeting that need on display in the toy-shop. A shopper in a supermarket will buy many items as they translate their physiological need for food into wanting various food products.

Our wants represent how we wish a need to be fulfilled, as conditioned by our past and present environment. As a need can usually be satisfied by a number of alternatives, we make a choice of how we wish a need to be filled and 'want' that particular option. A child's social needs can be met by a range of options from wooden toys to computer games. Our need for food can be met by a huge choice from pork chops to chop suey.

Which of the alternatives we choose is conditioned by our past and present circumstances. As well as current economic circumstances, our social and cultural background plays an important role. We would expect the food contents of a shopping basket in Manila to be very different to one in Manchester. These and other factors lead to a preference for a specific alternative and this choice constitutes a 'want'.

Demand

Wants are not always translated into actual purchases of a product or service. We may want many more products than we can afford. A demand for goods can only become effective when it is linked to an ability to obtain them, usually by paying for them. The economic concept of *demand* for a certain product assumes that those who want it can also afford its price.

Thus *effective demand* represents *affordable wants*. If we want a product but we are unable to purchase it, because we cannot afford it or for another reason, then this represents a *latent demand* for a product. I may need a drink and I want a glass of champagne, but I cannot afford it (latent demand) so I buy a glass of wine instead, thereby adding to the (effective) demand for that product.

In considering all of our possible wants, we give them some sort of priority order and satisfy them until our available resources are depleted. The problem for suppliers is to make sure their product is high enough up the priority list of sufficient potential purchasers. This is the role of marketing.

In summary:

❏ A *need* is something necessary for the maintenance of life at either a basic or more evolved level.

❏ A *want* is a choice of how that need is to be fulfilled.

❏ *Demand* is made up of the total number of those wanting a specific product who are also prepared to pay its price.

3. MARKETING MYOPIA

The significance of understanding these terms is more than just an appreciation of definitions. The role of marketing, at the interface between supply and demand, is to interpret our needs and make available wanted products and services that we can afford. However there is a danger that marketing can develop a myopic view about what is needed by customers. In supplying the existing demand for a product it is possible to believe it is 'needed', when in fact it is only 'wanted' until something better comes along.

Levitt's drill bits

Theodore Levitt, the well-known management writer, called this 'marketing myopia', giving the example of a supplier of drill bits. Because drill bits have been in demand for so long, a supplier can be forgiven for believing that their products were 'needed' by all their seemingly loyal customers. However those customers do not 'need' drill bits. They need what the drill bits produce – holes. Customers 'want' drill bits, but only so long as there is not a better way of producing holes. Once an affordable, superior product becomes available – a hand-held laser drill perhaps – then demand will shift to that product which will then become 'wanted' by those who 'need' holes.

● *The North American Railroads*

  Levitt demonstrated how this 'myopia' applied to whole industries citing the example of the American railroads. The development of the steam engine revolutionised transport systems during the nineteenth century. The North

American railroads were instrumental in opening up the whole continent and setting the USA on course to become the richest economy on earth. The railroad companies shared in that growth and by the twentieth century they had become one of the most prosperous and powerful industries in the country. Their decline was as spectacular as their rise; half a century later the industry was in ruins with services drastically reduced, often only surviving through government subsidies.

Levitt's judgement on their rise and fall is that railroad owners and managers mistook wants for needs, believing that people would always need their service, when in fact they needed the most effective, convenient, economic transportation system available. The invention of the internal combustion engine and the development of air transport provided alternatives to meet that need which became more and more attractive and therefore wanted in preference to rail.

- **The UK Coal Industry**

Many major industries, such as coal mining in the UK, have followed a similar pattern. Coal was the dominant form of energy as the industrial revolution began to transform manufacturing and communications in the nineteenth century. Mining companies struggled to keep up with demand and concentrated their efforts on becoming the most efficient extractors of coal. Alternative forms of power were soon to remind them that they were in the energy business, not the coal extraction business as first oil, nuclear power and then North Sea gas eroded their share of the market.

Overcoming myopia

Levitt's interpretation of the demise of once great industries like the railroads has been criticised because it does not necessarily indicate what can be done to correct decline. Even if the railroad owners had recognised early enough that alternative transport systems would develop, what could they have done about it? Alternative successful strategies are not obvious. However some important management concepts emerge from this example which influence how we think of customers and the demand and supply equation:

❑ Customers are loyal to the capabilities of a product to fulfil needs, not to the products themselves. They buy the end result, not the means to achieve it.

❑ Products are wanted only for a limited time before demand shifts to other products which represent a preferred means to the same end.

❑ Any organisation which limits itself to a product that represents only one means of achieving the desired result, is therefore limiting its own life expectancy.

We will discuss each of these propositions in turn in the next section on matching benefits and customers.

4. MATCHING BENEFITS TO CUSTOMERS

Features and benefits

As customers, we want products that fulfil our identified needs, and we buy them because of their capability to meet our needs. We buy products because of what they can do for us. In other words we are really interested in the *benefits* that a product offers us, not in the product for its own sake. We buy drill bits because we need holes, not because we like drill bits. We choose a particular type of drill bit in preference to another because it offers benefits that are appropriate to what we want: it is longer lasting and can make holes in masonry, for example.

Sales people are trained to distinguish between the *features* of a product and its *benefits* for the very reason that we only buy products to acquire the benefits that they offer us.

❑ The *features* of a product describe its characteristics. For example:

- *A mountain bike has the features of a sturdy frame, thick tyres and fifteen gears.*

- *A business loan account has the feature of a fixed rate of interest.*

❑ The *benefits* of a product describe the value that its features provide to a customer. For example:

- *The features of a mountain bike give it the benefit of being able to travel more easily over rough hilly terrain and withstand this type of use for longer.*

- *The feature of a fixed rate of interest gives this type of business loan account the benefit of predictable repayment amounts and therefore more certainty in planning the cash flow.*

We want products only if the benefits offered match what we need. If we want a bike in order to travel over rough terrain we will be attracted by the benefits of the mountain bike. If however we want a bike for use only on flat roads then some of these benefits disappear and become disadvantages. We may prefer less sturdy but lighter bicycles. Similarly, if our business needs the lowest possible rate of interest then we may not see an account with a fixed rate as beneficial and prefer a more flexible type of account. Our loyalty to a fixed interest rate account lasts only whilst it fulfils our particular need.

Product mortality

If customers buy benefits rather than the products themselves, then the demand for a product is determined by its success in providing benefits which customers prefer to those offered by alternative products. However changes to both supply and demand restrict the length of time that those benefits will be preferred.

❑ The supply of new or improved products quickly makes existing products obsolete when superior benefits are offered.

- *The microchip offered benefits to electronics manufacturers through*

> *superior performance and smaller size which could not be matched by the
> transistor components which had hitherto dominated the industry. Just as
> the railroads offered benefits of speed, economies of scale and comfort over
> the stagecoach services which they replaced, so they in turn were dislodged
> by the superior convenience of the automobile.*

❏ The demand for products or services may also decline because of changes in the
circumstances of the marketplace.

- *A decline in the consumption of beers and lager in the UK has been caused
  not by the emergence of a new product but by changes to the age profile of
  the population and tougher laws on drinking and driving.*

Like living organisms, products seem doomed to an inevitable cycle which foresees
eventual decline after initial phases of growth. This so-called *product life cycle* is
described more fully in Chapter 8, as it is an important concept in the management
of the product ingredient in the marketing mix. Customers are fickle and owe no
loyalty to products themselves, only to the benefits which they provide.

What business are we in?

If an organisation aligns itself closely to *the means* of fulfilling a need (for example, a
specific product), rather than to the need itself then it is linking itself to the same
inevitable cycle of growth and decline. Levitt's railroad managers myopically saw
themselves in the railroad business, thus tying their fortunes to that one particular
means of fulfilling our transportation needs. Their business declined with the product.

In order to avoid the same myopia, some guidelines are recommended:

❏ Organisations and companies define their activities by asking *'what are we
really here for?'* or *'what business are we in?'* It is important that the answer
refers to customer needs, *not* a specific way of meeting them. The drill bit
supplier is in the business of providing a means of making holes, not the
business of manufacturing drill bits. Many organisations in the public as well as
in the private sector have drawn up statements of 'mission', or organisational
objectives for this reason.

❏ Organisations need to know what their customers are seeking *in terms of
benefits*. They also need to know if the benefits their products offer are still
relevant and how they rate compared to competitors.

❏ This process of matching product benefits to what customers want is a
continuous one as changes to both supply and demand are inevitable.

5. │ WHO ARE CUSTOMERS?

We have so far referred to customers as if they receive products and services direct
from the original suppliers. We have also assumed that the purchaser of a product
is also the user of the product. This over-simplified view and the exchange of
product between producer and user is in reality a long and complex chain involving
many parties and influences.

Customers or consumers?

Customers are not always the *consumer* of the product that is purchased. Shoppers buying food do not necessarily eat it all themselves; the person paying for the contents of a supermarket trolley is unlikely to consume it all alone. We buy many products which we share with others or offer to them as gifts. Parents frequently purchase goods which are used by their children. This applies not only to products such as toys and clothes but also services such as education and leisure activities which are often chosen by parents for their children.

This complicates the question of needs and benefits. Whose needs should the supplier aim to meet – the purchasers' or the users'? Who determines which benefits are most important – the child demanding fun and excitement from their toy or leisure activity, or the parent looking for safety and economy?

Both sets of demands are important in assessing how to match product benefits with customer choice. The role of marketing is to take into account all the important influences on the decision to purchase or to use a particular product or service.

Customer chains

Before a product is finally 'consumed' it usually passes through several stages of manufacture, preparation and distribution. At each stage, suppliers pass on products to the next customer down the line until they reach the final consumer. Customers exist in chains that stretch from raw material producers to high street shoppers.

- *A chain of peas*

  Even a relatively simple product such as a tin of peas passes through several types of supplier and customer. Farmers may sell their crop of peas direct to one customer, a canning factory. The canner is under contract to their customer, a national company marketing tinned food products, which in turn sells the product to a national supermarket chain via their wholesaler. The wholesaler distributes the product to the retail store where the final consumer or end-user buys the product.

  Any assessment of customer needs and the matching benefits to be offered has to take account of the benefits required by the next link in the chain and the needs of their customers further down the chain, as well as the requirements of the ultimate consumer. This is illustrated in Figure 4.2.

- *The farmer has to meet the needs of the canning company which has specified what it will accept in terms of the size and tenderness of the crop. The farmer decides that the benefit most appreciated by their customer is the dependability of producing regular crops matching the required standards of pea size and tenderness.*

- *The canning factory has been guided by its customer, the food company for whom it has to meet specifications relating to canning and labelling operations. It believes it was awarded the contract by the food company because it offered the benefit of the lowest price for production according to the specification.*

Benefits offered in respect of	Customer chain	Benefits offered to customers

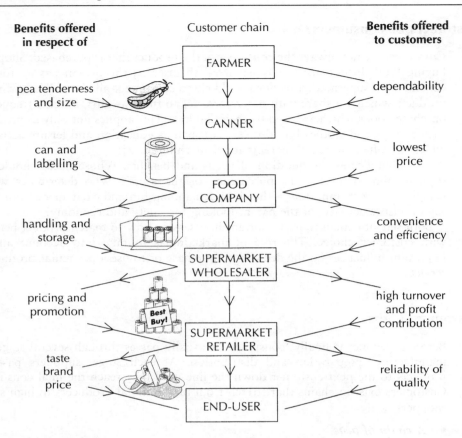

Figure 4.2 *Changing benefits in the supply chain of a tin of peas*

- *The national food company convinces the supermarket chain to stock their product because it provides benefits to both wholesale and retail divisions.*

- *The wholesale division of the chain wants to be assured of the ease of handling the finished goods. They are happy because the packaging offers convenient storage and efficient distribution.*

- *The retail division wishes to stock only those items which sell quickly so it prefers products which are supported by promotions and priced competitively. They benefit from the high turnover of this fast-moving product which contributes to their profit objectives.*

- *The supermarket chain believes that their customer, the end-user, selects their preferred product on the basis of taste and the brand name at an affordable price. They therefore offer their shoppers the benefit of reliability of quality associated with purchasing a nationally advertised brand of peas.*

This is a simplified version of the many influences on customer choice at each stage of the chain. Its purpose is to illustrate that customers and the benefits they are seeking represent '*moving targets*' dependent on their position in the chain. The farmer's perspective of what their customer wants and the benefits to be offered is different to that of others in the chain, although all the links influence each other and depend ultimately on the preferences of the final user.

Complex chains

Many chains are much more complicated than the example given which uses relatively few stages of production and distribution. For example:

❑ *Some manufacturing customer chains are extensive and complicated.* The various products which finally make up a car from the rubber of the tyres to the electronic components of the ignition system pass through lengthy and complex chains of suppliers and customers.

❑ *The distribution chain of a finished product can also involve several customers in different stages.* A car assembled in one country and sold in another passes through various levels of exporters, importers, agents and distributors before reaching the end-user.

❑ *Subsidiary chains exist which provide goods and services to the organisations in the main customer chain.* The car manufacturer requires equipment and machinery which is supplied by a subsidiary chain of design engineers, equipment manufacturers and suppliers.

Each link in a customer chain buys other products or services to help them fulfil their role in the chain; they become someone else's customer. In the example of the pea chain, the farmer is the customer of fertiliser producers and farm equipment manufacturers. The canning factory buys pre-formed cans and labels. The food company is the customer of an advertising agency. The supermarket is the final customer in a chain of architects, surveyors, planners and building contractors whose end product is a new out-of-town retail store.

The relevance to marketing lies in understanding the impact of these complex relationships on customer needs. The producer of fertiliser has to understand the needs of other customers in the chain of a tin of peas in order to understand the needs of their direct customer, the farmer. The farmer needs to provide the benefit of a dependable pea crop to their customer, the canning factory, and they judge the fertiliser they buy on its ability to help deliver this benefit. The problem for the fertiliser producer is that other customers have different priorities. For example, other farmers may put freedom from harmful environmental effects as top of their list of required benefits, as this is demanded by the customers in their particular chain.

Internal customers

Customers can also exist within an organisation. Internal relationships may be organised on the basis of suppliers and customers.

❑ Larger businesses sometimes trade between operating divisions by treating the receiver of goods or services as a customer. For example:

• *The management of a factory manufacturing electrical goods regards the overseas company responsible for assembling and selling its products in a particular country as its customer even though they are both part of the same multi-national corporation. This decentralised approach attempts to overcome complacent attitudes towards captive markets of internal customers who have no choice of supplier.*

- *The wholesaler and retailer in our earlier example may be owned by the same supermarket group which organised its operations on the basis of arm's-length trading between units, treating each other as customers or suppliers in the normal way.*

❑ Recent reforms of many public services have attempted to create supplier-customer relationships. Reorganisations have separated 'providers' from 'purchasers' of services within the same public authority.

- *Doctors within NHS community buying groups of GPs are allocated money to purchase the health care needed by their patients. Although they are most likely to specify their local hospital, they can opt to send a patient to other institutions for treatment. So a hospital now has several types of 'customers':*

  - *purchasing agents within the NHS (e.g. GPs) that buy a range of health care services from the hospital on behalf of the residents of a certain area;*

  - *other purchasers external to the NHS, such as health insurance companies (e.g. BUPA), which pay for private patient services in the hospital;*

  - *the end-user or patients who are the consumers in the sense that they receive the care that has been purchased on their behalf.*

❑ Organisations have an internal market of 'stakeholders', or people with an interest in the organisation, (as we have seen in Chapter 3, 'Stakeholders'). These interest groups act in some ways as customers because they influence how much income, investment or other resources an organisation receives even though they do not directly pay for or receive products or services from the organisation.

- *The board of directors of a company decide which of its operating divisions receive major investments for new projects or equipment. Divisions make 'bids' to the board by putting forward their case for an allocation of money in a similar way to making a sales presentation to persuade a prospective customer to spend money on certain products.*

- *The elected councillors of a County Council allocate taxpayers' money between the various services for which they are responsible. Such services as education, highways and the fire brigade compete for funds on the basis of the benefits they provide to the taxpayer. The Council decides which benefits have greatest priority and therefore receive most funds, just as an individual spends their income by deciding which benefits via products and services they most wish to purchase.*

6.	MARKETS

Markets old and new

Markets originated as places where buyers and sellers met to exchange goods. The term is now used in a variety of ways to describe:

❑ a grouping of customers with similar needs (for example, the 'teenage market');

❑ the total demand for a certain product, service or process (the 'jeans market');

❑ a combination of the two (the 'teenage jeans market').

In marketing, the term also has some important derivatives.

Market share

The demand for one particular product as a percentage of the total demand of the market is an expression of that product's *market share*. It is a particularly important measurement of success in marketing. Competitors seek to become the *market leader* by enjoying the largest percentage share of a market. A large market share for a product indicates a high level of customer acceptance which in turn can give the supplier several advantages including:

❑ lower production costs through longer runs;

❑ cheaper raw materials and components because of bulk purchasing;

❑ other economies of scale because fixed costs such as rent are apportioned over more units sold, thus lowering the cost per unit;

❑ greater product awareness in the marketplace because of high sales;

❑ greater influence over other customers in the chain to achieve preferential treatment (such as better display in retail outlets).

These and other advantages make the achievement of high market share a very desirable marketing aim. They can be translated into higher profits, or used to increase customer satisfaction by, for example, lower prices or more investment into the research and development of new products.

Potential markets

The role of marketing is to look for potential new customers as well as satisfying existing ones. This means exploring how to enlarge the total market by adding new types of customers. A high share of one market can provide the resources and incentive to look elsewhere for customers. It has also allowed 'blind spots' to develop through over-concentration on a particular group of customers and their needs. The extension of the computer market from business customers to users in the home was not pioneered by the existing dominant forces in the market such as IBM, but by newcomers like Sinclair and Amstrad.

Immature markets

Markets pass through different stages of development mirroring the life cycles of the products which are sold in them. New or immature markets tend to be fragmented between many suppliers seeking to benefit from the technological or other change which has created it. In this formative stage, the market provides high growth and high profit margins for the supplying organisations, although this does not usually translate into positive cash flows because of the levels of investment required.

Mature markets

Markets become mature as growth slackens and weaker suppliers are shaken out. Radical innovation of products tends to give way to modification and minor improvements as the small number of remaining suppliers fight for market share. Price competition erodes profit margins but cash flows can be positive for suppliers who often seek to take the benefits of their original investment at this stage.

Organisational and consumer markets

Customers form many different markets but a distinction can be made between two basic types: organisational markets and consumer markets.

Organisational markets

In some markets the customers are organisations such as businesses or public sector institutions. They buy goods and services for use in their own processes and production, or for resale to other customers. Most products pass through organisational customers before reaching the final consumer; in some cases, organisations are the final user:

- *The tin of peas in our earlier example passed through several organisational customers before it reached the shopper, including the canning factory, the food company, and the supermarket wholesaler and retailer.*

- *The supermarket company was the final customer in the chain of organisations which built the retail store, a 'product' which was only ever involved in organisational markets.*

- *A service provided by a hospital, such as an X-ray of a patient, is at the end of a chain of several organisations, including a research organisation which developed the technology of the X-ray process, a manufacturer which built the equipment, an agent who sold it, the health authority which bought it, and the hospital that used it.*

Organisational markets can be further divided into three main types as illustrated by our examples.

❑ *Industrial markets* consist of customers who buy products and services which are further processed or used in the production of new products and services. The canning factory is part of an industrial market involved in the processing and packaging of foods. The X-ray equipment manufacturer is part of the industrial market for electro-magnetic equipment and medical supplies.

❑ *Intermediary markets* are made up of customers who buy products or services for resale to others. They do not change the products purchased but add value to them in some other way, often by providing a distribution service. The supermarket wholesaler and retailer bought tins of peas in their finished form for re-sale to their customers to whom they offered the additional benefit of a convenient, centralised shopping facility. An agent sold the X-ray equipment to the health authority because the manufacturer was an overseas company which needed the services of an intermediary responsible for importing and selling in certain markets.

❏ *Government markets* consist of public sector organisations which buy products and services as part of their provision of services to the public. School catering services are customers in a local government market, which purchase tins of peas and other food products (probably in bulk from the food company). The X-ray equipment was sold to a public health authority for use in a hospital, both customers in a government market responsible for health services.

Consumer markets

We are all involved in consumer markets as individuals or part of a household purchasing goods and services. We may be a *direct* consumer buying for our own personal consumption or an *indirect* consumer purchasing on behalf of others (for example, purchases of food for a household or gifts for friends). Consumer markets are often broad with a wide range of customers (such as those who exist for our tin of peas). However some are more specialised, consisting of customers with special interests and needs (stamp collecting, health foods).

Although individual markets vary considerably, organisational and consumer markets exhibit some generalised differences between them.

❏ *Demand in organisational markets is derived* from other customers in the chain and ultimately the end user. Changes in consumption patterns further down the chain eventually effect those higher up.

- *For example, the widespread introduction of refrigerators and freezers into households reduced the demand for tinned products as more consumers purchased frozen foods in packets. Retailers such as the supermarket chain adjusted their stocks accordingly which affected the sales of the food company and the canning factory.*

❏ *Purchasing patterns are usually different.* As consumers, we tend to buy a large number of relatively small value products on a frequent basis. Consumer markets therefore tend to be made up of large numbers of customers spending small amounts reasonably often. The marketing implications are that the suppliers of consumer markets cannot deal on a personal basis with their customers. They tend to rely on advertising to communicate with customers, and wholesalers and retailers to distribute their products to the marketplace.

❏ *Organisational customers tend to be relatively small in number, purchasing in larger amounts, sometimes on an infrequent or contractual basis.* For example, the market for X-ray equipment is limited to a few customers who do not buy very often but who spend large amounts when they do. The production capacity of the canning factory is sold to a small number of companies who place high value contracts on an annual basis. Marketing to these customers therefore relies on personal contacts in which long-term relationships are very important.

❑ There are exceptions to these generalisations. Some consumer markets involve infrequent purchases of high value products by a few customers (Rolls Royce cars, ocean-going yachts). There are several million organisations in the UK alone, so products which are used by most of them (stationery, office furniture) are sold into relatively large markets.

❑ *The decision-making process is often different.* Customers in consumer markets tend to make individual decisions with only the most important purchases referred to more than one person (e.g. buying a house). Organisations frequently involve more than one person in a buying decision of any importance. The composition of a decision-making unit (DMU) varies from a board of directors (for important capital equipment investments) to less formal groups of managers and assistants (for more routine purchases of materials).

How consumers and organisations buy is covered in more detail in Chapter 5. Organisational and consumer markets and some generalised characteristics are illustrated in Figure 4.3.

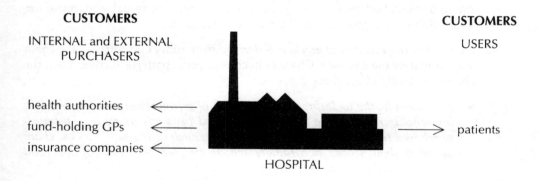

CUSTOMERS

INTERNAL and EXTERNAL
PURCHASERS

CUSTOMERS

USERS

health authorities

fund-holding GPs

insurance companies

patients

HOSPITAL

Figure 4.3: *Organisational and consumer markets*

7. | NON-CUSTOMER MARKETS

We have seen how organisations can have customer groups that are not necessarily the end users or consumers of their products or services. Some enterprises have internal markets in which one business unit sells services to another. We have also noted (in Chapter 3) that other organisations in the marketing environment, such as suppliers, have an important influence on marketing strategies. Theories of relationship marketing emphasise the importance of these non-customer groups that can be described as types of markets in which an organisation operates. The aim of relationship marketing is to build a supportive network around an organisation through partnerships not only with customers, but also with influential groups in these other markets.

The six markets model

These have been summarised as six markets which potentially play an important role in determining an organisation's success:

❑ *Customer* markets remain a primary focus, although the emphasis is on developing long-term relationships rather than short-term transactions.

❑ *Internal* markets refer to stakeholders within the organisation, particularly employees. *Internal marketing* has been described as 'the philosophy of treating employees as customers – indeed wooing employees' (Berry and Parasuraman, 1991). As internal communications are frequently cited as a key management issue, selling the organisation to existing staff is becoming more important.

❑ *Recruitment* markets consist of potential, new employees. Companies, particularly those in service industries, have become dependent on attracting and retaining motivated staff. Influencing the best people to apply for vacancies is a key marketing task.

❑ *Suppliers* can be crucial to an organisation's ability to meet customer demands as they control access to equipment, components, materials, services and finance. They are also an important source of market intelligence.

❑ *Referral* markets include anybody who is likely to make recommendations about the organisation's products or services. Referrals are an important source of new customers for many companies – often *the* most important source of new business, especially for smaller firms. Recommendations can come not just from existing customers, but also other organisations in the marketing environment (e.g. accountants, solicitors, bank managers, friends and acquaintances). The Internet has added a new dimension to such word-of-mouth marketing as positive and negative recommendations can be communicated widely through chat groups and emails.

❑ *Influence* markets are made up of organisations and individuals able to influence the marketing environment of an organisation positively or negatively. They include central and local government, pressure groups, consumer watchdogs and trade associations.

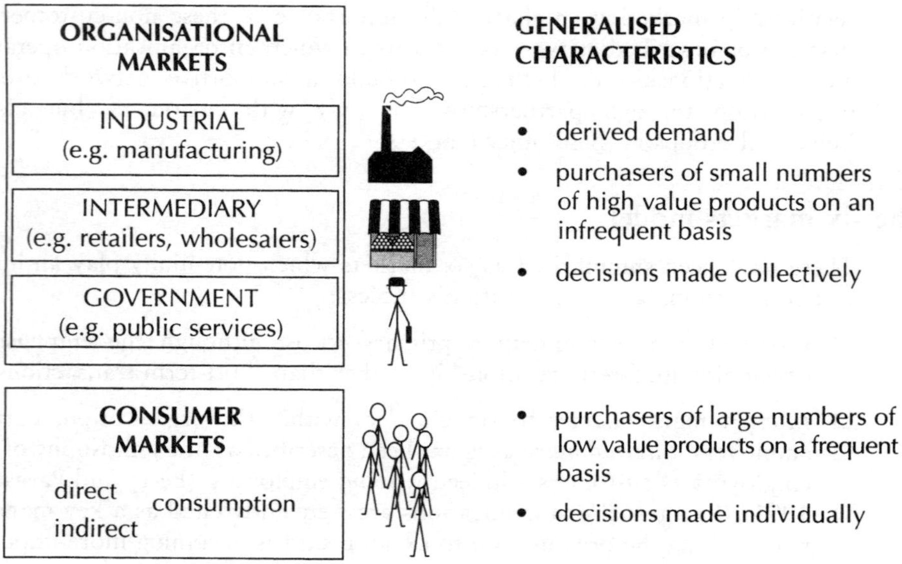

Figure 4.4: *The six markets model*

---

8. | COMPETITIVE FORCES IN THE MARKETPLACE

The five forces model

Markets vary in their attractiveness to supplying organisations. Some seem to provide healthy profits or resources for any well-managed supplier. Other markets are supplied by organisations who are all struggling to survive. The underlying economic structure of the market and the intensity of competition within the supplying industry cause these differences. Analysing the forces which affect the competitiveness of the marketplace is an important step in deciding on appropriate marketing strategies.

The management writer, Michael Porter (1980) put forward a model of competitive forces which is widely used. In this, five basic forces determine the state of competition in an industry. These are illustrated in Figure 4.5.

These forces of entry, rivalry, substitutes, buyers and suppliers govern the intensity of competition in an industry and the ability of organisations to meet profit or other objectives. It should be noted that these forces go beyond the common definition of competition that is normally restricted to the rivalry between the existing suppliers. Porter's idea of 'extended rivalry' includes not only potential new entrants into the marketplace and substitute products, but customers (buyers) and suppliers as well. This reflects the fact that if customers or suppliers have a relatively powerful position they can influence strongly the profitability of the market by, for example, driving down prices or increasing costs.

The focus of power shifts in different markets and industries.

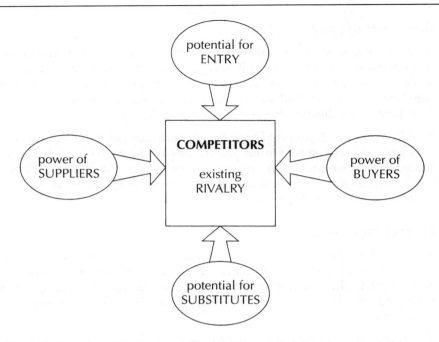

Figure 4.5: *Porter's five forces model of competition*

- *The power in the food industry has tended to centre on the buyer power of the large supermarket chains. It is their influence over suppliers which is the dominant force influencing marketing decisions on products, pricing and promotion rather than the direct competition among rival food producers.*

- *In the early days of office copiers, Xerox's patents prevented anyone else from marketing plain paper copiers. This unique position as a supplier gave them the necessary power in the marketplace for their marketing strategies to predominate. Customers had so little influence that they could only rent, but not purchase, machines, allowing Xerox to use long-term rental schemes to prevent them from switching to another supplier.*

The relative power of each of the five forces is determined by a number of characteristics which we now examine.

Potential for entry

New suppliers entering an industry increase competition and affect the viability of the existing organisations. Some markets are relatively difficult to enter and tend to be dominated by a small number of larger companies. Other markets are relatively easy to enter and tend to be supplied by a high number of small firms. Car manufacturing is an expensive market to enter and therefore dominated by a few international companies whereas it costs relatively little to set up as a consultant, hence the large numbers of consultancy firms.

The potential for entering a market depends on the barriers to entry that exist. These barriers to market entry include:

Economies of scale

If significant cost reductions are available from high levels of output in an industry, new companies will find it difficult to compete as they start from low output levels. In the 1960s, it was believed that the increasing existence of such economies in mass markets would lead to the inevitable decline of smaller firms. In many manufacturing industries this has proved to be the case.

- *The spinning of yarn and weaving of cloth was once undertaken by a large number of mill owners in Lancashire and Yorkshire. The UK industry is now highly concentrated with very few manufacturers, such as Courtaulds, who concentrated production to achieve the economies of scale required to compete with overseas textile producers.*

Product differentiation

Established suppliers build up loyalty with customers who identify with their particular product. This differentiation takes a considerable investment in time (to prove the reliability and quality of a product) and money (on branding, advertising, packaging) and therefore represents a significant barrier for any new entrant to overcome.

- *Some companies have attempted to overcome this barrier to entry by using the loyalty to the brand name of a product in one market to enter a different market. For example, Mars used the well-established name and look of Mars Bars when they entered the ice cream market in order to compete with the differentiated products already offered by suppliers such as Walls.*

Capital requirements

A very tangible barrier to entry into some markets is the large set up costs involved. Some industries, such as banking and insurance or heavy industrial goods are dominated by long established, larger firms for this reason.

Switching costs

When users change from one company's products to another, they may incur one-off 'switching costs'. These may be in the retraining of staff – in the change-over from one computer system to another for example. Existing stock may become obsolete – if a manufacturer changes from one raw material to another for example. Where significant switching costs exist this presents a barrier for any new entrant who has to offer more than just marginal benefits to replace an existing supplier.

- *Manufacturers know the importance of keeping a distribution pipeline filled with their stock in order to create switching costs for any retailer who is thinking of changing over to a different supplier. For example, Letraset distributed their patented rubdown lettering products through specialist graphic art shops. The marketing strategy was to develop the distribution system as fully as possible whilst their products were protected by patents so that when the patents eventually expired new entrants would still find it difficult to enter the market because the retailers were fully stocked with*

Letraset. This deterred new entrants and limited the progress of those that did enter the market.

Access to distribution channels

Unless they can sell direct to the user, new entrants need access to the established methods of distributing products. Distribution channels may not be readily available, (as we have seen in the case of the graphic art retailers stocked with Letraset). The competition for shelf space in high street retailers is fierce and new products have to win the right to be displayed. Failure to secure display in the major newsagent chains such as WH Smith and Martins would effectively block the launch of a new magazine for example.

Other cost disadvantages

Some cost advantages enjoyed by existing suppliers are independent of scale. For instance, a manufacturer may benefit from a plentiful local supply of cheap labour which makes new entrants from outside of the area uncompetitive. An established supplier may have advantages of 'economies of experience' because they have learned the most efficient ways of making products over a significant period of time, a learning curve that will have to be replicated by any new entrant.

Government policy

Certain markets are controlled by national or local government regulations which create total or partial barriers to entry. Some postal services have only recently been opened to new entrants and the Royal Mail monopoly is still preserved for some services such as domestic letter deliveries. Regulations control the number of outlets allowed to serve alcohol in public places; new entrants have to overcome the barrier of satisfying local magistrates and police of the need for an additional outlet and their own suitability to run it.

Rivalry among existing firms

Familiar forms of competition such as promotional campaigns, special offers, new product launches, or opening of new distribution outlets is evidence of existing rivalry between established firms. This rivalry tends to intensify when:

❑ the market is divided between competitors of roughly equal size;

❑ the market is maturing, involving a shake out of existing rivals;

❑ new entrants or market changes have created excess capacity;

❑ the industry has high fixed costs and suppliers prefer to maintain their capacity even at lower prices; or

❑ the industry has high 'exit barriers' which keeps existing rivals fighting to the bitter end. These exit barriers include the high cost of closing down some types of production, redundancy costs, or emotional attachment to a particular industry.

- *The competition among the large breweries in the UK illustrates several of*

95

these points. The market for beers and lagers in the UK has matured with demographic and social changes. There is over-capacity among the small number of big brewers who dominate the market. The high fixed costs of brewing create a powerful financial incentive to maintain capacity and exit costs are increased by the integration of the brewers into the pub trade. Major brewers such as Bass and Whitbread have attempted to exit the industry by selling their brewing operations, although they met with shareholder opposition.

Threat of substitute products or services

Suppliers compete not only with products similar to their own but also with substitute products. Substitution can come in a number of ways:

❑ *A substitute product which performs the same function.* The American railroads competed eventually with other types of transport such as road and air which met the same need. Coal has been substituted by other forms of energy such as gas and nuclear power. Theatre audiences were offered a substitute form of entertainment with the introduction of the cinema, which in turn was threatened with substitution by television and home videos.

❑ *A substitute way of spending money.* The competition for the disposable income in consumers' pockets comes from widely differing products and services. Theatres compete not only with cinemas, television and videos, but a whole range of other leisure opportunities, from restaurants and wine bars to evening classes and sports clubs. They also compete with very different uses of disposable income such as vacations and hobbies.

Industries where there are fewer real substitutes (for example, basic food such as bread) tend to be more stable than those that can be easily substituted by other products (for example, forms of leisure) or those that rely on disposable income (for example, tourism).

The power of buyers and suppliers

Buyers, or customers, 'compete' with suppliers by trying to get the best deal from them. They try to negotiate discounts, additional services, higher quality, more after-sales support and other benefits which are added costs to the supplier. Suppliers naturally try to resist the efforts of buyers which reduce their profitability. In some situations buyers have the upper hand; as a supplier marketing to Marks and Spencer your options are limited because of the power of this buyer. In other circumstances suppliers have more power; manufacturers of patented products have the opportunity to recover their development costs by charging high prices to customers as the monopoly supplier. This changing balance of power between buyers and suppliers varies depending on a number of factors:

Concentration of buyers or suppliers

If buying power is concentrated in the hands of a few organisations or individuals who are dealing with a relatively large number of suppliers, buyers tend to have more control. Conversely, if a small number of suppliers sell into a market of many buyers, then the suppliers have more power.

- *The DIY market was, until recently, a fragmented industry with a proliferation of independent retailers, builders' merchants and ironmonger stores. In these circumstances the suppliers had power to specify products and prices. The supply of paints, for example, was concentrated in the hands of a small number of large suppliers such as ICI who made marketing decisions on colour range, packaging and pricing in isolation from the retailer. The emergence of large out-of-town retailing chains such as Homebase and B&Q has concentrated buying power in the hands of relatively few organisations who now have much more influence over important marketing decisions. By introducing their own ranges of branded products these buyers have further increased their power over suppliers who are now forced to manufacture in-house brands to the retailer's specification or lose the business.*

Differentiation and switching costs

A supplier who has developed differentiated products or ones with high switching costs can exercise more power over the buyer. However if products are relatively undifferentiated and can be easily switched from one supplier to the next, then buyers have greater negotiating power.

- *Xerox once dominated the office copier market as we have already noted above. Their power stemmed from the differentiation of their patented plain paper copiers to competing coated paper machines and the high switching costs created by their marketing strategy of long-term rental agreements. In these circumstances they were able to charge premium prices and create a highly profitable business. Today, office managers have more buying power as other manufacturers entered the market on the expiry of the Xerox patents offering a variety of products available on flexible purchase and lease terms.*

Relative importance

Some purchases are crucial to the success of an organisation or the well-being of an individual, (for example the purchase of new premises or a house). In these circumstances the buyer is likely to shop around for the best possible deal and exercise their buying power to the full. In other situations a purchase is of relatively low value to the buyer and does not have any major impact on their organisational or individual welfare, (such as the purchase of paper clips or confectionery items). In this situation the buyer is unlikely to use their powers to the full and accepts suppliers' terms more readily.

Backward or forward integration

Buyers and suppliers are usually arranged in chains as we have seen (in 'Customer chains' above). This can give suppliers the opportunity of fulfilling the role of the next link forward in their chain themselves if they are dissatisfied with their immediate buyers. Likewise buyers can threaten to perform the role of the link before them in the chain if they feel their suppliers are not doing the right job. For example, a supplier selling through wholesalers to retailers may threaten to sell direct to the retailers if the wholesale terms are not acceptable (forward integration). A buyer who does not like the terms of their supplier may threaten to manufacture the product themselves (backward integration). The power that such threats carry depends on their credibility as realistic options for the buyer or supplier.

A summary of competitive forces

An analysis of the competitive forces at work in the marketplace helps an organisation identify its own strengths and weaknesses in relation to the competitive structure and evaluate the opportunities and threats which this reveals. Figure 4.6 is a summary of characteristics which determine the nature of these forces which can be used as a checklist for carrying out such an analysis.

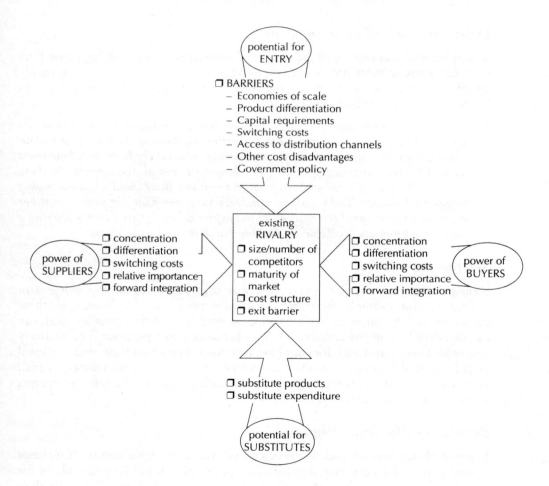

Figure 4.6: *Checklist for analysing the five forces*

9. | KEY POINTS

- ❏ Customer needs represent long-term necessities which Maslow categorised as survival, security, social, success and self-actualisation needs. They are not the same as 'wants' which are how we wish a need to be fulfilled as conditioned by our past and present environment.

- ❏ Organisations can suffer from 'marketing myopia' and mistake what customers want currently for long-term needs.

- ❏ In fact customers buy the benefits of a product (what it does for them) rather than its features (what it is) and change to alternative products which offer superior benefits.

- ❏ Customers are organised in chains linking producers to the end users. Benefits required from products change according to the position in the chain.

- ❏ Customers are served by markets and the industries or organisations within them. The characteristics of a market change as it develops from an immature to a mature state.

- ❏ There are consumer and organisational markets. Organisational markets can be further divided into industrial, intermediary and government markets. Distinctive characteristics of organisational markets include derived demand arising from buyers further down the chain, small numbers of buyers purchasing relatively large amounts, and multiple influences in the buying decision.

- ❏ Other groups or markets can influence marketing strategies. Relationship marketing theories have summarised these as the 'six markets' of customers, internal markets, recruitment markets, suppliers, influence and referral markets.

- ❏ The competitive structure of markets changes according to the balance of power between the five forces of existing rivalry, the potential for new entrants, the threat of substitutes, and the relative bargaining power of buyers and suppliers.

10. | DEVELOPING MARKETING SKILLS

Exercises

1. Think of a product you have purchased recently. Analyse the wants and needs that prompted your purchase. In what other ways could you have fulfilled the same need? What specific benefits prompted you to fulfil your needs this way rather than the alternatives?

2. Take an industry of which you have some knowledge (if only as a consumer such as the food or clothing industries). Draw a picture of the customer chains that exist within it, specifying the industrial, intermediary, government and consumer markets. What are the characteristics of these markets (in terms of

their immaturity or maturity, relative numbers of customers, purchase frequency, etc.)? Are their any signs or past examples of 'marketing myopia' amongst the suppliers?

3. Consider a leisure attraction that you have visited recently, or with which you are familiar (e.g. the local cinema, sports centre, a theme park or national attraction such as 'Madame Tussauds'). Analyse the competitive forces in which it operates using Porter's Five Forces model. Does your analysis indicate this is a favourable or unfavourable market to enter with new products?

Developing a marketing plan

Activity 4 An external audit

Complete the next stage of your marketing plan by undertaking the external audit and answering such questions as:

❑ Who are your customers? Who will be your customers?

❑ Why do they buy from you? Why will they buy in future?

❑ What are the features and benefits of your product(s)?

❑ What is the competitive environment?

❑ What are the key structural forces that act in this marketplace?

(See also Chapter 2 'The marketing audit'.)

FURTHER READING AND REFERENCES

General texts

Kotler, P. (2000) *Marketing Management*, 10th edition, Prentice Hall, part II.

Market needs and analysis

Deng, S. and Dart, J. (1994) 'Measuring market orientation: a multi-factor, multi-item approach, *Journal of Marketing Management*, **10**, pages 425–442.

Maslow, A.H. (1954) *Motivation and Personality*, Harper and Row.

Levitt, T. (1960) 'Marketing myopia', *Harvard Business Review*, July/Aug, pages 45–56.

Siu, N.Y.M. and Wilson, R.M.S. (1998) Modelling market orientation: an application in the education sector, *Journal of Marketing Management*, **14**, pages 293–323.

Relationship marketing

Berry, L. and Parasuraman, A. (1991) *Marketing Services through Quality*, The Free Press.

Cahill, D.J. (1996) *Internal Marketing*, The Haworth Press.

Christopher, M., Payne, A. and Ballantyne, D. (1994) *Relationship Marketing*, Butterworth-Heinemann.

Competitive analysis

Porter, M.E. (1980) *Competitive Strategy: Techniques for Analysing Industries and Competition*, Macmillan Publishing.

Mudie, P. (1997) *Marketing: an Analytical Perspective*, Prentice Hall, chapter 2.

CHAPTER 5

Customer Behaviour

This chapter examines how customers behave, particularly when they are involved in decisions to buy products or services. We will seek to answer the following questions:

❑ How do customers go about making a buying decision?

❑ What influences their decision to buy one product in favour of another?

❑ What differences exist between customers as individual consumers and customers as organisations?

1. CASE STUDY: FESTIVAL FOODS

'Can I introduce Paul Vidas from the marketing agency BFG, who is here today to present their promotional ideas for our hot cereal products.' David Bracewell, marketing director of Festival Foods indicated his colleagues around the table as he introduced them. 'This is Sue Morris, brand manager of 'Puritan', our new oats and honey porridge, Mazrene Richards, packaging manager for the company, and Graham James, purchasing manager.'

Paul Vidas began his presentation. 'Our detailed recommendations are in the report before you, but perhaps I can review the main considerations behind our proposals. Our brief was to develop a promotional strategy for your hot cereal product range to improve its sales compared to cold, ready to eat cereals. Looking at the market data, a number of factors are significant in influencing consumer demand for cereals. The high level of advertising expenditure by cereal producers which is currently running at around 9 per cent of total sales has ensured exceptional loyalty to the main branded products. Cereals are purchased by over 90 per cent of households, most of whom still prefer to buy well-known brands so that own-label products have not had the same success in cereals that they have had in other food sectors. However because the market for hot cereals is relatively small at around 5 per cent of the total cereal market, promotional spending has been traditionally lower in this sector and more erosion to own-branded products has taken place.' He turned to the next presentation board.

'Weather is a particular influence on hot cereals with sales peaking in the winter months and cold periods. There are also considerable regional variations with sales strongest in Scotland, the Midlands and East Anglia. This contrasts to cold cereals which are served most often in the South and least often in Scotland. Social groups also behave differently when buying hot and cold cereals. Cold cereals are favourite among the more affluent AB social groups and least popular among the poorer groups D and E. Hot cereals on the other hand are bought most frequently by group D, semi or unskilled manual workers. The economic climate does not seem to effect total demand for cereals although the last recession did help the less expensive products take a larger market share and it also slowed the growth of hot cereals more than cold.'

'The family unit is a crucial influence on all cereals as purchasing is highest among 25 to 34 year olds who are most likely to have children. And your own research indicates that children's preferences play a large part in determining which cereals are bought. Hot cereals do seem to have an older user profile than cold ones. They seem to appeal less to younger people – except for the under two year olds where they can be used as a first solid breakfast food.'

'Lifestyle changes have been a mixed blessing for hot cereals. On the positive side, the trend towards more healthy foods has favoured cereals containing oats. There has recently been considerable favourable press coverage about porridge on health grounds compared to the negative comments from the dental profession on sugar coated cold cereals. However, the increasing number of working women has hastened the decline of the cooked breakfast. The microwave has helped overcome most of the inconvenience of heating cereals in the morning but the decline in manual work and the increasing numbers of us who sit around indoors at work means that we no longer perceive the need for a big cooked breakfast every day.'

'Which leads me on to our proposals. We know that the big, cooked family breakfast is a thing of the past during the working week. But it is more common at the weekend as a special treat and this is the behavioural pattern on which we wish to capitalise. It is difficult for us to compete with ready to eat cereals for our key consumer group – the family – other than at the weekend. So we have designed some on-pack promotions designed to be an activity for all the family, not just individual members. We want to appeal particularly to parents by promoting the sociability of a hot but healthy family breakfast. The activities on the packs are fun but semi-educational and can involve adults as well as children – like this one which is the old card game requiring pictures and words to be matched, except that the words are in French and so it is best if a parent gets involved.'

'This means we have to stimulate recognition of a new need in the buying process. Cereals are normally a routine purchase with little time spent on the evaluation of alternatives. We will promote recognition of a new need at breakfast – the benefit of bringing the family together at the beginning of the day in a busy world in which individual family members often dash off to their own particular activity at the weekend and see little of their siblings or parents.'

'As you have the detailed proposals, perhaps I can leave other aspects to questions. Thank you.'

Sue Morris, manager of 'Puritan', one of the brands under discussion, spoke first. 'How do these proposals affect individual brands which currently have no standardised packaging?'

'Could I add to that?' asked Mazrene Richards, the packaging manager. 'Some of these on-pack activities are quite complex. Will they fit onto our current pack sizes and have you costed the extra items such as stickers?'

'These are only outline suggestions so we would have to work closely with you to make sure the final design conformed to your packaging requirements,' answered Vidas. 'I have included some costings from one supplier although you may be able to negotiate lower prices.'

'Yes, we would certainly want quotes of our own.' The purchasing manager was quick to agree. 'We now have a standard procedure that, once a new item has been specified and agreed between the relevant managers here, we invite suppliers for formal written proposals covering the areas outlined in these guidelines.' He handed Vidas a document headed, *Purchasing Procedures – Guidelines for Suppliers*. 'We then select a supplier and place an order which spells out the terms and conditions according to the procedures. Of course this only applies when we are purchasing a particular item for the first time. Repeat or modified purchases are more routine.'

Paul Vidas began to realise that selling this campaign to Festival Foods might be even more complex than persuading southerners to eat porridge on a sunny day.

Points to consider

1. What influences on consumer buyer behaviour are illustrated by this case? Classify the examples into:

   (i) Controllable and uncontrollable influences.

   See section 2.

   (ii) Social and personal or lifestyle influences.

   See section 3.

2. Consider how individuals buy compared to organisations. What examples of consumer and organisational buying processes are given in this case? What are the differences between them?

See sections 4 and 5.

3. What roles in the decision-making process concerning this proposed campaign do you expect those present at the meeting to play? For example, who will be the key decision maker and what type of influence will others have?

See section 5, 'The Decision Making Unit'.

4. Do you think the proposals made are relevant to the buyer behaviour outlined? What other suggestions can you make?

2. A CUSTOMER BEHAVIOUR MODEL

Marketing managers need to understand who their customers are in order to target their marketing activity as precisely as possible. Once they know who customers are, they also need to know as much as possible about how those customers behave. They would like to know what influences customers to make a buying decision and what processes they follow to select a product or service. They would particularly like to know how customers choose between one product and another so that they could use that information to increase the chances of their own products being selected.

The black box

To assist them, researchers have been trying for many years to find out why customers buy the products and services that they do. The many investigations which have been carried out have helped to suggest some general models of how customers behave, but very few universally applicable rules have emerged.

The 'black box' model

One reason for this is that we all make buying decisions in what has been described as a 'black box', an invisible processor in which the influences on the decision are assessed. As most of this processing takes place in our conscious and sub-conscious minds, the precise mechanics of the decision-making process cannot be observed – hence the mysterious black box. All we can do is observe what is happening around an individual or an organisation at the time of a buying decision and look at what inputs and influences the 'black box' might be receiving. These inputs can then be compared to the outputs from the black box in terms of buying decisions to see what impact the various influences may have had.

This general model of customer behaviour is shown in Figure 5.1.

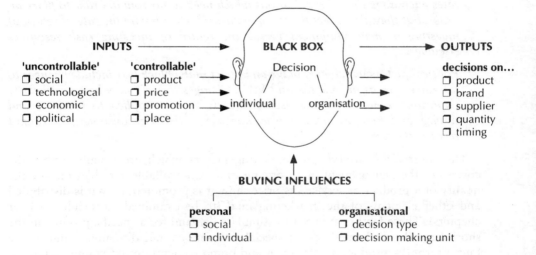

Figure 5.1: *A 'black box' model of customer behaviour*

Inputs (on the left of the diagram) in the form of controllable or uncontrollable stimuli enter the black box for processing. There are other influences on individual and organisational buying decisions, such as the personality of a customer or the structure of an organisation, which are shown as buying influences on the processing taking place in the black box. The results of this process are outputs in terms of decisions on what type of product to buy, if any, what brand of product, from which supplier, in what quantities and when.

The inputs

Inputs to the decision-making process take the form of stimuli, some of which can

105

be controlled by marketing management, some of which cannot.

The *uncontrollable stimuli* consist of many of the environmental forces that we have already discussed as impacting on the marketing organisation (see Chapter 3, 'The marketing context'). The prevailing social, technological, economic and political climates all affect our likelihood to consider buying certain products or services. These forces are usually beyond the control of marketing management. However it is important to know how customers may react to changes to this 'uncontrollable' environment.

- *Interest rates are an important economic factor in the purchase of high value goods such as cars and houses. Those people considering buying a new car or moving house are deterred by high interest rates if they need to borrow money because of the high repayment costs. They may also be deterred even if they have the cash available because the benefit of a good, risk-free rate of return on their invested money may outweigh the benefits of replacing a car or moving home. A fall in interest rates can therefore act as a stimulus on both groups to consider making a purchase.*

  Organisations considering investing in, for example, new plant and equipment are similarly affected by this economic stimulus. Not only do lower interest rates encourage those organisations which need to borrow in order to place an order, but they also affect those companies which compare the rate of return of investing in new equipment versus the return of investing cash resources elsewhere.

  Political factors which may make an impact in the black box include changes to tax rates such as income tax and VAT. Changes to VAT may be a particularly important input as an increase in rates is directly applied to products and services and therefore acts as a price increase for the final consumer who cannot recover the tax.

The *controllable stimuli* are marketing factors which are usually within the control of the management of an organisation. Controllable variables include the quality of a product or service, its price, how it is promoted, how it is distributed and other elements of the 'marketing mix' (to be examined more fully in later chapters). These factors are used to stimulate demand for a specific product in the short term (by such methods as special promotions and discounts), and in the longer term (by product development and brand recognition for example). One of the key tasks of marketing management is to assess the effectiveness of these marketing inputs on the outputs of the black box – the all important decisions to purchase certain products.

Together these uncontrollable and controllable factors form inputs into the buying decisions of customers. As we have seen customers can exist as individual consumers or as organisations and we will investigate the behaviour of these two categories separately in more detail.

3.	CONSUMER BUYING BEHAVIOUR

Purchases by individuals acting as the consumer are influenced by many factors including their own background and personality. We examine these under two classifications:

❑ the influences on the consumer as part of a social group; and

❑ the influence of more individual, psychological characteristics.

These can be further sub-divided as shown in Figure 5.2.

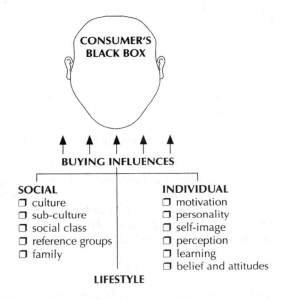

Figure 5.2: *Influences on consumer behaviour*

We will illustrate how each of these influences may operate by using the examples of a shopper buying shoes and a parent choosing a school for their child.

Social influences

Our membership of various types of social groups ranging from wider cultural groupings to narrower family units powerfully influences our habits as consumers.

Culture

The society in which we are brought up and the accepted beliefs, values, habits and attitudes which are handed on from one generation to the next as part of its culture are key forces in the marketing environment. Consumer behaviour is particularly affected by shifts in cultural beliefs and habits which present many opportunities and threats to marketing management.

- *Owen Williams decides that he needs a new pair of shoes for casual wear on informal occasions. His society, like most of Western Europe and North America, has become more concerned about the need for a healthier lifestyle in recent years; this has been reflected in preferences for clothing and footwear products portraying fitness and health. Owen opts to buy a pair of training shoes even though he does not intend to use them for any form of exercise.*

- *Susan Flynn has a daughter who will soon be five years old. As part of a society whose egalitarian principles make free education available to everyone from five to sixteen years old, Jane's daughter will soon be sent to a state funded school. However recent shifts within this cultural principle of equality have emphasised the responsibility of the individual to make their own choices rather than the collective provision of standard services by the state. Jane's mother had no real say over which school Jane attended; now for the first time she has to make a choice of Primary school for her own daughter.*

Sub-cultures

Within each social group sharing major cultural influences there are smaller groups, or sub-cultures, who have distinctive habits and tastes. These may be based on nationality, religion, race, or other beliefs and situations. These sub-groups can have particular needs which create distinct segments of a market.

- *Owen Williams is a vegetarian, a fast growing sub-group in the UK of approximately five million people. As well as avoiding meat products in his food, Owen is also active in promoting animal rights and avoids buying clothes which use animal furs and skin. This extends to his choice of shoes as he does not buy any goods containing leather. His choice of trainers is therefore limited to those made entirely from synthetic substances.*

- *Susan Flynn and her husband are of families of Catholic beliefs. Although she is not strongly religious, Susan wishes to avoid schools which are connected to religions other than Catholicism. This eliminates one local school which is controlled by the Church of England. As there is no local Catholic school, Susan is looking for a secular school with minimal religious overtones.*

Social class

Social class is a widely used method for classifying people into sub-groups. The population can be divided up into 'classes' in which the profiles of individuals tend to coincide. Criteria for making up these profiles include:

- ❑ income
- ❑ occupation
- ❑ education
- ❑ social status
- ❑ family background.

One common method of social classification is shown in Figure 5.3.

There is a strong correlation between these groups and their preferences to

GRADE CLASS	OCCUPATION	% OF ADULTS 15+
A upper/upper middle	higher managerial, professional or administrative	3.1%
B middle	intermediate managerial, professional or administrative	17.7%
C1 lower middle	junior managerial, professional or administrative; supervisory or clerical	27%
C2 skilled working class	skilled manual workers	23.5%
D working class	semi- or unskilled manual	16.2%
E those at the lowest level of subsistence	casual or lowest grade worker, unemployed, some state pensioners	12.4%

Figure 5.3: *Social classes in the UK*

purchase certain products and the way in which they buy them. The clothes or cars we buy, the types of holiday we take and the use of credit cards have been shown to be influenced by our approximation to one of these social classes.

- *Owen Williams has a middle class profile in terms of his education and family background. Like many of the social classes A/B/C1, he is very concerned that the clothes and shoes he wears create the right image. However he does not wish to appear elitist and emphasise his membership of a 'higher' social class, so his clothes have taken on a more egalitarian look. His lace-up, ankle-length shoes reflect styles traditionally worn by previous generations of working classes.*

- *Susan Flynn and her husband have a working class background and generally fit category C2 in terms of their income, occupation and education. Private education, like private health care, tends to be limited to the upper and middle classes (categories A/B), and Susan has not considered this for any of her children. However she is influenced by the concept of social mobility and hopes that her children can move to a more middle class social group. For this reason she is anxious that her daughter attends a school popular with C1/B class parents as well as her own social grouping.*

Reference groups

As well as these larger groupings of people, we are also members of smaller reference groups with which we have direct contact. In the case of these groups, we have regular interactions with other group members which can be very influential in our buying decisions. These reference groups are made up of people who are either inter-dependent on each other or who share common beliefs and values (or both). They can be further divided into:

❑ *primary groups* which communicate regularly face to face, such as families, neighbours, departments and teams at work, and students in the same class; and

❑ *secondary groups* which have less interaction and tend to be more formally structured, such as professional associations, unions, local community groups, religious bodies, and companies.

Reference groups are important to marketing because they influence our buying habits in a number of ways including:

❑ *The desire to conform to the group norms and 'fit in' fully.* This particularly affects visible products such as clothes which tend to conform to the style of a particular reference group. Many groups have their own acceptable 'uniform' which varies from dark suits to denims.

❑ *The transfer of new ideas and habits.* When we change reference group (by changing job, attending a new college, or moving to a new neighbourhood, for example) we encounter new behaviours and lifestyles which may influence our future purchasing decisions. If we change workplace from one where more formal dress was the norm to one where casual clothes are common, we will tend to dress accordingly and buy more casual clothes for work.

The family as a reference group

The family is a particularly important reference group to consider in making marketing decisions. Families, or households as they are sometimes referred to in marketing contexts, form a very common decision-making unit for purchases. Many products or services are bought for consumption by all or several members of the household. It is important therefore to establish exactly who is making the final decision of what to buy.

The married couple as a household unit make decisions in a number of ways which have been classified as:

❑ husband dominant;

❑ wife dominant;

❑ autonomic (partners make equal numbers of decisions but do so usually without consulting each other); or

❑ syncratic (partners mainly make joint decisions).

Families are not static in their composition. They evolve as the various family members grow older and their consumption patterns and buying behaviour change accordingly. Various stages in a common family life cycle can be identified as shown in Figure 5.4.

- *Owen Williams is a bachelor who no longer lives with his parents. His reference group of friends is a common influence on many of his purchase decisions. He has discussed shoes and trainers with them on several occasions and their experiences and opinions form an important input into his decision-making process.*

- *Susan Flynn is part of a 'Full Nest 1' as she has three young children. As she and her husband both have jobs they tend to live busy lives. This has lead to 'autonomic' purchase decision making in which they both make decisions but usually without reference to the other partner as time does not allow for much discussion. Susan has taken responsibility for choosing schools for their children and will inform her husband once she has made up her mind.*

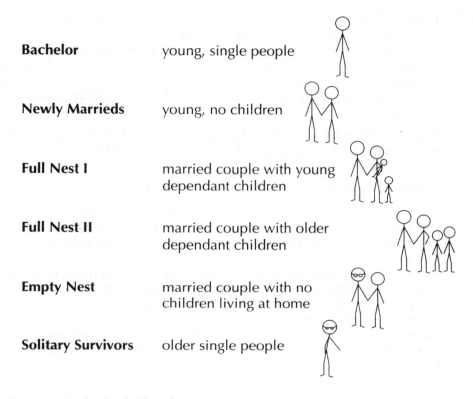

Bachelor young, single people

Newly Marrieds young, no children

Full Nest I married couple with young dependant children

Full Nest II married couple with older dependant children

Empty Nest married couple with no children living at home

Solitary Survivors older single people

Figure 5.4: *The family life cycle*

Individual influences

As individuals we have distinct characteristics which influence our buying decisions. Psychological factors such as our personality and attitudes as well as our personal situation are important clues to how we react in certain situations, and how we may respond to marketing stimuli.

Individual motivation

What motivates us to buy the products and services which we do? We are motivated to want products and services because we have needs to satisfy. These can be basic physical requirements for food, drink and shelter – needs which override all others if they are not satisfied. Once satisfied, other needs such as our desire to socialise with others, gain respect and status and achieve self-fulfilment can be considered (see the more detailed outline of Maslow's Hierarchy of Needs in Chapter 4, 'Needs').

- *Owen's motivation to buy shoes was originally the physiological need to avoid the discomfort caused by walking around without them. However he already has several pairs which can fulfil this basic requirement and his recent desire to buy a new pair of trainers is mainly motivated by status needs to keep up with his friends.*

- *Susan Flynn recognises that in our society education influences not only how we meet our basic needs through our ability to earn money, but also our ability to attain higher needs such as social acceptability, prestige and a satisfying career. She is therefore motivated to obtain a good education for her daughter because of the many benefits which this may bring her daughter and the corresponding satisfaction and esteem which a successful daughter will bestow on her.*

Susan and Owen are motivated – they are ready to act. How they act as individuals is influenced by a variety of other factors as discussed below.

Personality types

We are all different from one another in that we are unique combinations of different personality traits. But there are some traits within us that tend to predominate in certain situations. Some people, for example, have a compulsive trait which leads them to respond to certain events in a consistently compulsive way. Others only take decisions after careful analysis of all the factors. Such traits are dominant in that they regularly appear in certain situations. This can mean that we respond to our external environment in a consistent way.

Our personalities exhibit several types of dominant traits which act as a regular influence on how we behave. Many attempts have been made to classify these traits into personality types (sometimes referred to as stereotypes) such as the one shown in Figure 5.5.

Classification of Personality Types

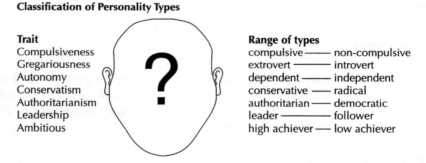

Trait
Compulsiveness
Gregariousness
Autonomy
Conservatism
Authoritarianism
Leadership
Ambitious

Range of types
compulsive —— non-compulsive
extrovert —— introvert
dependent —— independent
conservative —— radical
authoritarian —— democratic
leader —— follower
high achiever —— low achiever

Figure 5.5: *Classification of personality types*

If definite links can be established between people's personality type and their likelihood to purchase certain products or respond to marketing programmes, this could provide valuable information for making marketing decisions. Despite considerable research, correlations have been hard to establish, indicating that personality traits are perhaps only a marginal factor influencing consumer choices. Researchers have proven strong links in some situations however.

- *One investigation into the drinking habits of young men in Britain showed that impulsive, venturesome extroverts consume more beer and cider in public bars and restaurants than more introverted types. This information could be useful to marketing management in a range of decisions from the selection of* advertising for specific brands to the creation of the most conducive atmospheres in pubs.

Self-image

Related to classifications of personality type is the concept of self-image which sums up how we think about ourselves. We all have complex images about ourselves – a mental assessment of how we look and behave in given situations. We may believe we are better at certain types of activities (such as meeting people or dressing well) than others (dealing with figures, making speeches). These images are made more complicated by an assessment of the viewpoint from which they are taken, such as:

❑ *Real self*: you as you really are.

❑ *Ideal self*: you as you would like to be.

❑ *Looking glass self*: you as you think others see you.

❑ *Self image*: you as you see yourself.

How we see ourselves in this way influences how we react in purchase decision-making circumstances.

- *Owen Williams has a gregarious personality, and he is very conscious of the image he projects to those he meets. He believes he is a 'modern man' who selects products which make statements about his dislike of overtly materialistic attitudes whilst reflecting the up-to-date fashion tastes of his young age group. He is not at all impressed by one boutique he visits which has an exclusive atmosphere of thick carpets, luxurious fittings and attentive assistants. He feels relaxed in a more utilitarian shop with only basic furniture and minimal service but a large selection of canvass and non-leather shoes on display.*

- *Susan Flynn visited the local schools in order to make a choice between them. In each case she met the head teacher. From her own schooldays she has a strong mental image of herself in a very subservient role to her head teacher; she starts from a position of a poor self image which colours how she reacts in these meetings. She is most impressed by one head teacher who makes a deliberate effort to put her at ease and talks to her as an equal. She finds another meeting uncomfortable because the head teacher uses some educational jargon which she pretends to understand for fear of showing herself up.*

Perception

We interpret information received through our senses in an individual way. Our perception of an event differs from someone else's interpretation of the same situation. Two people listening to the same salesperson, looking at the same product, and sensing the atmosphere of the same shop end up with different perceptions of this same experience.

Our perceptions are coloured not only by our backgrounds and personality but also our ability to selectively receive only the information or stimuli which interest us. We screen out messages that we believe do not concern us and tune in to ones

113

that do. Parents can sleep undisturbed by the noise of a busy street outside, yet awake at the slightest cry from their baby in the next room. In a similar way we can ignore most of the marketing communications that bombard us every day, whilst retaining the one that triggers a specific interest. It has been estimated that we perceive less than 1 per cent of all the advertisements to which we are exposed.

For this reason, marketing managers often aim for a high number of repetitions of advertisements to make sure that the message has been received. Similarly a good salesperson frequently asks questions during a presentation to a prospective customer in order to obtain feedback on their perspective of what has been said so far. It is all too easy to assume that what we say or do is perceived by others in the same way as we perceive it ourselves.

- *One head teacher confused Susan with educational jargon during their meeting. He may have perceived that he was demonstrating his professional competence by using specialised language. Susan's perception was that he was probably not a very good teacher as he could not make himself understood even by an adult.*

Learning

We learn from actions and decisions we have taken in the past. Our future buying decisions will be influenced by what we have learned during past buying experiences.

Learning theorists believe that much of human behaviour is learned either from direct personal experience of a trial and error nature, or through seeking solutions based on a more reasoning approach. The implications to marketing management are that demand and repeat purchasing of products can be built up by reinforcing consumers' positive associations and experiences of a product and correcting any negative ones.

- *Owen has never purchased a pair of trainers before. However he is favourably disposed towards some brands of trainer as he has learned about their quality standards by buying other shoes of the same make. He also has a mental picture of some types of trainer which he has either admired or disliked when he has seen them worn by others.*

Beliefs and attitudes

Through our background and experiences we build up beliefs and attitudes which influence our buying behaviour. A *belief* is an opinion or viewpoint we hold about something. It may indicate a degree of like or dislike which conditions our purchase decisions.

- *Owen holds some current beliefs about trainers – specific thoughts about some of the products and the images which they project. He will tend to act on these beliefs unless specific marketing activities change them. An advertising campaign may shift his opinions or a sales assistant in a shop may be able to influence his beliefs about a certain make.*

An *attitude* is a body of opinions which represent a way of thinking or an outlook on life. They act as a framework on which we build our thoughts and beliefs – likes and dislikes – about specific products. We may have an attitude that top quality products always cost more, or that it is always desirable to buy British. This influences our belief about the quality and desirability of certain products.

Attitudes are harder to change as they represent a mind-set of beliefs and opinions that require several adjustments to alter.

- *Susan's attitude is that education is a serious business which requires firm discipline and hard work. In looking around schools, she tends to like those that are quiet with children working purposefully at their desks. She particularly dislikes one which is full of noise and bustle even though the teacher explains that they encourage this more natural atmosphere to make learning fun and stimulate creativity.*

Lifestyle

So far we have looked at both social and individual influences at work in the 'black box' where consumer purchase decisions are made. Marketing commentators have relied heavily on the disciplines of economics, sociology and psychology to help explain these forces. Marketing researchers have developed one concept which combines these various approaches under the heading of *'lifestyle'*.

Lifestyle is a summary of how we live. It embraces our activities, interests, opinions and aspirations. The concept of lifestyle goes beyond the separate influences of culture, social class, personality or attitudes, yet combines them all. People of the same sub-culture or personality type do not necessarily share the same lifestyle, although these factors do influence which one they choose.

Psychographics

Psychographics, the technique of measuring lifestyles, has developed several classifications of lifestyle groups. Once identified, these groups can be targeted with products and communications designed to appeal to their composite profile. For example, one psychographic study divided men into eight lifestyle categories as illustrated in Figure 5.6 below.

- ❑ 'The Quiet Family Man': self-sufficient, shy, focus on family life, shuns community involvement, high TV viewing, marked fantasy life, practical buyer, low level consumer.

- ❑ 'The Traditionalist': secure, high self-esteem, conventional, respectable, altruistic and caring, conservative shopper, selects known brands.

- ❑ 'The Discontented Man': dissatisfied at work, feels bypassed by life, dreams of better things, distrustful and socially aloof, price-conscious buyer.

- ❑ 'The Ethical Highbrow': concerned, sensitive, puritanical, content with family friends and work, interested in culture and social reform, buys quality and prepared to pay the price.

- ❑ 'The Pleasure-Oriented Man': emphasises masculinity, self-image as leader, self-centred, seeks immediate gratification of needs, impulsive buyer, likes products with masculine image.

❑ 'The Achiever': hardworking, dedicated to success, prestige, power and money, adventurous hobbies, stylish, likes good food and music, status-conscious consumer, discriminating buyer.

❑ 'The He-Man': gregarious, likes action, excitement and drama, bachelor-type even if married, buys products with 'man of action' image.

❑ 'The Sophisticated Man': intellectual, socially concerned artistic and intellectual achievements, wide interests, wants to lead, attracted to unique and fashionable goods.

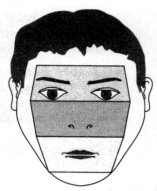

Figure 5.6: *Male lifestyle categories*

4. | THE BUYING PROCESS OF CONSUMERS

We have examined some of the many influences on consumer buying decisions from the marketing inputs to group and individual factors. This section looks at how consumers make decisions – the processes that are followed in order to buy a product or service.

Types of decision

The process of deciding what to buy is affected by the importance of the decision to the consumer. Some decisions become routine and automatic (buying a loaf of bread, or a postage stamp, for example). Others are irregular and more impulsive, triggered by a sudden desire (buying an ice-cream from a street vendor, or a bar of chocolate on display at the checkout of a supermarket). Others require more selection, but are regularly carried out (buying some types of clothes such as socks and underwear, selecting a magazine, or fruit from a street market). Some decisions are infrequent and require more thought even though the value may not be high, (presents for a friend, books, some types of clothes such as a pair of shoes); other infrequent decisions become even more significant to the purchaser because of their high value, (buying a house, choosing a holiday, arranging a pension).

These types of buying decisions differ in the amount of involvement the consumer has in the process. In some there is very little active involvement; in others there is a high degree of participation. This can be represented as a spectrum ranging from high to low involvement in the decision-making process, as shown in Figure 5.7.

We do not necessarily become more involved as the value of the purchase item increases. A present for a friend may not cost very much but takes a long time to select. Involvement changes through:

❑ *familiarity*: as purchase decisions are repeated they become quicker and simpler; and

❑ *significance*: important decisions which have a greater significance in the purchaser's life go through a more elaborate process (although this does not always mean they are better decisions as a result).

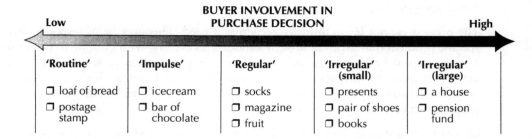

Figure 5.7: *A spectrum of decision-maker involvement*

Models of decision processes

Early composite models

Several models have been put forward which attempt to describe the various components in the consumer decision-making process. Early models, such as those developed by Engel, Kollat and Blackwell (1968) and Howard and Sheth (1969), amount to complex maps which describe all the possible components of a purchase decision. However these models do not explain how the various components relate to each other, or how they can be measured. They also assume that purchase decisions are a thought-out series of logical events. Whilst this may be true of decisions with high purchaser involvement, it is less applicable to low-involvement decisions.

The stages of a buying process

Models are useful, however, in describing the possible stages that a buyer might go through in making a decision. In some cases, particularly where there is low involvement, stages are missed out or the order is changed. But it is important for marketing management to recognise the possible stages because each one represents an opportunity to influence the outcome of the decision. Figure 5.8 shows the potential stages in a buying process which we will examine in more detail.

Figure 5.8: *The stages of a consumer buying process*

The first three stages represent a decision process before buying; the fourth stage is the actual act of purchase, followed in the fifth stage by a period of usage and evaluation of the product or service. This implies that the consumer is involved in the marketplace before and after buying the product, not just during the actual time of purchase. As we have seen the level of this involvement varies greatly.

117

Need recognition

The process cannot begin until we recognise a need. This may be in response to a specific problem that arises (a broken window, an evening with nothing to do) or a common need that regularly arises (hunger, companionship, prestige). The need may be triggered by internal stimuli (a physiological need such as thirst) or external stimuli (TV adverts, shop displays). It is important that marketing management understands several aspects of this stage:

❑ the factors that may stimulate the recognition of a need for their products;

❑ how to use these factors to full advantage;

❑ how to deal with the response to the recognition of need.

- *Owen's desire for a pair of trainers had not reached a high level of priority among the various needs and wants that competed for his financial resources. However, a shop window caught his attention as he passed by because trainers were displayed in a way that reminded him of his desire to buy this particular product. The retailer had recognised that an interesting window display could prompt recognition of need.*

- *Susan was prompted to begin selecting a school for her daughter by a general letter from the local education authority reminding her and other parents that a decision on a preferred school had to be notified to them by a certain date. One local school was not prepared for the response that this caused when many parents rang to arrange a visit on receipt of this letter. Susan was initially put off this school as it required several attempts to get through and when she did the replies to her questions were curt and hurried.*

Information search

The recognition of a need may prompt the search for more information. This may be active, or more passive, or in some cases not carried out at all, as Figure 5.9 illustrates.

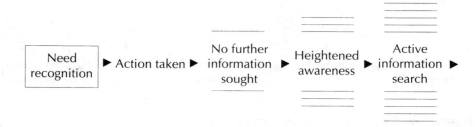

Figure 5.9: *A range of levels of information search*

The level of information search reflects the degree of consumer involvement. At one extreme, the need is recognised but no further information is sought as the consumer moves straight to the act of purchase. At the other extreme, an active search for information is instigated by reviewing product literature, reading consumer reviews, talking to friends or seeing product demonstrations.

Another possibility is that the consumer acknowledges the need but takes no deliberate steps towards fulfilling it. Instead their awareness of products or services fulfilling the need is heightened and they become more receptive to communications about those products including advertising and promotions, and conversations among friends.

In the case of both active searches by consumers and the more passive state of heightened awareness, the intervention of marketing activities at this stage can be crucial to the decision-making process.

- *Owen's awareness of trainers was further heightened as he passed the shop with the interesting display for a second time. He decided to seek additional information on prices and styles available by going inside.*

- *Susan's search for information on schools is much more deliberate and structured as she considered this to be a key decision in her young daughter's life. She talked to friends of their experiences and recommendations, collected school brochures, and made arrangements to visit those schools she considered most suitable.*

Evaluation of alternatives

The consumer processes the information which has been gathered actively or passively and in a competitive market evaluates the alternatives. At this stage the consumer is trying to assess which product will best deliver the benefits they are seeking.

Marketing activities that seek to influence this evaluation can only be effective if they focus on the benefits which interest the consumer. If targeted consumers are looking for high quality, it may not be helpful to advertise low prices. If shopping convenience is the highest priority, it may not be appropriate to offer the most extensive range of products if this detracts from ease of access.

- *Owen was shown several pairs of trainers by an assistant. He was initially put off some of the brands which presented a sporting image which was not what he wanted. He became more interested when the assistant empathised with his desire for fashionable, non-leather trainers which fitted his self-image of a modern yet caring man.*

- *Susan evaluated schools primarily on their ability to deliver the basic curriculum of the '3 Rs' of reading, writing and arithmetic which she saw as the key benefit her daughter needed from her first school. She used word-of-mouth reputation as her main method to evaluate this. She was not impressed by one school where the head teacher continually emphasised the quality of their music teaching as this was of little interest to Susan.*

Purchase choice

The evaluation of alternatives leads to an intention to purchase a certain brand of product or take up a particular type of service. This intention is normally followed by a confirmation of the purchase choice unless new factors intervene such as:

❑ The intervention of other people.

119

- *Owen made up his mind to purchase a pair of the trainers he had tried on in the shop once he received his monthly pay cheque. He told a friend who warned him of a bad experience regarding the quality of the same type of trainers. Owen decided to think again.*

❑ The intervention of the unexpected.

- *Susan chose a local school and informed the local education authority. She was taken by surprise when she was later informed that her first choice school was over-subscribed and her daughter could not be admitted. Instead she was offered a place at a school lower down her list of preferences.*

Post-purchase experience

When a consumer buys a product they do so with a set of expectations in mind concerning the performance of their purchase. These expectations are derived from their own research and the claims that the suppliers make for the product. They expect it to deliver the promised benefits.

Their level of satisfaction with the purchase is derived from a comparison between these expectations and the actual performance of the product. If it fails to deliver the promised benefits then the dissatisfaction caused can affect future sales in two important ways:

❑ the consumer does not repurchase that particular product but switches to another make;

❑ the dissatisfied consumer tells other people who are less likely to purchase the product as a result. This is particularly important for services which are difficult to test or experience prior to purchase and therefore rely heavily on reputation to encourage new customers.

- *Research among restaurant users found that dissatisfied customers invariably told their friends but rarely complained to the management of the restaurant. It also found that the most frequent method of choosing a new restaurant was word-of-mouth recommendation, especially from friends. These findings have significant marketing implications: satisfied customers are the most influential form of advertising for restaurant owners. Conversely, dissatisfied customers work as a potent invisible force, deterring new customers undetected by management until the damage has been done.*

The relationship between expectations and performance places a responsibility on marketing management to avoid making exaggerated claims for their products and services. If expectations are raised beyond the normal capabilities of the product by unrealistic or over-enthusiastic marketing communications prior to the sale, then levels of satisfaction are decreased in the post-purchase period, with a consequent adverse effect on future sales. If, on the other hand, product performance exceeds expectations then this is likely to be noticed and have positive effects.

Many retailers now offer a 'no-quibble' refund policy for these reasons. They know that a dissatisfied customer has a potential negative worth far exceeding the value of the lost sale.

- Owen returned to the shoe shop and told the assistant that he would not be going ahead with the purchase of the trainers reserved for him because of the quality problems experienced by his friend. The assistant countered by saying that the trainers were now a totally new product which were widely acclaimed for their quality standards, equivalent to much more expensive shoes. Owen was persuaded by an eloquent selling performance and purchased the shoes. Although he did not experience the problems described by his friend, a small defect did develop. This would not normally have bothered him, but because he was expecting perfection following the sales assistant's high praise for the product he was dissatisfied and complained to his friends.

- Sue was pleasantly surprised at the happiness and progress of her daughter in her new school. This was at the level she had anticipated from her first choice of school, but exceeded her expectations for this school which had been lower down her list of preferences. This unexpected satisfaction made her even more enthusiastic when she discussed schools with other parents.

Summary of consumer buying behaviour

We can now summarise the influences on consumer buying behaviour that we have explored in this unit. These are shown in Figure 5.10.

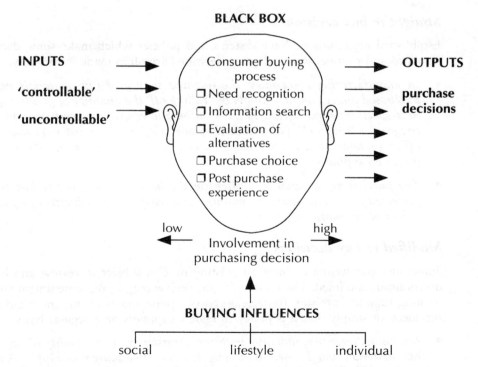

Figure 5.10: *A summary of influences and stages in consumer buying*

5.	**ORGANISATIONAL BUYING BEHAVIOUR**

In Chapter 4, 'Organisational and consumer markets', we saw that markets can be divided into two basic types:

❑ consumer markets of individuals buying mainly for personal consumption; and

❑ organisational markets in which organisations buy goods and services for further processing or for resale to others. We further sub-divided these organisational markets into industrial, intermediary and government markets dependent on the activities of the organisation.

Does buying in organisations differ from consumer buying behaviour? Organisations are made up of people who are still influenced by the social and individual forces we have already explored in this chapter (see section 3, above). However, the nature of the decisions and the processes for decision making are often different in organisations.

Types of organisational buying decisions

Different types of organisational buying decisions follow different buying processes. Early research in this field (e.g. Robinson, Faris and Wind, 1967) recognised three main types of decision, or 'buy classes'.

Straight re-buy decisions

Established organisations have systems and policies which make some decisions standard and routine. Repeat buying decisions are often made in this way.

- *In manufacturing companies, the ongoing supply of raw materials may be purchased under contract simply by 'calling off' the quantity of goods required in a specific period. Retailers have automatic re-ordering systems which are triggered when stocks fall to a certain level. Offices often order stationery and office supplies on a routine basis by emailing requirements regularly to one preferred supplier.*

- *The purchasing of services is often on the basis of a straight re-buy from a preferred contractor such as a maintenance company, an advertising agency or a firm of accountants.*

Modified re-buy decisions

Sometimes purchasing to meet an existing need is subject to review and buying decisions are modified. The reasons for the review may be discontentment with an existing supplier, pressure to decrease costs, opportunities to buy more advanced products, or simply that it is policy to review suppliers on a regular basis.

- *A manufacturer was unhappy with the consistency of the quality of one of its raw materials and decided to investigate alternative sources of supply. Another company had a policy of always involving more than one supplier when purchases of any product reached a certain level to protect the security of their supplies and improve their negotiating position. A wholesaler was unhappy with the margins they made on one product line and decided to look for an alternative. A charitable organisation had a policy of reviewing its major suppliers at least once every three years to ensure that it was still receiving value for money.*

'New task' purchasing decisions

An organisation takes a 'new task' buying decision when it purchases a particular type of product or service for the first time. The reasons for this include the launch of a new product or service, the need to acquire a new technology, or an internal reorganisation.

- *A retailer decided to diversify by adding a new range of products which involved dealing with a completely different type of supplier. A growing business computerised its accounts and payroll systems that involved investigating software packages for the first time. New regulations forced a hospital to put a service, which had hitherto been provided in-house, out to tender by private sector companies.*

Stages in the organisational buying process

As in consumer buying, various stages, or 'buy phases', have been identified in the process of buying in an organisation. Buy phases are not always activated in some types of buying decision but the full eight stages are outlined below, with two examples of the process in action.

Problem or need recognition

Many factors can trigger the recognition of a buying need including most of the situations described above. These include internal stimuli, such as dissatisfaction with existing purchases, and external factors such as a visit from the salesperson of a new supplier.

- *A manufacturer was dissatisfied with the productivity of one of its processes, and began to consider alternatives for improvement.*

- *A charitable organisation was alerted to a new fund-raising possibility by the advertising of telephone selling agencies in a magazine.*

General description of need

Recognition of a need leads to a general description of what is required in terms of the characteristics and quantity of items likely to fulfil the need. The principle benefits from any purchase are identified.

- *The production manager of the manufacturer identified some new types of equipment which could make its problem process more efficient and began an evaluation of the benefits versus the costs.*

- *The campaign director of the charity organised internal discussions of the fund-raising potential of telephone selling to its supporters and the implications for the organisation.*

Specification of product required

A specific description of the characteristics of what is required is the next stage, often involving wide consultation with other departments in larger organisations.

- *The engineering department of the manufacturer drew up a detailed specification of the type of equipment required after meetings involving production, engineering, purchasing and financial management.*

- *The fund-raising managers of the charity detailed the type of telephone sales operation they envisaged with cost budgets and revenue targets.*

Search for suppliers

The buying organisation looks for potential suppliers of the product or service they require.

- *The manufacturer's purchasing manager phoned equipment suppliers already known to the company.*

- *A fund-raising manager of the charity was given the responsibility of researching and contacting telephone sales agencies which could meet their brief. This was done largely by searching the Internet and using trade directories.*

Request for proposals

Buying organisations normally identify a short list of possible suppliers and ask them to submit a quotation to supply the product or service specified.

- *The purchasing manager asked for quotations for the supply of the specified equipment from three sources, including details of delivery times, guarantees and after-sales service.*

- *The fund-raising manager talked to several marketing agencies with telephone sales operations and asked each for a written proposal of the service they could offer and the terms.*

Selection of supplier

Proposals and quotations are evaluated and a supplier is selected.

- *The purchasing manager discussed the quotations he had received with the production and finance managers and together they put forward a recommendation to the manufacturing director who had the decision ratified by the board of directors.*

- *The fund-raising manager reported back to the management committee of the charity with proposals for a telephone sales campaign and a recommended agency to carry out the work.*

Specification of terms and conditions

The order is finally placed with the terms and conditions of supply agreed and specified.

- *The purchasing manager signed a contract for the supply of the equipment and organised the leasing finance previously agreed by the finance department.*

- *The campaign director signed an agreement with a marketing agency for the supply of a specified amount of telephone selling and the parameters for carrying this out.*

Performance review

Finally the buying organisation reviews the purchased product or service and evaluates the outcomes against their expectations. For example:

- *Reports from the production manager indicate that the new equipment has improved productivity substantially and recommend the purchase of another machine.*

- *The fund-raising management of the charity review the telephone selling operation and conclude that a combination of poor results and complaints from supporters objecting to being approached in this way indicate that the campaign should be discontinued.*

A framework for organisational buying situations

The classifications outlined above of the types of buying decisions (or 'buy classes'), and the stages in the buying process ('buy phases') can be amalgamated to form a framework, or grid, of organisational buying situations. This 'buy grid' is shown in Figure 5.11, which also indicates which buy phases are likely to be implemented in each of the buy classes.

The Decision Making Unit (DMU)

One of the characteristics of organisational buying is that more than one person can be involved in the decision-making process. As a result, marketing to organisations often involves targeting more than one individual. Identification of the membership of the so-called 'Decision Making Unit' (DMU) or 'Buying Centre' is a key part of marketing to organisations.

Participation in buying decisions

Several types of decision makers participate in buying. Some of these have already been illustrated by the various participants in the buying decision of the manufacturer and charitable organisation described above. These include:

❑ *Collective bodies*: boards of directors, management committees, governing bodies.

❑ *Individual*: director, manager, other delegated decision maker.

❑ *Department*: department manager, departments (e.g. production, engineering, fund-raising).

Participation in buying decisions depends on several factors:

125

Stages of buying process	Buy classes		
	Straight rebuy	*Modified rebuy*	*New task*
Need recognition	✘	?	✔
General need description	✘	?	✔
Specification of product	✔	✔	✔
Search for suppliers	✘	?	✔
Request for proposals	✘	?	✔
Selection of supplier	✘	?	✔
Specification of terms	✘	?	✔
Performance review	✔	✔	✔

From Robinson, Faris and Wind, 1967

✔ = yes, stage activated
✘ = no, stage not activated
? = maybe, stage sometimes activated

Figure 5.11: *The buy grid framework for organisational buying*

❑ *The size of the organisation*: for example, an owner-manager may make all the buying decisions in a small enterprise.

❑ *The culture of the organisation*: some entrepreneurial organisations encourage delegation of authority and buying decisions are predominantly individual. Other organisations are more bureaucratic and insist that even low-level purchasing is subject to checks and constraints by several participants.

❑ *The type of buying decision*: some decisions are routine (straight re-buy) and only need one person involvement. Other purchases are exceptional with potential risk to the organisation (new task), and merit careful consideration by several participants.

Roles within the Decision Making Unit

In buying decisions involving several people, the participants play different roles dependent on their position in the organisation, their specialised knowledge and personal motivations. These have been characterised as:

❑ *The Gatekeeper*, who acts as a filter for information concerning buying possibilities. Gatekeepers include buying departments which receive supplier and product information, specialised functions keeping up-to-date data in their area, or senior managers exposed to fresh ideas at meetings and conferences.

❑ *The User*, who ultimately is the consumer or recipient of the product. Users vary from production managers to post-rooms with varying levels of influence over what is purchased for their use.

❑ *The Influencer*, who has a say in the choice of product. This may be for a variety of reasons such as their technical expertise (e.g. the engineering department) or because they have the ear of the decision maker (e.g. a personal assistant).

❑ *The Decision Maker*, who takes the actual decision to purchase. As the player of this role changes according to the type of decision, the identification of this key person is an important phase in marketing to an organisation.

Summary of organisational buying behaviour

Organisational buying behaviour is a complex series of processes. Several models have been developed, but managers marketing to organisations have found it difficult to apply them in practice because there are so many variants.

However, successful marketing and selling to organisations starts with an understanding of the factors which may apply in any buying situation. A summary of those examined above is shown in Figure 5.12.

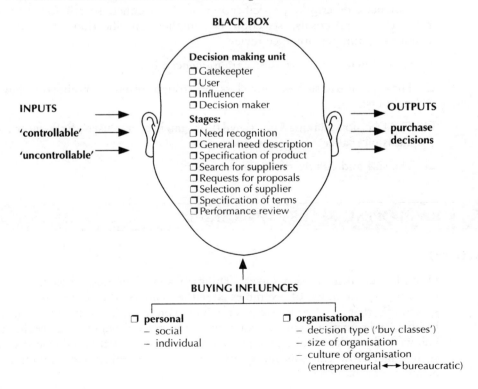

Figure 5.12: *A summary of organisational buying factors*

6.	KEY POINTS

❑ Customers make buying decisions in a way that cannot be directly observed. However inputs and influences into the decision-making process can be assessed by the buying decisions that result.

❑ Consumer buying decisions are influenced by:

❑ Social factors including culture, sub-culture, social class and reference groups, including the family.

❑ Individual factors including motivation, personality type, self-image, perception, learning, beliefs and attitudes.

❑ Lifestyle factors which combine social and individual inputs and can be classified into psychographic groups.

❑ Consumer buying can be divided into the five stages of need recognition, information search, evaluation of alternatives, purchase choice, and post-purchase experience. Some purchases require a lower involvement by the buyer and do not go through all the stages in the process (e.g. routine or impulse purchases).

❑ Organisational buying can be divided into the eight stages of need recognition, general need description, specification of the product, search for suppliers, requests for proposals, selection of supplier, specification of terms and conditions, and performance review.

❑ Organisational buying decisions are influenced by:

❑ The type of decision or 'buy class' of 'straight re-buy', 'modified re-buy' or 'new task'.

❑ The Decision Making Unit (DMU) of 'gatekeeper', 'user', 'influencer', and 'decision maker'.

❑ The size and culture of the organisation.

7.	DEVELOPING MARKETING SKILLS

Exercises

1. How do you behave as a buyer? Think of some purchases you have made recently; try to think of examples at either end of the 'buyer-involvement spectrum', that is a purchase over which you took considerable time and trouble, and something you bought without too much thought. Analyse the steps you went through to make each purchase and the factors that influenced you at each stage. How can this information help the organisations marketing the products you bought?

2. Imagine you have been appointed as the buyer of casual clothes for a chain of clothes shops. How would you go about selecting your ranges? Detail the

activities such as meetings and visits you would undertake and the information you would need before making any buying decisions. How could a potential supplier hope to influence your decision making in their favour?

3. How do employers recruit staff? Write down the process you might go through if you were about to recruit a new member of staff for an organisation for whom you worked. How similar is that process to the organisational buying process (described in section 5 above)? How could potential applicants influence the decision process by marketing themselves?

Developing a marketing plan

Activity 5 A SWOT analysis

Write an initial SWOT analysis of the product or organisation which is the subject of your marketing plan.

❑ What strengths and weaknesses are suggested by your internal audit?

❑ Which opportunities and threats appear from your external audit?

This initial analysis may clarify some further areas for research. Note what these are as they can be followed up in the next activity in Chapter 6.

FURTHER READING AND REFERENCES

General texts

Brassington, F. and Pettit, S. (2000) *Principles of Marketing*, 2nd edition, FT/Prentice Hall, chapters 3 and 4.

Kotler, P. (2000) *Marketing Management*, 10th edition, Prentice Hall, chapters 6 and 7.

Chaston, I. (1999) *New Marketing Strategies*, Sage, chapter 6.

Buyer behaviour

East, R. (1997) *Consumer Behaviour: Advances and Applications in Marketing*, Prentice Hall.

Engel, J.F., Kollat, D.T. and Blackwell R.D. (1968) *Consumer Behaviour*, Rinehart & Winston.

Howard, J.A. and Sheth, J.N. (1969) *A Theory of Buyer Behaviour*, John Wiley.

Robinson, P.J., Faris, C.W. and Wind, Y. (1967) *Industrial Buying and Creative Marketing*, Allyn & Bacon.

CHAPTER 6

Marketing Research

Marketing research is a specialised skill – one of the tools in marketing's bag of management techniques. It plays a key part in the analysis stage of the marketing process. This chapter explores marketing research by asking:

❑ What is the role and scope of marketing research. When is it useful?

❑ How is marketing research carried out? What are the processes involved?

❑ What are the various methods used in marketing research?

1.	CASE STUDY: FAST FOODS

Ray Greenwich had decided to open a fast food restaurant in the large urban area where he lived. As a specialist in the catering trade, he was attracted by the continued growth of this sector at a time when more traditional restaurants had seen a fall in their custom during the recession. However he had a number of choices to make before deciding on the exact form of his business.

First he had to decide on the type of food he would offer. He was considering the relative merits of traditional take-away foods like sandwiches or fish and chips against more recent innovations such as hamburgers, pizzas and pastas, chicken or ethnic foods stimulated mainly by developments in North America. He felt that whilst sandwiches could offer the stability of the largest existing customer base with around 30 per cent of the market, pizzas might offer more potential, if perhaps more risk, as it was the fastest growing sector.

He was also undecided on location. Should he go for a high street location where customers and competition abounded? Or should he try and attract travelling customers with a concession near the motorway or the railway station, or try one of the latest drive-through outlets?

The type of service to be offered was another decision he had to make. Whilst he was keen to make the emphasis on fast food, there were considerable variations on this theme. Take-aways were always popular but should he also offer table service? He had read that home delivery was a particular growth area.

The size of the menu was a further issue. He was unsure whether to target the core market of fast food customers or attempt to attract some other more specialist groups. He knew for example that vegetarians were becoming a significant market representing 10 per cent of the population and growing fast. Concern for healthy eating and for environmentally friendly preparations and packaging was increasing, particularly amongst the younger generation. Should he offer the very limited menu of most fast food outlets or look to a more extensive menu which some of the established chains seemed to be developing? This lead him to consider his pricing policy as some outlets aimed at the cheapest possible food whilst others seemed to justify higher prices by offering something different.

Finally he was considering whether to go it alone or take up one of the many franchises offered by either the large franchisors or more limited, innovative operators.

He decided to discuss these issues with Margaret deSilva, a marketing research consultant.

'The trouble is,' he told her, 'that most of the information available relates to the total market rather than the local picture. I know that nationally the main consumers of fast food are young – three out of four 16 to 24 year olds eat fast food once a month for example. Over 35 year olds seem to prefer to eat in more formal restaurants. But how does that help me here?'

'Yes, there is a lot of data from government statistics and other sources on the fast food market,' she agreed. 'The market grew very rapidly in the 1980s and 1990s. Although it has slowed down today, it has become very large with sales around £7 billion nationally. However there are some warning signs as young people are not only the largest customer group but the biggest element in the labour force as well – and 16 to 25 year olds are a shrinking proportion of the total population. It will be useful to build up a picture of national and regional trends. But you are right – we will also need some other research to see how this information applies locally.'

Points to consider

1. Consider the role that marketing research can play in this situation. How can research help Ray Greenwich and what types of information does he need?

See sections 2 and 3.

2. Assume you are Margaret deSilva. Outline the research plan that you would suggest to Greenwich:

   (i)   What objectives would you set and what areas would your research cover?

See sections 3 and 4.

   (ii) What research methods could you use?

See section 5.

   (iii) What existing, secondary sources of information would you use?

See section 6.

   (iv) What new, primary data would you collect and how?

See section 7.

3. Draft a questionnaire with the objective of painting a profile of the local consumer of fast food in Greenwich's area.

See section 7, 'The questionnaire'.

2. | THE ROLE OF MARKETING RESEARCH

Marketing information

In previous chapters we have looked at the various contexts in which marketing decisions are made, from general environmental and behavioural factors to specific market forces and trends in customer demands. A common theme throughout has been that marketing plans are made and executed in a complex world subject to constantly changing influences. As a result the marketplace is full of uncertainties which can influence the outcomes of marketing programmes. These uncertainties stem from various sources, from large-scale cultural or lifestyle shifts and economic trends, to specific market forces, competitive activity and customer changes.

The role of marketing research is to reduce this uncertainty as far as possible by providing relevant data and information as a basis for marketing intelligence.

Data, information or intelligence?

Marketing research uses several terms which need further definition as they carry different emphasis in their meanings:

❑ *data* is a collection of facts (for example, purchases recorded at a supermarket till);

❑ *information* is data which has been selected and sorted so that it can be analysed for a specific purpose (for example, sales as recorded through the till of one particular brand compared to other brands);

❑ *intelligence* is the interpretation given to the information through analysis (for example, recorded sales of the brand show an above average increase compared to competitive brands which correlate to a period of special promotion; the results of the promotion are quantified to provide a key input into future promotional decisions).

A *marketing intelligence system (MIS)*

Marketing research is part of an organisation's marketing intelligence system (MIS) which uses data and information from internal and external sources to better understand the interface between the environment and marketing activities. This is illustrated in Figure 6.1.

There are numerous sources for marketing intelligence to work on:

❑ marketing information from internal sources such as the sales force;

❑ marketing information from external sources such as trade fairs, conferences, and the trade press;

❑ accounting data from internal sources such as invoicing records and credit control reports;

❑ accounting information from external sources such as the Report and Accounts of competitive companies;

❑ information derived from public information (e.g. government reports);

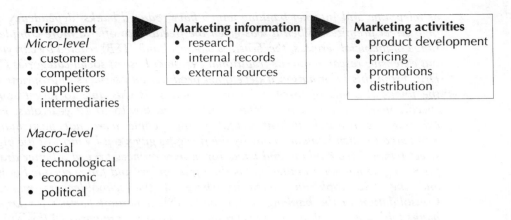

Figure 6.1: *Marketing intelligence systems*

❏ market intelligence reports on specific industries or market sectors, which can be purchased;

❏ information from the Internet, such as competitors' websites, online reports and newsgroups (online forums);

❏ marketing research which is privately commissioned to report on a specific problem or opportunity.

Marketing intelligence is used to tackle a wide spread of organisational issues including:

❏ *strategic long-term decisions* (Which market should we be in? What growth can we anticipate?);

❏ *tactical short-term decisions* (How do we promote this product in that market? How can we improve the coverage of our distribution?);

❏ *ad hoc decisions relating to one-off problems* (What do we do about this new competitor? How do we counter this price discounting?).

The application of marketing intelligence

Organisations use marketing intelligence in different ways with varying degrees of thoroughness.

Large companies

Marketing research is widely used by large companies who allocate substantial budgets to the collecting and analysing of information. Some make extensive use of consumer research before deciding their marketing strategies, which in turn determines the strategic direction of the entire organisation.

- *The banking sector has changed at great pace, stimulated firstly by the reduction of artificial barriers which used to separate such institutions as banks, building societies and insurance companies, and, secondly, by innovations such*

133

as telephone and Internet banking which have reduced banks' dependency on high street premises. When it was given the freedom to offer a more complete range of financial services, the Trustees Savings Bank (TSB) reacted by carrying out extensive research into its traditional customer base of social categories C2/ D/E. From this information it developed products and services appropriate to the financial needs of these types of customers. It was able to target some specific market areas such as senior citizens and the 15 to 19 year olds. For example, its research indicated that young people were not particularly motivated to open bank accounts by the free gifts given out by most of the high street banks. Free banking and value for money services proved a better draw for young people with limited funds than free folders and fancy cheque books, and the TSB took an increasing share of the school-leavers market. Consolidation in the banking sector made TSB a natural partner for larger banks with a more middle market profile, so that it is now part of LloydsTSB.

Other companies carry out less formal market research but rely on more informal methods for gathering market information.

- *Hi-Tec Sports became a significant player in the sports and leisure shoes market by closely associating the company with its marketplace. One of the key strands of its corporate strategy is to be 'better informed and wider awake than the competition'. They have achieved this by more informal intelligence processes, scanning their environment by paying close attention to expert opinion and competitors' activities. An understanding of lifestyle changes is crucial in their market but Hi-Tec have preferred a 'street-wise' approach to keeping up with fashions rather than use of formal market research. For example, it has developed strong links with the squash market through involvement with top players and sponsorship which helps the company to develop appropriate products as well as promote its image.*

Non-profit organisations

Although market research is traditionally linked to large private sector companies, non-profit organisations increasingly justify expenditure on research. As public services and charitable organisations have been exposed to competitive pressures and market forces, so they have responded by seeking fuller information about their clients, customers and supporters.

- *The London Borough of Richmond upon Thames conducted an exit survey into parents' opinions of primary schools. This was in response to concern in the Education Department that a high number of children left the Local Authority's primary schools to go into independent secondary schools. As part of their strategy to provide customer feedback to help market individual schools and monitor their progress, the authority undertook a survey of those parents whose children were about to leave primary schools in the Borough. This survey provided comparative data on parents' opinions of various aspects of school life which helped individual head teachers better understand what was expected of them. An analysis also looked at the reasons why a significant percentage of children leaving Richmond's state primary schools did not select a Richmond state secondary school.*

Industrial organisations

Marketing research is carried out not only by those organisations involved in consumer markets, but also by those marketing to other organisations or professions in the industrial or public sectors.

- *Letraset was founded when a graphic artist, Dai Davies, identified a need among his profession for a convenient and quick method of producing high quality lettering to replace the traditional, time-consuming hand lettering for professional display layouts and presentations. He did not need to research the market in any detail to come up with the idea and specification of rub-down transfer lettering as he knew the problems from his own experiences as a working professional. When the original product idea for Letraset turned into a high growth international business in the 1960s and 1970s, the managers of the company needed other ways of staying in touch with their customers. Letraset's products were distributed through agents and retail outlets so end-user contact was maintained by insisting that their own sales forces regularly visited the graphic artist consumer as well as the customers in the distribution network. The marketing intelligence resulting from these regular visits helped by some selective market research enabled Letraset to dominate its market until the advent of computer graphics made its 'instant lettering' products obsolete.*

Small firms

Research among successful entrepreneurs suggests that they develop a 'rich mental map' of their environment. They know their customers well; they watch competitive activity; they are aware of underlying social, economic and technological trends which could affect their business. They achieve this, not by commissioning research which they often regard as too expensive and time-consuming, but by developing extensive networks of contacts within their trade and by keeping 'an ear to the ground' in their chosen marketplace.

Researchers have further suggested that the survival of a fledgling business depends on how quickly new owner-managers take to properly understand their environment and then learn from their experience of dealing with it.

- *In the early 1970s a young couple decided to open a restaurant in a small seaside town. 'Paddingtons' restaurant opened in Littlehampton on the Sussex coast with a menu that reflected the backgrounds and concerns of its owners. It offered healthy food with many vegetarian dishes and Italian touches (vegetarian lasagne and quiches). Unfortunately the local market lagged behind the owners' early conversion to a healthy diet and customers stayed away. Rapidly reacting to this market information, the owners changed their menu to suit the mood of the times and were soon running a successful American-style hamburger restaurant.*

  The restaurant owners were Anita and Gordon Roddick who had to wait a few more years before their awareness of environmental issues developed into a more successful business venture when they opened the first Body Shop in 1976.

3. | THE SCOPE OF MARKETING RESEARCH

Whether the information gathering process is formal or informal, it has to start by asking the right questions. These questions can be divided into five major areas for marketing research as illustrated in Figure 6.2.

MARKETING RESEARCH

- Market and customer research
- Product research
- Promotion research
- Pricing research
- Distribution research

Figure 6.2: *Scope of marketing research*

Market and customer research

This looks at the size and structure of a particular marketplace, and the behaviour of buyers within that market, by asking questions such as:

❑ What are the parameters of the marketplace? What sort of customers are in it, where are they located and how many are there?

- *These are the kinds of questions that TSB had to ask about their customers before they could make decisions on developing their business. They discovered that their customers were concentrated in the C2/D/E social categories, a group who were potentially growing faster than the A/B/C1 categories who were the traditional customers of the main high street banks, such as Lloyds, TSB's eventual partner.*

❑ What are the competitive forces in the market? Who are the direct competitors and who provides substitute products? How successful are they and what are their strategies?

- *Hi-Tec have managed to challenge the leaders in a highly competitive market by carefully monitoring every move of the major players such as Addidas and Nike.*

❑ What are the behavioural characteristics of the market? How do the buyers in the marketplace behave? Who makes the buying decisions and how do they do it? What are the principle benefits they are looking for?

- *These were the kind of questions that Richmond Borough's research into the selection of secondary schools sought to answer. Were the decisions made by parents, or the children and what factors did they use to judge schools?*

Product research

New product ideas and concepts can be tested on a limited scale before they are put to the ultimate test of acceptance in the marketplace. The failure rate for new products is very high; nine out of every ten new product launches fail according to one estimate. To minimise this risk, concept testing is used to establish likely levels of demand. Improvements to existing products or changes to the packaging and presentation can also be tested for acceptability.

The lessons of failure often provide some of the secrets for future success. The Roddick's abortive venture as a health food restaurant provided them with valuable insights into consumer behaviour before they opened the Body Shop. But such insights can sometimes be less painfully and more quickly learned through research into the marketplace prior to launch.

Promotion research

Research provides important feedback on the impact of marketing activities. Marketing management need to know the effect of marketing interventions such as advertising in order to be able to plan future campaigns.

All forms of marketing communications can be made more effective by careful research and analysis of the results of past marketing efforts.

For example:

❑ Research among panels of TV watchers checks the impact of advertising campaigns.

❑ Analysis of the response rates to test mailings provides statistical evaluation of direct mail programmes.

❑ The effectiveness of special offers is researched before future activities are decided.

- *The Halifax uses marketing research as a way of reducing the risk in management decisions about its advertising. Halifax's corporate strategy relies on a strong association of values with their well-established brand name. It makes extensive use of its advertising campaigns which use the theme of groups of people arranged in various shapes (e.g. houses, wedding cakes) to create the desired image among consumers. A tracking study continuously monitors the effectiveness of this advertising, assessing its level of awareness among target customers and its ability to communicate key messages to them. This, in turn, informs decision making about the creative content of future advertisements, as well as how much should be spent on them and in what media.*

Pricing research

The acceptability of pricing levels can be researched in a number of ways. Experiments to assess the effect of changes to the price of a product give an indication of the relationship between price levels and sales. Attitude research among customers can be the basis of an organisation's pricing strategy.

- *Letraset's research into the buyer behaviour and attitudes of graphic artists found that purchases of instant lettering were not very sensitive to higher prices. As the rub-down letters actually reduced the time taken for a design, they were regarded as a cost saving and in any case the common practice was to pass on the cost of materials such as Letraset to the client who commissioned the work. Competitive products offered at substantially lower prices were regarded as poorer quality. Research confirmed that graphic artists worked to very tight deadlines so they needed the benefit of immediate availability of a high quality product rather than low prices. This information formed the basis of Letraset's strategy of pricing the product high and using the additional profits generated to improve the quality and availability of their products.*

Distribution research

Research can provide crucial information affecting the distribution of goods and services. For example, feasibility studies into alternative methods of distribution may involve:

❑ An analysis of the structure of the marketplace. What are the current distribution practices in this market? What is the best option for distributing this product: agents, wholesalers, or directly through the organisation's own operation?

❑ Research into store location. What is the optimum location for this retail outlet: prime high street, secondary off-high street, back street or out-of-town site?

- *Tesco Direct has become one of the world's leading online grocery services. It receives over 60,000 orders a week in the UK, predominantly on the Internet, for its home delivery service. After careful research into the logistics of establishing a reliable delivery system, it was decided to pick orders directly from existing Tesco stores, rather than follow the US model of separate, centralised distribution centres. With each order averaging £80 in value, this localised delivery operation has been one of the keys to the company's successful growth.*

4. THE MARKETING RESEARCH PROCESS

Marketing research is a process of several stages. These stages depend on each other; the neglect or unsatisfactory completion of one stage affects the quality of the entire research effort.

An overview of the process is shown in Figure 6.3.

Setting the objectives

The initiation of marketing research usually arises from management awareness of a problem or an opportunity (Why are we losing ground to competitors? How do we enter this new market?).

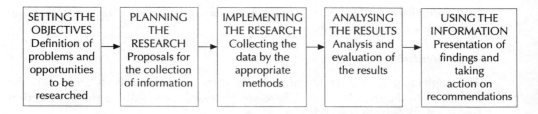

Figure 6.3: *The process of marketing research*

The translation of this awareness into a clear research brief or statement of objectives is not always an easy step. If research professionals are carrying out the work, the understanding between these researchers and managers commissioning the research is crucial in defining the problem to be investigated. Often managers do not have a clear idea of the issue that requires research; indeed the need for research may arise because problems are not understood.

- *Levi's wanted to move into the higher-priced clothes market as a way of diversifying away from the saturated market for jeans in the USA. They planned to introduce a range of high quality men's suits, jackets and trousers called 'Tailored Classics' under the umbrella of the Levi brand name. Research in the form of group discussions tested the acceptability of the new range. Although this reported that target customers did not perceive the Levi name to be in keeping with suits, the company decided they could overcome this problem by concentrating on separate jackets and trousers. The new range was not a success. Levi's marketing management had misread the market's fundamental objection to the Levi name on more formal up-market clothes. Their research objectives had not focused on this key issue as the diversification strategy aimed to maximise on the goodwill in the Levi brand.*

Planning the research

The next stage is to plan how to meet the research objectives. This normally requires defining the following areas:

❑ *The customer groups or markets to be investigated.* Which customers do we want to find out about? Which products are being considered?

❑ *The measurements to be made of these groups.* Do we want to know the value of their purchases, their attitudes to our products and the competitors, their decision-making processes, their buying patterns, or their exposure to various media?

❑ *The methods to be used.* How will we collect the data? What information already exists? Which research instruments, such as surveys or observations, will we use? Do we need to select a sample and if so how will this be done?

❑ *The costs and time involved.* How much is it going to cost? How long will it take?

139

In a formalised process involving professional researchers, a *research proposal* summarises this information.

Implementing the research

The implementation stage initiates the selected research methods and fulfils the collection of the required data. These are discussed more fully in the next section (section 5, 'Research methods').

Analysing the results

The data collected in the implementation stage is of little value without some processing to turn it into relevant information. Some data such as reports on markets or competitors may only require the selection of the relevant information. New data requires more processing involving such stages as:

❑ editing of survey answers to check for inaccuracies or omissions;

❑ coding of answers to help with the analysis; and

❑ tabulation of data into an understandable form. This can be assisted by computer processing.

Using the information

Once the collected data is converted into management information, it can be communicated in a way which is appropriate to the situation and the organisation, so that it can be effectively used. The form of this varies from informal briefings to written reports and presentations.

Research can only aid marketing decisions. It cannot make or implement those decisions, but it can ensure they are better informed. Ultimately the value of the research depends on specific actions which are guided by its results and recommendations.

- *Although market research can only analyse what has happened, not what is going to happen next, it does provide companies like the Halifax with information to make their advertising work harder in the next campaign. Their advertising research is presented not only internally but it is also shared with the agency that created it. Halifax management agree criteria on which the advertising is to be judged with their agency and later review the campaign using research to see what went well or less well. By analysing how their current advertising is working, they hope to learn how to make it even more effective in the future.*

5. | RESEARCH METHODS

Qualitative and quantitative research

Marketing research methods can produce qualitative and quantitative data.

Qualitative research

Qualitative research explores attitudes, perceptions and ideas. It seeks to find out why people make the choices they do, and what they believe their future needs may be. As it asks for opinions which are hard to quantify or reduce to simple questions, it usually involves face to face interviews with individuals or small groups. The most common qualitative methods are in-depth interviews or group discussions (see section 7, 'Primary data').

Quantitative research

Quantitative research seeks to measure or quantify factors for statistical analysis. It asks how many people buy certain products and in which ways. As it tries to build up a statistical picture of the marketplace, it usually involves taking data from many people in order to draw general conclusions from a sufficiently large sample. Common quantitative methods are therefore large-scale surveys and observations.

In practice, qualitative and quantitative research overlap and are often used in tandem in a research design. The wider sampling of quantitative data can reveal trends which more detailed qualitative research methods can try to explain. For example, quantitative data may show an unexpected increase in market share, and qualitative research can be used to find out why.

Primary and secondary data

Methods of collection depend on the type of information required. Two distinct categories of data exist:

❑ *Primary data*: new data specifically collected for the project through field research. It generates information specifically for the project in hand.

❑ *Secondary data*: data which already exists and can be collected by desk research. It is information relevant to the project, which already exists somewhere else.

This distinction is illustrated in Figure 6.4.

❑ *Desk research* is a passive form of marketing research. There is no interaction with the customer. Information is collected without the researcher leaving the desk by looking at both public sources, such as central and local government reports, and private sources such as the internal accounts of the organisation or data from a trade association.

❑ *Field research* is actively involved in the marketplace. It may be continuous research in which several organisations participate such as omnibus surveys. Alternatively it may be one-off ad hoc research commissioned by one

141

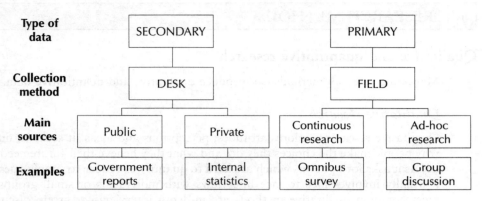

Figure 6.4: *Types of research data*

organisation to investigate a specific problem through discussions with a group of consumers.

Advantages and disadvantages

The comparative advantages and disadvantages of each type of data are shown in Figure 6.5.

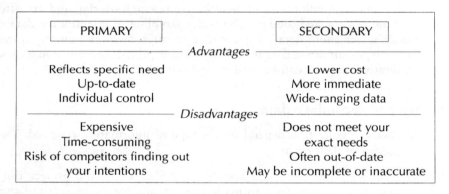

Figure 6.5: *Comparative merits of primary and secondary data*

6. SECONDARY DATA

Marketing research starts with desk research for secondary data. An evaluation of the many types of existing data may make further primary research better informed or even unnecessary.

A variety of sources exist for secondary marketing information, as outlined below.

Internal sources

The internal records and knowledge base of an organisation can provide unique, low cost data. There are several places to look for this including:

❑ *Internal marketing information*, such as the reports of salespeople in the field, or market surveys previously commissioned.

❑ *Accounting, production and other internal records*. The records kept by an organisation usually contain statistics on existing customers, sales by region and time period and the costs of specific products and processes.

❑ *Informal sources*. The knowledge and opinions of staff, particularly those dealing directly with customers, form an important information base. This is frequently accessed through informal communications although more formal research methods are used as well. Recent advice from management gurus which encourages managers to leave their desk and practise 'management by walkabout' recognises the value of gathering such information by observation and talking to others within an organisation.

Competitor sources

Organisations communicate constantly with their customers and their financial audience. This gives competitors information about the organisation and its strategies. Web-sites, promotional literature, advertising campaigns, press releases, financial reports and accounts and statutory returns provide data which other organisations can analyse in an effort to interpret their competitors' strategies and forecast their future activities.

External secondary sources

Many external bodies publish information which is relevant to marketing. These are usually available electronically, although not necessarily free. (See section 'Further reading and references' for examples of electronic databases and online reports).

❑ *Official information* is regularly published by governments at national and international level. In the UK, for example, the government provides a 'Monthly Digest of Statistics' on the population, housing, manufacturing and other key indicators. 'Business Monitors' summarise business statistics from a large database. The DTI publish a weekly guide to industrial trends and many other market reports. Summary statistics from the 2001 population census are available free of charge. These and many other official reports and statistics are often available online or through the Central Statistical Office and libraries.

❑ *Non-official sources* also publish a wealth of information. Many research agencies, such as Mintel, the Economist Intelligence Unit, Key Note Publications, Kelly's, and Dun and Bradstreet (D & B), sell reports and directories of markets and industrial sectors, either online or as hard copies.

❑ *The Press* is a regular source of information for any organisation whether it is the general press for financial and management information, or specialist publications reporting on specific trade sectors or professions.

❑ *Trade associations and professional institutions*, from the Confederation of British Industry (CBI) to local Chambers of Commerce, are further potential sources of information.

PRIMARY DATA

Research approaches

There are four different approaches to collecting primary data:

❑ observation;

❑ experimentation;

❑ surveys; and

❑ in-depth interviews.

Observation

Research in many fields from anthropology to astronomy uses observation as the basic method of investigation. Marketing research uses observation in a number of ways such as:

❑ *Mechanical observations*, which count activities like the number of shoppers in a street or the quantity of cars using a road.

❑ *Behavioural observations*, which note how people go about buying or using products by, for example, watching how people select brands in a shop or use products in the workplace.

❑ *Informal observation*, which keeps a 'weather eye' on the marketplace by, for instance, attending exhibitions and noting the activity level on competitive stands.

❑ *Internet observation*, through 'cookies', or small files inserted into end-users' computers, enabling web-sites to identify users and track their future behaviour. Organisations can identify visitors to their web-site, and build a profile of that visitor by observing their future Internet activity.

Experimentation

Experiments can assess the impact of variations to the elements in the marketing mix. Prices, promotions, packaging or other aspects of the product (e.g. taste, colour and size) are varied under controlled conditions to estimate the impact on buying preferences.

For example, retailers operating a chain of shops experiment with promotional discounts in one outlet and compare the impact on sales to outlets where the offer is not made. Organisations using direct marketing test response rates by mailing three different letters to separate samples of the same list.

Surveys

Surveys which collect data through the use of questionnaires are the most common method of primary research. They can be used to collect both quantitative and qualitative data depending on the structure of the questionnaire and the contact methods chosen.

A market survey asks questions of a number of respondents selected to represent the target market. Through the questionnaire, researchers can measure many factors such as:

❏ buying patterns and trends ('Have you purchased product X in the last 12 months/6 months/1 month?');

❏ competitors' performance ('Which of the following products have you purchased in the last 12 months?');

❏ expectations related to products and services ('Rate the following reasons for buying this type of product in priority order');

❏ attitudes to products and brand names ('How do you rate the performance of product X in terms of this benefit?');

❏ media exposure ('Which of the following newspapers do you read regularly/ sometimes/never?').

Surveys use personal contact, telephone and the post. (We look at the relative merits of each of these in 'Contact methods' below.)

In-depth interviews

For qualitative research, in-depth interviews probe more deeply for attitudes and motivations.

❏ *Individual interviews or 'depth interviews'* are informal and more conversational than the traditional questionnaires, allowing the respondents to talk about the subject in a less constrained way.

They may use techniques to open up respondents' deeper attitudes by asking them to project their feelings into hypothetical situations. These 'projective techniques' include word association and sentence completion tests. For example:

'What do you associate with the word Halifax?'
'The Halifax is ...'
'The Halifax ought to ...'
'The Halifax ought not to ...'

❏ *Group discussions, or focus groups*, guided by a trained leader can be both informative and creative. A small number of people (typically five to eight) from the target market are invited to discuss certain topics, concepts and products. The discussion leader may guide the group through their views on a specific market, its environment and the competitors before introducing a new product concept for reaction and comment.

  ● *The wide use of focus groups not only by consumer researchers but also by political parties has attracted critical comment. The Association of Qualitative Research Practitioners (1999) estimate that focus groups now account for two-thirds of qualitative research expenditure. This has prompted concerns that focus groups may be used inappropriately and have become part of a research 'methodolatry' or '... a preoccupation with selecting and defending methods to the exclusion of the actual substance of the story being told' (Denzin and Lincoln, 1998). Focus groups are not just*

145

a convenient way to get the outlook of a wider number of people. Their main advantage relies on the concept of group synergy – the group process generates a wider, more creative range of information than would result from a comparable number of depth interviews. Their main disadvantage stems from the tendency towards group consensus – a few, dominant members of the group may override the opinions of other, quieter members. Much depends on the skill of the moderators – researchers who lead and control the discussion. They walk a tightrope between allowing a free-flowing, creative discussion, and controlling conversations by reducing the participation of self-opinionated participants in order to encourage the more introverted group members to have their say.

Contact methods

Primary research is conducted by contacting a sample of respondents by mail, telephone or in person. Each method has advantages and disadvantages which are summarised in Figure 6.6.

CRITERION	CONTACT METHODS		
	Mail	*Telephone*	*Personal*
Quantity of data	poor	good	excellent
Interviewer effect*	good	fair	excellent
Control of sample	excellent	fair	poor
Speed	poor	excellent	good
Response rate	poor	good	good
Costs	fair	fair	poor

This refers to the possibility of bias in the results because of the preconceptions of the interviewer.

Figure 6.6: *Comparative merits of research contact methods*

Mail

Questionnaires by post can be inexpensive and reach geographically dispersed samples, but low response rates normally limit the effective size of the sample. Biases in the data are also possible because non-response is not a random process.

- *For example, 10 per cent of people respond to a mailed questionnaire and all of them state they are very satisfied with a specified product. Does this mean that they are a representative sample and that 100 per cent of people are satisfied? Or is it possible that those dissatisfied did not bother to reply and therefore only 10 per cent are satisfied? The truth is probably somewhere in between, but a mailed questionnaire cannot find out more precisely without further investigation.*

Telephone

Telephone surveys have become more popular as they can provide fast, convenient access to a relatively large number of respondents. The anonymity of the caller may induce a more open response, although the lack of visual clues and body language does hinder the collection of qualitative feedback.

Computer-Assisted Telephone Interviewing (CATI) can be used to guide the interviewer through the sequence of questions which appear on a screen and answers keyed directly into the computer system for analysis.

Electronic mail

The use of electronic communication methods for data collection is growing, but is still relatively limited. Survey data can be collected by emails to known addresses, or more passively via web-sites that ask visitors to volunteer information. It is also used in conjunction with other contact methods; for example, agreement to complete a survey form may be made on the telephone, or by post, but the questionnaire can be delivered and completed electronically. Whilst it can provide a convenient and fast method of data collection, research by electronic mail is constrained by the limited number of email address lists currently available. It is more frequently used to collect data from organisations rather than consumers, because of sampling issues arising from the inconsistent patterns of electronic mail usage in domestic households.

Personal

Personal, face-to-face interviewing is still the most popular method of collecting data for surveys. Although it can be expensive, because it is time-consuming, personal interviewing provides the opportunity for obtaining large quantities of high quality data.

Face-to-face research ranges from the highly structured interview with pre-determined routes through a planned sequence of standard questions to more open-ended discussions around the relevant topic. In either case the social interaction between the interviewer and the respondent is important for a successful outcome to the interview.

The questionnaire

The construction of a questionnaire in terms of what questions to ask and their form, wording and sequence determines how useful the resulting data is going to be.

What questions?

If questions are to be kept to a minimum, they are restricted to two types:

❑ Those that qualify the respondent in some way. Before proceeding with the rest of the questionnaire, the interviewer needs to find out more about the respondent (Do you own a house? Do you live within 20 miles of here?). Interviews are directed into a different route through the questionnaire depending on the response or in some cases terminated early. (If the questionnaire is about mortgages, the answer to the enquiry on house ownership determines whether to proceed to questions on attitudes to mortgage interest rates, for example.)

147

❑ Those that contribute to meeting the research objectives. In a well-designed questionnaire, every question has a purpose in line with the overall objectives of the research and is capable of contributing meaningful data.

What type of questions?

The form in which a question is asked influences the response. Questions can induce either an open or a closed response.

❑ *Open questions* leave the respondent free to choose how to answer; they invite an opinion (What do you think of ...?), or personalised information (Which books have you read recently?). Open questions are needed for qualitative surveys exploring attitudes and motivations.

❑ *Closed questions* attract only a limited response such as yes/no, or a rating on a scale. (Do you own a car? How do rate our service – good, average, or poor?). Closed questions are easy to ask and convenient to process afterwards. They are used for quantitative data collection, qualifying respondents or as multiple choice questions.

❑ *Multiple-choice questions* are closed in the sense that answers are predetermined, but they introduce more open elements by offering a longer list of responses than just yes or no.

Rating scales help to quantify opinions and attitudes that might otherwise be too imprecise if left totally open to the respondent. These take several forms, for example:

1. What is your general impression of the picture framing service of 'The Frame Centre'?

Expensive	☐	☐	☐	☐	☐ Cheap
High quality	☐	☐	☐	☐	☐ Low quality
Friendly	☐	☐	☐	☐	☐ Unfriendly
Fast	☐	☐	☐	☐	☐ Slow

2. Indicate in order of preference the features you would expect to find if the 'perfect' picture framing shop existed near your home:

A   Discount prices

B   Wide choice of materials

C   Good design advice

D   Quality workmanship

E   Easy to get to

F   Any other reason (state below)

1st ☐   2nd ☐   3rd ☐   4th ☐   5th ☐   6th ☐

What wording for questions?

The wording of a questionnaire requires careful thought to avoid bias or confusion in the response. Questions are best kept simple and direct, avoiding the obvious pitfalls of:

❑ *Leading questions* ('Does inhaling other people's harmful smoke in a restaurant concern you?' – the wording predisposes the respondent to answer positively even if it is not of great concern);

❑ *Confusing questions* ('What is your favourite dinner-time meal?' – 'dinner-time' to some is lunch-time to others);

❑ *Assumptive questions* ('Do you prefer pizza or pasta dishes?' – the respondent may not like either of them);

❑ *Ambiguous questions* ('Do you eat out frequently?' – definitions of 'eating out' can vary from a restaurant to a sandwich in the park whilst 'frequently' to some is infrequently to others).

What sequence for questions?

The order in which questions are asked is important for two reasons:

❑ The overall structure can influence the social interaction between the interviewer and the respondent. Questions which seem to be aggressive or intrusive in the early part of the interview (Why do you live in rented accommodation? How much do you earn?) can make respondents less than open in their later responses.

❑ Most questionnaires have a logical sequence which builds on data from previous questions. The need to ask irrelevant or inappropriate questions is eliminated if the order is carefully considered.

'*Funnelling*' is a common structure which starts off with wider, general questions often with closed responses to relax the respondent. Narrower, specific questions, especially those inviting more open responses, are left to the end.

Sampling

In some instances, information about an entire population is collected by a census (e.g. the 2001 UK Census of Population; a small number of manufacturers). However, most research is designed to draw conclusions about a larger group by studying a smaller sample that is taken to be representative of the whole. For qualitative data, samples are used with less concern for accuracy levels than in quantitative research. Qualitative samples tend to be small and chosen for the way in which they may *illustrate* key issues in the research brief (e.g. urban versus rural consumer opinions; manufacturing versus services management attitudes). For quantitative data, the sample has to be selected in such a way that it can be taken to *represent* the larger whole (e.g. percentages of rural dwellers shopping in urban centres; number of manufacturers buying a particular service).

Sampling involves a number of decisions:

The sampling unit

Who is to be studied? Who in the decision-making process is to be interviewed – the user, the purchaser or both?

- *For example, a manufacturer wishes to research the market for personal computers. These include domestic and commercial users. In the home there are several influences including husbands and wives and other family members. In the office there are also several potential decision makers and influences. Which people are interviewed?*

The sample size

How many people should be interviewed? How many activities should be observed? If properly selected for statistical validity, quite small samples can be chosen to be representative of a wider population or 'universe'. The exact number depends on the amount of variations within the population being studied (e.g. age ranges, sizes of firms), and the accuracy and confidence level required in the results produced. Formulae can be used to calculate the sample numbers needed, which are based on the smallest group in the sample to be analysed separately (e.g. an age range; manufacturers in a particular region). Normally, there would be at least 100 in the subgroup.

Sampling procedure

How should the sample be chosen? There are some options:

❑ *A probability sample* is chosen at random from the whole population being studied. To be truly random, every member of the population under consideration has an equal chance of being selected. It could therefore be expensive to conduct personal interviews of a random sample as they could be geographically distant from each other. A random sample may be modified by *clustering* into a small number of geographic areas in order to minimise this problem. A random sample may also be *stratified* to ensure it matches the population under study in some key respects. For example, target numbers of interviews can be set for particular age groups of people, or sizes of firms, within a sample in order to ensure that group is correctly represented.

❑ *Quota sampling* is the most commonly used method for quantitative consumer research. It involves selecting individuals who meet certain criteria (e.g. age, gender, social group), so that the complete sample matches known characteristics of the population. The interviewer is then given a quota of individuals who match these criteria (e.g. females between 15 and 25 years old in a certain town) to find and interview. Although quota sampling is less expensive than random sampling, it is also less accurate as bias can enter the selection procedures (e.g. the interviewer may look for 15–25 year females in a shopping precinct, approaching only those that looked willing to spend time on an interview. She was therefore excluding not only anyone that did not normally shop there, but also those in a hurry that day.)

- *Despite its popularity, quota sampling has its critics. It was widely blamed when the polls forecasting the results of the 1993 general election got it wrong. Days before the election, all the main opinion polls were predicting a narrow victory for Labour under Neil Kinnock. In the event, John Major became Prime Minister with a small Conservative majority. A key problem for the opinion polls was that Conservative voters were reluctant to declare themselves, and were therefore less likely to be selected for interview.*

❑ *A convenience sample* selects respondents on the basis of ease of access. It may be used in low-budget, qualitative research where representation of a wider population is relatively unimportant. For example, an interviewer may select on the basis of contacts already available, or may use the *snowball* technique of asking one respondent to recommend another.

Continuous research

Time frames for research depend on the information requirements but there is a choice between two basic types.

Ad hoc surveys

Surveys can be ad hoc or one-off pieces of research for a specific purpose.

Continuous surveys

Some research is conducted on an ongoing basis.

❑ *Omnibus surveys*: organisations can share in research by participating in an omnibus survey. Research agencies offer regular surveys of consumer groups of a consistent sample size. Participating organisations share general data and can also insert their own individual questions if they wish. Omnibus surveys are based on national samples (e.g. A/B/C1 adults) or more specialised groups (e.g. car owners).

❑ *Panels*: panels representing individual, household or industrial customer groups are set up and regularly asked for information about their buying behaviour. By reporting regularly on what products they have bought and when, or what advertising they have seen with what effect, these panels provide data on trends in purchasing patterns and the influences of marketing efforts.

❑ *Retail audits*: another way of regularly assessing demand is through retail audits in which research organisations analyse sales of various product lines in a sample of shops at regular intervals. Retailers now generate huge amounts of data on the purchasing behaviour of their customers through computerised recording of product bar codes through their tills.

This continuous research is particularly important for tracking the effectiveness of marketing activities. The impact of promotions, price offers, product changes and distribution efforts can be measured more effectively through regular surveys of the same sample to give comparable 'before and after' data.

8. A SUMMARY OF RESEARCH METHODS

We have examined many types of qualitative and quantitative research methods using primary and secondary data. These are summarised in Figure 6.7.

151

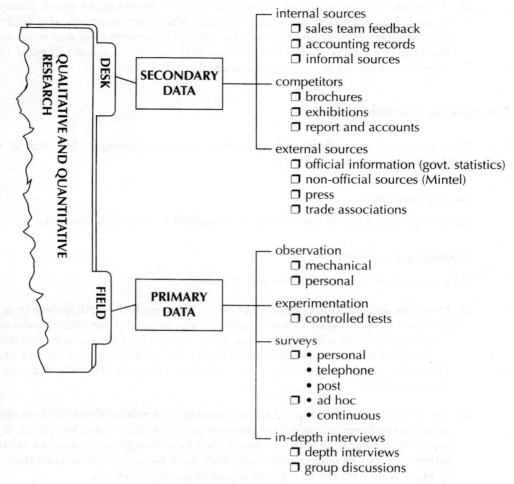

Figure 6.7: *A summary of marketing research methods*

KEY POINTS

❑ Marketing research collects data from a variety of internal and external sources and analyses it to provide information for marketing intelligence.

❑ Research varies from the formalised *marketing intelligence systems* which larger organisations use to track changes in their environment and the effects of their marketing campaigns, to the *informal networking* of entrepreneurs keeping a weather eye out for opportunities.

❑ Research can provide information on customers and markets or feedback on products, promotions, pricing and distribution issues.

❑ The research process first sets clear *objectives* before *planning* and *implementing* the research which can then be *analysed* and *used*.

- ❑ Research methods can produce *qualitative* or *quantitative* information from *primary* or *secondary data*.

- ❑ *Secondary data* already exists and can be collected from internal sources, such as accounting records, or external sources such as competitors' publicity or government statistics.

- ❑ *Primary data* is collected to meet specific research objectives through observation, experimentation, surveys or in-depth interviews.

- ❑ Respondents to surveys are contacted by mail, telephone or in person, on an ad hoc or continuous basis.

- ❑ Samples are used to represent (in quantitative research), or illustrate (in qualitative research), the population being studied. Methods include probability, quota and convenience sampling. Samples can also be clustered or stratified.

- ❑ Questionnaires use open, closed and multiple-choice questions, carefully worded to minimise bias, confusion and ambiguity.

10. | DEVELOPING MARKETING SKILLS

Exercises

1. Conduct some marketing research in an area in which you are interested. For example, this could be a hobby interest (e.g. recreation, health and fitness), a consumer product which you use (e.g. soft drinks, confectionery, clothes, fast food), or a career or work interest (e.g. healthcare, financial services, office equipment). Do not narrow your field of research too much at this stage as you may find it difficult to collect secondary data.

   (i) Analyse the existing secondary research data that exists on this market using libraries and other likely sources of information. In particular, try to find out:

   - ❑ the total revenue or income of this market, with any recent changes and trends;

   - ❑ the names of the principle 'players' such as manufacturers, suppliers and distributors, their market share and other measures of performance;

   - ❑ the structure of the market, investigating what products are bought or services provided and the distribution system that delivers them;

   - ❑ demographic information and trends among the principal buyers of the product or service;

   - ❑ international comparisons with similarities and differences between the UK and other markets, particularly in Europe.

   (ii) Develop a research brief for the market using primary research. Suggest a plan for the research that includes objectives, customer groups to be investigated and research methods specifying the sampling unit and the measurements to be made. Include a survey in your research methods and draft the structure and wording for this questionnaire.

(iii) Carry out the survey using your questionnaire and analyse the results. Consider aspects of your questionnaire which worked well and less well.

2. How could marketing research help you to develop the next steps in your career or personal life?

Developing a marketing plan

Activity 6 The research plan and implementation

The analysis stage of your marketing plan has looked at existing information and evaluated this as a SWOT analysis. Now consider how marketing research could help your project. This may fall into several areas such as:

❑ What other secondary information about the market and the competition do you need to complete your analysis? In what areas do you need more data to help clarify issues?

❑ In what areas is primary research required to clarify issues? What would be the objectives and methods of such research?

❑ What research methods would you use to evaluate the results of your marketing activities?

When you have considered these and any other opportunities for research, decide which you can implement as part of this project and plan how and when you will do this.

FURTHER READING AND REFERENCES

General texts

Hardaker, G. and Graham, G. (2001) *Wired Marketing*, John Wiley & Sons, chapter 3.

Hooley, G.J. and Hussey, M.K. (1999) *Quantitative Methods in Marketing*, Thomson Learning.

Mudie, P. (1997) *Marketing: an Analytical Perspective*, Prentice Hall, chapter 9.

Marketing research

Association of Qualitative Research Practitioners (1999) 'In Brief', March/April, page 2.

Denzin, N.K. and Lincoln, Y.S. (1998) *Strategies of Qualitative Inquiry*, Sage Publications.

Hague, P. and Jackson, P. (1995) *Do Your Own Market Research*, Kogan Page.

Morgan, D.L. (1998) *The Focus Group Guidebook*, California, Sage Publications.

Oppenheim, A.N. (1992) *Questionnaire Design, Interviewing and Attitude Measurement*, Pinter Publishers.

Proctor, T. (2000) *Essentials of Marketing Research*, Financial Times/Prentice Hall.

Webb, J.R. (2001) *Understanding and Designing Market Research*, Thomson Learning.

Research information web sites

Mintel: **http://www.mintel.com**

MORI: **http://www.mori.co.uk**

Economist Intelligence Unit: **http://www.eiu.com**

AC Nielson: **http://www.nielson.com**

Euromonitor: **http://www.euromonitor.com**

Key Note: **http://www.keynote.co.uk**

UKOP (UK Official Publications): **http://www.ukop.co.uk**

CHAPTER 7

Marketing Strategy

Strategic marketing management involves decisions in three key areas:

❑ Selection of customer groups, or segments of the market, that are relevant to an organisation's activities.

❑ Targeting of market segments in which an organisation can offer competitive benefits.

❑ Adoption of an appropriate market position which appeals to the selected segment.

These strategic decision areas of segmentation, targeting and positioning are the main subjects of this chapter.

1. CASE STUDY: BICYCLES

Over the last half-century, the British bicycle industry has experienced mixed fortunes. Not only has the bicycle become a much less used form of personal transport, but also the centre of production has shifted to the Far East. In 1955, the UK manufactured 3.5 million bicycles of which two thirds were exported. Producers in Hong Kong, Taiwan, Thailand and China, assembling mainly Japanese components have since taken over the world's mass markets. By the 1990s exports had fallen to 200,000 British bikes and imports of 1.5 million bicycles exceeded the total UK production of just over 1 million. Despite loosing share in the global market place, the British bicycle industry has begun to recover however from the relegation of the bike to a very secondary mode of transport. First the BMX (bicycle moto-cross) craze in the early 1980s showed the nation's youth that cycling could be fun and fashionable. Then in the late 1980s the mountain bike, or ATB (all terrain bike), appealed both to teenagers seeking more excitement and to the over 30 year olds looking for healthy and environmentally-friendly recreation. By 2000, ATBs accounted for over two thirds of all bicycle sales in the UK, helping the industry increase production to higher than mid-1980 levels.

Although cycling has made a comeback with one third of the population now owning a bike, its penetration varies demographically. More men own bicycles than women (38 per cent of men against 29 per cent of women). Ownership is highest amongst 15 to 19 year olds (55 per cent ownership) and the 35 to 44 year old group (40 per cent ownership) with dips in the intervening years and a considerable decline from 45 years on. The AB and C2 social groups own more ATBs than other groups. Ownership is highest where the terrain is flattest (East Anglia and the South) and lowest in hilly areas (Scotland and Wales) or urban centres where cycling is more dangerous (London).

Bicycles are owned for a variety of reasons. Exercise and recreation is the most common use today, ahead of making local trips such as shopping and travelling to work. A more varied product range attempts to meet the needs of the different customer groups. The ATB or mountain bike with its rugged frame and wheels and up to 21 gears has a more adventurous image than the conventional sports or touring bike that has thinner wheels, lighter frame and dropped handle bars. But a new hybrid, 'town and trail' variety has become increasingly popular. It combines some of the features of the ATB such as multi-cog gears and sturdy appearance with a more comfortable, efficient ride, recognising that most bicycles are still ridden primarily on roads. ATBs have also become the popular form of children's cycle superseding the junior BMX, although more conventional, small-wheeled cycles and 'trikes' are still sold to the youngest riders. Specialist road and track bicycles cater for the growing number of participants in the sport of cycling that received a welcome boost in the UK from the success of local riders and cycles in the 2000 Olympics. Other specialist products include the folding bike which can be put in the boot of a car, tandems and tricycles.

All of this was common knowledge to Rob McIntyre, managing director of one of the leading UK cycle manufacturers as he considered the strategic options that had recently opened up to his company. McIntyre had just concluded a deal with a major Japanese producer of cycle components to test market a new gearing system in the UK. The new product had ten gears, sufficient for most uses, but it was totally enclosed in the hub that protected it and made it easier to maintain and use. The producers claimed that it combined the benefits of the older hub gears and the newer derailleur, 'chain-jumping' systems popularised by the ATB. Although tests on the new product convinced McIntyre that it met these claims, his long experience in the bicycle trade also warned him that there would be resistance to it.

'Cyclists perceive the hub gear as rather old fashioned and utilitarian compared to the excitement of all those cogs and levers of derailleur gears, however impracticable they may sometimes be,' he explained to his fellow directors when they met to consider their marketing strategy for the new product. 'External gears are seen as an essential part of the ATB, and it may detract from its macho image if we give our range an internal gearing system. So we have to look carefully at the various sections of the market and decide where to target this innovation. Should we target buyers of our more traditional sports and touring cycles, as the gears are more in line with their image? Or should we go for the larger market of ATBs and try to re-position the enclosed gear in the marketplace as a technological innovation, far removed from the older systems? Perhaps the benefits of the new product has particular relevance to some types of cycle user above others and can help us develop new markets. We should be quite clear about which segment of users we are targeting and what particular position we wish to adopt in order to appeal to those customer groups. Whatever we decide we should remember that this product only gives us a short-term technological lead. For once, we are ahead of other overseas manufacturers who do not have immediate access to this product, but it will only be for another year or so. We must use our window of opportunity to the full.'

Points to consider

1. What do you think McIntyre means by a 'marketing strategy'? How does it differ from marketing 'tactics'? Give examples of strategic and tactical marketing decisions in this case.

See section 2.

2. Consider the different customer groups that exist in the bicycle market. In what ways could you divide this market into segments and sub-segments that might be meaningful to cycle manufacturers?

See section 3.

3. Evaluate the options open to McIntyre for targeting customer groups with the new product. What targeting strategy would you recommend?

See section 4.

4. Evaluate the likely market perceptions of cycles using the enclosed hub gear compared to the open, multi-cog, derailleur variety currently used on mountain bikes. How would you position the new product in relation to existing ones in the marketplace?

See section 5.

5. In what ways could the Internet have an impact on the marketing of an established product such as a bicycle?

See section 5, 'Impact of the Internet'.

6. What marketing methods would you use to support the position of the new product in the marketplace and how?

See section 6.

2. | STRATEGIES IN MARKETING

Corporate strategy

A strategy can be defined as a plan or pattern that brings together the objectives and activities of an organisation into a cohesive whole. It sets out the direction and the scope of an organisation over the long term.

Marketing strategies play a significant part in the formulation of an overall strategy for an organisation and it is difficult to treat them in isolation.

Strategic decision making represents a key stage in the translation of analysis and objectives into specific plans and activities. If we wish to climb a mountain, we start with research into likely conditions and optional routes in order to fulfil our objective of reaching the summit. We finish with the specific climbing and walking activities to get us there. In between we make strategic decisions such as the route to take; for example, we make a strategic choice between a direct assault up the steepest face or a more indirect approach. Similarly, corporate strategy determines the overall direction that an organisation takes to reach its declared destination.

- *The Burton Group (now re-named Arcadia) was the largest UK menswear retailer in the 1960s. Customers were mainly middle-aged men buying suits made to measure in one of Burton's garment factories as the company emphasis was on manufacturing clothes. However, fashions were changing rapidly; demographic and lifestyle influences in the late 1960s and early 1970s emphasised the younger fashions of Carnaby Street and the new pop star idols. The growth in menswear retailing came from the under 25 year olds who preferred ready-made casual clothes, hitherto regarded in an inferior light by Burton's management. Burton's strategy was no longer appropriate in this environment and a new management team changed direction. Instead of regarding the company as a manufacturer that operated its own retail outlets, the new strategy focused the business around retailing with more emphasis on ready-to-wear clothes.*

Marketing strategies and tactics

Marketing strategies are an integral part of an organisation's overall corporate strategy because they deal with the all-important interaction with the marketplace. Just as in Chapter 2, we saw that it is sometimes difficult to separate marketing planning from corporate planning, so marketing strategies are sometimes indistinguishable from corporate strategies. Burton's change of direction was a corporate decision dictated by marketing considerations.

Marketing decisions can be at a strategic or tactical level:

❏ *Marketing strategies* define a continuing basis for determining how an organisation interacts with the marketplace to achieve its broad objectives.

❏ *Marketing tactics* are short duration actions adapted to specific situations to achieve limited objectives in line with the general strategy.

- *In the 1970s Burton's marketing strategies included developing a product range to include more competitively priced, ready-made suits. The manager of a Burton shop undertook tactical activities including window dressing, in-store displays and staff training to merchandise this new ready-to-wear range in order to meet six monthly sales targets.*

Characteristics of strategic marketing decisions

Although the difference between strategic and tactical decisions depends to some extent on levels within an organisation (what is tactical at senior management level may become strategic at a junior management level, for example), strategic marketing decisions have some distinguishing characteristics, including:

❏ Defining the scope and nature of an organisation's marketplace by *segmenting* the market into customer groups: 'How can customers be grouped according to their needs and buying patterns?'

❏ Matching the activities of an organisation to the market in which it operates by *targeting* selected customer groups: 'What benefits do these particular groups of customers look for and how can we provide them?'

❏ Matching the strengths of an organisation to the needs of a customer group by

159

adopting an appropriate market *position*: 'What do we have to offer this customer group that is special in some way?'

These strategic considerations of segmentation, targeting and positioning are the subjects of the next three sub-sections.

3. MARKET SEGMENTATION

Buyer groups

Markets are often made up of buyers who have different needs and expectations from the products they buy. We are all buyers in the food market and the clothing market, but our diets and our wardrobes are not the same because our particular needs and wants are unique to us.

However, some people show similarities in what they choose because of their age, lifestyle or other distinguishing factors. The wardrobe of one teenage girl resembles that of another teenage girl in many respects and is certainly very different to that of a middle-aged man. The refrigerators of vegetarians contain many similar items and will differ from the food-store of the average meat-eating family. Different groups of buyers have broadly similar needs and wants from what they buy in specific markets.

Segments

Markets can be divided into distinct groups of buyers in this way. Each group has similar needs or expectations from the products or services they buy, which are different to other groups buying the same type of product.

- *The book market is made up of groups of buyers with different requirements including:*
  - *'recreational' buyers reading for pleasure and relaxation who choose easy-to-read fictional novels;*
  - *'knowledge' buyers wanting information on specific topics who buy non-fiction reference books; and*
  - *'display' buyers who regard books as a symbol of sophistication and culture and buy them for show in their homes or places of work.*

These distinctive buyer groups are referred to as *market segments*.

Sub-segments and niches

Market segments are often broad categories of consumers that can be further sub-divided into narrower *sub-segments*.

- *The book market segments described above can be broken down further. 'Knowledge' buyers consist of sub-segments including:*
  - *parents who buy reference books such as encyclopaedias for their children;*
  - *students who need textbooks for a particular course of study; and*

- *hobbyists who buy specialised information about their hobby.*

Some sub-segments contain groups of buyers who require very specialised products or services which sets them apart as a *market niche.*

- *Some hobbyists form niche markets. Stamp collectors buy specialised books, a market niche served by Stanley Gibbons, who have developed a range of catalogues and reference books specifically for the serious philatelist as well as the more amateur collector.*

Markets divided into segments, sub-segments and niches are sometimes represented by pie charts such as Figure 7.1.

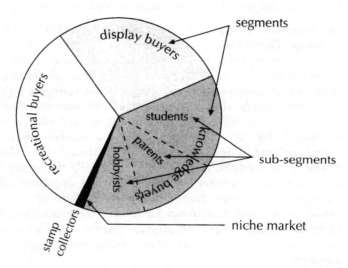

Figure 7.1: *Possible segments, sub-segments and niches in the book market*

The advantages of market segmentation

Market segments, sub-segments and niches form separate markets which require distinctive marketing strategies. Not only do they need different products but they may also respond differently to pricing policies, promotional approaches and distribution coverage.

- *Parents, students and hobbyists, the sub-segments we identified in the book market, all require different types of publications. Student textbooks usually command lower prices than hobby or reference books, and their promotion and distribution may be through specialised university bookshops.*

The manufacturer or supplier might see this as an inconvenience as it can lead to a multiplication of product lines and fragmentation of efforts in trying to reach the market segments.

However market segmentation offers the following important advantages to supplying organisations:

❑ *Closer matching between what is offered by the organisation and customer needs.*

It is possible through a combination of research and experience to develop a good understanding of the needs of a well-defined segment of customers and offer appropriate products and services to them. It is difficult to get close to customer groups that are widely defined as their needs have fewer common factors. In trying to please diverse types of customers, it is possible to end up pleasing none.

- *The Burton Group began changes to its approach to the marketplace in the early 1970s (as we have described in section 2 above). Shops were restocked with a much wider range of merchandise, including ready-to-wear suits and casual clothes as activities concentrated on the retailing of menswear. Valuable lessons, which were to transform the future of the group, were learned at this time from the results of these new strategies.*

  The menswear shops were competing in a marketplace that was rapidly changing. The driving force was the under 25 year olds who had become a much larger segment of the population because of the post-war 'baby boom'. A new type of retail outlet, modelled on the boutiques of Carnaby Street, which captured the atmosphere of the 'swinging 60's' with loud pop music and 'trendy' clothes, spread rapidly to cater specifically for the tastes of this large, new segment of the clothing market. Burton naturally wanted to attract this fast growing area of the market whilst retaining their traditional middle-aged customer base. Although their shops changed the profile of their stocks, they failed to meet fully the requirements of any of their different customer groups: they still appeared old-fashioned to younger buyers, who preferred the atmosphere of the new boutiques, whilst their more traditional customers were disaffected by the more fashionable merchandise on display. Burton could no longer appeal to a general menswear market as other retailers increasingly specialised in one segment.

  Elsewhere in the group, the lessons of this segmented retailing were being learned. 'Top Shop', a new venture consisting of outlets targeted specifically at the younger woman looking for the latest fashions, rapidly expanded. 'Evans Outsize', aimed at the segment of larger customers who did not fit standard garment ranges, proved a successful acquisition. As the men's shops struggled to identity with a market, Top Shop and Evans thrived in their well-defined segments. By the mid 1970s they were the only profitable businesses in the Burton Group.

❑ *Concentration of resources on areas of greatest advantage.*

By identifying closely with one segment of the market, an organisation can concentrate its resources on meeting the needs of that customer group in the fullest possible way. Larger organisations have learned that the key to success in competitive markets is to focus decentralised business units on specific segments. Smaller firms with limited resources survive by concentrating on what they do best for a targeted group of customers.

- *The Body Shop was another retail chain which developed in the 1970s, this time from the humble beginnings of one shop in Brighton founded by Anita Roddick in 1976. Its appeal was to a group of women opposed to the hype of the 'impossible dream' of perfect beauty symbolised by the advertising and packaging of the conventional cosmetic companies. Started with a small £4,000 bank loan, the new business concentrated its meagre resources on a rapidly growing segment of female buyers who desired more natural and less synthetic products. Hitherto, the established cosmetic companies had dominated the market with expensive packaging and extensive advertising. The Body Shop broke their stranglehold by concentrating on developing totally new products with 'exotic' names such as Seaweed and Birch Shampoo, and Honey and Oatmeal Scrub Mask. There was no money for advertising and fancy packaging, but environmentally-concerned customers preferred the Body Shop's plastic bottles and simple labels. Anita Roddick's limited resources in those early days focused the Body Shop on its greatest strength – the simplicity and naturalness of an organisation which respected rather than exploited the environment. By playing to this strength, the Body Shop found a gap in the market. Rather than take on the whole body care market on the terms of the existing dominant suppliers, Anita Roddick concentrated her resources to develop a marketing mix appropriate to a new, fast-growing segment. The Body Shop maintained its focus by franchising its original concept throughout the world. By 2001, it had become an international organisation of over 1800 shops trading in 49 geographic markets.*

❑ *Market leadership through domination of a narrowly defined market.*

It is becoming increasingly difficult to achieve and maintain leadership in large global markets as competition increases. One way to achieve leadership is through specialisation. If an organisation can spot a viable sub-market, it can concentrate on the needs of that segment and establish high customer loyalty and a position of market leadership.

- *Letraset developed a rub-down lettering product for graphic artists (as we have seen in Chapter 6, 'The application of market intelligence'). It successfully marketed this product world-wide and grew rapidly into an international company. To maintain growth it needed to diversify either its product range or its market base. There were opportunities to extend the applications of its instant lettering product away from the original market of graphic artists and into new areas such as office products or children's activities. Initially the company decided to continue to play to its strength, concentrating on developing new products such as markers for the graphic artist. This strategy allowed Letraset to dominate this particular market segment on an international basis as it understood the products and services needed. Only when the company strayed from this market base did it falter. A series of acquisitions in markets not understood by the company's management left it vulnerable to takeover. Letraset was acquired by the Swedish group Esselte who wanted to exploit further its domination of the graphic art market.*

❑ *Key to profitability in competitive markets.*

The examples discussed above show how the segmentation of markets is fundamental to establishing an edge over competitors. Burton lost out to more focused competitors, the Body Shop carved a new segment away from the dominant cosmetic suppliers and Letraset quickly dominated a market largely ignored by others. Research has also confirmed that segmentation is the key to profitability in competitive markets. Long-term profitability is associated with those companies that achieve leadership positions in viable segments or market niches.

The criteria for market segmentation

The need for segmentation arises when markets are neither totally homogeneous nor totally heterogeneous. Markets can be seen as a continuum between these two extremes of uniformity and non-uniformity, as illustrated in Figure 7.2.

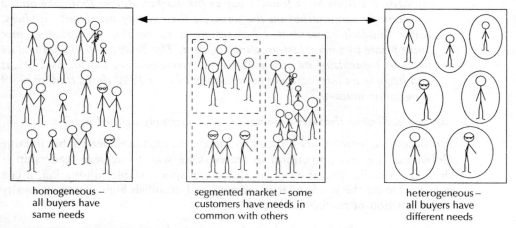

homogeneous –
all buyers have
same needs

segmented market – some
customers have needs in
common with others

heterogeneous –
all buyers have
different needs

Figure 7.2: *A continuum of market types*

Some specialised markets fall into the extremes at the end of the continuum:

❑ *Homogeneous markets* exist in commodities trading where traders seek to buy undifferentiated raw materials, such as metals (silver, copper) or basic foodstuffs (sugar, coffee) at the lowest possible prices.

❑ *Heterogeneous markets* exist in industrial buying situations when one organisation is a large enough buyer to be considered a market by itself. A manufacturer of aeroplanes, for example, might regard each major airline and each significant government purchaser as a separate market.

However most markets can be segmented in one of several ways. There is no single method of segmenting markets. A number of variables are possible in both consumer and organisational markets. These can be classified as illustrated in Figure 7.3.

Benefit segmentation

Benefit segmentation looks for the major benefits that are given priority by a significant number of customers and then seeks to identify with that group through

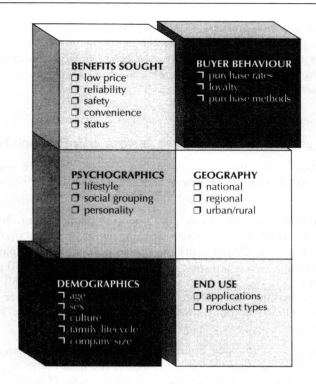

BENEFITS SOUGHT
- ❏ low price
- ❏ reliability
- ❏ safety
- ❏ convenience
- ❏ status

BUYER BEHAVIOUR
- ❏ purchase rates
- ❏ loyalty
- ❏ purchase methods

PSYCHOGRAPHICS
- ❏ lifestyle
- ❏ social grouping
- ❏ personality

GEOGRAPHY
- ❏ national
- ❏ regional
- ❏ urban/rural

DEMOGRAPHICS
- ❏ age
- ❏ sex
- ❏ culture
- ❏ family lifecycle
- ❏ company size

END USE
- ❏ applications
- ❏ product types

Figure 7.3: *Possible criteria for segmenting markets*

consistent marketing efforts. Some organisations seek to identify with segments attracted mainly by the best value for money (e.g. Woolworth), others with those seeking status (e.g. Rolex watches). It is often a long-term process to build the reputation of a company to the stage where it can be readily associated with a key market benefit.

- *Volkswagen have carried out one of the most successful long-term campaigns to segment a mass market by focusing on only one of the benefits sought by car buyers. The original Beetle had several major disadvantages over its rivals: it looked strange and did not go very fast. But it offered an important benefit over more complicated, larger cars – it was reliable. Advertising over several decades has consistently majored on this theme so that the Volkswagen name and reliability have become synonymous. Early advertising showed a VW starting first time on a wintry morning and travelling through a snow-filled landscape, with the caption: 'Have you ever wondered how the man who drives the snowplough drives to the snowplough?' Later, even the unchanging looks of the Beetle had become a dependable virtue in an era of change; one advert showed the lunar landing module of the Apollo moon mission with the caption: 'It's ugly, but it gets you there.' Advertising for other VW cars, after the demise of the Beetle, continued the same theme. The emphasis switched from car to driver in scenarios depicting a variety of human problems from gambling to divorce but the message was the same: 'If only everything in life was as reliable as a Volkswagen.'*

- *Another car manufacturer has used benefit segmentation with similar success. Volvo selected safety as the key benefit to offer and established itself as the market leader for a segment of buyers concerned about safe motoring rather than the high performance and style promoted by other manufacturers.*

Behavioural segmentation

Buyers can be grouped according to their purchasing patterns and behaviour.

❑ *Purchase rates* vary among customer groups. Markets are usually divided between a small number of heavy users and a large number of infrequent purchasers.

❑ The 'Pareto effect', or '80/20 rule', is a common phenomena in both industrial and consumer markets. This expresses the tendency for a small number of customers (as few as 20 per cent) to be heavy users of a company's products and account for a high proportion of sales (maybe as much as 80 per cent). The converse of this is that the majority of customers (the other 80 per cent) are lighter users making up a small percentage of sales (20 per cent). These segments of heavy or light users create a strategic choice for supplying organisations.

- *For example, a flooring contractor specialised in commercial contracts. Their marketing strategy was to focus on the heavy user segment of large company contracts and big office developments. However although the sales from successful tenders for these contracts was high, the market was extremely competitive and so prices and gross margins were very low. The company therefore investigated an alternative strategy of focusing on the more fragmented market segment of smaller businesses where there was less competition and higher prices to compensate for the problems of many lower value orders.*

In consumer markets, mail order marketing concentrates on the frequent buyer, making repeated offers to those who have already bought by direct mail, in the knowledge that they are the most likely group to use this purchase method again.

❑ *Loyalty to brands or companies* is another way of segmenting markets as some customers exhibit great loyalty to one supplier, whilst others switch more easily. By studying and identifying existing loyal customers, an organisation can target marketing efforts to groups of a similar profile.

- *Insurance companies found that teachers represented a group of very loyal, long-term customers. They did not pay the largest premiums and therefore did not fall into the heavy user category, but their loyalty made them a segment worth targeting.*

Identification of existing customers can also help prolong their loyalty. Season tickets have long been used by rail companies and football clubs to recognise and retain their regular customers. More sophisticated techniques are also now used to encourage repeat purchasing through promotions and loyalty programmes.

- *Information technology has helped organisations to pinpoint their loyal customers. Shoppers remained largely anonymous to the larger retailers such as supermarket chains. 'Smart' cards containing microchips which record the details and buying behaviour of individual customers (with updates at every purchase) have changed this. Shoppers now receive inducements to use a shop card as retailers allocate points for purchases, which reward their loyal customers through extra discounts or special offers. These loyalty programmes use information from the cards to monitor response rates, making them sophisticated exercises to lock customers into one retailer.*

❏ *Purchase method* is a way of segmenting organisational buyers. Some organisations such as local authorities purchase by asking for tenders on specific projects. Some purchase through committees, whilst others delegate to individual buyers. Each of these methods requires a different selling approach.

- *The work of central government has been opened up to private sector competition. Companies are now invited to bid for contracts to service Whitehall departments in such areas as information technology and computer services. This represents a large market segment for private sector companies that are forced to adopt distinctive marketing approaches to take account of a central government purchasing culture. For example, the Hoskyns Group, a large supplier of computer services in the UK, has a separate division specifically to deal with public services which, typically, adopt a procurement approach of asking for bids on a detailed specification of requirements and accepting the lowest price.*

Psychographic segmentation

In Chapter 5, we looked at the many social and individual influences on consumer behaviour from personality types and self-image to perceptions and attitudes (Chapter 5, section 3, 'Consumer buying behaviour'). Psychographics, a technique for classifying lifestyles, attempts to draw together some of these influences to describe 'typical' consumers who can then be regarded as segments of the market.

- *One classification of lifestyle groups includes a category described as 'the sophisticated adult' – intellectual and socially concerned people who like to lead and are attracted by unique and fashionable goods. This segment is the target market for ranges of exotic soft drinks, including Aqua Libra, a herbal drink of 'pure fruit juices, vegetable aromatic extracts, aqueous infusions of sunflower and sesame seeds, fresh tarragon and Siberian ginseng'. There are many others, including 'Original Norfolk Punch' and a revamped Lucozade, competing in this growth market segment of sophisticated adults looking for interesting, healthy alternatives to alcohol.*

Geographic segmentation

Geographic boundaries naturally divide many markets. Suppliers or customers determine geographic segments:

❏ Suppliers may decide to limit their market coverage to a geographically discrete area. Most companies only sell within their home nation and many within a more limited area such as a town or county. Small firms tend to operate on a limited geographic basis and very few export goods or services. Public sector organisations are usually limited by statute to a specific region; health care, education, social services and law enforcement are provided on a regional basis. Industrial marketing companies often segment their customers by dividing them geographically into sales areas.

❑ Customers may be divided into geographic segments on the basis of different localised needs or wants. This is most obvious on a national basis where cultural or climatic differences lead to different demands. Cool, blonde lagers were for a long time confined to hotter European and Antipodean climates whilst warm, darker beers were preferred in the UK.

Demographic segmentation

Demographic variables are a widely used basis for market segmentation. In consumer markets the demographic variables frequently used are age, gender, occupation and income. Industry classification and company size are often used in organisational markets. There are two main reasons for the popularity of demographic variables as a basis for segmentation:

❑ Customer needs often vary according to demographic differences; for example age and gender clearly differentiate demand in many markets including clothes, magazines and body care products.

❑ Demographics are usually well defined and above all, measurable. For example, we know what proportion of the population are over 60 years old, male and live in East Anglia. Government publications identify the numbers of organisations by industry type and region. Demographic statistics are widely available and a major source of quantifiable market data.

End use

The same product may be used for different applications, or specific types of the same basic product may be developed for distinct end-uses.

- *An office copier may be used by one customer group for large runs of the same original, and by another customer for many one-off copies of different originals. Although their total copy volume per month is similar, the needs of these customers in terms of equipment and costs per copy are not the same.*

4. TARGETING STRATEGIES

Alternative market strategies

What strategies can be used to direct marketing efforts following an analysis of the market and its possible customer segments? Three basic strategies can be considered, as illustrated in Figure 7.4.

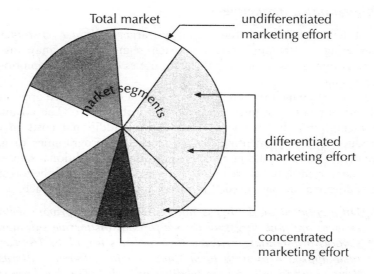

Total market

undifferentiated
marketing effort

market segments

differentiated
marketing effort

concentrated
marketing effort

Figure 7.4: *Alternative market strategies*

Undifferentiated marketing

An undifferentiated marketing strategy takes no account of market differences and applies the same marketing effort to the whole market. It relies on one basic product and marketing programme to attract sufficient buyers. This strategy has the advantage of lower costs because it can provide economies of scale in production or administration and lower distribution and marketing costs.

❑ In consumer markets, an undifferentiated strategy may rely on mass advertising and distribution methods. Guinness and Coca-Cola are examples of companies that originally offered only one product to their respective markets, relying on its unique, universal appeal, backed by extensive advertising and wide availability.

❑ In industrial markets, unbranded, commodity-type products are often marketed in an undifferentiated way. Suppliers of electronic components such as transistors, capacitors and resistors sell identical products to different markets using the same strategies.

Undifferentiated strategies are increasingly vulnerable to competitors willing to match the needs of segments more closely. Both Guinness and Coca-Cola have launched new products that recognise the importance of trends in segments of the market. Guinness is now sold in cans for the growing numbers drinking at home. Diet and caffeine free Coke are available for the health conscious. In industrial markets, large users of undifferentiated products, such as electronic components, try to become segmented by negotiating lower prices. The Burton (now Arcadia) Group found that their undifferentiated approach to the menswear market left them exposed to more targeted competitors.

Differentiated marketing

A differentiated marketing strategy targets *distinct customer groups* using marketing efforts appropriate to each segment. This may involve developing different products or offering different mixes of pricing, promotion or distribution arrangements.

A strategy which recognises the need for a differentiated approach benefits from the advantages of segmentation discussed above (see 'The advantages of market segmentation'). It has the disadvantage of additional costs in developing new products and implementing diverse marketing programmes to match individual segments. These should be recovered through the additional sales which a targeted approach brings, but there are limits; some segments may be too small to generate the additional income needed to justify a segmented approach.

- *Differentiated marketing is not restricted to the private sector. Many public services are now targeting their efforts at distinctive sub-markets. Secondary schools differentiate between their policies for 11 to 16 year old pupils and their approach to sixth form students with different patterns of attendance, dress requirements and the facilities provided. This has been stimulated partly by competition from sixth form and technical colleges which offer a different environment for the 16 plus age group. Similarly, hospitals and universities develop centres of excellence in a particular medical field or academic area, in recognition of the need to demonstrate specialised expertise to attract public funding.*

Concentrated marketing

If resources are limited an organisation may decide to limit its approach to only one segment of the market and follow a strategy of *concentration*.

Specialisation has the advantage of effective use of resources. Most small businesses need this focused market approach in order to survive the start-up period, as the Body Shop ably demonstrated.

There are risks in total reliance on one segment of the market, however. In its formative years, Letraset discovered that its chosen segment of graphic designers were particularly vulnerable to economic recession, as advertising is often the first activity to be cut back when the economy turns down. This almost stifled the fledgling company and led to a strategy of seeking diversification into other, more stable, markets.

Choosing target segments

How does an organisation choose which segments to target? The purpose of targeting a segment is to use marketing resources and effort more effectively than if they were applied to a wider base. Several criteria determine just how effectively this can be done:

❏ *Can the segment be identified?*

If a sub-segment is hard to identify it will also be difficult to measure and quantify for analysis. Targeting relies on precise definition and measurement, without which it becomes inexact and uncertain.

- *In the 1990s, many young people attended secretive 'rave' parties and were influenced by an underground rave culture. Although stories abounded about what rave culture involved, it remained illusive and ill defined because of its secretive nature. Some attempts were made to target this lifestyle segment by using psychedelic or irreverent advertising. But despite estimates that up to one third of all under 25 year olds had experienced a rave party of some sort, this segment proved extremely hard to access for marketing campaigns.*

❑ *Is it a relevant segment?*

Effective segmentation is based on criteria which are relevant to the buying decision of that subgroup of customers. There is no point in differentiating between customers on a basis which is irrelevant to how they make particular purchase decisions. A population segment of left-handed people is probably not relevant as a basis for segmenting the clothing market, for example.

❑ *Is the segment large enough?*

A market segment has to be capable of providing a satisfactory return on the investment made in it. Markets can be over-segmented into small groups of customers whose purchasing power does not warrant a distinctive marketing approach. An organisation can only survive if it is based on a segment which proves to be a viable commercial size in the long term.

- *Although we live in an age of increasing specialisation, a slackening of economic growth exposes suppliers who base their existence on a narrow marketplace. Many specialist retailers, such as the 'Sock Shop' and 'Tie Rack', targeted a sub-market in clothes accessories in the 1980s and were among the first to feel the effects of the recession at the end of the decade, resulting in the closure of many branches.*

❑ *Is the segment accessible?*

Targeting relies on accessibility. Marketing efforts can only be applied if customers in a segment can be reached through channels of distribution and communication in a cost-effective way. The rave lifestyle segment of the population have no established mass media or distribution outlets and so cannot be easily reached, for example.

Targeting segments in practice

In practice, organisations use a number of segmentation variables at the same time to target a marketplace. For example, geography and demographics (sometimes referred to as geo-demographics) are often used to pinpoint socio-economic groups living in a given district. Examples of consumer and organisational market strategies show a number of possible approaches.

Targeting consumer market segments

Managers marketing to consumers use a series of variables to target customer groups, often starting with demographic and geographic segments but recognising

171

lifestyle and other differences within them.

- *The Burton Group learned the lessons from their undifferentiated marketing to the menswear market in the 1960s and '70s. Under a new chief executive, Ralph Halpern, the company began to adopt a much more targeted approach by carefully segmenting the markets for both men's and women's clothes. A new chain of shops, 'Top Man', specialised in exciting fashion clothes for the younger man, to complement the successful 'Top Shop' outlets for young women. Shops still using the Burton name concentrated on a more mature segment of the menswear market and Dorothy Perkins provided good value fashion for 20 to 35 year old women. By the 1980s the group recognised the significance of an increasingly fashion conscious group – the 'baby boomers' of the post-war years. Although they were now aged from 30 to 45, this large segment of the population had been teenagers in the swinging sixties and still tended to look for more style from their clothes than preceding generations. 'Principles' and later 'Principles for Men' were launched to cater for the lifestyle needs of this segment, who had moved on from the brashness of boutiques and now wanted more sophisticated shopping and higher quality garments, without compromising on fashion and design. Market coverage of this older segment was further increased by the acquisition of Debenhams department stores to give a 'family' feel to the group.*

  Burton's strategies proved extremely profitable for a while, but the inherent dangers in a highly segmented approach proved to be the downfall of Halpern, who resigned in late 1990. The recession in high street sales and the slump in commercial property values caught Burton over-exposed in both markets. Demographics affected sales as the teenage population began to fall. Top Shop and Top Man were combined and shrunk in size to reflect the decrease in importance of the younger segment of the market. Burton's aim of complete market coverage through targeted outlets proved not only costly but unwieldy in adapting to changes, and the group found themselves over-concentrated in a shrinking youth market. In 1998, the Burton Group demerged with Debenhams, and renamed itself Arcadia. It has undergone a further re-structuring with the sale of hundreds of its shops. Its history provides a timely reminder that changes in the business environment can erode the effectiveness of a segmentation strategy.

Targeting industrial market segments

Larger organisations selling on a 'business-to-business' basis frequently use a succession of segmentation variables to target the various markets in which they operate. The structure of the salesforce often mirrors the adopted segmentation approach. Personal selling, like other aspects of the marketing effort, requires different approaches according to the targeted segment.

- *A reprographics company selling a range of printing machines, office copiers and speciality reprographic equipment targeted its markets by end-use, customer type and geographic region. This is illustrated in Figure 7.5.*

  This organisation first differentiated its marketing efforts according to the end use of the products sold. Separate divisions sold equipment suitable for

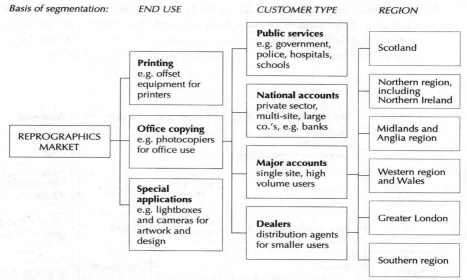

Figure 7.5: *Target market segments for a reprographic company*

printing, office copying, and special applications in the design and artwork processes.

The office copying division targeted its salesforce according to customer type and by region. One salesforce concentrated on the public sector such as national and local government departments, and the police, health and education authorities, as these customers required special contractual terms. Another salesforce targeted national accounts; these large companies operated from a number of premises but still bought office equipment centrally through purchasing managers who required strong personal relationships with their suppliers.

Major accounts were the customer targets of another salesforce as they represented heavier users but purchased locally in a decentralised way. Distribution agents or dealers bought stocks of equipment for forward sale to smaller users. Finally both the major accounts salesforce and the dealers were organised into six geographic regions.

Targeting public service market segments

Public services increasingly use differentiated strategies in order to meet the requirements of their markets. As one service competes with another for limited funds, public service managers have important internal markets to consider, as well as the external markets made up of the users of their services. These internal markets include stakeholders, who can influence the amount of resources dedicated to that service. Stakeholders include taxpayers and their representatives (politicians and pressure groups), local and central government bodies, employees and their representatives (unions, federations) and quasi-government organisations (ombudsman, regulatory authorities or 'watch-dogs'). Internal and external markets have different needs and therefore require differentiated marketing approaches.

173

- *A hospital first segmented its markets into different types of stakeholder, including those influencing the level of funds for health care as well as the patients requiring health care. Patients were further divided by the priority and type of treatment required. These segments are illustrated in Figure 7.6.*

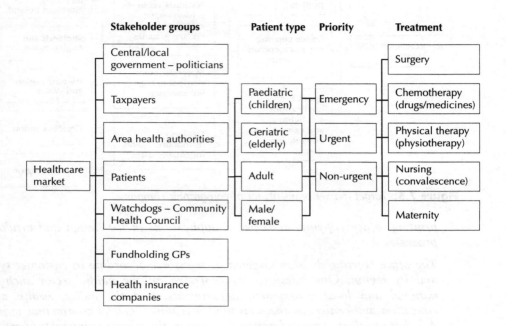

Figure 7.6: *Possible target market segments for an NHS hospital*

Stakeholders include direct fund holding agencies such as the district health authority and certain types of GPs, local watchdog groups, taxpayers and their local and national political representatives. These groups all have an influence on the well-being of the hospital, but have different requirements from it which justify separate marketing approaches. The District Health Authority, for example, may be mainly concerned with efficiency and economy, whilst watchdog groups may be more concerned with the effectiveness of the services provided.

Patients form different demographic markets, based on their age and sex, which are recognised in the way the hospital caters for them. They also differ in the priority of the services they need from emergency to non-urgent and in the types of treatment they require from surgery to nursing care. The achievement of high quality services depends on recognising the different needs between these and other segments of patients.

Targeting and databases

The power of information technology now enables even the largest enterprise to have a close relationship with individual customers or segments of the market. By using computerised databases, information can be acquired and stored on customer buying habits according to selected criteria. Marketing activities can then be focused on a specific group of customers by, for example, sending fully customised offers or information to individuals based upon an understanding of their past buying behaviour.

Database marketing involves building up a database of such information on actual and potential customers. Such database activities need to conform to the Data Protection Act (1984) which requires organisations which hold personal data to register with the Data Protection Registrar and to conform to rules about the accuracy of the data and the purposes for which it can be used.

Some of the advantages of using customer databases include:

❏ *It develops relationships with existing customers.* It can cost up to six times more to recruit a new customer than to retain an existing one. Database marketing helps to develop relationships with existing customers as well as to acquire them. It emphasises the *lifetime value* of a customer by collecting data on their purchases over a long period of time.

❏ *It allows a bottom-up rather than a top-down* approach to marketing. Market segments can be defined by groups of existing customers who have similar characteristics according to customer records. This is in contrast to segmentation based on information about the whole market which is often difficult to obtain.

  • *Tesco's Club Card has facilitated the collection of data on millions of customers and their purchases. This has been analysed to define groups of customers who are then sent various offers and promotions. Tesco overtook Sainsbury at the top of the supermarket league, not by gaining new customers, but by reducing the attrition rate amongst existing customers who stayed loyal to Tesco for longer once they had the card. Top spending customers have been invited to special events to keep them coming back. Competitive threats such as the opening of other stores have been monitored by looking at the purchasing patterns of the highest spending Tesco customers. Those whose spending has declined sharply are assumed to be trying a competitive outlet and specific offers can be made to woo them back.*

Targeting customer retention

Strategies targeted to *retain* customers by the development of long-term relationships can be conceptualised as a hierarchy of customer loyalty as shown in Figure 7.7.

❏ *Prospects* represent the target market. Traditional marketing strategies have tended to focus at this level of converting prospects into customers.

❏ A *customer* in this model is someone who has done business with an

175

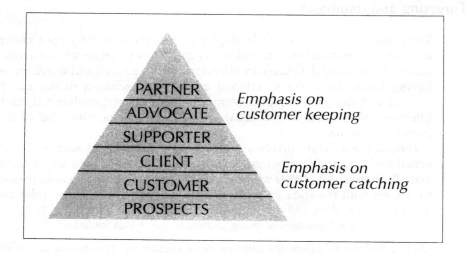

Figure 7.7: *A hierarchy of customer loyalty*

organisation once or occasionally. The aim is to develop customers into clients.

❑ A *client* is a regular, repeat customer. However, they may not think positively about the organisation, but come back merely through inertia or because of high switching costs. They are obviously vulnerable to competitors who can overcome these issues.

- *Historically borrowers rarely switched from one building society or bank to another once they had established a mortgage because it was an elaborate and costly procedure. Fierce competition amongst lenders has simplified procedures and large financial incentives have been offered to existing borrowers to move their mortgage. Retaining existing clients has become a key marketing objective for building societies and banks who traditionally have only marketed to new buyers (prospects) or existing customers about to take out a new mortgage because they are moving.*

To retain a client it is important to convert them into a 'supporter'.

❑ A *supporter* **thinks** positively about the organisation and is pleased to be a customer.

❑ An *advocate* **acts** positively about the organisation by recommending it to others. At this level up the hierarchy, the customer is not only more secure from competitive enticements, but also acts as an extra salesperson for the organisation by making recommendations through word-of-mouth communications.

❑ *Partnerships* of suppliers and buyers are at the pinnacle of this particular marketing model as organisations and individuals work together as partners to identify further ways in which mutual advantage can be gained from the relationship.

5. | POSITIONING

Positioning strategy

Customers perceive organisations and their products in a certain way. This perception is usually a simplistic impression: some products are perceived as 'up-market' and expensive (e.g. Rolex watches, Porsche cars); others are 'down-market' and inexpensive (Timex watches, Seat cars). Some companies give an impression of exclusivity (Harrods), technological leadership (IBM), or classic excellence (Burberry).

These perceptions describe the position of an organisation or a product in the marketplace. The 'position' represents a general impression given to customers in relation to competing organisations or products. To many book shoppers, Amazon.com represents convenience through technology while Waterstones is regarded as a more traditional browsing experience: we tend to position the countless suppliers that compete for our custom through generalisations in our minds such as these.

Positioning can be left to chance. Many companies earn a reputation which spreads by word of mouth and sticks with them. This may not be to their advantage and can require active steps to change. Jaguar cars were perceived as unreliable until the company took positive steps to change its market position to that of high performance, luxury motoring. The Labour Party was perceived as out-of-date until Neil Kinnock, and then Tony Blair, re-positioned it as modern 'New Labour'.

Steps in a positioning strategy

Targeting a market segment involves deciding what positioning strategy to adopt within it and making sure that the perceptions of the customer match the desired position. This involves several steps:

❑ deciding the positions which are relevant to the market segment and most likely to influence buying habits;

❑ evaluating which position the organisation can effectively deliver and which is hard for competitors to match;

❑ communicating the selected position through promotions and sales messages.

- *Buyers tend to perceive mass-market packaged holidays as commodities. They are most likely to be influenced by value-for-money considerations, with price the key purchase determinant. The UK tour operator and travel agency business consists of four main competitors: Thomas Cook, Thomson Travel, Airtours and First Choice. These companies have achieved market dominance through economies of scale in the supply chain which keep prices low, and competitors out. They have acquired travel agents to sell their holidays. They own many of the charter airlines that fly to their holiday destinations. Because they can generate the volume of bookings that enable them to offer prices and discounts which competitors find hard to match, they have taken market positions of economy and value for money in the perceptions of the consumer. They reinforce this position through extensive advertising of their mass-market holidays.*

- *Thomas Cook is an international brand which won a position of quality in the minds of consumers because of its reputation for offering more exclusive holidays. While this was an advantage in some market segments, this position restricted its ability to compete in mass-markets, where package holidaymakers perceive Thomas Cook primarily as a retailer of more expensive holidays. In order to expand its operations, the company acquired other operators such as Sunworld, Nielson and Club 18–30 in an effort to re-position the company.*

Positioning 'maps'

Products or organisations can be plotted on a market positioning 'map' and compared to the positions of competitive offerings or companies. A simple method is to represent two key customer perceptions on a grid. For example, the market for restaurants can be evaluated against perceptions of price and quality as shown in Figure 7.8.

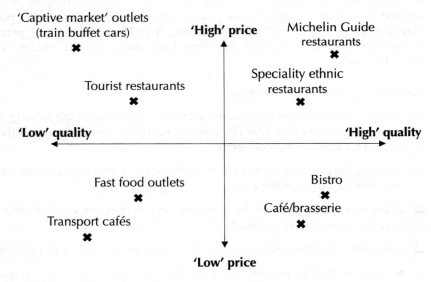

Figure 7.8: *A positioning map of the restaurant market*

Such a perceptual map can be used to plot the position of competitors so that any gaps in the market can be identified. For example, the perceptions of restaurants in a local area can be evaluated to see if there are any unfulfilled market needs. Figure 7.9 is an example which seems to indicate a gap in the 'high' price/ 'high' quality quadrant. However further research would need to establish if there was sufficient demand to sustain this type of restaurant in the area.

Positioning is not only by price and quality. Other parameters can be used such as positioning by application, type of use, benefits offered or customer type. For example, the market for chocolates could be evaluated against consumers'

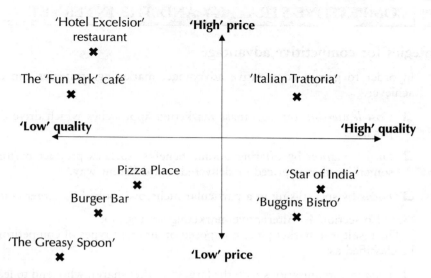

Figure 7.9: *Positioning of restaurants in town x*

perceptions of end-use (from 'special occasion' to 'everyday use') and application of the purchase (from personal consumption to a gift). Cars might be plotted against perceptions of image (from functionality to high image) and age range of customer types (older/younger). Some possible product positions for these markets are illustrated in Figure 7.10.

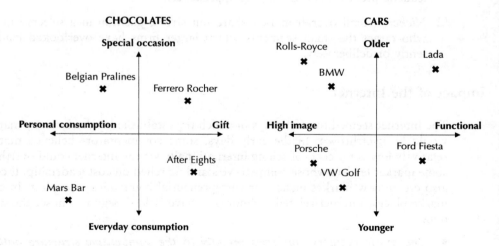

Figure 7.10: *Possible positioning maps*

Although every consumer has their own perceptual map of the markets with which they are familiar (do your perceptions fit with those given above?) – research can identify some consensus perceptions by aggregating all the individual impressions to give a total picture. This information can then be used to exploit and develop an established position or to change an unsatisfactory one.

6.	COMPETITIVE STRATEGY AND THE INTERNET

Strategies for competitive advantage

In order to gain a competitive advantage, marketing strategies can attempt to achieve:

❑ *Cost leadership* through mass marketing approaches which drive down costs per unit.

❑ *Differentiation* by offering unique benefits, such as product performance or something that is priced or delivered in a different way.

❑ *Focus* by specialising in a particular niche overlooked by larger competitors.

(See also section 4, 'Alternative marketing strategies').

The result is a market place composed of different types of competitors that can be classified as:

❑ *Leaders* (organisations with the largest market share), who tend to lead the way in new product introductions, price movements, distribution coverage and promotional expenditure.

❑ *Challengers* (substantial market share, but 2nd/3rd largest), who attempt to improve their position by either attacking the market leader or smaller competitors.

❑ *Followers* (large or small market share), who imitate, clone or modify the leaders' products and marketing approaches.

❑ *Nichers* (small overall market share but strong position in a selected niche), who target the small segments which larger firms have overlooked inadvertently or deliberately.

Impact of the Internet

The Internet seemed to offer ways in which the established order in many markets would be overthrown. In the early days, some commentators believed that the relatively low entry costs of selling internationally via the Internet could overthrow some market leaders whose competitive standing relied on cost leadership. It could also create new market niches for entrepreneurial companies to exploit. In some marketplaces, Internet-related technologies have indeed begun to upset the status quo.

• *The music industry conforms broadly to the competitive structure outlined above. Internationally, it is dominated by five companies, the 'leaders' and 'challengers' in all major markets who represent over 70 per cent of music albums sold worldwide. Market positions vary by country. In the UK market, EMI has become the 'leader' with over 25 per cent of album sales, helped by the acquisition of Virgin and Chrysalis and the success of artists such as the Spice Girls and Robbie Williams. The other big companies, BMG, Sony, Time Warner and Polygram, represent the 'challengers' with a further 55 per cent share of the market between them. Independent record labels and music publishers make up only 20 per cent, as the big five have tended to buy up any promising newcomers. Independent labels such as Telstar and Beggars Banquet have succeeded either as 'followers' by promoting new bands in existing markets or as 'nichers' developing a specialist music genre.*

New technology has threatened to destabilise these established positions. The development of digital recording techniques and the commercialisation of the Internet is affecting the music industry in a number of ways:

- *CDs and recorded music have become very popular online products in their existing, hard copy form. CDs are well suited to online retailing: they are a commodity product with little differentiation except for the musical content; they are small and light, and therefore inexpensive to ship; and customer selection from the huge variety available is made easier by computerised searching. Yet it is a newcomer to the music business, the 'e-tailer', Amazon, that is making the inroads against more traditional music retailers.*

- *Music can be digitised and downloaded onto computers, which means that musical products can be distributed directly over the Internet. Digital recordings of music can be encoded on the Internet using the MP3 format, compressed and distributed across computer networks. This means music can be copied and quickly distributed anywhere in the world. The big five music companies tried to ignore the new technology until Napster was founded in September 1999 to allow users to swap music files amongst themselves. As the service quickly developed a huge following of 70 million users, the market leaders' first reaction to this threat was legal action. Napster's operation was declared illegal in 2001 as it violated copyright laws. Recognising that the threat will not disappear, one of the big five, BMG, is now backing Napster in a legitimate, paid-for service.*

- *Many in the industry believe the future for music distribution will be 'streaming' – instant access to any music via pocket computers and advances in telephony. This opens up new opportunities for the music industry which may be exploited by existing organisations or new competitors.*

It was not only the music industry that seemed destined for a competitive shakeout. The early wave of Internet entrepreneurs setting up innovative new services such as eBay and lastminute.com seemed to indicate that tried and tested competitive strategies would be insufficient to save traditional organisations in many sectors. Since then, the pace of change has slowed. The domination of markets by existing brands and organisations now seems less at risk for a number of reasons:

❏ Sales of £13.5 billion were made over the Internet in the UK in 2000 (Keynote, 2000). Despite the rapid growth of e-commerce, most transactions are made business-to-business as existing organisations adopt the Internet as a purchasing mechanism. Sales to end-users, or business-to-consumer transactions, are still relatively small over the Internet, representing about 15 per cent of total sales.

❑ Existing major brands are popular products on the Internet. Consumers are concerned about shopping security on the Internet, and choose known brands to reduce the perceived risk of buying by this method.

❑ Existing companies may not have been the first to realise the potential of e-commerce, but they are likely to take advantage of subsequent developments on the Internet. Well-publicised casualties amongst new technology companies, such as the demise of Boo.com, has made investors more wary of Internet shares. New investment is likely to come from existing competitors buying into the new technology. The music industry model of a market leader (BMG) supporting an Internet newcomer (Napster) is becoming more common.

The full impact of the Internet on competitive marketing strategies has yet to be seen. Although it is revolutionising the way we do business in some respects, it is also reinforcing some of the principles behind marketing strategies. In particular, it is assisting the ability of organisations to accurately target customer groups with customised products and services.

7. THE MARKETING MIX

The 4 Ps

Marketing strategies are implemented through management of the *marketing mix*. The marketing mix consists of the controllable variables which marketing management can use to influence customer demand. It represents the methods by which managers seek to meet marketing objectives.

Traditionally, this mix of marketing methods has been categorised as the '*4 Ps*':

❑ *Products* are more than just physical goods. They include not only intangible products, such as services, but also intangible aspects of physical products such as image and market position. Product decisions therefore include a range of activities that affect both tangible and intangible factors, from new product development to packaging and branding.

❑ *Pricing* decisions can be strategic and tactical. The overall level of pricing is an important strategic ingredient in the positioning of a product, whilst discounts and special offers are used tactically to improve short-term sales.

❑ *Promotion* involves communicating to a target market about the benefits on offer. Marketing communications include personal selling, advertising, sales promotions and public relations.

❑ *Place* describes how products or services are made available to the target market. It includes decisions on distribution strategy which establish the appropriate channels through which products are marketed (such as agents, wholesalers and retailers). *Location* is a key ingredient in this element of the marketing mix in some cases (for retailers or hoteliers, for example).

Managing the marketing mix

We will explore each of these elements of the marketing mix in more detail in the following chapters. Before examining them individually, it is important to recognise that they are not independent of each other. Each element crucially affects the others:

❏ the attributes of a product help determine its price, how it is to be promoted and how it can be distributed;

❏ price adds to the intangible aspects of a product and may be an important promotional vehicle; pricing levels influence the channels of distribution available;

❏ promotions draw on product benefits and pricing strategies and often involve the channels of distribution;

❏ place is constrained by product, price and promotional decisions.

Rather than distinct elements, the 4 Ps represent inter-dependent variables symbolised by the overlapping circles in Figure 7.11.

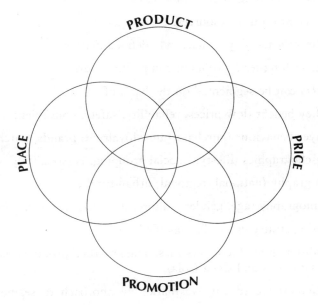

Figure 7.11: *The marketing mix*

Strategies bring together an organisation's activities into a cohesive whole. Marketing strategies therefore need to harmonise the elements of the marketing mix into a consistent approach to the marketplace. If the strategy is to adopt a position of exclusivity, this has to be projected consistently by the product, and its pricing, promotion and distribution.

Some commentators have modified this fourfold classification of the marketing mix in order to take account of specific contexts. For example, some have argued that the particular issues involved in marketing intangible services merit the addition of three extra 'Ps': People, Process and Physical evidence. The appropriate mix for marketing services, and other variations to the marketing mix arising from the specific marketing environment, are discussed in Chapter 13. First, however, we will examine each of the four elements of the marketing mix in greater detail in Chapters 8 to 12.

8. KEY POINTS

❑ A strategy is a plan or pattern that brings together the objectives and activities of an organisation into a cohesive whole.

❑ Strategic marketing decisions segment markets into customer groups, select target segments, and adopt appropriate market positions.

❑ Markets can be divided into segments, sub-segments and niches.

❑ The benefits to an organisation of segmenting its markets include:

  ❑ closer matching of customer needs;

  ❑ concentration of resources;

  ❑ market leadership of narrowly defined markets;

  ❑ higher long-term profits in competitive markets.

❑ Markets can be segmented on the basis of:

  ❑ a key benefit (low prices, reliability, safety, convenience, status);

  ❑ buyer behaviour (purchase rates, loyalty to brands, purchase methods);

  ❑ pyschographics (lifestyle, social grouping, personality);

  ❑ geography (national, regional, urban/rural);

  ❑ demography (age, gender, culture, life cycle, company size).

❑ Targeting strategies can be classified as:

  ❑ undifferentiated (commodities, 'mass market' products, e.g. early marketing of Guinness and Coca Cola);

  ❑ differentiated (distinctive marketing approach to segments, e.g. Burtons/ Arcadia);

  ❑ concentrated (a new or small business).

❑ Viable market segments are identifiable, relevant to the purchase decision, large enough to sustain the products offered, and accessible.

❑ Organisations operating in a variety of contexts, from the private to the public sector, from consumer to industrial markets, can target their customer groups through segmentation.

❑ Customers' simplistic impressions or perceptions of a product or company in the marketplace describe its 'position' (e.g. up-market/down-market).

❑ Positioning strategy seeks to:

  ❑ identify positions which influence buyer behaviour;

  ❑ select an appropriate, competitive position which an organisation can deliver;

  ❑ communicate this position through marketing messages.

❑ Competitors in a market can usually be classified as 'leaders', 'followers', 'imitators' or 'nichers'. In some industries (e.g. the music industry), competitive positions are being threatened by newcomers exploiting Internet-related new technologies. However, whilst e-commerce is well established in business-to-business markets, it has relatively low penetration levels in business-to-consumer markets.

❑ Marketing strategies are implemented through management of the *marketing mix* which can be summarised as 4 Ps: product, pricing, promotion and place.

❑ Effective strategies harmonise these elements of the marketing mix into a consistent approach to the target markets.

9. DEVELOPING MARKETING SKILLS

Exercises

1. Assume you have been asked to advise on the marketing strategy for your local leisure centre, cinema, museum or another local attraction with which you are familiar. Come up with recommendations covering the following areas:

   (i) The recommended bases for segmenting their marketplace.

   (ii) The priority targets you are assuming for their marketing activities.

   (iii) The position they need to adopt in the relevant segments for maximum competitive advantage.

   (iv) Draw a perceptual map using axes that are relevant to the marketplace and position your chosen attraction on it with its principle competitors. (If possible compare your own positioning to that of others and come up with a composite 'map'.)

2. Produce a perceptual map of some local clothes shops by plotting the national chains as well as local traders. What factors do you think make the most relevant axes? Again compare your own map with that of others if possible and develop a composite map. (If you are able to do this in groups, first decide together on the axes before individually plotting your perceptions – otherwise you may be comparing apples and pears.)

Developing a marketing plan

Activity 7 The marketing strategy

From the analysis undertaken in the first six activities of the marketing planning process, what strategies are you going to adopt?

❑ Which segment(s) of the market will you target (and why)?

❑ Which position will you adopt compared to competitors (and how)?

FURTHER READING AND REFERENCES

General texts

Brassington, F. and Pettit, S. (2000) *Principles of Marketing*, 2nd edition, chapters 5 and 20.

Dibb, S., Simkin, L., Pride, W.M. and Ferrell O.C. (2001) *Marketing Concepts and Strategies*, Houghton Mufflin, chapters 7 and 21.

Hannagan, T.J. (1992) *Marketing for the Non-Profit Sector*, Macmillan, chapter 2.

Kotler, P. (2000) *Marketing Management*, 10th edition, Prentice Hall, chapters 9 and 10.

Strategic marketing management

Dalgic, T. and Leeuw, M. (1994) Niche marketing revisited: concept, applications and some European cases, *European Journal of Marketing*, **20**(1), pages 39–55.

Doyle, P. (1998) *Marketing Management and Strategy*, Financial Times/Prentice Hall.

Hooley, G.J. and Saunders, J. (1998) *Marketing Strategy and Competitive Positioning*, Prentice Hall.

Ries, A. and Trout, J. (1986) *Marketing Warfare*, McGraw-Hill.

Internet marketing strategy

Chaffey, D., Mayer, R., Johnston, K. and Ellis-Chadwick, F. (2000) *Internet Marketing*, Pearson Education, chapter 5.

Chaston, I. (2001) *E-Marketing Strategy*, McGraw Hill, chapters 5 and 6.

Hardaker, G. and Graham, G. (2001) *Wired Marketing*, John Wiley & Sons, chapters 5 and 7.

Keynote (2000) *Internet Usage in Business*, 4th edition, Keynote Ltd.

Trimmers, P. (1999) *Electronic Commerce: Strategies and Models for Business-to-Business Trading*, John Wiley & Sons, chapters 3, 5 and 6.

CHAPTER 8

Products: Characteristics and Strategies

This chapter explores strategies relating to one element of the marketing mix – the product or service on offer. The boundaries of a product extend well beyond physical features to include benefits to consumers and other intangible features. Branding is an important intangible element, key to the success of many products and services. We examine the concept of the product life cycle, emphasising the changing resource requirements of products over time, and some techniques for analysing product portfolios as a way of managing these changes.

1. | CASE STUDY: THE PRODUCTS OF A SCHOOL

The 1988 Education Reform Act delegated significant powers to individual state schools and their managers in England and Wales. Previously, local education authorities had allocated resources and pupils to individual schools from the centre. The legislation required education authorities to delegate substantial authority and resources to the board of governors and the headteacher. In addition, governors and parents of a school were granted powers to opt out of the control of the local education authority and become even more self-managed. At the same time, parents and children were given greater freedom to choose their school. Theoretically they could choose to attend any state school, although in practice their choice was limited by the places physically available. As annual budgets for each school were allocated mainly on the basis of how many pupils attended the school, education managers were obliged to market their services in order to maximise the resources at their disposal.

Saxon Park School decided to opt out of local control when it was threatened with closure by the County's education authority. For a secondary school taking pupils from ages 11 to 18 it was relatively small with a total of 720 pupils of whom 120 were in the sixth form. Situated in an unfashionable residential area, the former Saxon Park council housing estate, the school lost pupils to larger comprehensives in more affluent parts of town. When the local education authority threatened it with closure because of its high proportion of empty places, numbers fell even more until existing parents voted to save the school by opting out. However unless the problem of falling numbers could be overcome, this only represented a temporary reprieve. Even demographics were working against Saxon Park as 'customers' requiring secondary education were decreasing; there were less under 19 year olds in the region than there had been for decades and numbers were not predicted to rise for several years.

A new headteacher, Jack Shannon, had set about improving academic standards at Saxon with notable success. The tangible outputs of the school in the form of GCSE and A level results were now comparable to the best of the other local schools. 'The issue is no longer one of academic standards', he told a meeting of the governors, 'but one of image. The basic education a child receives here is as good if not better than anywhere else in the area, but parents still associate our name with something inferior. We have removed a fundamental negative and now we need to consider how to give ourselves an edge.'

Shannon was asking the governors for guidance on measures to boost the declining pupil numbers and revenues of the school. To overcome their image problems, one idea was to change the name of the school to 'The King Alfred School', as the famous Saxon ruler had once held court close by. But Shannon believed that getting the product right was going to be their most important marketing activity, which no amount of clever publicity could equal.

'There are several options we can consider,' he told his board of governors. 'We need to achieve a higher share of the local market for the first of our main curriculum areas – subjects leading to GCSE qualifications. For example, almost all our students live nearby, yet we are very close to the train station and bus depot. We should be able to attract more children from the neighbouring villages. We could also consider more mature students – for instance older students re-taking some of their GCSEs, although we may need to modify the courses we offer them. We can consider developing some areas of the curriculum as a speciality. For example, many schools have decreased their sports activities because of time-tabling pressures, but we could use our new astro-turf pitch to develop this school as a centre of sporting excellence.'

'A particular issue we have to address is our sixth form which is small compared to other schools and colleges, so we cannot offer the range of subjects that others can. However some subjects are growing very fast. Science, for example, has always been popular here and we attract quite a few pupils from other state and independent schools because we have excellent laboratory facilities. The subjects are growing in popularity generally so our pupil numbers are increasing quite quickly each year. I'm pleased to see the extra pupils, but on the other hand I worry about the effect on our resources – our laboratories are fully used at the moment so if we increase our numbers we will have to invest in new facilities.'

'I would prefer some growth in our real problem area of music and drama. We have very few takers for these subjects and no signs of growth, so the courses are not really viable at the moment. In the past we had a poor reputation for the social sciences like economics and politics, and many of our students who were attracted to those subjects tended to go elsewhere. But our new head of department has changed all that and from a very small base she is increasing pupil numbers rapidly. Again, it means considerable investment, as we have to buy new specialised books and materials.'

'If only we had more subject areas like the humanities – history, geography and the like – which have always been popular here. Numbers are high but reasonably constant because there has been no real growth in demand for some time. We don't have much new investment to make in these subjects because we have all the books and materials we need and they are easier to plan because of the predictable numbers.'

'As we have very limited resources, we have to make some choices to balance both our finances and the portfolio of courses we offer. Your advice would be most welcome.'

Points to consider

1. Consider the 'products' or services that a secondary school offers.

   (i) What are their main tangible and intangible aspects?

   See section 2.

   (ii) How does Jack Shannon group some of his school's individual 'products' together?

   See section 3.

   (iii) What are the basic benefits which are expected from them? What are some additional benefits which might attract pupils to one school in preference to another? What is the headteacher proposing in this case?

   See section 4.

2. Do you think the school is right to consider re-naming the school to change its 'brand image'? What other branding options should the school consider?

   See section 5.

3. Evaluate the sixth form subjects according to their growth, market share, and use of resources. Classify them according to their attractiveness to the school and suggest strategies for their future.

   See sections 6 and 7.

4. Do you agree that 'getting their product right was going to be their most important marketing activity'? What types of product strategies would you recommend for Saxon School?

   See section 7.

2. | WHAT IS A PRODUCT?

A definition

A product is quite simply anything that is capable of fulfilling customer needs. This broad, basic definition has several important implications.

❑ *Some products are more tangible than others.* We sometimes think of products in a restricted way, as objects which have definite physical attributes which can be evaluated by our senses; they can be seen, touched and sometimes heard, smelled or tasted. In consumer markets they can be tins of food, children's toys, bottles of perfume, video recorders. In industrial markets they may be machine tools, chemicals, electronic components, or barrels of oil. These represent a sub-division usually referred to as tangible products because they can be touched and appear to have clearly visible boundaries.

❑ *Some products are intangible services.* A bank or building society offers consumers a range of services, such as deposit accounts and mortgages. A firm of accountants provides business services, such as an annual audit of accounts

189

or a payroll service. These services are 'products', according to the marketing definition of the word, because they are clearly capable of meeting customer needs. Services like these that are hard to touch because they have no obvious physical dimensions are sometimes referred to as intangible products.

❑ *Products are not limited to traditional objects and services. Other 'products' include:*

    ❑ *People:* pop stars, politicians and sports personalities are all frequently marketed like more traditional products.

      • *Tiger Woods has become the biggest sporting personality 'product'. In 2000, his annual revenues were over £30 million, but only £5 million was directly from golf. Sponsorship by Nike, General Motors, Rolex, American Express and Disney is worth far more than the prize money that he wins playing golf.*

    ❑ *Places:* towns, counties and countries are increasingly 'packaged' and sold as an entity to encourage tourism or business investment, or to attract one-off events such as the staging of the Olympic Games.

    ❑ *Organisations:* many businesses have long recognised the need for a consistent corporate image because they are inseparable from the products they sell; there is effectively a total company 'product', offering a variety of individual products. Supermarket chains such as Sainsbury and Tesco are good examples. Other organisations, from charities and educational establishments to political parties and pressure groups, are now also marketing themselves as a package of 'products' with a consistent presentation. In the last General Election, the Conservative, Labour and Liberal Democrat parties offered voters their manifesto of policies, which amounted to presentations of competing products.

❑ *Perceptions of products relate to the benefits they offer rather than the features they present.* As we have emphasised in earlier chapters, customers buy benefits not products. Our perception of a product is therefore coloured not so much by what it can do, but by what it can do for us. A large estate car capable of seating seven people may seem desirably convenient to the parents of a large family, but off-puttingly sluggish and hard to park to a single city dweller. We can only define individual products by taking account of customer perceptions of the benefits of that product.

❑ *Even tangible products have intangible aspects.* The emphasis of our definition is on meeting customer needs, but these are often met by benefits which are intangible, even for products that appear very tangible. As we have discussed in earlier chapters, customers buy for obvious and not so obvious motives. We need a car to travel from point A to point B but this need alone will not determine our choice of vehicle; other considerations, including our attraction to the 'image' of different models, come into play. Thus even a product as tangible as a car has intangible qualities in the design and brand name which form a significant part of the perceived benefits that it offers.

The tangible/intangible spectrum

Products are thus a mixture of tangible and intangible factors. The relative mix of these factors varies considerably. It can be described as a spectrum ranging from products that are predominantly tangible to those that are mainly intangible, with many different combinations in between. Figure 8.1 illustrates this.

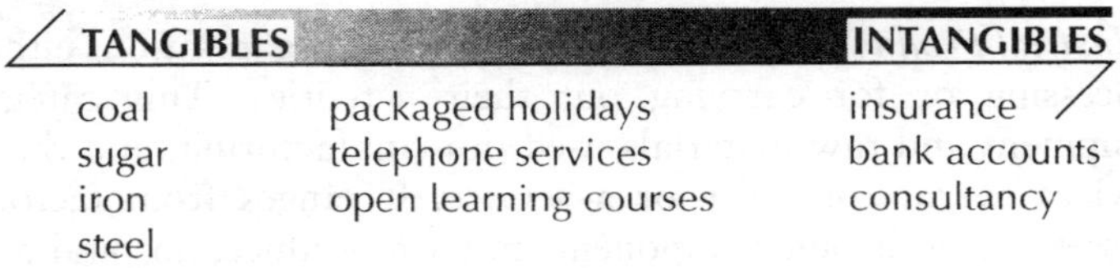

TANGIBLES		INTANGIBLES
coal	packaged holidays	insurance
sugar	telephone services	bank accounts
iron	open learning courses	consultancy
steel		

Figure 8.1: *The tangible/intangible spectrum*

At one extreme are products with tangible features and obvious intangible benefits. Commodities such as coal and sugar, or raw materials such as iron and steel fit this category. At the other extreme are products with only intangible features and benefits. Products such as insurance policies or bank accounts are examples here. In between are products with tangible and intangible features and benefits. A packaged holiday combines intangible services, such as the arrangements for travel and accommodation, with tangible products like the meals served in the hotel. A telephone service requires the tangible hardware of telephone handsets and cabling as well as intangible transmitter and operator services.

3. PRODUCT CLASSIFICATIONS AND THEIR SIGNIFICANCE

Basic classifications

As well as tangibility, products are classified according to their durability and end-use:

- ❑ *Tangibility:* we have seen how products can be divided according to our ability to divide them into

  - ❑ tangible products; and

  - ❑ intangible products or services.

- ❑ *Durability:* tangible products are often further sub-divided:

  - ❑ *Non-durable goods* are consumed relatively rapidly and usually re-ordered regularly. Food, drink and toiletries are major categories of non-durable products.

  - ❑ *Durable goods* survive many uses (or should do) and are replaced infrequently if at all. They include so-called 'white goods' such as refrigerators and washing machines, and 'brown goods' such as videos and music stations, as well as industrial equipment from machine tools to computers.

191

❑ *End-use:* A fundamental distinction can be made between products that are intended for the ultimate user and those that will be processed further:

❑ *Consumer products* are bought or taken up by the final consumer for their own use. This is a very wide category, including most (but not all) products that are advertised on television or sold in high street outlets such as clothes, food, electrical products and banking services.

❑ *Industrial products* are used by businesses or organisations either for further processing or for carrying out their activities. This category includes equipment and raw materials used in manufacturing, and the supplies and services to run an office or a service. It ranges from factories, printing presses and electronic components to farm produce, hospital beds and office copiers.

Figure 8.2 illustrates these basic product classifications.

	TANGIBLE		INTANGIBLE
CONSUMER	Durable	Non-durable	Services
INDUSTRIAL	Durable	Non-durable	Services

Figure 8.2: *Product classifications*

The significance of product classifications

The significance of these classifications lies in the effect they have on marketing strategies.

❑ *Consumer goods* frequently have wide appeal which justifies the use of national advertising media such as television and the national press. In order to maximise demand, indirect distribution channels such as wholesalers and retailers are often used.

❑ *Industrial goods* are often more limited in their market appeal and use more targeted marketing methods such as direct selling or exhibitions. This is not always the case however; there are over three and a half million small and large businesses in the UK alone and products that have a generic appeal to all of them, such as office furniture, computers and copiers, enjoy a market bigger than many of the more specialised consumer products.

❑ *Tangible goods* are easier to display and demonstrate than intangible products. For these goods, design and appearance can take on more importance than the functioning of the product itself. The packaging of a brand of perfume or a child's toy is often the crucial marketing decision. In industrial markets, sampling (of raw materials, for example) and demonstrations (of office equipment, for example) are frequently used marketing tools.

❑ *Intangible goods and services* have several important distinctions:

❑ Being intangible makes them difficult to demonstrate or sample. This makes the reputation of the provider of a service a crucial ingredient in the buying decision, and word-of-mouth a powerful advertising force. Professional services offered by accountants, solicitors, medical practices, schools and universities are often selected by personal recommendation.

❑ Services depend crucially on the people that provide them and are often viewed as inseparable from them. Hairdressers, advertising directors and consultants can take their clients with them when they change from one firm to another.

❑ Services cannot be stored. They cannot be produced in advance and held in stock until required. An empty seat on a train or an aeroplane is a lost sale forever; an unfilled place on a course or in a school is an opportunity lost for good.

❑ Services are often 'tailor-made' to suit the customer. Sometimes the product is a unique solution to a customer's requirements, such as a consultant's report, a dental filling or a haircut. At other times the choice is limited to a 'menu' of services on offer, for example a house mortgage, a car service or office cleaning. Even so there is likely to be considerable 'personalisation' of the service to meet an individual customer's requirements: the amount, term and interest rates of a mortgage vary from customer to customer within the overall guidelines of the building society or bank, for example. This lack of standardisation of the final delivered product makes personal contact between the supplier of a service, or their agent, and the customer desirable and often inevitable.

Product aggregations

Organisations offering more than one product sometimes *aggregate*, or collect together, various products into one classification:

❑ *Product mix or product portfolio:* all the products offered by an organisation (e.g. all the pet products sold by a manufacturer; all the courses offered by a school).

❑ *Product group or category:* several related product lines (e.g. all tins of pet food; all GCSE courses offered).

❑ *Product line:* several products which are related by specification or markets (e.g. all tins of cat food; all GCSE language courses offered).

❑ *Product item:* a single, identifiable product or service (e.g. a tin of chicken and liver cat food; a French GCSE course).

These groupings may be necessary to facilitate management decisions (a product line or group may be managed by one 'product manager' or their equivalent in other organisations – such as the Head of Department in a school) or to focus marketing strategies (a product line may be advertised under one brand name or in one marketing campaign).

4. THE AUGMENTED PRODUCT: FEATURES AND BENEFITS

As well as having boundaries that are less obvious than might at first appear, products can be described on several different levels.

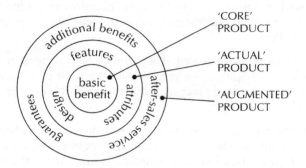

Figure 8.3: *The layers of a product*

❑ *The core product* describes the fundamental reason for the acquisition of the product. This is the benefit which underlies the decision to purchase a product or use a service. In a competitive market it will almost certainly not be a unique benefit offered by any one product, but rather a generic description of the core benefit of a number of competitive offerings. Although it is the real stimulus for the demand for a product, it is not necessarily the main reason for the choice of one product in preference to another.

- *The core benefit for buying a ticket for an airline flight is usually to travel from one place to another, safely, conveniently and comfortably.*

❑ *The actual product* describes the key features that a customer expects from a product. It represents the level of quality and type of features that enable a product to deliver the core benefits desired. Therefore, these often represent the minimum required for a product to survive in a competitive environment.

- *The actual features expected of an airline flight as a product might be regular scheduling, non-stop flights, good seating arrangements, in-flight services, and a reputation as a reliable and safety-conscious airline.*

❑ *The augmented product* represents additional benefits and customer services that have been built around the basic product, often in an attempt to differentiate it from competitive offerings. These are methods of adding value to the core product, which in themselves do not represent the reason for purchase, but may well be the reason for choosing one product over another.

- *The augmented product of an airline flight might include such extras as:*

  - *free transport to and from the airport;*

  - *discounted travel insurance;*

  - *refund guarantees on flight arrival times;*

- *free extra tickets for regular business class users;*

- *wide choice of in-flight entertainment at no additional charges; or*

- *reclining, bed-style seats on long haul flights.*

Product:	A Pencil	Office Cleaning Service	Dental Check-up
Core product	Enables graphic communications in words or pictures.	Clean working environment with minimum disruption and effort.	Healthy and attractive teeth by prevention of problems.
Actual product	Choice of lead hardness. Easy-to-grip barrel. 8 inches in length.	Daily and weekly cleaning routines. Fixed price contract. Self-managed. Honest reputation.	Modern equipment and facilities. Reputation as skilful dentist. NHS patients accepted.
Augmented product	Eraser at one end. Personalised message on barrel.	Penalties for non-performance. Security checks. Preventative maintenance.	Free parking. Appointment reminders. Stickers for children.

Figure 8.4 *Examples of the augmented product*

5. BRANDING: DEVELOPMENT AND STRATEGIES

The power of branding

The name of a product, and symbols associated with it, can be more significant in determining consumer choice than the product itself. The branding of products to give them distinctive images differentiating them from competitors, has turned mundane products into ways of life.

- *'Carbonated drinks' do not sound the most exiting product category, yet Coca Cola has turned a fizzy drink into a symbol for the friendship of global communities. The peoples of the world certainly have one thing in common: they all drink Coca-Cola, the world's top selling brand of fizzy drink sold throughout 185 countries. 'Coke' is now the most recognised word on earth, it is claimed. In the UK it is the biggest consumer brand with over £1 million worth of Coke consumed every day.*

A definition of branding

Several terms are used in conjunction with the branding of products:

❑ A brand is a combination of name, symbol and design that clearly identifies one product from another.

❑ A brand name is the written or spoken word(s) used to distinguish the brand (e.g. Mars Bar, Kellogg's, Rolls-Royce, Apple Macintosh).

❑ A brand mark (or logo) is a distinctive symbol or form of lettering which is always associated with the brand (e.g. the red lettering of Mars, Kellogg's K, the RR of Rolls Royce, and Macintosh's multi-coloured apple with a bite out of it).

However branding means more than just the labelling of products to distinguish one from another. Successful branding has other aspects that make it one of the most powerful tools of modern marketing:

❑ *It represents an assurance of a level of quality and product performance.* A key objective of branding is to build a relationship with customers which keeps them loyal to the product. Such a relationship can only be based on the consumers' trust that a product will do what they expect it to do. The marketing of branded products builds on an expectation of performance which is known to be relevant to the customer. 'Beanz meanz Heinz' because they taste in a way which is appreciated by their target market. As long as the expected performance is consistently delivered, consumers can repurchase the product safe in the knowledge that the satisfaction derived from the last purchase will be repeated. Companies such as Heinz and Mars faithfully reproduce the taste of their products to protect the customer goodwill that has taken them decades to build up.

- *Supermarkets usually stock around 20,000 different product lines, giving consumers a bewildering choice of alternatives. Research indicates that when consumers are faced with a lot of information about competing products, they pay most attention to brand names. Brands are thought to be the best indicators of performance and are purchased in preference to unbranded products unless there are compelling reasons to do otherwise. 'Generic' products – unbranded, simply packaged and lower priced versions of popular products – became more common in supermarkets. These were initially successful in taking market share from branded products, but have now become branded products themselves as chains such as Sainsbury and Tesco use their own brand name to endorse products. These 'private-label' brands are now estimated to represent almost 40 per cent of the UK grocery trade as the big retailers have recognised the power of branding their own products to develop consumer loyalty.*

❑ *Brands are selected for what it says about the consumer as well as for what the product does for the consumer.* Brand names have become increasingly symbolic of lifestyle and emotional aspirations. Products are differentiated not only by what they taste like or how they operate, but also by what they symbolise and imply about their purchasers.

- *Kellogg's cereals offer not just a tasty breakfast but the promise of a fun-packed, healthy life as well. Persil washing powders symbolise caring mothers and responsible parenthood. Managers buying IBM office products can be perceived as reliable and rational decision-makers. Rowntree markets Black Magic chocolates to couples aspiring to elegance and romance, and After Eight to those who want to be associated with gracious living.*

The development of branding

The original meaning of the word brand is to burn a mark onto an animal to establish ownership. In this sense products have been branded from the earliest days. For example, ancient potters put a mark on their wares to denote the place of origin. If a potter's reputation grew by word of mouth, then items with their mark on them became more sought after and therefore more valuable.

The explosion of economic activity associated with the industrial revolution in the nineteenth and twentieth centuries was accompanied by the rapid development of branded products. Differentiated, branded products of high quality survived and prospered in increasingly competitive markets, particularly when early market growth slackened and weaker products were squeezed out.

Many of the brands developed in those early years still predominate in their markets. Kodak film, Wrigley chewing gum, Gillette razors, Coca-Cola, Campbell's soup, Goodyear tyres and Burberry coats all became established brands in the late nineteenth or early twentieth century. They are still market leaders today, testifying to the value of consistent branding.

Key developments

Legal systems throughout the world have worked increasingly hard to stop imitations of brand names and logos. Trademark, copyright and patent laws have established the sellers' right to protect the intangible value of their products. Enforcement is still difficult. Although the European Customs Code now permits officials to impound suspected goods, there is a thriving trade of counterfeit brands in Europe estimated to be approaching £100 billion in 2001. Most established brands have defended their name vigilantly against any impostors in order to protect the intangible value that is at stake.

Winners are not always the big brands as the law is there to protect smaller companies as well.

- *The Halifax dropped its plans to launch a service offering motor insurance because the High Court ruled it could not use the word Halifax in conjunction with motor insurance policies. A local insurance company, Halifax Insurance Ltd won an injunction against its more famous namesake, the court recognising that the local company had sold insurance since the 1960s under the Halifax name.*

Services as well as tangible products are now branded. For example, suppliers in the increasingly competitive financial services industry such as the Halifax, Barclaycard, and Norwich Union have recognised the value of branded products.

Brands have expanded geographically and organically. Coverage has become increasingly global, whilst variety and local choice has developed within brands.

- *Coca-Cola expanded rapidly as a single product into almost every country in the world. It then added variations to the main theme with products such as*

Diet Coke, Caffeine-free Coke, and Cherry Coke. However, in the late 1990s the company ran into problems. Pepsi took market share in the USA and European markets began to react against symbols of uniformity in global markets such as Coke. In 2000, a new CEO, Douglas Daft, introduced a strategy of 'thinking local, acting local'. This involves responding to changes in consumer tastes quickly by developing new products as the drinks market becomes increasingly fragmented. Coke now consider that they compete against four categories of products: refreshment drinks (main brands such as Pepsi), hydration products (mainly waters, such as Perrier), energy and stimulation drinks (e.g. Lucozade and Red Bull), and juices and health drinks (e.g. Five Alive). They plan to offer appropriate products in each of these areas, dependent on local tastes. For example, a new drink 'Alchemy' is targeted at those who want a sophisticated non-alcoholic alternative to traditional cocktails. The ingredients are activated by shaking in a container in the form of a personal cocktail shaker – a far cry from Classic Coke.

The sale of products at low cost on the Internet was initially seen as a threat to the domination of branded goods. But e-commerce is still full of unknowns, especially in the areas of payment and quality control, and in those circumstances, consumers have opted for the products they already know – the established brands.

Branding strategies

As organisations developed and products proliferated, managers were faced with a choice of strategy over the naming of branded products: should the same name be used for all products to give them an authoritative stamp of approval? Or should products be individually branded and left to develop their own loyal following? Both strategies have been used successfully and less successfully.

'Umbrella' branding

Umbrella branding makes the maximum use of a well-established brand name by using it on all the organisation's products. This strategy has two main variants:

❑ Use of the company name on all products, often with more descriptive, individual product names.

- *Kellogg's Frosties, Kellogg's Rice Crispies and Kellogg's Fruit 'n Fibre all use the name of the founder Will Kellogg who launched the original corn-flakes in 1906. The company's simple, focused approach help it to dominate the cereal market with a 42 per cent market share and eight out of the top ten selling brands in the UK in 1998 (Kellogg's Corn Flakes was the top selling product with Weetabix and Shredded Wheat the only non-Kellogg's branded products in the top ten).*

❑ Use of one brand name for all products or a group of products which is different to the company name. For example, Marks and Spencer used the St. Michael label for their own products. However, some organisations take the use of their brand name too far.

- *Bic became a very successful brand name for pens, razors and lighters. When the company diversified into toiletries, the Bic brand was used on a perfume product, this time without success as the cheap, disposable image of the name was not appropriate for a more exclusive, luxury item.*

A 'portfolio' of brands

Some organisations are involved in diverse markets that require different brand names.

- *Reckitt Benckiser (formerly Reckitt and Coleman) market a wide variety of household products under many individual brands, many of which have their own variants. They range from health products such as Lemsip and Disprin to cleaning products such as Vanish, Mr Sheen and Dettol. It would be difficult to see how their products – as diverse as Coleman's mustard and Harpic toilet cleaner – could be marketed under the same brand.*

❏ Other companies acquire branded products or develop their own competing brands to maximise their share of one market. In these circumstances, the strategy is to developing a portfolio of different but complementary brands.

- *Proctor and Gamble and Lever Brothers between them dominate the market for washing machine powders. Both companies market overlapping brands to ensure complete coverage of the market. Proctor and Gamble own Ariel, Daz and Bold which compete with each other as well as Lever's Persil and Surf.*

6. | THE PRODUCT LIFE CYCLE

The life of a product

Products have a finite existence in the marketplace. Many are short-lived fads or failures; others go on for many years before they are overtaken by new developments. However long they last, products, like people, are mortal. They do not live forever; some have a brief moment of glory, others persist in relative obscurity, but they all wax and wane in popularity.

Their 'lives', like ours, can be divided into several distinct stages:

❏ products are 'conceived' and developed by their innovators until they are ready to be launched;

❏ they are 'born' and introduced into the marketplace;

❏ they 'grow' to the limits of their sales potential;

❏ they 'mature' as their markets become saturated and more competitive;

❏ they decline and 'die' as demand falls and alternative products are 'born' to begin the cycle over again.

This is the concept of the product life cycle (PLC) which is usually illustrated graphically as shown in Figure 8.5.

Not all products follow this classic curve closely. Products can miss out stages or they can be rejuvenated to earlier stages of the cycle. For example:

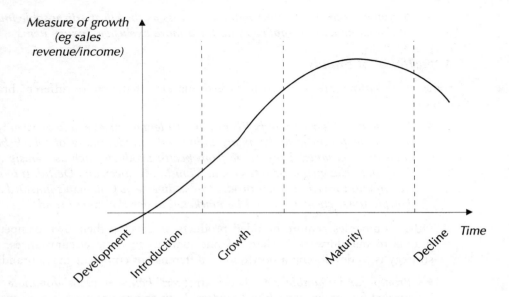

Figure 8.5: *The product life cycle*

❑ Unsuccessful products may not have any significant growth stage, but go into decline soon after their introduction (e.g. the Sinclair C5 electric car, most music bands).

❑ Some products exist because of a short-lived fad or craze. The speed of their introduction and growth is matched only by the rapidity of their decline which leaves no time for a period of consolidation and maturity (for example, the Hula-hoop, Rubric's cube, a 'one-hit' pop group, and many children's 'heroes' from the 'Teenage Mutant Hero Turtles' to 'Pokemon').

❑ Products are sometimes rescued from an earlier decline by a revitalisation as growth slackens and markets mature. This could be the result of marketing efforts to restimulate demand by re-presenting or re-packaging the product (for example, the relaunching of 'Marathon' chocolate bars as 'Snickers', the re-packaging of many soap powder brands from 'Blue Daz' to 'Green Persil', the changing images of pop stars such as Kylie Minogue, the enhancement and re-launch of the Star Wars movies). Products are also helped by technological changes that may enhance their demand. Film making was given a new lease of life through the development of videos and DVDs, which has given many films a second opportunity for generating revenue; the market for watches had matured until the introduction of quartz crystal digital mechanisms created a new growth stage; similarly, domestic demand for computers and peripherals was stimulated by the development of the Internet.

The *product life* cycle can be used to describe generic classes of products (computers), and their sub-divisions (personal computers), or the specific product lines of one organisation (Macintosh PCs) or their individual product items or brands (the iMac). This produces some differences in the application of the concept.

❑ Generic products tend to have longer life cycles than individual products. Coal as a generic form of energy in the UK has been through a long cycle, lasting hundreds of years; it was introduced during the industrial revolution, grew rapidly in the nineteenth century to reach a peak of production soon after the First World War, matured as markets saturated and other forms of energy such as oil, gas and nuclear energy were introduced, and has now suffered a substantial decline in output. Many generic product classes (cars, office copiers, University degrees) stay in the mature stage for a long time because there is no better alternative.

❑ Within a generic product's life cycle, sub-groups exhibit a variety of different curves. Although the overall market for coal had matured by the 1960s, house coals returned to a phase of modest growth as house owners rediscovered the benefits of an open fire.

❑ Individual products are much more susceptible to rapid change in their fortunes because of competitive forces and shifts in consumer preferences. Some branded products survive, virtually unchanged, for decades (Mars bars, Oxo cubes), but these are the exceptions rather than the rule. Most long-living brands change as a product (e.g. Gillette razors, Kodak film), so that the brand lives on in the shape of a new product.

The life cycle stages

The development stage

In the development stage, new product ideas are researched and taken through to readiness for the marketplace. No sales are made during this stage (except perhaps during a market test), so it is an unprofitable, cash absorbing phase in a product's life. Two aspects of product development need emphasising as they can work against each other:

❑ The most important element in the marketing mix is getting the product right in the first place. No amount of clever promotion, sophisticated pricing, or extensive distribution can compensate for a weak product that is not in tune with customer needs.

❑ Speed of new product development is becoming more and more important in competitive international markets. It is no longer enough to get there first; continual improvements to existing products are required just to maintain market share.

• *The Range Rover was the first rugged four-wheel drive vehicle to be sold as a luxury car, but the world market has been dominated by Japanese manufacturers who developed newer versions more suited to mass markets.*

Rank Xerox once dominated the UK office copier market with the only plain-paper machines available. After the expiry of their protective patents, Xerox saw their leadership eroded as competitors, such as Canon, introduced more versatile and compact copiers to give customers the decentralised copying facilities that they preferred.

Given the overwhelming importance of getting the product right, organisations can suffer from inertia in developing new products to take over from successful existing products. The result is that they lose out to more agile competitors. Some companies, such as 3M and Hewlett Packard, have developed deliberate policies to overcome these negative forces. These include:

❑ *Keep divisions small*. There is evidence that smaller business units provide a more innovative, working environment than larger groupings.

❑ *Tolerate failure*. One success usually comes from many rejected concepts which nevertheless contribute something to help progress an idea. This implies that risk-taking and experimentation is to be encouraged even when it means high failure rates.

❑ *Look for innovations, not just inventions*. The two are often confused, but they are not the same. Invention involves creating new ideas; innovation takes new ideas but puts them to practical use as desirable products or services.

❑ *Encourage some 'disorder'*. Creativity is often sparked when ideas that are normally not connected are 'accidentally' linked. This is the basis for processes such as brainstorming which attempt to encourage creative thinking. Unfortunately, most management activities strive for order and predictable policies as the only way of coping with complex structures and markets. 'Thriving on chaos' does not come naturally, particularly to well-established organisations.

❑ *Systematically search the most likely sources of opportunities*. New products rarely come as a one-off flash of inspiration. Organisations that are most successful in new product development seek out innovation continuously and methodically. Changes to existing markets and customer habits often leave clues which the innovator can pursue. For example, demographic changes often signal opportunities for new products as well as threats to existing ones. We know, for example, that the UK population profile is set to become older as the percentage of over 70 year olds increases. This is already creating opportunities for those offering services such as sheltered housing and nursing homes for the elderly. Conversely, the decline in numbers of young people poses product problems for those dependent on youthful markets (for example manufacturers of fashion clothes, leisure shoes and trainers, alcoholic and non-alcoholic drinks).

In an established marketing organisation, product development usually goes through a number of processes, which take a new idea from a position of unknown risk through to reasonable prospects of success. This is illustrated in Figure 8.6.

The introduction stage

In this stage the product is introduced into the marketplace and made available to customers. Most new products are relatively unknown at this stage and, therefore, demand is slow; there are exceptions such as films or West End plays which use pre-launch publicity to generate the immediate, substantial demand which these products need to be financially successful.

The common themes (although not hard and fast rules) of the introduction stage are:

UNKNOWN RISK	
GENERATION OF NEW PRODUCT IDEAS	Systematic search for innovative opportunities among employees, customers, competitors and other sources, using analysis, research and 'creativity techniques' eg brainstorming.
SCREENING OF IDEAS	Unsuitable ideas rejected often by reference to a checklist of criteria for acceptable product parameters and performance.
TESTING OF CONCEPT	The idea of new product is tested conceptually on a group of target customers before it is taken further.
PLANNING OF STRATEGY	Marketing objectives for new product established. Financial and other implications analysed in a business plan.
DEVELOPING THE PRODUCT	Development of a successfully working prototype product.
TESTING THE MARKET	Product is tested and evaluated in the market place by limited exposure in selected areas prior to more extensive launch in the introduction stage.
REASONABLE PROSPECTS	

Figure 8.6: *A new product development process*

❑ If the product is at all innovative, competition will be limited.

❑ The product specification remains basic as refinements are not yet needed and may be undeveloped.

❑ The need to develop awareness of the product makes promotional effort the highest priority in the marketing mix, whether this comes from advertising, personal selling, PR, or other methods.

❑ Pricing pressures are downward because of increased output and more competition.

❑ Distribution is widened (e.g. geographically) and deepened (e.g. to smaller retail outlets) to maximise sales potential.

❑ Financially, growth leads to profits as revenue increases and unit costs decline. This may not be reflected in a positive cash flow however as increased debtors and stocks, or other investments necessary to cope with growth, absorb surplus cash. Profits may also be re-invested in product improvement or other marketing activities in order to capture more market share.

The maturity stage

As markets become saturated and competition increases, growth peaks and sales begin to stabilise. This is the onset of maturity, the most common stage for products as it tends to last longer than other phases. Common themes in this stage are:

❑ The slackening rate of growth leads to a shake out amongst competitors. At first competitive activity may increase as rival suppliers try to maintain growth by increasing market share through promotional activities, product improvements and price-cutting. The resulting decline in profit margins usually forces weaker competitors to exit from the market. This may allow for a period of relative stability among the few established organisations that emerge as the final market leaders.

❑ Products become more refined as rivals seek to gain competitive advantage through improvements to performance and presentation and by the addition of new features. It is in the maturity stage that the added value of the augmented product becomes a more and more significant determinant of demand. Additional benefits, such as longer guarantees, after-sales service, financing deals, give-away extras and incentives are required to attract buyers.

❑ Promotional activity is no longer targeted at creating awareness but at maintaining loyalty to a brand or product. Some promotions may seek to develop new, secondary market segments.

❑ Pricing becomes more sophisticated as markets mature. Discounting may threaten margins in the short term, and in the longer term if over-capacity remains a permanent feature of the market. However suppliers often try to protect margins by offering a more attractive 'bundle' of benefits for the same price.

❑ Distribution spreads even wider in an attempt to improve sales. It may be at this stage that international markets become more attractive for the first time as demand in the home market slackens. New channels of distribution may be opened up to gain access to different segments.

❑ Financially, profits tend to decline as sales level off, although they can improve again if a shakeout of competitors stabilises the market. However the maturity stage can be sufficiently cash positive for successfully managed products to recoup the investments made in earlier stages. Indeed it is important to prolong this stage for as long as possible to ensure satisfactory financial returns.

Managing the mature stage is a key marketing management task as manipulation of the marketing mix can delay the beginning of decline or stimulate a return to growth.

The decline stage

Eventually the sales of an individual product or group of products may go into decline. This can represent a gradual shift or a more rapid decline in demand, caused by the introduction of better or substitute products, or a change in consumer attitudes. Choices for marketing management include:

❑ Maintain the product by concentrating on segments where there is evidence of continued demand.

❑ Revitalise the product so that it can be re-launched as 'new' in some way.

❑ 'Harvest' remaining profits from the product by reducing expenditure on it to a minimum.

❑ Delete the product from the range.

- *The 35-year-old doll 'Cindy' was phased out by its makers Hasbro, who withdrew all marketing support in 1997. Cindy was the casualty in the battle with 'Barbie' who proved the more durable doll, and a relative newcomer, 'Polly Pocket'.*

Effects of the product life cycle on the marketing mix

This description of the product life cycle illustrates how the evolution of a product changes the use of the marketing mix over time:

❑ More emphasis is placed on product changes as the cycle advances. Whereas the basic product is acceptable in the introduction stage, features are added in the growth stage; additional benefits of the augmented product are needed in the mature stage, and finally the product may be totally revamped in the decline stage.

❑ Promotions vary in both extent and objectives. During introduction and growth extensive promotion may be required to generate awareness and to capture market share. In maturity and decline promotional activity may be reduced to improve profitability and targeted at increasing customer loyalty. Alternatively, it maybe increased temporarily to promote a re-launch of the product.

❑ Pricing can be high for innovative products during their introduction but prices are increasingly subject to competitive pressure as the cycle progresses. Substantial discounting may be required to maintain market share in maturity and decline.

❑ The place element of the marketing mix can also change as distribution policies reflect a product's fortunes. Restricted distribution in the introductory stage usually gives way to wider geographic coverage and deeper penetration of specific channels of distribution as markets grow and mature.

The implication for marketing management is that the effective use of the elements in the marketing mix varies according to the stage of the life cycle. What works well at one time may fail or be inappropriate at another stage.

7. | PORTFOLIO ANALYSIS AND STRAGEGY OPTIONS

Life cycles of a product portfolio

Most organisations offer more than one product or groups of products at a time. They offer a portfolio of different but often related products. Each of these products has its own life cycle and, at any given time, they will be at various stages of their cycle. Figure 8.7 illustrates the life cycles of the portfolio of products of one organisation. On a specific date – Time X – in this organisation's history, one product is in decline, another has entered maturity, one is growing fast, whilst one is just being introduced.

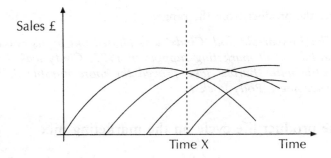

Figure 8.7: *Life cycles of an organisation's product portfolio*

The potential impact of this combination of life cycles is an important ingredient in the organisation's product decisions.

Resource implications of the product life cycle

Financial and other resources are affected by the product life cycle.

❏ *Profits* which are non-existent during development and introduction, should emerge with growth, and may then plateau or disappear altogether in maturity and decline.

❏ *Cash investment* is required to develop new products and to finance their introduction. Products often remain cash negative during high growth, only generating a positive cash flow as growth slows into maturity. The decline stage can be cash positive or neutral if products are well managed and support for them is removed in line with sales; eventually decline inevitably absorbs cash if significant losses occur before deletion of the product.

❏ *Other resources are also affected by the life cycle.* For example, more management time may be required to cope with the rapid changes likely during introduction and growth than is needed once more predictable patterns have emerged in maturity. The production of a new product probably needs more operator and machine time than an equivalent, established product where 'economies of experience' have begun to be realised.

The implications of this analysis is that an organisation requires a portfolio of products which is balanced in line with the resources available and the growth objectives of the organisation. In order to finance the development, introduction and growth of newer products, a business needs more mature products which provide the necessary cash flow. In order for a business to continue to grow overall, it has to introduce new products to replace the growth lost by mature and declining products.

Competitors, market share and life cycles

The competitive situation is likely to change with the life cycle of the products in the marketplace:

❏ An innovative new product may have little competition when it is introduced but many competitors emerge as growth of the market is confirmed.

- In the growth stage, a large number of organisations with relatively small individual shares of the market can survive, many of them dependent on the increase in the total market to provide them with new customers rather than any specific competitive advantage.

- As market expansion slows down, the survivors are likely to be those who have gained a relatively high market share because they have demonstrated a competitive advantage. This may come from lower costs which give bigger profit margins to invest in promotions or product development, or to withstand the effects of a price war. Or it may stem from a superior product which is able to differentiate itself from competitors.

- Once markets have matured and become dominated by a few, well-established organisations, it is usually more difficult to gain market share. Market leaders should have a lower cost base as they produce more than their competitors and can benefit from economies of scale and experience. Research and development to produce a superior product can be expensive as competitors have already introduced sophisticated or technologically advanced modifications.

These characteristics imply that taking a relatively large market share in the growth stage can be critical to success and survival in the maturity stage. In an expanding market, growth may be relatively easy to achieve. But if the growth of a product is below the rate of increase in the rest of the market, this could spell problems later as that product is loosing ground to its competitors and may end up with a relatively small market share. Complacency during the earlier stages of a product may shorten its life expectancy.

The BCG growth-share matrix

These influences of growth and market share have been brought together into a matrix by the Boston Consulting Group (BCG). Products are labelled according to their likely impact on an organisation's resources.

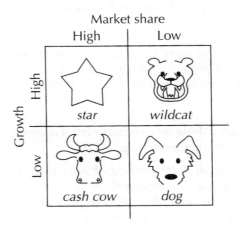

Figure 8.8: *The growth-share matrix*

❑ A *Star* product is growing fast and has achieved a high market share. Although it generates high revenues and is profitable, it uses lots of cash to fuel its growth and maintain its competitive position. It is well placed to survive and prosper when growth slackens.

❑ A *Cash Cow* has a high share of a market which has matured. Because of their dominant market position, they are able to exploit maturity and generate plenty of surplus cash from their sales. Cash Cows 'evolve' from the Stars of the growth stage and are a critical source of cash and other resources to develop new products.

❑ A *Wildcat* (sometimes referred to as a Problem Child or Question Mark) is in a growth stage but has achieved a relatively small market share. As this makes the product unprofitable at present and could put it in an even weaker position when the market matures, it requires some changes and probably investment to improve its market position. Wildcats are therefore net users of cash resources. They may be managed into Stars but they can also degenerate into Dogs if market growth disappears.

❑ A *Dog* has the worst of both worlds having a low share of a market with no or low growth. They represent a drain on an organisation's resources often at the expense of other products and are candidates for deletion unless they can be transformed into a Wildcat through growth.

The growth-share matrix emphasises the need for a balanced portfolio of products if an organisation is to grow and be self-sufficient in resources. Once the portfolio profile has been established four basic strategies for each product are possible:

❑ *Build*: increase market share to strengthen the future position at the expense of shorter-term profits and cash flow, for example turning Wildcats into Stars.

❑ *Hold*: maintain current market share to make sure maximum profits and cash is generated now or in the future, for example by sustaining and milking a Cash Cow.

❑ *Harvest*: increase short-term cash flow even at the expense of longer term profits, for example by taking profits from Stars and Wildcats rather than investing in them and milking Cash Cows dry if market conditions seem set to worsen.

❑ *Divest*: cut off a drain on resources even if it means taking short-term losses, for example by terminating a Dog.

Critics of the growth-share method of analysing product portfolios point to its simplistic assumption that market share is always the key measure of a product's competitive position and that market growth is always the most important indicator of an industry's attractiveness. In particular, it overlooks the large number of highly successful products that occupy niche positions in larger markets and the diseconomies of scale in providing some services which undermine the value of a high market share.

Market attractiveness/competitive position matrix

To overcome these and other criticisms, different models have been developed to help guide product strategies. In one approach (developed by General Electric and McKinsey), products are rated against two principle dimensions: attractiveness of the market and their competitive position.

❑ *Market attractiveness* is a measure of the profit potential in a market for all participants including not just growth but also other factors such as market size, level of competition, historic profit margins, rate of technological change, and the political and legal constraints.

❑ *Competitive position* is assessed not only by market share but also product quality, perceived image, distribution network, management strength, patent protection and other significant factors.

This multi-factor model can be drawn as a grid as shown in Figure 8.9.

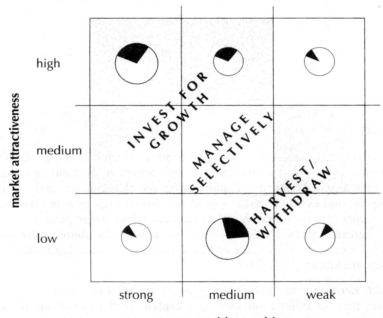

Figure 8.9: *The GE multi-factor portfolio model*

Products are plotted on the grid according to their rating against the established criteria. They can be drawn as parts of circles where the size of the circle represents the size of the total market and the product's market share is shaded. The cells of the matrix fall into three distinct areas:

❑ those justifying investment for growth;

❑ those requiring more selective management and cautious investment; or

❑ those needing a policy of harvesting or divestment as they represent unattractive options.

Ansoff's classification of product strategies

We looked briefly at alternative marketing objectives which specify the relationship between products and markets in Chapter 2 (see Chapter 2, section 6 'Controls'). This introduced the four basic, alternative strategies of Ansoff's matrix which links products to the markets they are targeted to serve, as shown in Figure 8.10.

Products

	Existing	New
Markets Existing	Penetration	Development
New	Extension	Diversification

Figure 8.10: *Ansoff's matrix*

❑ *Product penetration* develops existing products within existing markets. The underlying assumption is that there is still untapped demand or competitive advantage that can be further exploited without changing either the product or looking beyond existing market segments. This strategy usually involves use of other elements in the marketing mix, such as an increase in promotional effort, more aggressive pricing policies or more extensive distribution. Providing the potential exists, it is the strategy of least risk because both products and markets are known.

❑ *Product development* introduces new products into existing markets. It assumes that an innovation will be accepted by the organisation's existing customer group. Product development can be radical with the introduction of an entirely new product, or moderate involving only the modification of existing products in some way such as performance, presentation or quality.

❑ *Market extension* takes existing products into new markets. This strategy assumes that existing markets are fully exploited or that new markets can be developed concurrently with existing markets. New markets may be defined geographically (for example, potential export areas), or by customer grouping (a different age or social group), or other parameters (e.g. purchasing patterns, industrial classification or sectors).

❑ *Diversification* develops new products and offers them to new markets. As it represents a departure from an organisation's existing product and market involvement, it is the strategy of highest risk.

The use of portfolio and product strategy analysis

Although portfolio analysis using these and other models has been much discussed amongst theorists since the 1970s, research has indicated that they are little used in practice. Some managers have not heard of them, others do not understand them and some have tried them and found them wanting as management techniques.

Defenders of portfolio analysis claim that the tools are frequently misapplied and often too much is expected of them. They are intended as techniques which can help the product planning process by providing ideas on the value of various strategic options but they are not methods which on their own can determine product strategy.

8. KEY POINTS

- ❏ A product is anything that is capable of fulfilling customer needs. It is therefore not limited to physical objects, but includes intangible services, people, places and organisations.

- ❏ Products are classified into *consumer* or *industrial* products, and *tangible* or *intangible* products. Tangible products are sub-divided further into *durable* or *non-durable* goods.

- ❏ Individual product items are aggregated into *product lines*, *groups*, and finally *portfolios* or *product mix* – all the products offered by an organisation or unit.

- ❏ Three distinctive elements of a product need consideration: the *core product* of basic benefits to meet customer needs, the *actual product* of features which create those benefits, and the *augmented product* of additional features and benefits (such as guarantees and after-sales service) which often differentiate competing products.

- ❏ Branding has become an important, intangible aspect of many products, representing an assurance of quality, and a statement of aspirations of the purchaser.

- ❏ Branding strategies can follow an *umbrella* or *portfolio* approach.

- ❏ The '*product life cycle*' concept (PLC) divides the lifespan of a product into stages of development, introduction, growth, maturity and decline.

- ❏ The *development stage* takes new product ideas from concept to market readiness. This development process can be under-emphasised without deliberate policies to generate, screen and test new ideas that can then be planned, developed and tested as products in the marketplace.

- ❏ Typically in the *introduction stage*, a basic product is launched with limited competition, promotional activity, higher prices, restricted distribution and sales, and negative cash flow.

- ❏ The *growth stage* is typified by rapid market acceptance, more competition, product improvements, additional promotional effort, and downward price pressures. Although profitable the product continues to absorb cash.

❏ In the typical *mature stage*, growth slackens, products and pricing becomes more sophisticated, distribution becomes wider and deeper and promotions seek to maintain loyalty. The pressure on profits and market share shakes out weaker competitors although cash flow becomes positive.

❏ In the *decline stage* decisions are needed to either revitalise, harvest or delete the product.

❏ A balanced *portfolio of products* is required to cope with the resource and marketing implications of the product life cycle. The *growth-share matrix* of the Boston Consulting Group typifies products as 'stars', 'cash cows', 'wildcats' and 'dogs' according to their market share and growth characteristics.

❏ The *multi-factor model* measures the market attractiveness and competitive position of a product.

❏ *Ansoff's matrix* classifies product strategies as market penetration, market extension, product development or diversification.

9.	DEVELOPING MARKETING SKILLS

Exercises

1. Consider a non-durable, durable and intangible product you have recently purchased, been given or used. How would you describe each according to the three elements of the core benefits, the actual product features, and the augmented product of additional features and benefits? In which stage of their life cycle would you place each of these products?

2. 'The age of branding as the dominant force in consumer goods marketing is over.' Evaluate the evidence for and against this statement both from developments you have witnessed in retail stores, mail order catalogues and other consumer outlets, and from your own buying behaviour.

3. Choose a high street retailer which sells a variety of different lines and with whose products you are familiar (such as Top Shop, Boots, Woolworths or a local trader).

   (i) Draw your impression of the life cycles of their products and consider the implications of this analysis.

   (ii) Suggest a portfolio analysis for their products using the growth-share and multi-factor matrices

Developing a marketing plan

Activity 8 The product strategy

How will your product strategy reflect the objectives and market strategies you have decided to follow?

❑ What are the core benefits, the actual features and the augmented aspects and other benefits of your principle products?

❑ What is the anticipated mix of products in your portfolio?

❑ What is the implication of the mix on resources?

❑ How will you develop new products?

❑ How will your products be differentiated from the competition?

❑ How do you assess the attractiveness of the market?

❑ What will be your strategy – penetration, market extension, product development or diversification?

FURTHER READING AND REFERENCES

General texts

Brassington, F. and Pettit, S. (2000) *Principles of Marketing*, 2nd edition, chapters 7–9.

Cowell, D. (1993) *The Marketing of Services*, Butterworth-Heinemann, chapters 2 and 6.

Doyle, P. (1998) *Marketing Management and Strategy*, 2nd edition, Prentice-Hall.

Gabbott, M. and Hogg, G. (1997) *Contemporary Services Management: a Reader*. Thomson Learning, part 1: 'The Classics' (includes seminal articles such as Shostack, L. 'Breaking free from product marketing').

Kotler, P. (2000) *Marketing Management*, 10th edition, Prentice Hall, chapters 13 and 14.

Branding

Aaker, D. (1995) *Building Strong Brands*, Free Press.

Bainbridge, J. and Curtis, J. (1998) 'The UK's biggest brands', *Marketing*, 30th July, pages 22–25, and 6th August, pages 20–23.

New product development

Adair, J. (1990) *The Challenge of Innovation*, Talbot Adair Press.

Henry, J. and Walker, D. (1991) *Managing Innovation*, Sage Publications, sections 4–6.

CHAPTER 9

Pricing: Influences, Strategies and Methods

This chapter investigates various influences on another key element in the marketing mix – pricing. A number of internal and external factors help determine the optimum price for a product or service:

❑ Internal factors include the marketing and financial strategies of an organisation.

❑ External factors include the type of customers, the state of the marketplace and more general environmental influences such as taxation and the economic policies of the government.

The two generic pricing strategies of market skimming and penetration are examined in the light of these factors. Finally the chapter considers specific pricing methods and techniques under the categories of the 3Cs of cost-based, customer-based and competition-based pricing.

1. CASE STUDY: PRICING BICYCLES

Monica Bogaert, product manager for all-terrain bicycles (ATBs, or mountain bikes as they were more commonly known) at one of the top UK suppliers had an important task to complete. She had to recommend a pricing strategy for a new model to be launched by her company. It was a hybrid 'town and trail' bicycle, so-called because it had all the off-road features of a mountain bike but was comfortable and efficient for on-road use as well. It incorporated some important new features: a super-light aluminium frame to minimise the pedal power required, front suspension forks to cushion the ride, and most innovative of all – hub gears. Unlike the old three-speed variety which had become outdated by external, cog-changing derailleur gears, the new enclosed hub gears provided ten speeds and were much easier to use and maintain.

The marketing strategy for the new bike was to target some market segments which the existing ATBs in their range had not fully penetrated, notably the over 35 female group, whilst having appeal to the core market of 15 to 19 year olds and men over 35. Although the new features gave it considerable advantages, the bike's technical leadership was likely to be short-lived as the innovations were the result of developments not by Bogaert's own company but by component manufacturers.

To take advantage of advances made by Far Eastern producers and to keep fixed costs to a minimum, all the components of the new product were to be imported with final assembly only taking place in the UK. Bogaert had received estimated costings for the components and manufacturing. Assuming an order for quantities of at least 10,000, the total cost of components approximated to £80 per bicycle which Bogaert knew to be very competitive, considering the new features. Even the price of the lighter aluminium frames had fallen considerably in recent years although they were still more expensive than the hi-tensile steel models. The costs of setting up each bike in the UK would add a further £30. There were fixed costs that would be charged to the new model as well. The promotional budget had been set at £200,000 for the first year to cover advertising and sales promotions and an allocated cost for group publicity such as catalogues and exhibitions. A further allocation to central overheads including R&D, central services and finance costs had been estimated at £300,000 per annum. In any pricing decisions, Bogaert would have to observe the key financial measures used by her company such as a profit to sales ratio of at least ten per cent.

The final price of the bike to the user would have to take into account the distibutors' margins and of course VAT. Bicycle distribution in the UK was still very fragmented with most sales going through independent retailers although superstores such as Halfords had grown in popularity to an estimated 25 per cent of retail bike sales. Most retailers added a mark-up of between 35 and 45 per cent to their buying price, depending on the volume of their purchases and how keenly they wished to price their products.

Over a million adult ATBs were still being sold in the UK, but Bogaert knew that the market had become very competitive. The growth of the ATB market had attracted many competitors and imports of lower priced bikes had grown steadily. Now 'bargain' ATBs started at £99, with reasonable bikes for the more serious rider in the £199–£250 bracket. Aluminium-framed models continued to drop in price and were now available at £300 and under. For the enthusiast there was a growing choice of mountain bikes over £500 with a top of the range price of £1500–£2000. As growth of the ATB sector had slackened, manufacturers tried to differentiate their products through improved features and the use of branding with names such as 'Dirty Dog', one of Bogaert's own models which had achieved something of a cult following. Although Bogaert's company and one other supplier controlled over 50 per cent of the UK bicycle market between them, there were a dozen or so other serious competitors offering a variety of models.

'I must decide first what my pricing strategy will be,' thought Monica Bogaert. 'Do I take advantage of the technical superiority of my new product and make good profits as quickly as possible by pricing up in the market segments that I know will pay? Or do I look for longer-term profits, keep my price down and broaden my appeal to more segments in the hope that I can take a significant market share?'

(Note: this case can be read also as a follow-on from the case 'Bicycles' in Chapter 7 which has additional market information.)

Points to consider

1. What types of influences on pricing decisions are discussed here? Are there others that should be taken into consideration?

See sections 2 and 3.

2. Consider the possible impact of these influences:

(i) Which internal influences will be most important and why?

See section 4.

(ii) Which external influences will be most important and why?

See section 5.

3. Consider the questions Monica Bogaert is asking herself about the pricing strategy to adopt. What are the advantages and disadvantages of the alternatives she suggests? What pricing strategy would you recommend?

See section 6.

4. What selling price would you recommend for the new model and why? What is the break-even volume of sales at your recommended price?

See section 7.

---

2. PRICING IN THE PRIVATE AND PUBLIC SECTORS

New products and economic growth in many market sectors has increased the significance of non-price variables, such as branding, advertising and distribution channels, on customer preferences. Maturing markets and economic downturns reaffirm pricing as a crucial marketing tool. The introduction of market forces into the delivery of public services and growing competitiveness amongst other non-profit organisations has also emphasised the importance of pricing as a management function.

In the private sector, pricing has a crucial impact on the profitability of a business. In the public sector, the importance of the pricing mechanism is less obvious because users of public services do not often pay directly for each service received. However pricing is still an important management function in both sectors although there are differences in its application.

❑ In the *private sector*, prices charged need to cover at least the costs of providing products if an organisation is to survive in the longer term. Pricing is unique among the 4 Ps of the marketing mix in that it produces income whereas the other elements incur costs. The total income or sales revenue of a business can be represented by the formula:

$$R = V(P)$$

where:

R is sales revenue,
V is the volume or quantity of units sold,
P is the price per unit sold.

Pricing strategies therefore not only represent an important marketing consideration, but also play a direct role in the financial viability of a private sector company.

❑ In the *public sector*, organisations receive revenues from a mixture of charges to customers and allocations of public funds from tax receipts. A state-owned corporation is expected to cover its costs mainly from prices charged to consumers with increasing pressure to minimise any subsidies from taxes; pricing operates in much the same way as it does in the private sector except that it is subject to more political scrutiny. However public services such as the health, police and education services are mainly funded by allocations of tax receipts as there are few direct charges on consumers.

❏ These allocations of tax receipts are increasingly made on the basis of the delivery of a specific service which therefore takes on a notional price.

- *State schools are allocated annual budgets primarily on the basis of the number of pupils attending the school, thereby giving a notional price to the provision of a year's education to a child.*

- *Hospitals are awarded contracts for the provision of certain services by a district health authority which effectively puts a specific price on the provision of those services. Some departments (such as physiotherapy) within a hospital can be used by patients paying directly through a medical insurance scheme and so those services have to be priced separately.*

- *Some public services such as refuse collection are subject to competitive tendering; if a public authority (such as a district council in the case of refuse collection) wishes to continue to provide the service itself, it must submit a price in the form of a tender for the contract.*

Within many public services there is a division between the purchaser of a service who controls the allocation of public funds and monitors the quality of delivery, and the provider who delivers the specified service for a set price. Managers in today's public services have to understand pricing either from the side of the purchaser assessing competitive bids for a service, or from the context of a provider of services for a specific price.

3. INFLUENCES ON THE PRICING PROCESS

The setting of prices for products and services varies from a relatively simple to a very complicated process. However, pricing decisions are rarely easy in practice because they are subject to many different, often conflicting, influences and constraints inside and outside of an organisation.

Historically, buyers and sellers arrived at a price through a process of bargaining. Both parties searched for a price by making offers and counter offers until they decided on a level acceptable to both, or made no deal. Prices arrived at by this method were often different for each transaction even if the product was essentially the same, reflecting the individual needs and negotiating skills of the bargainers.

Although elements of this process can still be found on the floors of commodity and stock exchanges where prices for the same item change by the minute, most modern sellers set one price for all buyers, or groups of buyers. Retailers normally establish a price for each product and buyers either accept it or leave it. Some organisations do offer differential pricing for the same product: an industrial seller may accept lower prices for bulk or regular purchases; travel companies and hotels offer discounts for off-peak users of their services. However these prices are subject to uniform policies which qualify the buyer. In our society, individual negotiation is the exception rather than the rule, limited to larger one-off deals between organisations (negotiation of a long-term contract) or individuals (buying a house). The majority of items sold are pre-priced before they are offered to the market-place, with little room for bargaining thereafter.

Internet pricing

The Internet does allow for more individual negotiation of prices. Auctions have recently been given new impetus by the Internet with the success of Net auction houses such as eBay. The system of bidding is usually the same as the traditional format but the Internet makes the process more convenient and easier to join in. Internet auctions have also developed some pricing novelties. A buyer can state how much they wish to pay (e.g. for airline seats) and see if a seller wishes to accept (for example at eWanted and lastminute.com). Other sites use collaborative buying power to attempt to achieve lower prices for specific items (e.g. LetsBuyIt.com). Some sites act as an intermediary seeking to find the best price on your behalf, whilst on others you can barter for a better price. For consumers, these systems are still in their infancy. The key issues to overcome before extensive expansion of individual bargaining is to increase the security of payments over the Internet, and to develop more cost-effective methods of delivery of products. Most individual buyers are still wary of giving credit card details over the Internet, and are cautious about the value of bargains which prove expensive to deliver.

Buyers in organisations increasingly use e-procurement to achieve lower prices. This may be done in conjunction with other companies forming a virtual marketplace of buyers and suppliers (such as the WorldWide Retail Exchange of over 100,000 suppliers and major retail buyers). In most cases procurement is still through an electronic catalogue, so that there is little effect on pricing. However, companies are also using 'reverse auctions': the buying company indicates what it wishes to purchase, and suppliers bid for the order, successively lowering the price. Such methods facilitate communications between buyers and suppliers so that players in the marketplace are better informed. However, pricing decisions are still influenced by a series of internal and external factors, whatever the communication or negotiation mechanism.

Influences on pricing

Pricing decisions are subject to a complex series of influences arising not only from the needs of buyers and sellers but also from the market and general environment around them. Figure 9.1 illustrates some of these influences which might be taken into account by an organisation when pricing its products.

❑ *Internal* influences comprise both the *marketing and financial strategies* of an organisation. Marketing strategies are likely to stipulate the markets that an organisation targets, the position it takes within them and the marketing mix strategies adopted. Financial strategies dictate the cost base for providing

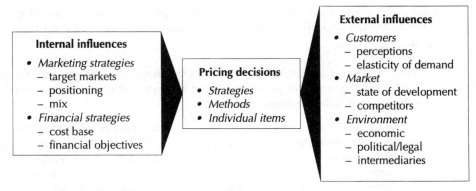

Figure 9.1: *Influences on the pricing process*

products and services and the returns expected from them. All are fundamental influences on pricing decisions.

❑ *Customers* influence pricing decisions by their perceptions of the relative importance of price in the marketing mix which establishes the elasticity of demand for particular products.

❑ *Market* influences take into account the state of development of the market and the strategies and activities of competitors.

❑ *Environmental* influences on pricing include the applicable levels of taxation, the state of the economy, existing legislation and current government policies.

❑ *Pricing decisions* eventually set prices for each item, but they also establish a strategic framework within which the method of selecting individual prices can operate.

Each of these influences in the pricing process is considered in more detail in the following sections.

4. INTERNAL FACTORS: MARKETING AND FINANCIAL STRATEGIES

Prices are frequently determined by a mixture of marketing and financial factors. The price of a product is a key part of the marketing mix and needs to be in line with other elements of marketing strategy if the customer is to be given consistent messages. The price achieved by a product is also a significant ingredient in the financial equation which determines the profitability or efficiency of an organisation. Thus, pricing is a function of concern to both the marketing and financial management of an organisation.

Marketing strategies

Different marketing strategies can lead to different pricing decisions. For instance, a strategic objective to penetrate the market as rapidly as possible is more likely to keep prices down than the aim of maximising profits at the expense of growth.

Prices are particularly influenced by the following marketing decisions:

❑ *Target markets.*

The decision to segment a market into customer groups and target one particular segment with a differentiated approach affects pricing as well as the other variables in the marketing mix.

> • *In the early years of passenger travel by air, the airlines differentiated only between those passengers able to pay for first class seats and regular fare payers. However, an important segment of business travellers emerged who expected some of the luxuries of first class without the high price tag. Airlines began to target this segment by charging premium rates over economy passengers for extra comforts and services. Although the basic benefit of rapid transportation from point A to point B was the same for all passengers, the business class segment was offered a package of additional benefits including the status and comforts of a separate seating area which avoided the extravagance of a first class ticket but was still priced higher than economy class.*

❑ *Positioning strategy.*

Customers' perceptions of the position of a product or organisation in the marketplace is influenced by pricing strategies. The exclusive position of cars made by Rolls Royce or Ferrari is maintained by making sure only a few customers can afford the price. Most organisations do not have such an obvious connection between their prices and market position but still need to establish a clear identity that is created or confirmed by their pricing policies.

> • *Woolworths shops have always aimed at the bargain position in the marketplace. Their original strategy offered shoppers the convenience of extensive ranges of lower priced products from buttons to bath taps sold in one town centre store. Large stocks of cheap items no longer made economic sense as the costs of high street retailing escalated in the 1970s and 1980s and retailing became more targeted. Woolworths refocused its operations in the UK under the umbrella of the Kingfisher group that also included the B&Q DIY chain. The traditional Woolworth shops concentrated on limited popular lines such as toys, children's clothes, music and videos. However they retained their historic position as the bargain basement retailer. Although this proved popular in the recessionary times of the early 1990s, shoppers grew weary of year-round sales and became confused by the variety of in-store promotions offered by all retailers fighting to retain their share of shrinking markets. Woolworth's decided to re-affirm their position by a radical, consistent pricing scheme called 'Street Value'. This gave customers the simple promise of the lowest prices on items marked with the 'Street Value' logo. The aim of this price branding scheme was to position the group as the retailer who offers permanent value for money.*

❑ *Marketing mix strategies.*

Pricing decisions are part of a marketing mix strategy that can only be effective if all the ingredients blend together. Decisions on price need to be consistent with those made about other elements of the mix.

- *The Arcadia group (formally Burtons) approach fashion retailing by targeting demographic segments, differentiating between younger buyers of both sexes, and older age groups (as described in Chapter 7). This involved changing the proposition of each element in the marketing mix in a consistent way to each market segment:*

  - *Top Shop sells fashion ranges appropriate to the younger female and male clothes buyer. This age group typically likes to keep their clothes up-to-date by frequently changing what they wear. Product quality can therefore be compromised as long as prices are low enough to allow the buyer to repurchase relatively quickly. The place of purchase and promotional messages which emphasise low prices for high fashion are also consistent with the lifestyle of the youth market.*

  - *Principles target the 30 plus age group and offer fashionable clothes with a longer life expectancy. Prices are correspondingly higher, relating to the higher quality merchandise offered in a more sophisticated shopping environment with appropriate promotional communications.*

Financial strategies

Pricing possibilities are constrained by the financial structure and objectives of an organisation:

❑ The financial structure determines the cost base of the products to be priced.

❑ Financial objectives indicate targeted revenues to be achieved by products through a combination of volume and price.

The cost base of an organisation is a particularly important influence on pricing strategies. Whilst the overall level of costs compared to income determines the profitability or viability of an organisation, it is the *types* of costs within the total cost base that often determine the pricing strategies adopted. Two basic types of cost can be defined: fixed costs and variable costs.

Fixed costs

Fixed costs refer to expenses that do not vary with the level of products sold or the quantity of service provided. They are overhead costs such as rent, rates, insurance, heating, lighting and management salaries which, within limits, do not change irrespective of whether there is one customer or one thousand.

A manufacturer incurs the same costs to finance its plant and equipment whether they produce ten units per week or ten thousand. A retailer has to pay at least one person to serve in a shop even if there are no customers for long periods. A school has to pay the same to heat and maintain its buildings whether there are five or five hundred students enrolled.

As these fixed costs have to be recovered from sales or income, a crucial element in the pricing decision is the volume of production or quantity of services that can be allocated to cover these overheads, as the following two examples illustrate:

- *Two manufacturers of the same product line had identical fixed overheads of £10,000 per week. Company A estimated that their sales would average 1000 units per week, whilst Company B budgeted for 2000 units sold each week. Company A therefore allocated fixed costs of £10 per unit when calculating the cost base of a product whilst Company B worked on the basis of £5. This allowed Company B to offer substantially lower prices than Company A, or generate more profits from the same prices assuming the forecasts were met.*

- *Two secondary schools had similar fixed costs (which excluded teachers' salaries) of £200,000 per annum. School X had 1000 students on roll but School Y was less popular with 800 students and several empty classrooms. Fixed costs at School X were therefore £200 per student whilst at School Y they were 25 per cent higher at £250 per student. The education authority paid each school the same grant for educating one student irrespective of total numbers. Both schools received £2000 each year per pupil from which most costs (fixed and variable) had to be met. This meant that School X could spend £50 more on each of its students for resources such as books or more teaching hours.*

Economies of scale are said to operate when an organisation can spread its costs across more units of production, or quantities of service provided, in this way. Economies of scale mean that the largest seller in a particular market should have the lowest costs per item, providing they are at least as efficient as their competitors. This is why gaining market share is such an important objective for many producers. Taking a large share of a market can create economies which provide competitive advantages through a lower cost base. This facilitates lower prices, or it may be transferred into other advantages.

- *Company B in our example above decided to price its products at the same level as its competitor, Company A. The economies of scale provided by its higher output meant that it generated more profits than its rival. Company B reinvested some of this extra profitability in product development and promotional campaigns to give it a more permanent competitive advantage.*

- *School X in our example above was able to spend £50 per pupil more than the neighbouring School Y because of the economies of scale from its higher student numbers. The extra teaching resources that it was able to provide helped it to register better examination results and attract even more pupils as a result. School Y on the other hand found itself in a downward spiral: less pupils meant that even more of the per-student financial allocation had to be spent on fixed costs and even less on classroom resources, which in turn meant it was less able to attract students for the future.*

Variable costs

Variable costs are expenses that do change in proportion to the level of sales or the amounts of services fulfilled. They are the costs of raw materials for manufactured products, the price of stocks sold by a retailer or the materials used by a service organisation.

As activities in an organisation increase, so do the variable costs. The manufacturer has to buy more raw materials which make up finished products if sales increase; a retailer has to buy more stock as items sell; a school has to buy more books as student numbers increase.

The relationship between the variable costs and the selling price of a product is often expressed as a mark-up or a gross margin:

❑ *Mark-up* expresses how much is added to the variable costs to reach the selling price. It is often given as a percentage of the variable costs.

  • *A clothes retailer buys a garment from the manufacturer for £20 and gives it a selling price of £50. The mark-up is £30, or 150 per cent of costs. In a sale the item is reduced to £40; the mark-up is now £20, or 100 per cent of costs.*

  This can be represented by the formula:

  $$\% \text{ Mark-up} = \frac{\text{selling price} - \text{variable cost}}{\text{variable cost}} \times 100\%$$

❑ *Gross margin* is also an expression of the difference between the selling price and the variable costs of an item. However it takes the selling price as its reference point, expressing how much of the revenue from the selling price is left after deducting variable costs. It is often given in percentage terms, expressing the difference between price and cost as a percentage of price.

  • *The retailer in our previous example priced a garment for £50 that had been bought for £20, thereby aiming to achieve a gross margin of £30 or 60 per cent (of the selling price). It was sold in the sale for £40 at a gross margin of £20 or 50 per cent (of the selling price).*

  This can be represented by the formula:

  $$\% \text{ Gross margin} = \frac{\text{selling price} - \text{variable cost}}{\text{selling price}} \times 100\%$$

Mark-ups and gross margins are often used to provide guidelines in the pricing process, establishing minimum or budgeted levels.

  • *A retailer prefered to work with mark-ups because it was easier to start with the cost of an item which was always known from purchase invoices. The retailer adopted the policy of always adding at least a 100 per cent mark-up to items purchased, as this was the minimum required to cover the fixed overheads of premises and salaries on the current level of turnover.*

  • *A manufacturer budgeted for a 45 per cent gross margin on their sales as this had historically been achieved and gave a reasonable profit after fixed overheads were deducted. When pricing new products, the marketing manager knew that they had to achieve an average gross margin of at least 45 per cent.*

Flexibility in pricing

Some organisations have less pricing options than others because of financial constraints. One important influence is the mix of fixed and variable costs in the total cost base. Where most costs are fixed, there will be more chances to offer differential prices for the same product once the fixed costs are covered. If variable costs are the major cost element and represent a high percentage of prices charged, there is less room for manoeuvre and opportunities for using flexible pricing policies are limited.

- *The tourist industry illustrates extremes of flexible and inflexible cost structures. Travel agents receive a commission of approximately 10 per cent for booking holidays provided by tour operators; thus their gross margin on sales is effectively only 10 per cent. They have little flexibility in their prices to customers if they wish to cover their costs, and usually pass on the full prices charged by the tour operators.*

  Conversely, hotels have mainly fixed costs with a low percentage of variable costs; premises and staff costs remain similar irrespective of guest numbers so that the key indicator of success for a hotelier is room occupancy rate. Once fixed expenses are covered, it costs relatively little to accommodate more guests. Special prices offering large discounts can be used to attract customers during off-peak periods.

Financial objectives

As pricing has a direct impact on the financial performance of an organisation, pricing decisions are constrained by financial objectives and policies. Examples of financial objectives and their impact on pricing strategies include:

- ❑ *Short-term profits*: if a company sets ambitious targets for the profits it expects from any investment in new products, then the pricing of those products may have to be aggressively high in order to achieve the financial targets. Because of their limited resources, smaller companies often adopt short-term financial targets for new investments.

- ❑ *Longer-term profits*: some organisations are prepared to adopt longer-term financial strategies allowing products more time to develop profitability. In these circumstances, prices can be set at lower levels to maximise penetration of the marketplace and build profitability from a position of high market share. Historically, Japanese companies in the automobile and electronic markets have tended to follow this strategy.

- ❑ *Cost recovery*: successful new products often have to recover the costs of products that failed or were never launched; prices also have to take account of development costs. Pharmaceutical companies, for example, invest heavily in the research and development of new drugs, the cost of which has to be recovered from the profits of the small number of successful new products that are launched.

  - *The mobile phone industry has been over-burdened by debt because of the introduction of 'third-generation' (3G) telephones. This development offers users exiting new features such as high-speed Internet access and video clips for which the phone operators can charge higher prices. However, companies, including British Telecom, Vodafone and France Telecom, paid over £80 billion to buy the licences to operate the new network in Europe. Technical problems have delayed the introduction of 3G handsets that are effectively mini-computers. As a result, the income from the sale of the new product, which is needed to service the debts from the licences, has been delayed. This has caused financial problems and a pricing dilemma: the 3G phones can either be priced up in order to recover the high fixed costs of the new system, or priced down in order to generate cash as quickly as possible to pay off the debts.*

❑ *Survival*: in industries suffering from surplus capacity or changes in customer demand, organisations are forced to regard survival as their overriding objective. Normal financial criteria become secondary as prices are cut in an effort to stay alive until the market achieves a better balance between supply and demand.

● *Price wars often erupt when demand in a market sector turns down. Chip makers and personal computer (PC) manufacturers saw the Internet-led boom disappear during 2000/2001. As PC sales declined, they soon became caught up in a price war that is expected to reduce the number of players in the market-place. The battle was triggered when the two largest chip makers, Intel and AMD, responded to sluggish sales by repeatedly reducing prices. This in turn reduced the costs of PC manufacturing and gave the PC makers an opportunity to join the battle. Compaq became the largest PC maker when it overtook IBM in 1994, but Dell's decision to cut prices by over 20 per cent in early 2001 allowed it to become number one in terms of market share. Compaq responded with cuts of its own and, although the major companies can probably withstand the financial effects of the price war, inevitably there have been casualties as smaller companies are taken over or close down.*

❑ *Non-profit objectives*: some organisations such as charities and public services do not have the profit objectives of private sector businesses. This does not necessarily make their pricing levels lower. A charity tries to maximise the funds available for its chosen cause, and may therefore even price products it sells at a premium. If public authorities charge for any of their services they are usually required to obtain prices which fully recover all of their costs so that there is no possible hidden subsidy from public funds.

5. EXTERNAL INFLUENCES: CUSTOMERS, COMPETITION, AND THE BUSINESS ENVIRONMENT

Whilst influences internal to an organisation establish parameters for pricing decisions, the final judgement on the acceptability of a price is made in the market-place.

Customers' perceptions and demand

Customers surrender something of value (the price) in order to acquire the product or service that they are purchasing. The level of price they are prepared to pay depends on the value they place on the benefits on offer. Customer-oriented pricing decisions therefore involve an investigation into the customer's perception of the value of the benefits of a product.

In some cases the benefits which a customer obtains from purchasing a particular product can be valued directly because they reduce costs in other areas.

- *Energy saving devices can be used in connection with a variety of electrical installations such as lighting. Sellers of these devices target heavy users of electricity and sell their product on the basis of the benefit of lower energy costs. They can measure the savings to be made with some precision and therefore quote customers a sum of money they will gain in exchange for paying the price of the product. Pricing of the energy saving device is related to this valuation.*

In most cases the benefits which a customer receives are harder to value in this way. Many products offer benefits that are difficult to evaluate because they are intangible and relate to customers' perceptions of a product.

- *The purchaser of a new car buys some benefits that may have an obvious value; for example, the benefit of low running costs can be quantified in comparison to competitive vehicles. Some of the benefits perceived by a customer are intangible such as the prestige and pride derived from new car ownership. Moreover these perceptions vary from customer to customer; the status of ownership of a Jaguar perceived by one customer may be perceived as inappropriate materialism by another.*

Pricing decisions therefore involve an understanding of the motivations behind a purchase decision and how much the customer is prepared to pay for the benefits which they perceive.

Elasticity of demand

In some cases customers are prepared to pay almost any price to obtain the benefits they perceive. In other cases they are sensitive to even small price movements which can change their buying decision. The demand for a product is influenced by many factors of which price is only one. The relative importance of price compared to other factors varies according to the type of product, and the circumstances of the marketplace.

- *Letraset's rub-down lettering product was targeted at graphic artists who needed to present layouts of advertising and other artwork to clients. This customer group usually worked to very tight deadlines which demanded the production of high quality, creative artwork in a short time. The cost of the materials involved in the production of this artwork was usually a tiny proportion of the costs of the total advertising campaign under consideration. In any case the graphic artist invoiced the client, not only for their own time, but also for the costs of any materials such as instant lettering. These factors combined to put price as a low priority in the purchase motivations of the graphic artist. As the deadline for the finished job approached, availability of the required typeface for the presentation became more significant than how much it cost. The price of materials such as lettering was so small compared to labour and media costs that it was not a consideration in the final choice of advertising campaign. The graphic artist as a purchaser of Letraset's products was therefore relatively insensitive to how much a sheet of instant lettering cost and much more influenced by the range and rapid availability of typefaces.*

Letraset adopted a high price strategy which priced instant lettering at levels which bore little relationship to its production costs. The high gross margin was used to provide the benefits of wide range and fast availability which the customer valued so greatly. As the market leader offering a good quality product, Letraset was also able to use its brand name to justify prices higher than those of competitors.

Letraset was also involved in another market in which customers had a very different perception of the relative importance of price in the marketing mix. Rub-down transfers of cartoon characters were key components in a type of activity game for children which were distributed either as boxed games in toy shops or featured as special offers in breakfast cereals. These products were perceived by consumers as low in value as they were non-essential items with a very limited life and frequently given away with other products. The producers of the activity games therefore priced them at pocket money levels which put the emphasis on volume of sales rather than high margins to generate profits. Letraset offered few advantages over other manufacturers supplying this market other than a low price made possible by the economies of scale of their production facilities. The Letraset name did not command a premium price as it was less relevant to consumers in this market and rarely featured in the branding of the end product. Letraset's strategy to this market was therefore to price low, ensuring only that there was a margin on variable costs as fixed costs were assumed to be covered by other product types.

These are examples of the different *elasticity of demand* for products. Elasticity of demand measures how much the demand for a product changes with movements in price:

❑ *Inelastic demand* indicates that quantities sold are likely to change very little as prices move up or down.

  • *The demand for Letraset's graphic art products could be described as inelastic as customers were much less sensitive to price than other elements in the marketing mix.*

❑ *Elastic demand* indicates that quantities sold are likely to be significantly affected by prices changes.

  • *The demand for Letraset's children's activity products could be described as elastic as price was the most important influence in the marketing mix.*

Different circumstances make customers relatively insensitive to small price changes and therefore exhibit inelastic demand:

❑ *Products that have few competitors or substitute products*: Letraset enjoyed patent protection for its instant lettering product and there were no competitive substitutes until computer graphics developed. Lack of direct competitors is not itself sufficient to produce inelastic demand if there are substitutes. For example, railway companies often enjoy a monopoly service having no direct competition on their routes, but this does result in inelastic demand; if prices are raised more customers use substitute methods such as road transport.

❑ *Exclusive products sold for benefits of status and prestige*: a high price is part of the image of some products such as perfumes and luxury cars which are expected to be expensive.

❑ *Well branded products*: some established brands of products have a higher inelasticity because of the loyalty of existing consumers.

❑ *Expenditure on a product is a small part of total costs or income*: when one product represents a very small part of the overall costs of a project, the price of that product has less significance and demand is more likely to be inelastic. Although Letraset priced instant lettering at a high price in comparison to its own variable costs, the price to the customer still represented a very small part of their total costs; price increases did not affect the profitability of the buyer's work as much as the improved efficiencies offered.

Demand curves

The relationship between price and the number of units bought can be shown graphically as a 'demand curve'. Figure 9.2 below shows the 'normal' demand/price relationship for many products.

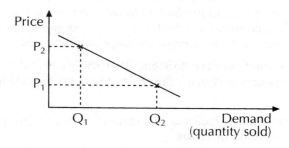

Figure 9.2: *'Normal' demand/price relationship*

In this case, there is a straight-line relationship between price and demand. The higher price (P_2) leads to the lower quantity sold (Q_1); the lower price (P_1) leads to the increased demand (Q_2). Each change in price leads to a corresponding change in demand. This may be the relationship for many non-essential products such as confectionery and magazines.

However, it is not the relationship for all products. Figure 9.3 shows the demand curve for more essential goods such as certain basic foods (e.g. bread, potatoes).

The lower price (P_1) again leads to higher demand (Q_2) and demand decreases as price levels rise. But in this case the rate of decline slows and eventually stops (Q_1) as demand reaches the minimum required for survival whatever the price (P_2 and above).

In other cases, the curve may be inverted as demand rises with price. This may be the case for certain types of luxury goods (e.g. jewellery, perfumery, and 'top-of-the range' products such as exclusive cars) where the perceived value increases at price levels which make the product a status item.

In this case, demand is smaller (Q_1) at the lower price (P_1) and then increases (Q_2) at the higher price (P_2), before declining again as further price rises put the product beyond the purchasing power of significant numbers of customers.

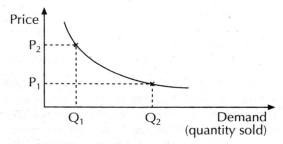

Figure 9.3: *Demand curve for essential goods*

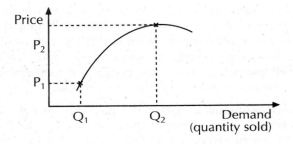

Figure 9.4: *Demand curve for some luxury goods*

It is important for organisations to understand the price/demand relationship for their products if they are to optimise their prices. In practice it is difficult to eliminate other influences on demand in order to study the effect of price changes only.

- *A retailer tried to calculate the effect on turnover of their annual sale in which they discounted a variety of goods. Although they knew that turnover had increased during the sale, they were unsure how much of this was due to lower prices and how much due to the increased advertising to promote the sale or improvements to the economic climate. Another retailer with a chain of stores was able to produce more accurate estimates of the relationship between demand and price changes as they could monitor the effect of lower prices in one store against the results in a similar store where prices were not changed.*

Market and competitive influences

The competitive structure of a market plays an important role in determining prices. Economists have classified markets into different categories according to the type and level of competition:

❑ *Perfect competition* exists when many buyers and sellers collectively determine prices at the point where supply equals demand. In this hypothetical situation, no seller has advantages over another as products are uniform and equally available. Sellers cannot therefore charge more than the going rate which buyers are prepared to pay to obtain all they need; nor do they have any incentive to charge less as they can sell all they have at these prices.

Although some markets, such as fresh fruit and vegetables and commodities trading, come close to these conditions, this type of pure competition is largely a hypothetical concept as many factors such as product differentiation and shortages or surpluses of supply distort 'pure' competition in the marketplace.

❑ *Monopolistic competition* describes the markets in which there is a range of prices for similar products because sellers differentiate what they offer and buyers are prepared to pay different prices for the perceived differences. This is the usual situation in most of our consumer markets, for example, where branded products often command a price premium over non-branded goods because of their higher perceived value.

❑ *Oligopolistic competition* exists in markets in which the high cost of entry restricts the numbers of competitors. The small number of sellers compete actively however, often following each other's pricing strategies to protect their customer base. For example, petrol companies and high street banks rapidly adjust their prices and charges to match any competitive movements which look like having an impact on customer demand.

❑ *Pure monopoly* means a market in which there is only one seller. This may develop because of government intervention (e.g. the National Lottery), or because of patent protection (the early days of ICI's Terylene and Letraset's instant lettering). Prices are not necessarily high in these circumstances: nationalised industries were subsidised in the past and now are regulated by watchdog committees even after they have been privatised; monopoly private sellers often use their advantage to penetrate the market as fully as possible with lower prices before competition develops.

The level of influence of competitive pricing therefore varies according to market conditions. For example, in oligopolistic markets of non-differentiated products, pricing is a more crucial element in the marketing mix than it is in monopolistic markets of differentiated goods and services.

However significant their influence, competitors' pricing strategies and activities form a key part of marketing intelligence. Collecting information on competitors' prices can be done formally or informally:

● *Retail audits, often carried out by specialised research agencies, collect data on the prices of a wide range of products at the point of purchase. For instance, a confectionery manufacturer may collect information on the prices of competitive chocolate bars on display in retail outlets.*

● *Firms of accountants price their service of the annual audit of a company on the basis of individual quotations. It is therefore difficult for one firm to monitor the prices of other accountants as the information is not generally made available. Instead they rely on informal information gathering methods such as talking to customers who have received quotations from other firms.*

Environmental influences

Other factors in the external environment influence prices:

❑ The state of the economy plays a part in most markets with prices weakening in recessionary times and hardening as boom times return.

❑ Taxes on goods and services such as VAT form part of the price paid by the final consumer and act as a constraint on the flexibility of suppliers' pricing strategies. A manufacturer may think again about a planned price rise following an increase in the rate of VAT on their products.

❑ Government intervention influences prices directly and indirectly. The pricing levels in some recently privatised industries such as gas, electricity and telephones are subject to direct regulatory control by watchdog agencies. Government insistence on increased competition in some markets has a more indirect but often significant impact on prices. For example, the enforced loosening of ties between public houses and breweries lead to intensified price competition between rival brewers with surplus capacity.

❑ Intermediaries in the chain between the manufacturer and the end user have varying levels of influence on prices. Some intermediaries have more power than the manufacturer to determine prices. Large retail groups such as the supermarket chains dictate prices to their suppliers. More fragmented wholesalers and retailers have only marginal influence on pricing levels.

6. PRICING STRATEGIES: SKIMMING AND PENETRATION

The internal and external influences discussed in the previous sub-sections shape pricing decisions in the context of pricing strategies. Organisations can adopt two generic types of strategy:

❑ *Skimming*: a higher price strategy to 'skim the cream' off the market.

❑ *Penetration*: a lower price strategy aimed at penetrating the market as thoroughly as possible.

Skimming

Price skimming aims to develop a market by attracting the least price sensitive segment of customers first, and satisfying their demand with high prices. If demand begins to fall or further growth is required, then prices are lowered to attract the next segment of customers who are attracted at slightly cheaper prices. This process can be repeated until all potential markets are satisfied, although competition may hasten the development of sales to new customer groups at lower prices.

● *The first personal computers developed by Apple and later IBM were targeted at business applications and pitched at prices which companies could afford. As the only comparison was with bigger, more expensive computers, there was little price resistance among larger companies who were the first to see the potential of PCs. As prices were gradually lowered, smaller businesses also became interested in the benefits versus the costs of the new equipment. In the UK, new entrants into the market such as Sinclair and Amstrad forced the pace by cutting prices so dramatically that a much wider home computer market was opened up. The development of the Internet allowed the biggest manufacturers such as Compaq and IBM to offer faster, more powerful machines at higher prices. Dell Computers decreased prices because of its lower costs through direct delivery and lower stocks through its made to order service. This in turn created new demand as more businesses and households bought upgraded equipment.*

Favourable factors for price skimming

Circumstances which favour price skimming strategies include:

❑ Products that have unique advantages (e.g. light, portable laptops still command a premium over PCs with a higher specification). High initial prices may be needed to recover the investment in research and development, and the best time to do this may be when competition is likely to be at a minimum.

❑ Mature or saturated markets that can be segmented with differentiated products or services. The travel industry is now well developed with distinct pricing strategies for different customer segments. We have already described how airlines adopted a high price strategy for business class travellers by offering a few extra luxuries (see 'Marketing strategies' above). Railway companies have also increased their revenues by charging premium prices for Inter-City and peak hour commuter travel.

❑ Suppliers with limited resources who wish to maximise revenues from the capacity they have. This might apply particularly to smaller organisations.

- *A small company built up a reputation as a high quality printer specialising in relatively short run jobs such as company reports which commanded premium prices. They maintained a high price strategy by avoiding the temptation of taking on lower margin work which would keep their presses more fully occupied but detract from the fast, flexible service which they could offer to the higher price segment of the market.*

Skimming strategies have a number of potential advantages and disadvantages which are summarised in Figure 9.5.

Penetration

Pricing to achieve market penetration means keeping prices as low as possible to achieve the highest potential level of sales. This may be achieved by taking market share from competitors, or growing the total market rapidly, or a combination of both.

New products

Some new products need to develop rapidly into their marketplace to consolidate their position before competitive products arrive and to achieve economies of scale through larger production volumes. To achieve this a low price strategy may be chosen.

- *An electronics manufacturer designed an innovative fuel injection system for*

Advantages	Disadvantages
✔ Fast payback of investment in new products, research and development etc.	✖ Encourages new entrants into the market.
✔ High profits while less competition.	✖ May produce diseconomies of scale as volumes kept low.
✔ Prices can be gradually reduced.	✖ May limit sales potential.
✔ Less investment and resources required, as output limited.	
✔ Positive image and status associated with high prices.	

Figure 9.5: *Potential advantages and disadvantages of skimming strategies*

cars. Although the product had important new benefits, the company priced the product in line with existing systems on the market in order that the major car manufacturers could specify the new product into their existing production of vehicles without increasing their cost base. In this way the company was able to penetrate the market quickly, rather than wait for their product to be specified into new models as they were launched. This rapid build up of demand overcame the problem of a reduced initial profit margin as it gave them two important advantages. First, they achieved a high market share which protected their position when competitors caught up with their technology as their product was already designed into existing models. Secondly, the high production volumes created economies of scale which eventually improved their profitability.

Existing products

Penetration pricing may be used also as a strategy to improve the competitive position of existing products.

* *Tabloid newspapers declined in popularity in the 1980s and early 1990s. In July 1993 one of the market leaders, the Sun, decided to cut its cover price from 25p to 20p in an attempt to win back lost readers. The strategy had two aims: to improve circulation figures for the total market and to gain market share from the other tabloids. Sales of tabloid newspapers had fallen from a peak of 12.6 million per day in 1983 to 10.6 million by 1993. Rupert Murdoch, chairman of News International which owned the Sun, believed that the decline was partly in reaction to the cover price of papers which had increased by an average of 11 per cent a year since 1983. The industry had believed hitherto*

233

that sales of newspapers were price inelastic and regularly increased prices above the rate of inflation. However, Murdoch had watched the daily sales of the Sun decline from 4.3 million in 1989 to less than 3.5 million by 1993, and felt that the market had become price sensitive. The 20 per cent price decrease was designed to tempt back some of those who had stopped buying papers on a regular basis as well as take circulation from competitors particularly its close rival, the Daily Mirror. The Mirror responded by taking its own price down from 27p to 10p for a day as a one-off promotion. Murdoch at least proved that newspaper sales are price sensitive: the Sun gained daily sales of 200,000 in the first week at its lower price, and the Mirror sold an extra 500,000 copies on its special-price day.

Favourable factors for price penetration

Circumstances which favour market penetration pricing strategies include:

❑ Markets in which demand is price elastic. There is no point in offering lower prices if demand is unaffected (which was the collective wisdom of the newspaper industry before Murdoch changed its pricing strategy.

❑ Industries which offer economies of scale to the largest producers or suppliers. The large retail chains and supermarkets look for this benefit when offering low prices as they know that they can replace lost margin by spreading their fixed costs over higher volumes of sales.

❑ The launch of new products where rapid adoption and awareness is a key marketing goal. This may apply, for example, to products expected to enjoy a market advantage for a limited period only.

   • *Pricing strategies on the Internet have generally followed penetration strategies for this reason. Internet Service Providers (ISPs), such as AOL, Compuserve, BT Internet, Virgin Net, and NTL, needed to attract a critical mass of users as quickly as possible. At first, providers such as AOL offered unique on-line services via the Internet for which they could charge a monthly subscription. However, the Internet now offers far more than single providers can hope to match. Free Internet access has become the norm, as the ISPs compete for market share and take revenues instead from the telephone companies who make the connection. Market share has become so prized that providers have offered reduced price and even free phone connections.*

❑ In markets dominated by a small number of major suppliers (oligopolies). Price wars are often the trigger to the elimination of weaker suppliers with subsequent gain in market share by the survivors. *Today*, a loss-making title amongst the tabloid press, was a casualty of the newspaper price war when it closed in 1995.

The potential advantages and disadvantages of penetration pricing strategies are summarised in Figure 9.6.

Advantages	Disadvantages
✔ Fast sales growth.	✖ Reduces profit in short term.
✔ Wide product awareness.	✖ May be difficult to put prices up.
✔ Build strong market position.	✖ More investment and resources required to build high volumes.
✔ Economies of scale through higher volumes.	
✔ Deters new entrants into the market.	

Figure 9.6: *Potential advantages and disadvantages of penetration strategies*

7. PRICING METHODS

In this chapter we have so far considered the main internal and external influences on pricing decisions and the generic strategies that can be followed. But how are pricing decisions made in practice? There are a number of methods and techniques that can be used to help determine the optimum price to offer the customer. These are sometimes categorised as the 3Cs:

❑ cost-based pricing;

❑ competition-based pricing; and

❑ customer-based pricing.

Cost-based pricing

Cost-based pricing methods take the costs to produce and supply a product or service as the starting point and add what is considered to be an adequate element of profit, or contribution to revenues, to arrive at the final price. Although cost-based pricing methods have disadvantages, most organisations do take costs into account in setting prices. Even when prices are not calculated directly from them, costs remain a significant influence.

Cost-plus pricing

Cost-plus pricing is a simple and very common way of pricing items. A standard percentage mark-up is added to the variable costs of an item. The standard amount added is calculated in such a way as to cover fixed costs and produce some profit.

The advantages of adopting a cost-plus formula include:

❑ It is simple to understand and operate, providing that costs can be calculated accurately.

❑ It ensures that costs are at least covered, providing sales volume targets are met.

However, there are several limitations to this method, including:

❑ It does not take account of competitive pricing or what the customer is prepared to pay.

❑ It is often difficult to allocate costs to specific products, particularly when costs vary with volume or they are shared with other products.

❑ It can ignore capital requirements or return on investment criteria.

This method is widely used in retailing where variable costs can be easily identified. Customer preferences and competitive activity can be taken into account by using the system flexibly.

● *A jeans boutique has a standard pricing policy of adding a mark-up of 200 per cent to the cost of garments purchased from the manufacturer. Thus a pair of jeans invoiced at £15 from the manufacturer is sold for £45 to the consumer. The mark-up is £30, or 200 per cent of the cost of the garment to the retailer. Experience has taught this retailer that such a mark-up is needed to cover the fixed costs of running the shop, such as rent, rates and staff wages, and to provide a reasonable profit. Although the 200 per cent mark-up is the rule for normal trading, sales and special offers are used throughout the year to stimulate sales and counter competitive activities. The annual trading accounts of the shop can be analysed therefore as follows:*

	£s
● *Total sales at full prices*	*150,000*
● *Discounts*	*25,000*
● *Costs of garments sold*	*50,000*
● *Gross profit*	*75,000*
● *Fixed costs*	*50,000*
● *Profit contribution*	*25,000*

This indicates that the standard cost-plus policy provides a benchmark to arrive at the full retail selling price. This is then adapted to market conditions by offering discounts from the full price.

Gross margin pricing

A variation on the cost-plus method is to use a standard gross margin rather than a mark-up as a means of arriving at the final selling price. (If you are unsure of the difference between gross margin and mark-up, review section 4, 'Financial strategies'.)

● *Sci-Scope, a manufacturer of scientific instruments, priced its products to give an overall target of a 50 per cent gross margin on its sales. The marketing manager worked within pricing guidelines which required at least a 50 per cent gross margin after taking account the variable costs. Thus if a selling price of £30 was required, the normal gross margin would be at least £15, or 50 per cent of the selling price, leaving £15 to cover the costs of parts and labour.*

This system was used flexibly, the gross margin calculation being used to provide a baseline from which to assess other pricing options.

Break-even analysis

One of the problems in the cost-plus methods we have described above is that prices do not reflect changes in the volume of items sold. A break-even analysis helps to add this further dimension as it is a method of exploring the relationship between costs, prices and volumes.

The first step is an analysis of fixed and variable costs.

- *Sci-Scope were launching a new optical instrument. Fixed costs of £500,000 per annum were apportioned to this new product. Variable costs were £25 per unit, or £25,000 per thousand units. From this information the total costs per unit at various volumes could be calculated:*

  If 10,000 units were produced, the costs equalled:

Fixed costs	£500,000
Variable costs	£250,000
Total costs	£750,000
Total costs per unit	£75

  If 20,000 units were produced, the costs equalled:

Fixed costs	£500,000
Variable costs	£500,000
Total costs	£1,000,000
Total costs per unit	£50

This can be illustrated graphically as shown in Figure 9.7.

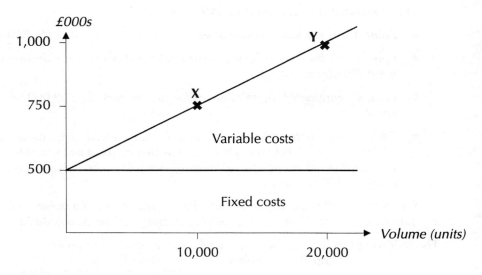

Figure 9.7: *Fixed and variable costs*

- *Point X = total costs to produce 10,000 units.*
- *Point Y = total costs to produce 20,000 units.*

The next step in a break-even analysis is to calculate the sales revenue obtained from certain prices at varying sales levels.

- *Sci-Scope wished to consider the price/volume relationship at a price of £50 per unit. This indicated that at 20,000 units revenues equalled the total costs of £1,000,000 and that at 30,000 units sales reached £1,500,000 – the targeted revenue for the product. A sales revenue line could now be added to the graph to show the break-even point, and levels of profitability at various volumes (Figure 9.8).*

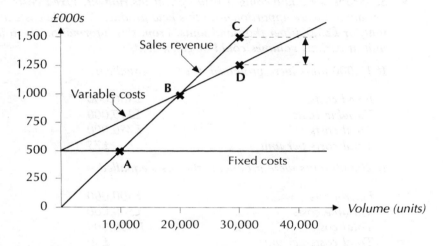

Figure 9.8: *Break-even analysis*

This illustrated that at a price of £50 per unit:

- *Point A was the sales volume at which fixed costs were met (10,000 units).*

- *Point B was the sales volume at which total costs were met – the break-even point (20,000 units).*

- *Point C represented the sales target for the product (£1,500,000 or 30,000 units).*

- *The distance between points C and D represented the profitability at 30,000 units (£250,000 net profit after deducting fixed and variable costs or £750,000 gross profit after deducting variable costs only, a gross profit margin of 50 per cent).*

Sci-Scope used this technique to study the financial effect of a number of pricing options before deciding on their pricing strategy for the new product.

The following formula can be used to calculate a break-even point:

$$\text{Break-even volume} = \frac{\text{Fixed costs}}{\text{Gross margin per unit}}$$

Marginal costing

The break-even analysis described above ensures that both fixed and variable costs are covered by the price of a product. In some circumstances, it may be necessary to ignore fixed costs and price products on their variable costs only. A contribution can be made towards profits, providing there is a margin between the selling price and the variable costs and assuming fixed costs are covered by other sales.

- *Sci-Scope's sales of its new optical instrument achieved their target of 30,000 units ahead of schedule through its normal distribution channels. Noting the success of the new product, a major distributor asked Sci-Scope to produce a very similar product for them, but under their own brand name. As the distributor had to make their own profit margin on the product, they asked for a maximum price of £35, compared to Sci-Scope's normal selling price of £50, in return for large orders. A selling price of £35 left Sci-Scope with a gross margin of £10 on their variable costs, or 28.6 per cent – well below their target margin of 50 per cent.*

  However, the marketing and finance managers advised the company to accept the deal on the basis of marginal costing. The fixed costs were already covered by normal sales of the product and this contract would generate a contribution to profits of £10 per unit which they would forgo if they did not take the business.

Time and materials

In the public sector and increasingly in the private sector, organisations are offering services for which the most important cost ingredient is the time spent by people in fulfilling the service. In the education and health care services up to 80 per cent of total costs can be the salaries and wages of staff. The pricing of professional services, such as solicitors and accountants, is dominated by the costs of the time of staff allocated to jobs. In these circumstances, pricing is normally calculated by charging hourly rates for the staff involved plus the cost of any materials spent on the job.

- *Garages normally price car repairs on the basis of time spent on the work multiplied by an hourly rate plus the cost of any parts used. The hourly rate is calculated to cover not just the costs of the mechanic but also to make a contribution to the fixed costs and profits of the garage.*

  Many other services from physiotherapy to plumbing are charged on the same basis.

Customer-based pricing

Consumers rarely judge the price of a product by attempting to work out what it may have cost to make. We tend to assess prices on the basis of what products are worth to us. We have a perception of the value to us of the benefits of a product, and we compare its actual price to this perceived value.

Customer-based pricing uses this notion of perceived value as the starting point and attempts to set prices on the basis of what the market is prepared to pay. This may be more influenced by either the circumstances under which the product is sold, or the particular environment in which it is offered, rather than a generalised idea of the value of the product itself.

Product shortages or restrictions on supply may create circumstances in which demand exceeds supply if only on a temporary basis and suppliers increase prices to a level at which available stock can be sold.

- *The Morgan car company produce their specialised cars at a rate well below market demand. The length of time between placing an order for one of their new, hand-built cars and taking delivery extends at times to several years. This tempts some buyers to sell their newly delivered cars at a quick profit to someone lower down the waiting list who is prepared to pay more for an earlier delivery. The family-owned Morgan company was criticised by John Harvey-Jones in one of his 'Troubleshooter' television programmes for not raising its prices to reflect the perceived value of customers rather than their own costs, nor automating its production to meet the higher levels of demand. But the company prefers its traditional methods to more commercial practices.*

In other situations, the environment in which a product is sold add to, or detract from, its perceived value.

- *The price of a cup of tea varies considerably. A tea bag in a plastic cup from a vending machine may cost 50p. The same product sold in a railway station cafe may be priced at 70p, or £1 if it is purchased from the buffet car on the train. In a family teashop, a pot of tea normally costs over £1. In an up-market restaurant, the same product could be priced well over £2. Why the differences? Variables other than price establish perceived value differences to the consumer. These may be product quality perceptions (e.g. the difference between a tea bag in a plastic cup, and a silver teapot and china crockery), or they may be related to the environment in which the tea is consumed (standing on a railway platform or sitting in a comfortable restaurant).*

Customer-based pricing relies on finding out how much customers are prepared to pay for the product or service on offer. Although market research can help to understand the value in a customer's mind of various products, in practice it is often experimentation which is used to align prices with what customers are prepared to pay.

Psychological pricing

Psychological factors are often used in advertising prices to customers. These include:

- ❑ *Price break-points*: some prices points form important pyschological barriers which suppliers try not to break. £9.99 or £9.95 is a much more common price than £10, or £10.05p.

- ❑ *Discounts*: many customers place great importance on receiving a discount on the original price of a product. Some suppliers pitch their initial pricing high in the knowledge that they can enhance the perceived value of their offer by bringing prices down at a later date.

- ❑ *Loss-leaders*: pricing can be used as a promotional tool to gain customers by offering them low prices for one product on which little or no profit is gained in the hope that they will buy other products. For example, direct mail companies use this technique in offering 'continuity programmes' of reference publications and other products in which the first instalment is priced at a fraction of the price of subsequent instalments. Retailers use the same ploy to tempt customers into their premises.

Competition-based pricing

Costs may fix the minimum price for a product, and customer demand may reflect the maximum price that can be charged, but competitive pricing acts as a third influence, that often sets prices somewhere between these two extremes.

Direct competition between a limited number of suppliers often results in the most aggressive use of pricing as a marketing tool. We have already described two industries in which the leading suppliers competed directly on price: the tabloid newspapers who tried to win over customers by reducing their cover prices, and the major PC manufacturers attempting to cope with a downturn in the personal computing market. In both cases a small number of major suppliers tried to gain a larger share of a market by reducing their prices.

Price competion may also be indirect. Customers may select among products which are not the same, but which offer similar benefits.

- *Cinemas used to compete directly with similar establishments in the same town. Except for larger towns and cities, it is now rare for more than one cinema to exist within a convenient geographic area. Far from representing a cosy local monopoly, cinemas fight for their customers with a host of other forms of entertainment and price is a major determinant of demand. Video hire is a form of direct competition which costs less than cinemas, but is less immediate in offering the latest films. Theatres tend to be more expensive, but offer live entertainment. There are also a whole host of alternative ways of spending money on leisure and entertainment from eating-out to concerts. In selecting their choice of entertainment, customers consider the value to be gained from the various options, even though they are in some respects dissimilar.*

8. KEY POINTS

- ❑ Pricing is a key ingredient in the marketing mix of private and public sector organisations and one that has a direct financial effect.

- ❑ The Internet has increased the potential to lower prices through improved communications between willing buyers and sellers. Consumers can benefit through the development of individual bargaining (e.g. through auctions), and organisations through virtual marketplaces and reverse auctions.

- ❑ Prices are derived from a mixture of internal and external influences.

- ❑ *Internal influences* include:

- ❑ targeting, positioning and marketing mix strategies;

- ❑ the cost base of fixed and variable costs; and

- ❑ the financial objectives of the organisation.

- ❑ *External influences* include:

  - ❑ customers' perceptions of the value of a product and elasticity of demand;

  - ❑ the competitiveness of the marketplace (defined by economists as perfect, monopolistic and oligopolistic competition, and pure monopoly); and

  - ❑ environmental factors such as the economy, taxes, government intervention and the power of intermediaries.

- ❑ The two generic pricing strategies are:

  - ❑ *skimming*, which has the possible advantages of fast payback, high profits, possibility of price reductions, less investment, an up-market image, and the disadvantages of encouraging new entrants, diseconomies of scale, and limitations on sales volume potential; and

  - ❑ *penetration*, which has the possible advantages of fast sales growth, wide product awareness, strong market position, economies of scale, deterring new entrants, and the disadvantages of reduced profits, difficulty in increasing prices, and more investment required.

- ❑ Pricing methods include:

  - ❑ cost-based pricing (using break-even analysis);

  - ❑ competition-based pricing; and

  - ❑ customer-based pricing.

9. | DEVELOPING MARKETING SKILLS

Exercises

1. Think of a purchase that you make regularly (e.g. confectionery, books) and a significant purchase you have made recently (e.g. clothes, computer equipment). What role did price play in your purchase decision in both cases and how did you evaluate it? What lessons might suppliers draw from your experiences?

2. You have just taken over a pizza restaurant and need to price your menu. How would you go about this? Suggest some prices for menu items with your reasons.

3. Investigate the different prices charged in your local area for essentially the same product (e.g. a pair of jeans, a pizza, a cup of tea, or a drink of coke). What is the range of prices and what justifications can you give for this?

Developing a marketing plan

Activity 9 Pricing strategy

Define your pricing strategy taking into account the appropriate internal and external influences. Will you use a skimming or penetration strategy?

- ❑ How will you price your product(s)?
- ❑ What methods will you use?
- ❑ What will be your recommended prices?
- ❑ What is your break-even point?

FURTHER READING AND REFERENCES

General texts

Dibb, S., Simkin, L., Pride, W.M. and Ferrell O.C. (2001) *Marketing Concepts and Strategies*, Houghton Mufflin, chapters 18 and 19.

Mudie, P. (1997) *Marketing: an Analytical Perspective*, Prentice Hall, chapter 5.

Pricing strategy

Blois, K.J. (1994) Discounts in business marketing management, *Industrial Marketing Management*, **23**, page 94.

Nagle, T. and Holden R. (1995) *The Strategy and Tactics of Pricing*, Prentice Hall.

Internet pricing

Chaffey, D., Mayer, R., Johnston, K. and Ellis-Chadwick, F. (2000) *Internet Marketing*, Pearson Education, chapters 11 and 14.

Chaston, I. (2001) *E-Marketing Strategy*, McGraw Hill, chapter 9.

Kennedy, A.J. (2000) *The Rough Guide to the Internet*, Rough Guides Ltd.

Wheatley, M. (2000) Supplies on de-mand, *Supply Management*, **21** (September), pages 11–12.

CHAPTER 10

Promotions I: Marketing, Communications and Selling

The promotional element in the marketing mix can be further sub-divided into personal selling, advertising, sales promotion and public relations. This chapter looks at selling, and Chapter 11 considers advertising, sales promotion and public relations. All of these types of promotions form 'marketing communications' and first we evaluate a general model of how these work, and the use of the Internet for such communications.

1. CASE STUDY: INSURING THE MESSAGE

For once Philip Creed sat down in front of his television specifically to watch the adverts. Normally he would 'zap' the commercial breaks with his automatic control, but tonight was different. His company, one of the largest sellers of insurance and pensions in the UK, was screening its first advertisement for several years. As sales director, Creed had a particular interest in watching this opening instalment of a campaign which would include £10 million of media advertising, supported by mailings of special offers, new-look leaflets, press releases and sponsorship deals. All would feature a common, consistent theme, as research had revealed confused and contradictory customer perceptions of the company and its products.

Positive marketing communications were much needed after a run of bad publicity for both Creed's company and the insurance industry as a whole. Accusations of sharp practice by insurance salespeople had culminated in allegations that the regulatory standards had been consistently breached in the selling of personal pensions to people transferring out of occupational pensions. The decision to set up a single personal investment authority to regulate the whole industry had helped overcome some of their image problems. Creed hoped that the government's stakeholder pension scheme would restore confidence further. Selling insurance was hard enough without adverse publicity. Customers were now receiving sales approaches from their banks and building societies to add to their weariness of the 'hard sell' from conventional insurance companies. Direct selling of policies by telephone or over the Internet was also threatening the tradition role of the salesperson offering face-to-face information on pensions and insurance.

Creed had organised a conference to launch the new campaign to his salesforce. He was particularly concerned to ensure his salespeople reinforced rather than undermined the themes of the campaign, especially after the expressions of public unease over standards in the insurance industry. The very size of his company made this a daunting task: over £10 billion funds under management, over 1 million customers and a 3000 strong, direct sales force. Each one of those salespeople had their own way of communicating with clients that could mean very fragmented messages about the company. The conference would attempt to unify their overall communications without stifling individual styles. As well as suggesting answers to some of the more common objections arising from the bad publicity, Creed would be insisting on a more consultative sales approach by his salesforce.

Although he did not wish to encourage salespeople to learn scripted presentations, he had decided to give his version of a sales presentation of one of their products. He had chosen their new 'Personal Property Protection Policy' insurance scheme to demonstrate the image they wished to convey. The policy was designed to provide insurance for the loss of any personal possessions inside or outside of the home, and included a scheme for protecting credit cards and cheque-books against false use after loss. A special feature was the databank of customer's possessions, credit and bank card numbers, passport and other important details so that the relevant authorities could be notified immediately from one central point in the event of loss. In his presentation, Creed would try to present the benefits of the product in a way that would generate attention, interest and desire for the policy so that a prospective customer would action its purchase willingly – without being pushed.

'I wish I could reach millions of homes with a consistent communication like that', Creed thought as he watched the advert, 'but I have 4000 different voices speaking to customers and delivering the appropriate message every time is not going to be easy.'

Points to consider

1. Consider the marketing communications process in the insurance market. How do prospective customers receive information and other messages about the policies available? Why is Creed so concerned to develop a consistent message?

See sections 2 and 3.

2. Creed's company is using several different types of promotional methods in its campaign. What are these? What will be the different objectives of each type?

See section 4.

3. The image and professionalism of selling are subject to widespread concern in this marketplace. How would you advise Creed to develop a more professional approach amongst his own salesforce?

See section 5.

4. How would you structure the sales presentation on the 'Personal Property Protection Policy' that Creed will make? Write out what you consider to be the basis of a sales presentation for this product to a prospective customer.

See section 6.

2. THE DAILY BOMBARDMENT

For most of our waking hours, we are subject to an almost constant bombardment of marketing communications. How many different types of promotional activities can you recognise in this everyday example?

- *As you sit down to breakfast, your attention is drawn briefly to the free offers and nutritional information on the packets of cereal brands before you on the table. In the background, a radio jingle repeats the sponsor's message before an announcer reminds you of forthcoming programmes. You open the newspaper, scanning reports of the election campaigns of the political parties, before turning to the sports news and Tiger Woods's latest golfing victory. Checking emails on your mobile phone, you are irritated by a company that has 'spammed' you with an unsolicited offer. You make a note in your diary that boasts the name of a pharmaceutical's company on the front cover, writing with a pen embossed with the sponsor's name. As you prepare to go out, even the label of your coat discreetly reminds you of its maker. You leave the daily delivery of mail shots on the floor, to be opened or thrown away later.*

  Your journey takes you past rows of shop windows inducing you to buy the merchandise inside, and even the refuse bins in the street carry notices reminding you of the activities of the local council. You walk into the station past poster hoardings recommending something so subtly that you only guess what it is by the government health warning. Avoiding the attention of a salesperson offering you a leaflet from a mobile exhibition stand, you are advised on the cheapest train ticket for your journey by a sales assistant whilst another employee of the railway company explains changes to departure times over the public address system. As you wait for your train, a friend chats to you about how long they have waited to see the consultant at the local hospital, the problems with their new car, and a film which they recommend you to see. Your day has hardly begun and already you have been inundated with a profusion of marketing communications! (Sixteen different types in fact, as categorised in Figure 10.3.)

It has been said that advertising has filled in 'all the cracks of people's lives' so that we can no longer escape from this daily encroachment. Certainly promotions have infiltrated into every aspect of our lives. Hospitality tents and sponsors' logos have invaded even the most traditional of sporting events. Public toilets are now seen as appropriate places in which to advertise, and telephone and Internet selling penetrates the privacy of home life. Branded products are not only promoted overtly but are seen more subtly as props in films and television programmes.

This promotional saturation has lead to two conflicting concerns:

❑ *Social concern* that advertising is ruining the environment whilst it brainwashes us into buying what we do not need and cannot afford. The Advertising Standards Authority, the regulatory body in the UK, does have powers to prevent misleading or unfair advertising but they cannot limit its extent.

❑ *Marketing concern* that the competition for consumers' attention has become so intense that extreme measures are required in order to be noticed. One study indicated that a typical consumer was exposed to 550 advertisements in one day and yet paid attention to less than one per cent of them. Some advertisers are using more sensational advertising to get their message heard.

- *Benetton, the retailer of colourful fashion clothes, achieved some notoriety and considerable publicity for their series of controversial posters depicting graphic scenes such as a new born baby and oiled seabirds which have no obvious connection to Benetton's products. Entrepreneurs such as Richard Branson and Anita Roddick who have a natural flair for publicity have become even greater assets to their companies as the competition for air space has intensified. Some companies still overdo it: for example, the Advertising Standards Authority upheld complaints against a poster campaign for International Distillers and Vintner's 'Cockspur Golden Rum'. The headline ran: 'She can take my jeans, she can take all the duvet, but she can't take my Cockspur'. The complaint was on the grounds that it emphasised the strength of the drink in the deliberately ambiguous final clause.*

Marketing communications have become such an integral part of everyday life in our society that they are often inseparable from other types of communication and they work in a similar way.

3. MARKETING COMMUNICATIONS: THE PROCESS AND OBJECTIVES

A communications model

Marketing communications flow from an organisation to its customers, potential customers and other groups who may influence its success. They involve many types of communications: some deliberate (e.g. advertising), others unplanned (personal recommendations). The communications may be supportive (personal selling) or critical (adverse press comments). In total, these communications form an overall impression, or image, which determines how people think about an organisation and how they may act in relation to its products.

Whatever their origin and effects, marketing communications work like any other forms of communication: they are concerned with *who said what, in which way, to whom, and with what effect.*

This process can be represented as a model with a number of components as illustrated in Figure 10.1. This shows how any message might be transmitted – whether it is a message in a bottle from a shipwrecked sailor, a mail shot from a charity or a sales presentation by a manufacturer.

The stages and participants in the communications process can be categorised as follows:

❑ The *Sender* (who?) – the person or organisation sending the message. For example:

    ❑ a shipwrecked sailor;

    ❑ a national charity; or

    ❑ a manufacturer of office equipment.

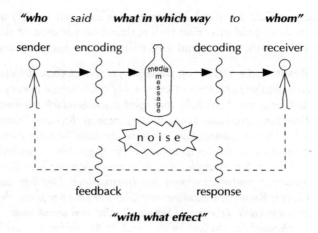

Figure 10.1: *The communications process*

❑ *Encoding* is the process of putting abstract ideas into a form that can be understood by others – the process of putting thoughts into words or pictures.

  ❑ The shipwrecked sailor writes a message on a piece of paper asking for help.

  ❑ An agency working for the national charity puts together a mail shot asking for donations to a specific cause.

  ❑ A sales representative of the office equipment company prepares a presentation to a prospective customer.

❑ The *Message* (what?) – the written or spoken words, pictures and other symbols that are actually transmitted.

  ❑ The sailor keeps it simple and writes 'Help!' with an indicator of position.

  ❑ The charity uses its well-known name to authenticate the written message that is reinforced with photographs of those in need.

  ❑ The salesperson gives a verbal presentation supported by visual aids and a demonstration of the product itself.

❑ The *Media* (in which way?) – the channels of communication that are used to take the message from the sender to the receiver.

  ❑ The sailor uses the traditional bottle thrown in the sea.

  ❑ The charity employs direct mail – a letter and leaflet sent through the post.

  ❑ The salesperson delivers the message in person and leaves a written report and quotation to reinforce the verbal message.

❑ *Decoding* is the process by which the receiver interprets the message encoded by the sender.

  ❑ Someone spots the bottle, takes out the paper and reads it.

❑ The direct mail shot is opened, the name of the charity recognised and the letter read.

❑ The presentation is watched by committee members who also consider the written report and quotation.

❑ The *Receiver* (to whom?) – the person or group of people who receive the message.

❑ A passer-by who finds the bottle.

❑ A supporter who is on the charity's mailing list.

❑ The committee with responsibility for a particular office equipment purchase.

❑ *Response* represents the attitudes and actions of the receiver in answer to the message.

❑ The passer-by cannot decipher the message in the bottle and throws it back in the sea.

❑ The charity supporter is sympathetic and makes a mental note to make a donation.

❑ The committee defers their decision because they find they have spent their allocated budget for the year.

❑ *Feedback* is that part of the response which is received back by the sender of the message.

❑ The sailor waits in vain for a response.

❑ The charity receives a returned coupon and donation from the supporter.

❑ The salesperson hears that the committee has postponed making a purchase until next year.

❑ '*Noise*' can interfere with the message that is being sent, and distort or block out the original communication.

❑ Water leaked into the bottle and made the message illegible.

❑ The supporter received many requests for donations from a variety of charities and ignored all but a few of their requests.

❑ The sales presentation was interrupted by an urgent phone call to one of the audience, whilst other committee members were distracted by their own preoccupations.

The objectives of marketing communications

Communication processes such as these seek to establish a common understanding between the sender and receiver. The term 'communication' derives its meaning from making ideas 'common'. Information is transferred between the parties with the objective of establishing a 'commonness of thought' between them. Some communications take this a stage further by trying to establish not only understanding but also response from the receiver: the sailor wanted not just an awareness of his or her predicament but some rescue action. Similarly, marketing communications provide a stimulus aimed at inducing a desired response: in the examples above, the charity's objective was to obtain donations and the salesperson was seeking an order.

Not all communications can go this far. Although the ultimate objective of a marketing communications process is to induce a purchase (or its equivalent, such as a donation), some advertising, or sales calls, have more limited initial objectives. It may take several types of communication to achieve a sale. In our example, the charity may have used marketing communications in the form of information to the press to create a favourable reception for the mail shot by heightening public awareness of the need for their work. The salesperson had to make the appointment for the sales presentation by letters, phone calls and other communications. Even impulse purchases, such as buying a bar of chocolate at the checkout point of a supermarket, are pre-conditioned by advertising which creates recognition of a brand.

Marketing communications have a wide range of objectives.

❑ In *consumer* markets, the objectives of marketing communications may be to:

   ❑ introduce a new product (such as the launch of a new brand of cereal or the opening of a new retail outlet);

   ❑ remind customers of the product's existence (by in-store displays for products or street signage for shops, for example);

   ❑ encourage repeat purchases (by offering points towards gifts and other 'loyalty' promotions);

   ❑ give information about special offers (such as three for the price of two, or free credit deals);

   ❑ correct misunderstandings and problems (explaining the withdrawal of products and actions taken to replace defective goods, for example);

   ❑ improve a company or product image (by corporate or brand name advertising);

   ❑ educate customers (for example, 'social' advertising about drinking and driving); or

   ❑ give information and advice (as given by shop assistants or product leaflets).

❑ In *organisational* markets, the objectives of marketing communications may be to:

   ❑ obtain the name of the decision-maker (often by 'cold' canvassing);

   ❑ make an appointment with the decision-maker (by personalised letters, email and other approaches);

   ❑ arrange a sales presentation (usually through telephone calls or personal visits); or

   ❑ provide follow-up information and advice (for example, a detailed quotation or after-sales service).

Communication stages

The choice of tasks which marketing communications seek to fulfil depends on what stage the customer has reached in their decision-making process towards a purchase. In some cases, customers have made up their minds about what they want and only need further details from a sales assistant to complete the purchase. In other circumstances, the consumer is not even aware of the existence of a particular product, let alone of their need for it, until they see an advertisement which arouses their interest.

In Chapter 5 (section 4, 'Models of decision processes') we listed the five stages of a consumer buying process as:

- ❑ need recognition;
- ❑ information search;
- ❑ evaluation of alternatives;
- ❑ purchase choice; and
- ❑ post-purchase experience.

During this process of making buying decisions, customers adopt various attitudes, or are in various states of mind, in relation to products on offer. It is the job of marketing communications to influence these attitudes or states of mind so that the customer completes the process in favour of a particular product. As this state of mind changes through the buying stages, so the nature and objectives of marketing communications change to match.

The AIDA model

Various models of the stages of the communications process have been advanced to illustrate these changing objectives as the consumer progresses from a position of unawareness of a product to one of willingness to purchase it. The simplest of these is the **AIDA** model, in which marketing communications seek:

- ❑ first, to gain **Attention** (an awareness of the benefits of a product);
- ❑ second, to create **Interest** (by an understanding of those benefits in relation to a personal need);
- ❑ third, to arouse **Desire** (when the benefits are wanted to fulfil a need); and
- ❑ finally, to obtain **Action** (by arranging for the customer to acquire the product).

Figure 10.2 illustrates these stages along with some possible barriers to effective communications.

The AIDA model can be illustrated by the three examples we have already used:

- ❑ The message in the bottle gained attention from someone who was unaware of the sailor's need. Although this lead to interest as the bottle was opened, the communication process did not go any further as there was lack of common understanding between sender and receiver.

- ❑ The mail shot obtained attention when it arrived and created interest when it was read by developing awareness of a problem and an understanding of how it

251

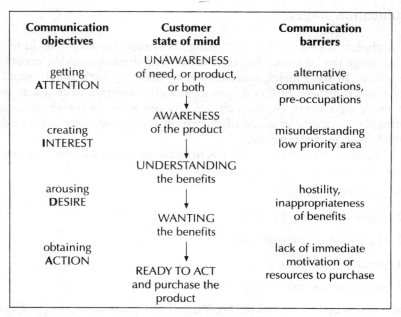

Figure 10.2: *The AIDA model of communication stages*

could be tackled. This induced a desire to help which was finally translated into the action of making a donation. A number of obstacles were overcome in this process including indifference to the cause and inertia to do anything even when the benefits of acting had been accepted.

❑ The salesperson's communication process stalled at the last stage of translating desire into action. Although the communications convinced the committee of the need and the desirability of the benefits on offer, they could not overcome the lack of resources to make the sale at that time.

More elaborate models have been suggested to describe how marketing communications work. These include the five-step adoption model of *awareness, interest, evaluation, trial* and *adoption* used particularly in new product marketing. The common theme is that marketing communications need to be staged to match the progression of the buyer through their decision-making process.

The flow of marketing communications

So far, the communications model presented has assumed direct contact between the sender, or source, of the marketing communication and the intended receiver, or audience. In practice, the process is more complicated as intermediaries often interpret marketing messages for others. The influence of 'opinion leaders' whose views we respect, and 'word-of-mouth' communications that we believe to be impartial, are particularly important.

❑ *Opinion leaders* and their effects were recorded by researchers who carried out a famous study during the 1940 presidential elections in the USA which investigated the influence of the mass media on voting intentions. They discovered that messages about the candidates did not always travel directly from the media to the voter but often went via an intermediary or 'opinion leader' who filtered and interpreted messages and influenced others for or against the candidates. Although the existence of opinion leaders has been confirmed by other research, they have proven very difficult to identify as a group that can itself be targeted by marketing communications.

Opinion leaders are those that others turn to for opinion and advice. They owe their influence to:

❏ *Who they are*. They may personify certain values which are looked up to by others (e.g. social and family values).

❏ *What they know*. They may have knowledge in certain areas, which is highly regarded by others who see it as more impartial than other expert advice.

❏ *Who they know*. They may need extensive personal networks to obtain information and to be influential they need to be accessible to lots of people.

❏ The influence of '*word-of-mouth*' communications from family members, friends and neighbours stems from their assumed impartiality. Our natural suspicion of anything we are told when we believe there is an ulterior motive is an important barrier for all marketing communications to overcome. We are naturally resistant to accepting information that we believe to be part of a selling process. Independent, but often amateur, advice from acquaintances is more trusted than expert recommendations from those in the business. One study even found that if subjects believed they were 'merely overhearing' a message, they were more likely to be influenced by it, as the senders could not be suspected of ulterior motives.

These two factors – the influence of opinion leaders and the perceived impartiality of word of mouth recommendations – help to create a *diffusion* of marketing messages as communications are passed on from one person to the next, rather than a direct flow from the sender to the intended audience.

- *A new wine bar opened in town amid a fanfare of publicity in the press and special offers to entice the first customers through the doors. Those that tried the bar liked the atmosphere and told their friends who also made a visit and passed on favourable comments to other acquaintances. It became known that some of the minor celebrities of the town were seen there which further improved the bar's popularity almost to the status of a cult. Even those who were not in the habit of drinking in wine bars felt obliged to make a visit to find out what they were missing.*

This *diffusion process* has been used to explain how new products become accepted. A small percentage of people are more likely to try innovative products. These so-called '*early adopters*' are likely to be opinion leaders and therefore a prime target for marketing communications aimed at introducing new products and ideas. Early adopters are likely to be young, socially mobile and of high education and income. They influence the '*early majority*' of other users, who adopt the product before the '*late majority*', together making up about two-thirds of all final users. The final category of '*laggards*' then adopts the product.

4. THE COMMUNICATIONS MIX: SELLING, ADVERTISING, SALES PROMOTIONS AND PR

Controllable and uncontrollable communications

Organisations communicate with their publics and consumers through many forms of marketing communications. Some they control directly themselves; others are less controllable. Some communications are delivered personally by representatives of an organisation, or other people who talk about it; other messages are delivered by impersonal methods in print or other media. This 'mix' of marketing communications is summarised in Figure 10.3 (with some examples in each of the categories taken from the story of the 'daily bombardment' in section 2 above).

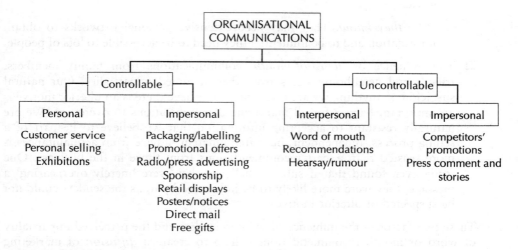

Figure 10.3: *The marketing communications mix*

Uncontrollable communications

The image of an organisation and the demand for its products are affected by communications outside of the control of its managers. These may be directly communicated face-to-face, by email, telephone or letter, as customers discuss their experiences of dealing with an organisation. They can also be impersonal communications, such as news reports in the media or messages posted on an Internet newsgroup site. These uncontrollable communications can be very influential, as we are more likely to believe them than communications received directly from the supplying organisation. However, such communications do not always promote the cause of the organisation under discussion in a positive way.

- *A well-known restaurant chain launched a promotional campaign to attract new customers and improve declining sales. Press advertising, leaflets and posters offered free bottles of wine to couples dining in the evening and discounts to families eating lunch. The campaign was evaluated through market research among users and non-users. The campaign seemed successful as sales in the group's restaurants increased during the campaign, but the follow-up evaluation revealed deeper problems. The research revealed a high level of dissatisfaction amongst customers over the standards of service, particularly the waiting time before food was served. Further research revealed an even more damaging picture, for although only a small minority of customers actually complained to the management about the poor service, a majority mentioned it to their friends and acquaintances. One customer had even posted advice to avoid the restaurant on an Internet newsgroup about eating out. This implied that potential customers were more informed about the problems than the restaurant managers! Any plans for further promotion were stopped until the service problems were overcome as the management realised the disadvantage of attracting large numbers of new customers who were likely to act as a negative marketing force among their friends.*

This illustrates some important truisms about marketing communications:

❑ Uncontrollable communications (which may or may not promote a product) are more powerful in many cases than controllable promotions. Many causes have been lost through bad publicity, and many organisations have succeeded relying only on word-of-mouth recommendations. Small enterprises often rely on word of mouth to increase their customer base: research has consistently shown that the vast majority of small firms cite recommendations as their number one method of attracting new customers (Stokes *et al.*, 1997).

❑ Word-of-mouth marketing communications are no longer restricted to face-to-face conversations with friends and neighbours. The telecommunications revolution means that people exchange views on their buying experiences in a number of new media including text messaging and email. Internet newsgroups (online discussion forums) now involve millions of people around the world exchanging news and views over a huge range of topics. This often includes positive or negative stories about buying experiences, or a product's performance. The scope for uncontrollable, word-of-mouth marketing communications on the Internet is enormous.

- *Usenet news is the Internet's prime discussion area. It is a network of over 85,000 discussion groups, each dedicated to a specific topic. These range from the serious (e.g. tips on mortgages and pensions) to the weird (e.g. messages from aliens). Usenet users often react against attempts to use their site for commercial purposes by 'flaming' anyone who posts overt advertising – that is, by sending them abusive messages in return. However, users frequently make positive and negative recommendations about products and services. Some entrepreneurs use groups to subtly inform others about their business (e.g. by contributing informative postings, and signing off with a website address and contact details).*

❑ Advertising and promotions have helped a large number of organisations to become successful, but it is not enough on its own. Even the most intensive, well-conceived advertising campaign cannot compensate for a deficient or unwanted product. The Sinclair C5 electric car and the De Lorean sports car both received enormous publicity when they were launched yet both failed because they were found wanting in other crucial respects.

Controllable communications

An organisation can choose to use various forms of promotions such as personal selling, advertising and special offers to try and influence the demand for its products and services. The organisation's management pays for and controls these communications by selecting the type, quantity and timing of the promotional methods. In subsequent sections of this chapter and Chapter 11 we will look at the various types of promotions in more detail.

However promotions are not the only element in the marketing mix to communicate to an organisation's customers. Product, pricing and place strategies also communicate messages that form part of the overall image projected by an organisation:

❏ A tangible product's design and packaging communicate important impressions. Intangible products communicate through the physical evidence of their delivery. For example, a credit card projects an image of the banking service that is behind it.

❏ Pricing can communicate a variety of messages from exclusivity or high quality to 'cheap and cheerful' or value-for-money images. For example, the bargain air travel prices of EasyJet and Ryanair are a crucial part of the 'power-to-the-people' message inherent in their strategy of opening up short-haul routes to a wider customer base.

❏ The place in which a product is sold or distributed communicates further images. For example, the waiting room of a surgery often leaves a lasting impression in a visit to a doctor (often because the most time is spent there).

Communication strategy

An organisation has to consider several aspects of marketing communications if it is to have an effective strategy for communicating to its customers. These include:

❏ Consideration of uncontrollable communications: how to use word-of-mouth recommendations as thoroughly as possible and how to limit the possibilities of damage done by negative communications.

❏ Planning controllable communications: how to ensure that all the elements of the marketing mix are giving consistent, not conflicting, messages to the public.

❏ Use of the 'promotional mix': how to optimise the use of specific promotional opportunities and techniques available to an organisation.

The promotion mix

The term 'promotion' is used in a variety of contexts and meanings. Here we are using it to describe controllable communications to customers or potential customers which, in conjunction with the other elements of the marketing mix, support the marketing objectives of the organisation.

Promotions have a 'mix' of their own because wide choices of promotional methods are available. Most organisations employ a variety of these methods in differing mixtures.

Major categories of the promotion mix can be identified as:

❑ *Personal selling*: personal presentation of the organisation and its products to customers or prospective customers.

❑ *Advertising*: a paid form of non-personal presentation, using various media such as the press, TV, radio, cinema, posters and the Internet. Advertising agencies sometimes refer to these methods as 'above-the line' advertising.

❑ *Sales promotions*: inducements or incentives outside of the normal terms of trade to encourage sales within a specific time period. This non-media, or 'below-the-line' advertising, includes loyalty cards, free gifts, competitions and other special offers which add value to the original product.

❑ *Public relations (PR)*: attempts to gain favourable, unpaid publicity, usually in the media, and to limit any potentially unfavourable comments or activities. PR is concerned primarily with influencing as far as possible the various 'uncontrollable' communications that affect the image of an organisation.

A promotional campaign may embrace all four elements in an integrated effort.

• *British Airways uses a combination of PR, advertising, sales promotions and personal selling to counter competitive activity and launch new services. The company suffered considerable adverse publicity following revelations of a 'dirty tricks campaign' by BA against Richard Branson's Virgin Atlantic. This allegedly included accessing computer information relating to Virgin Atlantic flights and poaching passengers at airports. BA's public relations department worked hard to minimise the damage in the media by emphasising their corporate pedigree and popularity with customers. More recently, the airline sought to gain a competitive advantage by focusing on premium customers through an integrated communications campaign involving TV and press advertising, direct mail, sales promotions and personal selling. BA's business service was upgraded with the introduction of bed-seats. The changes were advertised in the press, on BA's website and on TV. Frequent travellers were mailed newsletters detailing the new service. Sales representatives visited and telephoned travel agents to encourage them to sell the benefits of these new services to their customers.*

Promotion mix decisions

Decisions about which element in the promotion mix to use are affected by the type of purchase, the objective of the communication process and the product life cycle.

Type of purchase

In general, personal methods of promoting such as personal selling and exhibitions are more suited to communicating to markets made up of a relatively small number of large customers. Conversely, impersonal methods of communicating are more appropriate to promoting to a large number of relatively small buyers. A complex, infrequent purchase is more likely to need personal attention than a simple, frequently made one. These variables can be shown as a spectrum of purchase types: at one extreme in-depth personal contact is needed; at the other extreme, impersonal communications such as advertising, influence the buying decision (see Figure 10.4).

- SIMPLE PURCHASE
- FREQUENTLY MADE
- LOW PRICE PER ITEM
- RELATIVELY LARGE NUMBER OF BUYERS
- EXAMPLES: food & drink; newspapers & magazines; underwear; office stationery; musical recordings (CDs, cassettes); choosing a fast-food restaurant.

▲

ADVERTISING

■

PR

■

SALES PROMOTIONS

■

PERSONAL SELLING

▼

- COMPLEX PURCHASE
- INFREQUENTLY MADE
- HIGH PRICE
- RELATIVELY SMALL NUMBER OF BUYERS
- EXAMPLES: houses; industrial equipment; made-to-measure suits; office copier; musical equipment (e.g. piano); choosing a school/university.

Figure 10.4: *Types of purchase and the promotion mix*

This means that the order of preference of promotional methods changes, particularly between industrial and consumer markets:

❏ In consumer markets, advertising and sales promotions tend to receive most resources, followed by personal selling and public relations.

❏ In industrial markets, personal selling is usually the most used method, followed by sales promotions, public relations and advertising.

Objective of the communication process

As buyers progress along their decision-making process, marketing communications seek to achieve different objectives. As we discussed earlier in this chapter (section 3, 'Communication stages'), these objectives can be summarised as attention, interest, desire and action – the AIDA model. When awareness of a product is low, communications need to gain attention and advertising and public relations are often the most effective at this stage. PR and sales promotions are widely used to generate interest in a product as well as advertising. When awareness and understanding of the benefits on offer are higher, sales promotions and personal selling are the more effective methods to increase desire, whilst some form of personal selling is normally required to complete the necessary action to make a purchase.

The relative effectiveness of each category of promotion in the stages of the AIDA model is illustrated in Figure 10.5.

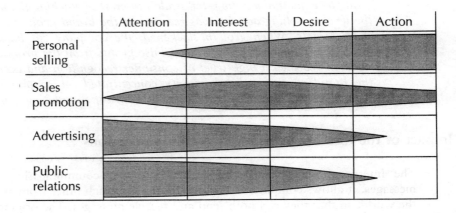

Shaded areas indicate relative effectiveness of the promotional method to achieve that objective of the communication process

Figure 10.5: *Communication objectives and the promotion mix*

Product life cycle

The stage a product has reached in its life cycle influences the choice of promotional method.

❑ In the *introduction stage*, personal selling is important to introduce the new product to the supply chain to gain exposure. Advertising and public relations are used to generate awareness and understanding of the product. Sales promotions are used to attract the 'early adopters' to try the product.

❑ In the *growth stage*, sales promotions and selling may be less needed as advertising and PR maintain the momentum.

❑ In the *maturity stage*, the product is usually well known so that the level of advertising may be cut back with more reliance on sales promotions to provide a stimulus to sales.

❑ In the *decline stage*, expenditure on promotion is usually reduced to a minimum, although sales promotions may still be used to prop up sales.

• *These various influences on the composition of the promotion mix can be seen at work in the launch and subsequent management of new products. For example, a large company launched a new brand of toothpaste. A special conference trained and motivated the company's own salesforce to introduce the product into the toiletry trade so that it received good display and shelf space particularly in the large multiple retailers. A TV advertising campaign attracted the attention and interest of the target buyer groups. Free samples and discount coupons, some given away by company*

259

representatives during in-store promotions, introduced customers to the product. Press releases told the story of the new product to the trade and national press. The strong growth and continued national advertising of the toothpaste maintained the retail trade's interest in stocking the product, so the level of selling activity was reduced as the brand achieved its market share targets. When growth slackened, the company cut back on their advertising budget in order to maximise profits from the product. Market research revealed a high level of consumer recognition and acceptance of the brand so promotional activity concentrated on coupon offers and competitions to win free holidays as a means of stimulating demand.

Impact of the Internet on marketing communications

The Internet provides a variety of new ways of communicating marketing messages. It allows computers to communicate with each other from anywhere in the world, so that they can both send and receive messages. The origins were not commercial; the system was developed initially by the US Defense Department during the Cold War, and adopted by academics as a way of sharing information. In the 1990s, business managers began to realise the potential of the Internet for commercial applications. Despite exaggerated expectations in the late 1990s, the Internet has emerged as an important marketing tool, particularly for promotions. Three types of marketing communications have become popular over the Internet:

❑ *Electronic mail:* email can be in the form of personalised marketing messages (e.g. from a customer service department to a client), or impersonal 'spams' (unsolicited commercial email, apparently named after a sketch in the TV programme, 'Monty Python's Flying Circus', in which everything on the menu was the same: Spam). Email can be used for controllable marketing communications (e.g. company newsletters) or uncontrollable messages (e.g. positive or negative word-of-mouth recommendations).

❑ *World wide web*: the development of the web has made the Internet user-friendly. It consists of millions of graphic and text documents published on the Internet, connected through 'hypertext' links. A website is a collection of inter-linked documents, or web pages, which might contain, for example, information and news about a company and its products. Sites have become interactive; for example, a visitor may order, or look up information on a product type on one visit to a website and be presented with tailor-made information on related products on a subsequent visit. In some cases, customers gain access to an organisation's intranet via the website in order to answer specific questions about the status of their order or other information hitherto provided by a customer services department.

For marketing communications, the web offers a remarkable combination of international coverage with individual targeting: it is already used by over 300 million people around the world, yet it is also able to deliver messages targeted at one individual. A website can also provide information on its effectiveness as a communications medium; small files, or 'cookies', inserted into computers by a web server, track data on the numbers and activities of visitors to a site.

The problem with the world wide web is that it is extremely difficult to get noticed. Millions of companies and countless individuals have websites in a relatively uncontrolled, unstructured system. The first marketing issue is to ensure that potential customers find your site before the rest. When looking for information about products and services on the Internet, most buyers and consumers use 'search engines' (a database of websites that can be interrogated to find something on the Internet) such as Yahoo! and Ask Jeeves. If your site is not listed in the first twenty or so results of keyword searches relevant to your product, it is unlikely to be visited. As the number of sites expands, such listings are increasingly difficult to achieve. Companies are now using traditional marketing communications such as advertising and direct mail to 'drive' visitors to their sites.

❑ *Newsgroups* are online discussion forums of people exchanging news and views on their particular areas of interest over the Internet. They have become informal yet important ways of spreading positive and negative communications about products and services. (See also example on Usenet above in section on 'Uncontrollable marketing communications'.)

These new forms of marketing communications are evolving constantly, creating new forms and nuances as they do so. Some represent controllable communications from websites and banner advertising. Others are less controllable messages via chat rooms and emails. They have become particularly important because of their ease of access for all types of business; creating a website and sending marketing messages on email has become relatively straightforward and inexpensive, despite the jargon and hype.

We will now consider each of the four major categories of the promotional mix in turn. The rest of this chapter looks at personal selling and Chapter 11 considers the impersonal promotional methods of advertising, sales promotions and public relations.

5. PERSONAL SELLING

The sales stereotype

Until sales are made, nothing else can happen in business for very long. Sales in most organisations depend at some stage on a personal presentation of the product. These simple facts ought to make personal selling a cherished and respected role. In fact, selling fell into such disrepute that those who did the job stopped calling themselves salesmen or saleswomen and adopted euphemistic titles such as 'account representative', 'marketing consultant', 'field engineer' and 'customer service executive'. Other business professions, such as accountancy and production management became more respected than personal selling, which developed a reputation, not as a profession, but as a manipulative activity carried out by fast-talking extroverts. Selling is one of the largest professions in Europe and North America but it still has fewer specialist journals or societies devoted to it than other, less numerous professions – an indication of its low esteem.

Factors that fuelled this poor image of selling include:

❑ *Sales-orientation*. Many organisations concentrated on finding as many new customers as possible irrespective of the underlying needs of the market. Sales training focused on teaching salespeople techniques to get new orders at any cost rather than improve the level of service to existing customers. Successful salespeople were judged on their ability to sell anything to anybody – the proverbial 'refrigerators to Eskimos' – rather than on their efforts to meet customer needs.

❑ *Polarisation of salespeople and customers*. This emphasis on sales at all costs by suppliers created a protective reaction from potential buyers. Fearful of falling prey to persuasive selling, customers made themselves less accessible to the sales approach. Hostile receptionists and professional buyers put up barriers to the now, unwanted sales call. Salespeople rose to the challenge and looked for new ways to break through. Seller and buyer became adversaries as salespeople adopted military-style tactics to 'find the weak spot' and deliver the 'knock-out blow' to clinch the deal.

❑ *Wide range of selling situations*. 'Salesperson' is a term applied to many different sales situations ranging from shops to international negotiations. This has not helped the profession develop a consistent image capable of attracting the most able recruits. Instead, selling has been perceived less as a profession and more of a trade to be fallen back on if qualifications are inadequate for other jobs.

❑ *Characteristics of successful salespeople*. Countless different personality types enjoy successful careers in selling. Whilst attempts to correlate sales success and character traits have failed generally, research in North America has indicated that salespeople differ from non-salespeople in the following respects:

❑ Salespeople are more likely to persuade rather than criticise.

❑ They act on intuition rather than analysis.

❑ They are more energetic.

❑ They are more motivated by money, prestige and power.

These characteristics can, of course, be interpreted positively or negatively. Some salespeople have not always been good advertisements for their profession and live up to the stereotyped image of the charming, adaptable, fast-moving performer always ready to take your money. However, more salespeople differ from the popular stereotype than conform to it, as selling is a complex and demanding job that relies on positive, personal qualities as well as organisation and technique. Unfortunately, the low status image is hard to change and helps to perpetuate the myth by making recruitment into the profession harder.

The changing face of selling

There are signs that the relatively low status of selling is improving, helped by some changes to the sales environment:

❑ *Increased costs of personal selling*. Increased labour costs have reduced the numbers involved in selling at the retail level and forced manufacturers to look for maximum productivity from their salesforce. The jack-of-all-trades role has become more sharply focused as organisations count the cost of making a sales call.

For example, the total annual costs of a salesperson including their salary, commission, travel and other overhead costs may range from £30,000–£100,000 per annum. The effective selling time of a salesperson may represent 200 days in the year once time has been deducted for holidays, training, internal meetings and administration. In one day, the number of sales calls that are possible varies according to industry and market from one per day for complex sales (such as sophisticated industrial equipment) to ten or more per day for simpler calls (such as merchandising to retailers). This gives the following range of costs per call:

Costs per annum	Costs per day (200 days)	Calls per day	Costs per call
£30,000	£150	10	£15
£40,000	£200	7	£29
£50,000	£250	4	£63
£60,000	£300	2	£150
£100,000	£500	1	£500

With costs ranging from £15 to £500 per call, selling has had to become a more focused, specialised activity to justify its expense.

❑ *Increased buyer power*. Buyers have become more powerful in certain markets as their purchasing power has increased. For example, the concentration of retail sales in the hands of fewer companies and outlets has placed more emphasis on negotiating larger contracts with multiples and retail chains, rather than one-off local sales, with a commensurate increase in the level of skill and knowledge needed from the salespeople involved.

❑ *Increased competition*. National and international markets are becoming more and more competitive. Salespeople are no longer order-takers, but order-makers who have to win business in the face of local and overseas competition. The increased emphasis on quality standards and agreed minimum specifications means that products are often similar in performance, price and other respects. The main differentiation is the relationship with the selling organisation and in particular their representative – the salesperson. This has put more pressure on organisations to recruit, train and retain high calibre sales professionals.

❑ *Professional involvement*. The growing influence of market forces in the public services and professions such as accountancy and law has brought selling into some unfamiliar environments. Bank managers, accountants, solicitors and architects now make sales presentations to secure clients. Headteachers openly acknowledge their selling role when they show prospective parents round their school. The acceptance of selling into these more traditional surroundings has helped legitimise it as a professional activity.

Types of selling

Personal selling can be defined as the personal presentation of the organisation and its products to customers or prospective customers. This can take many forms, from the doorstep deliveries of the milkman to the presentation of computer equipment to a multinational corporation, as illustrated in Figure 10.6.

Description	Aims	Examples	Possible customers	Job requirements
Delivery selling – the delivery person who also sells	Increase sales to the existing customer base by using customer visits that are already being made	The milkman, van drivers	Housewives, receptionists	Friendly personality, a driving licence
Retail selling – serving customers who visit the company's premises	Show customers what is available, offer advice and complete the transaction	Sales assistants in shops, waiting staff in restaurants	Shoppers, visitors to showrooms	Some product knowledge, patience and stamina
Trade selling – selling products into the relevant distribution chain	Ensure adequate, well displayed stocks are held at the wholesale and retail level, provide promotional assistance with in-store displays and point-of-sale merchandising	Sales representatives for food and drink companies	Shopkeepers, buyers for multiple chains	Limited technical knowledge, good understanding of customer practices
Technical selling – providing technical assistance and advice	Identify, analyse and solve customer problems, develop relationship with existing customers	Sales engineers of electronic or industrial equipment manufacturers	Other manufacturers, public services	Good technical and product knowledge essential
New business selling – 'creative' selling to new customers or markets	Find new customers for existing or new products, create sales where an established market does not exist	New account executive for an advertising agency, insurance and office copier salespeople	Office managers, public service managers, consumers	Good selling technique and experience, resilience to rejection
'Missionary' selling – promoting to endusers or specifiers of a product	'Pull' products through the distribution system by demonstrating them to ultimate users or those who specify a product for others to purchase	Graphic art salespeople demonstrating products to artists who then buy them from their local retailer, medical reps selling to doctors who prescribe medicines dispensed in chemists	Art directors, general practice doctors	Low pressure selling but to large numbers – therefore articulate and energetic

Figure 10.6: *Types of selling situations*

The role of personal selling

The role of selling and the requirements of the job, change according to the situation in which it takes place. The list of selling situations shown in Figure 10.6 illustrates just how different the selling role can be. Two variables in particular have a significant effect:

❑ *The complexity of the product or service*: selling a mainframe computer system obviously requires a different approach to presenting a line of confectionery products.

❑ *The experience of the buyer*: in some markets, the buyers have little or no internal expertise of the product and it is a 'new task' purchase (because of the newness of the product or their newness to the market). In other cases, the buyers are very experienced at purchasing the type of product under consideration as in a straight re-buy or modified re-buy situation (see Chapter 5, section 4 'Types of organisational buying decisions' for clarification of the terms 'new-buy', 'straight re-buy' and 'modified re-buy'). Again, very different sales approaches are required.

This can be illustrated as four different selling roles as in Figure 10.7.

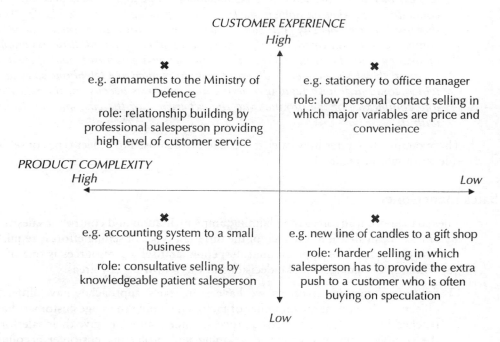

CUSTOMER EXPERIENCE
High

✖
e.g. armaments to the Ministry of Defence

role: relationship building by professional salesperson providing high level of customer service

✖
e.g. stationery to office manager

role: low personal contact selling in which major variables are price and convenience

PRODUCT COMPLEXITY
High ←————————————————————→ *Low*

✖
e.g. accounting system to a small business

role: consultative selling by knowledgeable patient salesperson

✖
e.g. new line of candles to a gift shop

role: 'harder' selling in which salesperson has to provide the extra push to a customer who is often buying on speculation

Low

Figure 10.7: *Selling roles by customer experience and product complexity*

The changing nature of the selling role influences the skills and types of salespeople required and how they are organised.

• *An electronics company, Deltronix, sold two types of product. The first was custom-made electronic designs that varied according to the needs of individual customers who were themselves usually manufacturers of consumer or industrial durables. The second was a range of ready-made electronic components which were stocked by the company and sold to other manufacturers as they required them. The company organised itself into two separate divisions, each with two different types of sales team. One division sold the custom-made products – complex designs using specialised, new technologies of which customers had little experience. Initially, sales engineers used consultative selling approaches to demonstrate the potential benefits of their design and production methods to the technical design departments of potential customers. At this stage, a complex product was being sold to an inexperienced customer. However, once the Deltronix sales engineer had achieved acceptance of their proposal and the new circuit was designed into the customer's own product, the sales role changed as the customer's purchasing department took over the ordering of the circuit. Although the product was still complex, the customer had experience of what it was and the quality standards they expected from it. Deltronix built relationships with these existing customers through a second sales team responsible for technical support.*

The products of the second division were standard electronic components sold from a catalogue that specified the performance features of each product type. A 'new business' sales team was responsible for opening up new accounts in a competitive market in which many similar products were available. They therefore relied heavily on sales technique to introduce their range to companies often satisfied with their existing suppliers and with little experience of dealing with Deltronix. Once the new business salesforce had opened an account, they handed over its day-to-day maintenance to a telephone sales team which could deal with regular ordering and enquiries because of the relatively low complexity of the product and the experience of the customer in dealing with it.

This example illustrates how sales teams can be organised to reflect types of selling role as shown in Figure 10.8.

Sales management

Sales management involves the planning, implementation and control of salesforce activities. The evaluation of which of the different types of selling effort is required and the deployment of appropriate salespeople and selling resources is one of its key roles. Sales managers make decisions in the following key areas:

❑ *Setting selling objectives*: as we have seen, sales approaches have different objectives dependent on a number of factors including the stage customers have reached in their decision-making process. Some companies give their salesforce the complete job of opening, developing and protecting customer accounts. Others divide the sales function into more discrete roles as in the example of Deltronix above. As well as quantifying objectives into sales forecasts, sales managers make judgements about what needs to be achieved in the various stages leading up to the final sale.

❑ *Establishing the selling strategy*: is a consultative, technical selling strategy required, or a relationship-building approach? Does the situation need 'harder'

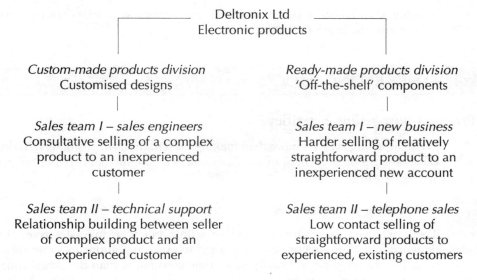

Figure 10.8: *An example of organising selling by roles*

selling or low personal contact? Sales managers determine the appropriate strategic sales approach.

❑ *Deciding the salesforce structure*: salespeople can be given responsibility for a territory based on geography (e.g. by counties or major towns), on customer types (e.g. in retail selling, customers might be grouped into 'national accounts' of large supermarkets, 'major accounts' of large regional stores and 'standard accounts' of independent retailers), product ranges (e.g. custom-made or ready-made product divisions in the example of Deltronix above), or a combination of these (e.g. the product range of one division in a geographic area).

❑ *Recruiting and training the required salespeople*: once the objectives are agreed, the strategy set and the structure decided, the implementation of these decisions revolves around selecting the salespeople and training them in both product knowledge and selling technique. This can be done at formal training sessions or in the field. In practice only the larger companies regularly train their salespeople 'off-the-road', smaller companies relying more on learning whilst doing the job.

❑ *Motivating and controlling the sales team*: sales managers are responsible for monitoring and controlling the performance of their salespeople and their selling activities. Selling can be a very lonely job: many salespeople spend over ninety per cent of their time out of contact with others from their own organisation. They can experience high levels of frustration and rejection: they often spend long periods trying to contact a busy customer or waiting for appointments, and when they do finally see someone a high percentage of answers are 'no thank you'. The ability of a sales manager to motivate salespeople in these difficult circumstances is crucial to success. As well as personal advice and counselling, managers organise sales team meetings to provide opportunities to discuss common issues. A variety of incentives from regular commission payments to one-off contests with prizes can help maintain enthusiasm and momentum.

---

6. | THE SELLING PROCESS

Pre- and post-selling activities

Personal selling is much more than making presentations to customers. Making the sale is the tip of an iceberg of activities which create the opportunity for personal selling to work.

Prospecting for customers

These activities vary with the type of selling but in many sales roles they are designed to find prospective customers and to make appointments to see them. This so-called 'prospecting' is usually more time consuming than the actual time spent selling in front of customers.

- *For example, Jack Coltman, a salesman selling office copiers, analysed the average number of activities which he undertook to secure a sale. He found that for every order he took, he made an average of five product demonstrations. For each demonstration made, he averaged two other appointments with customers, equivalent to ten appointments for each sale made. To make those appointments, he used a combination of 'cold canvassing' (or unannounced visits to customers' premises), phone calls, sales letters and mail shots. For each sale, he needed an average of fifteen cold calls, fifty phone calls and one hundred mailings. (see Figure 10.9)*

  Coltman used this information to work out the amount of each type of activity he needed to meet his annual sales targets of fifty copiers. He then broke this down into a daily target assuming he had a maximum of two hundred and fifty working days a year. He found that he needed to be making an average of one presentation, two appointments, three cold calls, ten phone calls and twenty mailings each and every day – and this did not take into account time for travelling, administration, training, meetings, illness or holidays!

The lessons from this type of analysis are:

❑ *Selling is a 'numbers game'*: persistence in prospecting for customers is as important to sales success as eloquence in front of customers. In many selling situations, the opportunities to make persuasive sales presentations depend on systematic and regular prospecting. The salesman in our example will meet his sales target if he remembers the 'numbers game' and makes the required number of telephone calls, sends the necessary number of mail shots which give him the right number of appointments and demonstrations to make sales. He can reduce the numbers of these activities by improving the ratios between them and the final sale but the most successful salespeople maintain activity levels whilst also improving their effectiveness.

❑ *Rejection* is a fundamental part of selling: every acceptance is built on several

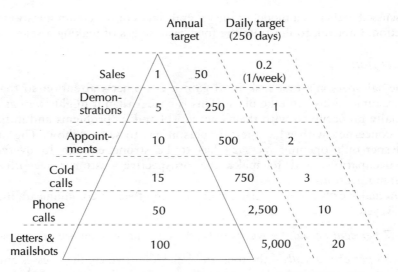

		Annual target	Daily target (250 days)
Sales	1	50	0.2 (1/week)
Demon-strations	5	250	1
Appoint-ments	10	500	2
Cold calls	15	750	3
Phone calls	50	2,500	10
Letters & mailshots	100	5,000	20

Figure 10.9: *An example of activities required to make sales*

refusals. In our example, for every 'yes' after a demonstration there were four 'nos', and many other rejections during cold canvassing and telephoning. Whilst the new salesperson can become disheartened by this amount of negativity, the experienced salesperson knows that it is part of the job.

❏ *Time management* is essential to successful selling. The high level of pre-selling effort needed to generate consistent sales can only be achieved by a careful allocation of time to each of the important activities and a minimisation of time spent on non-productive tasks. Travel for example often accounts for a high percentage of a salesperson's time but can be reduced if sales calls are grouped geographically.

Post-selling activities

The conclusion of one sale often signals the beginning of other activities:

❏ *Referrals*: we have already emphasised the importance of word-of-mouth communications in marketing (see section 3). Successful salespeople make these work in their favour by asking existing accounts for introductions and referrals to new customers.

❏ *Account maintenance and development*: satisfying existing customers so that they are prepared to make repeat purchases is usually a more economic and productive way of making sales than finding new customers.

The stages of making a sale

Like other forms of marketing communications, personal selling takes the prospective customer through several stages, or states of mind, before they are ready to buy. Sales trainers frequently use the mnemonic AIDA, which we discussed earlier as a model of the general stages of the communication process (in section 3 above), to illustrate the four basic stages of making a sale.

Attention

The salesperson's first task is to gain a customer's attention so that effective communications can take place. This is harder than it might seem as buyers are usually preoccupied with their own world and its problems and initially not at all concerned with what the salesperson has to say or show. The impact of a salesperson's opening message has to be strong enough to overcome these preoccupations and to make the prospective customer receptive to their communications.

Actual words are not what count most in effective communications. Impact is conveyed:

❑ *7 per cent verbally* – words only, the content of what we are saying;

❑ *38 per cent vocally* – the tone and inflexion of voice, the stresses and pauses in our presentation; and

❑ *55 per cent non-verbally* – gestures, postures, facial expressions and visual aids.

This implies that:

❑ *Non-verbal* gestures and expressions are often the key to gaining attention. A positive, smiling salesperson speaking enthusiastically is more likely to gain our attention than one repeating a prepared script. It is not what is said, but how it is said and the expressions and gestures that accompany it that are important, particularly in the opening moments of a sales interview.

- *For example, the eyes are particularly important in establishing initial contact as they are indicators of trust, as some of our common phrases indicate. 'Seeing eye to eye' implies agreement whereas 'shifty eyes' signify lack of trust. 'Looking a person in the eye' is needed to establish trusting communication. To establish a good level of trust our eyes should meet the other person's very regularly during a conversation or presentation. However, eyes can also signify hostility if contact is prolonged into a stare, so regular but short bursts of eye contact are desirable.*

❑ *Visual aids*, such as demonstration kits, computer-generated presentations, and written material all help to gain attention. These are particularly important in the presentation of intangible products which cannot be physically demonstrated. Insurance salespeople for example are trained to draw graphs, present written figures, and show newspaper articles as testimonials to visually support their presentations.

Interest

A sales presentation does not keep attention for long unless it also arouses interest. We become interested when can relate personally to what is being said. Attention once won only lives on through the self-interest of the customer who begins to identify with what is being sold. This stage of the sale needs therefore to demonstrate to the customer that the product or service presented is relevant to their problems by identifying the customer's particular needs and matching the benefits of the product to them.

❑ *Questions* are often the best way to involve and interest the customer, as well as providing essential information to identify their requirements. In answering questions about themselves, their organisation and its needs, a customer has to focus their attention onto the subject of the presentation and away from their other preoccupations.

❑ *Listening* carefully to the answers is the only way the salesperson can learn more about the customer. However, listening takes many forms and can be shown as a spectrum of 'listening modes', as in Figure 10.10.

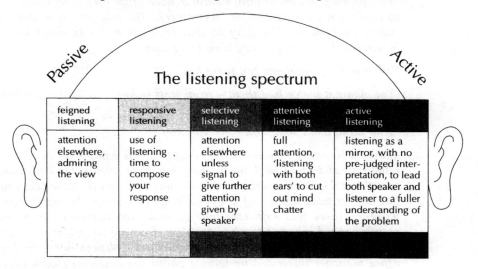

feigned listening	responsive listening	selective listening	attentive listening	active listening
attention elsewhere, admiring the view	use of listening time to compose your response	attention elsewhere unless signal to give further attention given by speaker	full attention, 'listening with both ears' to cut out mind chatter	listening as a mirror, with no pre-judged inter-pretation, to lead both speaker and listener to a fuller understanding of the problem

Figure 10.10: *A spectrum of listening modes*

In selling, the temptation is to adopt responsive or selective listening modes to think about the next part of the presentation, or the answer to a query, whilst the customer is speaking. To fully engage the customer's interest, attentive, and sometimes 'active' listening is required to help find the benefits that most closely identify with customer needs.

❑ *Attentive listening* concentrates fully on the words and ideas being presented so that the response will be appropriate and informed. 'Mind chatter' – the ever-present temptation to let the mind wander to topics other than those directly in front of it – is kept to a minimum.

❑ *Active listening* takes attention a stage further by adding an element of participation designed to help the customer articulate what they need. The aim is to help both prospective buyer and seller to reach a common understanding of a situation.

● *For example, Jack Coltman, the copier salesman, had an appointment with an office manager and during the course of the meeting, he asked: 'Do you have any particular copying requirements?' The office manager replied:*

'We operate to very tight deadlines. Everything has to be copied by a certain time.'

This could be taken as a signal to interest the customer in the product by presenting a time-related benefit with a statement such as, 'Our fastest machine makes ninety copies a minute which makes sure everything is copied on time.'

But Coltman was experienced enough to recognise he had not got to the root of the problem. He adopted an active listening mode to probe further:

'You have to copy to a deadline?'

'Yes, although we email information to head office on a daily basis, we have to confirm it with hard copies every week. The courier has to have all the copies by 6pm on Thursday so that they are in Switzerland by Friday. Whatever the problem, they have to be there.'

'What sort of problems can there be?'

'You name it we've had them – from staff sickness to equipment breaking down at the last minute.'

'Your equipment sometimes lets you down?'

Coltman went on to present the benefits of his equipment in terms of its reliability and rapid back-up in the event of problems. He had found out that the real issue of interest to the customer was not the time taken to copy but the critical nature of the deadline. Providing the equipment was working, there was sufficient time to make the required copies, so that copying speed was not the key problem. Keeping the equipment working however was essential to meet the deadline. Coltman not only kept the office manager interested by talking about the customer's own problems, but he found out a key area of need which allowed him to pass to the next stage of making the sale.

Desire

Interest in a specific problem has to be translated into desire for a particular solution before a sale can be made. Desire is aroused when the benefits of the product or service on offer are understood and accepted as viable answers to a customer need. For example, Coltman aroused the desire of the office manager for his product by presenting the benefits of its reliability and a guaranteed minimum call-out time in the event of breakdown.

Desire for certain benefits of a product are not always a guarantee of a sale however, as other constraints and objections may condition the desire.

❑ *Objections* are negative attitudes that threaten the conclusion of a sale. They may be fundamental problems, hesitations, or particular problems.

- *Coltman convinced the office manger that his product was a preferred solution, but there may have been a fundamental objection such as the unexpired lease of the existing equipment or the lack of budget for new equipment. Perhaps the office manager wanted to put off a decision to confer with others. Or there may have been a specific issue that still bothered the office manager. Coltman's previous experience told him that desire can decline rapidly after a sales interview so that any objections needed to be dealt with as quickly as possible.*

❑ *Empathy* with the customer's problem is important if objections are to be answered. Empathy is trying to understand the other person's point of view rather than denying it has any validity.

- *For example, after agreeing with Coltman's summary of the benefits of the copier the office manager brought up a new concern:*

  'Your cost per copy is more expensive than other suppliers.'

  Objections like these can be the signal for an expression of disagreement with the customer with a reply such as: 'I think if you include all the relevant costs we are less expensive.' Coltman's training had taught him that winning arguments with customers did not win orders. So his answer tried to show understanding of the customer's problem before answering the objection:

  'Yes, if you compare the cost per copy in our price lists, we are more expensive. Our prices include free service and call-outs. Competitor's prices exclude this as they charge separately for maintenance and breakdowns. If the machine never needs attention, we are more expensive. But as reliability and fast repairs are important to you, then our pricing system could well turn out less expensive – as well as giving you a predictable all-inclusive price.'

Action

Once desire is aroused and objections dealt with, the last stage of the sales process can begin. Some form of action or 'closing' of the sale is required. Closing a sale is to ask for a buying decision. This may seem straightforward but salespeople often find this the most difficult stage because of the fear of being turned down. As customers often feel uncomfortable during decision-making, the close can be a difficult moment for both buyer and seller. To help smooth the way to a final decision, several closing methods can help the salesperson test the customer's readiness to buy:

❑ *The assumptive close*: if all the stages of the selling process are obviously complete, the salesperson may use an assumptive close such as: 'I can arrange delivery of this model next week if we can complete the paperwork today.'

❑ *The question close*: questions can provide 'trial closes' which find out how near a customer is to ordering. They are often used in conjunction with an assumptive close such as: 'I can arrange delivery of this model next week. Would this be early enough?'

❑ *The alternative close*: another type of closing question is to ask the customer to choose between alternatives such as: 'Do you think this model will cope with your requirements or do you need the high-speed version?'

❑ *The testimonial close*: this method refers to a satisfied customer who is already

273

using the product: 'One of your neighbours has used this model to transform their office systems. Don't you think it makes sense for you too?'

❑ *The direct close*: a direct request for an order is sometimes all that is needed: 'Can I ask you to sign a purchase order for this model as I think we have agreed it is what you need.'

7. KEY POINTS

❑ Marketing communications are concerned with *who* (the sender), says *what* (encoding the message), in which *way* (media channels), to *whom* (the receiver), and with *what effect* (decoding, response and feedback).

❑ The AIDA model of Attention, Interest, Desire and Action summarises the stages necessary for successful communications.

❑ Marketing messages often travel by a process of diffusion because of the influence of *opinion leaders* and *word-of-mouth* communications.

❑ The marketing communications mix consists of *uncontrollable* and *controllable* communications. Controllable communications form a promotional mix consisting of:

  ❑ personal selling;

  ❑ advertising;

  ❑ sales promotions; and

  ❑ public relations.

❑ The selection of the appropriate method depends on the objective of the communication influenced by the product life cycle stage.

❑ The commercial development of the Internet has had a major impact on the scope of marketing communications. It offers a number of new media opportunities for promotional activities, including:

  ❑ *electronic mail* in the form of personalised marketing messages or impersonal 'spams';

  ❑ the *world wide web* for information, advertising and online ordering; and

  ❑ *newsgroups* (online discussion forums) consisting of millions of people around the world exchanging news and views about products and services.

❑ *Personal selling* has suffered from a poor reputation as a marketing tool, but factors such as increased costs and competitiveness are making it a more professional activity.

❑ Selling covers many types of activity from household deliveries to complex presentations. Customer experience and the complexity of product sold divide the role required into:

  ❑ *consultative selling* (complex product, inexperienced customer);

❏ *relationship building* (complex product, experienced customer);

❏ *harder selling* (straightforward product, inexperienced customer); or

❏ *low contact selling* (straightforward products, experienced customers).

❏ *Sales management* involves establishing selling objectives, sales strategy and the salesforce structure, and recruiting, training, motivating and controlling the sales team.

❏ The *selling process* involves many time consuming and potentially demotivating activities as well as making sales presentations.

❏ The stages in making a sale follow the AIDA model:

❏ *Attention* is gained 55 per cent non-verbally, 38 per cent vocally and 7 per cent verbally.

❏ *Interest* comes from careful questioning and attentive or active listening.

❏ *Desire* has to overcome objections with empathy.

❏ *Action* means closing the sale.

---

8. DEVELOPING MARKETING SKILLS

Exercises

1. Think of a recent occasion when you ate in a restaurant. Analyse the marketing communications used and their relative success or failure. Rate the sales performance of your waiter or waitress: if you were the restaurant owner, how would you improve it?

2. Evaluate some of your experiences of personal selling as a potential customer. Consider some negative and positive experiences and evaluate the key differences between them. (These may have been in shops, dealing with trades-people, customer services, door to door or telephone selling.)

3. You have been asked by a prospective employer to make a short sales presentation about yourself. Make notes on and practice such a presentation, if possible in front of others. How could you make use of the AIDA model?

Developing a marketing plan

Activity 10 Planning the marketing communications

❏ What objectives will your marketing communications have and how will you achieve them?

❏ Which elements of the promotional mix will you use and why?

❏ How will your marketing communications attract attention, gain interest, arouse desire and generate positive action?

❏ What role will personal selling play and what style will you adopt?

FURTHER READING AND REFERENCES

General texts

Brassington, F. and Pettit, S. (2000) *Principles of Marketing*, 2nd edition, chapters 14 and 17.

Dibb, S., Simkin, L., Pride, W.M. and Ferrell O.C. (2001) *Marketing Concepts and Strategies*, Houghton Mufflin, chapter 17.

Marketing communications

Blythe, J. (1999) *Marketing Communications*, Financial Times/Prentice Hall.

Monye, S.O. (ed.) (2000) *The Handbook of International Marketing Communications*, Blackwell Publishers.

Pickton, D. and Broderick, A. (2001) *Integrated Marketing Communications*, Financial Times/ Prentice Hall.

Word-of-mouth marketing communications

Arndt, J. (1967) Word-of-mouth advertising and informal communication, in Cox, D. (ed.) *Risk Taking and Information Handling in Consumer Behaviour*, Havard University.

Bayus, B.L. (1985) Word of mouth: the indirect effects of marketing efforts, *Journal of Advertising Research*, **24**(3), June/July.

Bone, P.F. (1995) Word-of-mouth effects on short-term and long-term product judgements, *Journal of Business Research*, **21**(3), pages 213–223.

Buttle, F.A. (1998) Word-of-mouth: understanding and managing referral marketing, *Proceedings of the Academy of Marketing Annual Conference*, Sheffield Hallam University, pages 100–106.

File, K.M., Judd, B.B. and Prince, R.A. (1992) Interactive marketing: the influence of participation on positive word-of-mouth and referrals, *Journal of Services Marketing*, **6**(4), pages 5–14.

Rodger, E.M. (1983) *Diffusion of Innovation*, 3rd edition, Free Press.

Stokes, D.R., Fitchew, S. and Blackburn, R.A. (1997) Marketing in small firms: a conceptual approach, *Report to the Royal Mail*, Small Business Research Centre, Kingston University.

Wilson, J.R. (1996) *Word of Mouth Marketing*, New York, John Wiley & Sons.

Personal selling

Jobber, D. and Lancaster, G. (2000) *Selling and Sales Management*, Financial Times/ Prentice Hall.

Manning, G. and Reece, B. (2001) *Selling Today*, Financial Times/Prentice Hall.

Internet marketing communications

Chaffey, D., Mayer, R., Johnston, K. and Ellis-Chadwick, F. (2000) *Internet Marketing*, Pearson Education, chapter 5.

Chaston, I. (2001) *E-Marketing Strategy*, McGraw Hill, chapter 8.

Hardaker, G. and Graham, G. (2001) *Wired Marketing*, John Wiley & Sons, chapter 4.

Trimmers, P. (1999) *Electronic Commerce: Strategies and Models for Business-to-Business Trading*, John Wiley & Sons, chapter 3.

CHAPTER 11

Promotions II: Advertising, Sales Promotions and Public Relations

This chapter looks at further elements in the promotional mix – advertising, sales promotions and PR (public relations). It describes the five basic steps that can be used to plan and implement a campaign of media advertising. It examines sales promotions that use incentives and inducements to push or pull sales through the distribution system. The chapter concludes by evaluating PR activities that promote an organisation to its various publics.

1. CASE STUDY: PROMOTING 'KIDKARE'

Jane Allen was pleased with her latest project. She worked for a marketing agency and had been asked to manage a new client, a charity called 'KidKare' which had been set up by Metropol Health Authority to raise £50 million towards the rebuilding and re-equipping of its children hospital. She looked forward to working for a cause rather than a business, but her investigations soon indicated that this was no easy assignment.

She discovered that charities worked in an increasingly competitive and controversial environment. There were simply too many chasing an insufficient supply of funds. Many of the larger national charities were beginning to use aggressive promotional tactics to communicate their appeal and maintain their flow of funds. As charitable giving had not increased in line with national wealth, there was a feeling among some of the smaller charities that they were being left behind and forgotten in the deluge of requests for help. Medicine and health was the largest charity sector attracting about one third of all funds. But this itself had been subject to some controversy. Some people felt that they were being asked to finance through charitable donations what had previously been provided out of taxes. NHS hospitals were allowed to raise money from charitable sources and critics suggested that health authorities were increasingly using fund-raising for projects that should be paid for by the government. The National Lottery was an added complication. It did provide an additional source of revenue, but it also created complacency amongst some potential donors who assumed it was providing all the money that good causes needed.

Jane's initial brief was to come up with proposals for advertising, promotions and PR. She considered first the market she was targeting. It consisted of three different donor groups: individuals, companies and public bodies such as local authorities. She knew from statistics on other, similar ventures the likely percentage that the sources of funds contributed:

Voluntary fund-raising	20 per cent
Covenants	5 per cent
Legacies	15 per cent
Other gifts	30 per cent
Corporate donations	10 per cent
Local government grants	15 per cent
Trading	5 per cent

She had not been given a total promotional budget. Rather she had been allocated £25,000 to test promotional approaches. Those that proved cost effective in bringing in funds could then be used more extensively.

'We are happy to consider any types of advertising and promotions to raise money as long as it is in keeping with the values of a professional health service', the director of the charity had told her, 'and we also need some positive publicity for the project to counter some of the criticism aimed at the lack of government funds.'

Points to consider

1. What advertising would you recommend? Consider the objectives, the media to be used and the creative strategy. How would you evaluate the results in order to decide what to repeat and what to discontinue?

See section 2.

2. Make some proposals for sales promotions in the form of inducements and incentives that could be made to the target markets.

See section 3.

3. What PR activities would you recommend? What message would you try to communicate, to whom and how?

See section 4.

2. ADVERTISING: PLANNING AND IMPLEMENTING A CAMPAIGN

One of the leading practitioners of advertising, David Ogilvy (1995), said that he did not want his advertisements to be judged by their creativity but by their effectiveness in making people buy the product. This practical approach stands in contrast to some of the mystique that surrounds advertising which is perceived sometimes as an art form rather than a management tool. In general, carefully managed advertising campaigns are the most successful. Creativity plays a major part but there are other more systematic functions.

Planning and implementing an advertising campaign covers five important decision-making areas:

❑ setting objectives;

❑ estimating the budget;

- ❑ deciding the creative strategy and message;
- ❑ selecting the media;
- ❑ evaluating the results.

We look at these steps in more detail below.

Setting objectives

The particular objectives chosen for a campaign depend on the overall marketing strategy, taking account of such factors as the target market, the desired product position and its life cycle stage. Advertising can achieve one or more of three main types of objective:

- ❑ to inform;
- ❑ to persuade;
- ❑ to reinforce.

Information

Advertising can inform target customer groups and build awareness of the existence of a product or service – a particularly important objective when new products are launched.

- *The Queen announced that she was opening Buckingham Palace to the public to help pay for the restoration of Windsor Castle and reduce the taxpayers' contribution to the costs of the Royal Family. The management of the Royal Collection Trust which was set up to manage access to the royal residences decided on an informative rather than a promotional campaign in daily newspapers. It was felt that publicising information about the arrangements, rather than inducements to make use of them, was more in keeping with royal protocol and the marketing needs of a new service added to a well-established tourist attraction.*

- *'Le Shuttle', the company originally set up by Eurotunnel to operate the channel tunnel, ran an information campaign to tell potential customers about the service. The first advertising objective was to inform rather than to excite, particularly as the campaign started after many delays to the completion of the tunnel and over a year before it opened. This was followed by a brand building campaign featuring Le Shuttle's mascot Marcus the Mole in a more segmented approach targeting weekend breaks and business trips. More recently, Eurotunnel have broadened their approach by informing regular users of other services they offer such as insurance and breakdown cover. Their website not only offers information on prices and promotional offers but also an online booking service.*

Persuasion

Once a product has gained the awareness or attention of potential customers, it needs to persuade them to purchase it in preference to anything else. This is achieved by emphasising the benefits that products offer.

In his book *The Hidden Persuaders*, Vance Packard (1963) exposed an advertising industry which he claimed was dictating what we eat and drink, what we wear, how we spend our leisure time and even who we elect to run our affairs. Advertising certainly can persuade and there have been notable success stories.

- *By the early 1980s, denim jeans had become dated. Their popularity as the symbol of youthful rebellion in the 1950s and '60s had faded over the years as they became more synonymous with middle-aged conformity. Sales dropped, including those of the leading brand, Levi's. After unsuccessful attempts to diversify into other clothing markets to replace the lost sales, Levi Strauss decided to return to their original product and re-market 501 jeans. 501s were first manufactured as hard-wearing, working trousers in California in 1873, the '5' referring to the original factory production line that made up denim cloth, product code '01', into the functional trousers with five pockets that have not changed to this day. The objective of the advertising campaign was clearly stated in the brief to the advertising agency: 'to make 501s from Levi's compulsory equipment, establishing them as the definitive, classic jean'. The target group of 15–19 year old males was to be shown the product in a way that associated the original jean with the beginnings of teenage culture in the 1950s. The result was a series of advertisements that fulfilled David Ogilvy's criteria of success: they sold a lot of jeans. By 1987, 501s were selling at fifteen times the volume of the pre-advertising levels in 1985. The campaign has also become part of the creative history of advertising, featuring scenes such as 'Launderette' in which a young man waits in his boxer shorts for his 501s to wash to a background of nostalgic 1950's music.*

Although the Levi's campaign may indicate the extent to which consumer demand can be influenced by advertising, success at this level is the exception rather than the rule. Research indicates that much advertising fails to persuade, that sales do not increase with advertising expenditure. Those products that do respond to advertising are more likely to show small gains rather than dramatic changes.

Advertising can attempt to persuade with a number of end results in mind:

❑ *To increase sales by increasing the total market.* Levi's advertising benefited not only their own brand but other manufacturers as well because the total demand for jeans increased (even the sales of boxer shorts went up as a result).

❑ *To take market share from competitive products.* British Airways' advertising of its business travel facilities is designed to take away customers from competitive airlines in a market that is constrained by flight routes from Heathrow, its major airport.

❑ *To persuade a target audience to a point of view.* Advertising is not only concerned with increasing sales of products. It is also concerned with promoting a whole range of social issues from ideas and attitudes to specific charities and political parties.

- *The Norwegian government demonstrated how advertising could be used to address social problems when it launched a campaign with the objective of reducing alcoholism among teenagers. Headlines such as 'The average Norwegian 16/17 year old drank 155 bottles of alcohol last year' achieved record levels of readership, including 70 per cent of all Norwegian parents.*

The advertising sparked off a national debate and the heightened awareness of the issues helped reduce the upward trend of drinking among teenagers. This type of success has encouraged UK governments to use advertising to promote its policies from the wearing of seatbelts to the muzzling of dogs.

Reinforcement

Advertising is also defensive in that it attempts to keep existing customers by reminding them of favourable attitudes they have towards an organisation or its products. Campaigns can have the objective of reassuring customers that the choice they have just made is a wise one. For example, research indicates that car advertisements are more likely to be read by existing owners of the promoted model than anyone else; manufacturers use this information to build up repeat purchasing habits by reminding customers of the benefits behind their original buying decision.

Organisations can sometimes arrest the decline of their product by reminding customers that the satisfaction they once gained is still available.

- *By 1990 the end of the milkman seemed in sight. Every year approximately one million customers cancelled their home delivery of bottles of milk and opted to buy the cheaper cartons in their local supermarket. Although a promotional campaign in the mid-1980s had been unable to halt the switching, the National Dairy Council launched a TV campaign in 1991 to remind viewers of what they were giving up. Animated milk bottles emphasised the friendliness and convenience of home deliveries by jumping into milk crates outside people's homes according to personalised milk orders. The award-winning advertisement worked, halting the decline of home deliveries of milk, at least temporarily. The Milk Marketing Council recently launched a new campaign with the same objective – to reinforce the value and convenience of British traditions such as the milkman.*

Estimating the budget

Advertising is more difficult to budget than most other costs because it is often difficult to know how much to spend and quantify the benefits. An organisation has no choice over some costs such as wages and rent, but how does it know how much to spend on advertising? The decision becomes increasingly difficult as the objectives become less tangible and more long term as, for example, in corporate advertising aimed at building up a favourable image over a number of years.

In practice, several different methods are used:

❏ *Percentage of income*: as most advertising is aimed at increasing the income received by an organisation, a common method is to set a budget as a certain percentage of existing or expected sales. Percentages vary widely from above 20 per cent of sales for some fast-moving consumer goods, to less than one per cent of income for some public services. Whilst this may be a convenient method in stable market conditions, it does not provide resources for opportunities which lie outside of the existing business.

❏ *Competitive expenditure*: in competitive markets, products often need to ensure they receive an equal amount of advertising as competitor products. Market share objectives can also be translated into an equivalent share of the total advertising expenditure on similar products: a product with the sales objective of a 20 per cent market share can be assumed to need 20 per cent of total advertising expenditure on the product category.

This method is reactive, assuming that competitors have got their expenditure levels right and can lead to an escalation of total expenditure as suppliers all try to increase market share.

❑ *Objectives and tasks*: promotional budgets can be set by defining specific objectives, then establishing the tasks required to meet the objectives, and finally costing those tasks as a budget. This logical approach assumes that a relationship between objectives (e.g. an increase in sales) and advertising tasks (e.g. media exposure) can be defined. However, this method does have the advantage of linking planned expenditure to the accomplishment of specific tasks so that performance can be more easily evaluated.

❑ 'What can we afford?' Many organisations set their budget based on what they think they can afford rather than any other, more sophisticated measure. This is particularly common among smaller organisations with limited resources.

The cost of advertising

Advertising costs can be split into two main types:

❑ *Media costs*: the price of buying the relevant media space or time. Advertising agencies are normally paid their fee for creating an advertisement as a percentage (up to 15 per cent) of this media expenditure. Media expenditure varies from millions of pounds spent on a national TV advertising campaign to a few hundred pounds to buy space in the trade press.

❑ *Production costs*: the costs of producing the final advertisement. For a television campaign these might include directors, actors, camera operators, location, filming, music, and studio time. These costs have escalated as advertisers have used increasingly elaborate productions to attract viewers' attention. For example, the National Dairy Council's advertisement in support of home milk deliveries cost £5.1 million to make.

Deciding the creative strategy and message

Once objectives and budgets have been set, the next two steps of deciding the creative strategy and selecting the media can be implemented. Although we treat them separately here, in practice these two steps are simultaneous rather than sequential as the selection of the message and the media influence each other and cannot be treated in isolation.

A creative strategy is designed to fulfil the advertising objectives in the selected media by transmitting the appropriate messages to the target audience. The approach selected depends on the aims of the campaign in relation to the target audience:

❑ *If it is to inform*, then a straightforward, factual strategy may be used. The message may give target customers the information they need to use the product or service, for example the dates and hours in which Buckingham Palace is open to the public. It can sell more overtly by offering information as a USP – a unique selling proposition – that makes the product more competitive.

- *This headline appeared in the national press: 'Stay in a Forte city centre hotel on business and wake up with 35 per cent off your bill'. The Forte hotel group were running a summer promotion to attract the business traveller and stated the benefit in a clear and direct way which informed the reader of what was on offer in the headline whilst the copy went on to explain where and when.*

❏ *If it is to persuade or reinforce*, a more subtle, psychological approach may be necessary. Advertising uses images of lifestyles and emotions to appeal in a more indirect way. Levi's communicated nostalgia and teenage non-conformity to sell 501s. The National Dairy Council reminded us that the friendly milkman delivering bottles to our doorsteps is part of the British heritage, a valuable national institution that we throw away at our peril. Persuasive advertising offers attractive lifestyles, but ones which need to be in tune with the aspirations of the target audience if they are to work.

- *British Airways' business class advertising took a new creative approach in its re-launch of its business class service. Previous promotions had majored on the theme of the 'office in the sky', showing how BA could give hard-nosed business executives a competitive edge over their scheming rivals. Whilst this may have been appropriate to the enterprise culture of the Thatcher years, BA's research indicated that a softer approach was now needed. A new campaign conjured up images of comfort and relaxation as the business traveller used flying time for personal reflection rather than clinching deals. This theme was continued in the launch of BA's bed-seat service in 2001 which emphasised home comforts whilst travelling.*

  Virgin Atlantic responded to BA's advertising by revamping its own appeal to business travellers. Originally, Virgin had launched its trans-Atlantic service as a no-frills, cut-price alternative to the major carriers. As airfares dropped generally in response to the new competition and over-capacity on the route, Virgin had to offer something more, particularly to the less price-sensitive business traveller. They launched TV and press ads which conjured up images of a self-indulgent, luxurious lifestyle whilst retaining echoes of their earlier low price appeal with headlines such as: 'You know those rotten, pampered so-and-sos who travel first class? Become one for the price of a business class ticket'.

Selecting the media

Media selection requires choices not only between different media (e.g. press or posters) but also within each medium (e.g. *The Times* or the *Daily Telegraph*; poster site locations in which towns).

In the UK, approximately £12 billion ($17 billion) is spent each year on the different display advertising media. The media is broken down as shown in Figure 11.1 with comparisons to some other European countries.

	Total expenditure US$ million	Press	TV	Radio	Outdoor	Cinema
France	9,761	47%	34%	7%	12%	0.5%
Germany	19,853	66%	25%	4%	3%	1%
Italy	6,524	38%	56%	4%	2%	–
Spain	4,828	45%	40%	9%	5%	0.5%
UK	17,354	58%	33%	4%	4%	0.5%

Figure 11.1: *Media shares of display advertising expenditure in US$ million (1998)*
(Source: World Advertising Research Center (WARC))

In every country, except for Italy, the press takes the biggest share ahead of television.

Press

Press advertising has a long history dating from the first English newspapers in the seventeenth century. Despite the advent of radio, TV, and the Internet it remains more popular than any other media because it is the most flexible. It can be used as a permanent reminder of a small business in Yellow Pages, as a targeted approach to a specific industry in the trade press or as part of a national campaign in the Sunday papers.

Its share of media expenditure can be broken down further as shown in Figure 11.2.

Regional newspapers	32%
National newspapers	24%
Magazines – business and professional	16%
Magazines – consumer	9%
Directories	11%
Press production costs (on advertising)	9%
Total	**100% = £6.5 bn**

Figure 11.2: *Breakdown of expenditure on UK press advertising*
(Source: *Advertising Statistics Year Book, 1999*)

Press advertising has several advantages compared to other media:

❑ *Broad, targeted coverage*: the diversity of press publications ensure that they provide a wide yet targeted coverage of customer groups suited to segmented marketing campaigns. National papers offer lifestyle focus (the Sunday colour supplements); the regional papers give a local, geographic breakdown (the *Surrey Advertiser*); magazines offer advertisers demographic segments (*Seventeen*) or special interest readers (*Gibbons Stamp Monthly*); the trade press targets a profession (*Physiotherapy*) or an industry (*Electronics Weekly*).

❑ *Permanence*: it provides a permanent record so that the reader can refer to information more than once.

❑ *Responsive*: the press can carry coupons for direct response or telephone enquiry numbers which are more likely to be retained than other media.

The limitations of press advertising include:

❏ *Limited impact*: print does not have the same potential sensory impact as multi-dimensional media such as cinema, TV and the world wide web. The reproduction qualities of newsprint are poor, and high quality colour advertising is still limited to the more glossy magazines.

❏ *Fragmentation*: the diversity of the press can make in-depth coverage of some customer groups difficult and fragmented across many publications. For example, a consultancy practice wishes to advertise their services to the business community. Do they chose national press for wide coverage, regional papers for local contacts, trade press and professional journals for specific customer segments, or a combination of them all?

Television

Television is the advertising medium with which we tend to be most familiar as consumers, yet a relatively small percentage of organisations use it. Small organisations cannot afford it and industrial products do not need its wide coverage. TV is heavily used by larger companies, particularly the suppliers of branded consumer goods seeking impact and coverage who can spread the high production and media costs over a substantial turnover.

● *Thirteen per cent of the UK population is aged between five and fifteen, a group of over 7.5 million consumers (Annual Abstract of Statistics, 2001). These young people represent the core market for many leading branded products from Coca-Cola and Tango to Sega and Lego. Advertising to this segment of consumer goods such as snacks, confectionery, soft drinks, music, videos, toys and computer games is largely carried on TV. Satellite and cable TV has given advertisers a new option as this group watch more of it than adults. It is capturing an increasing percentage of their viewing time with complete channels such as 'Children's Channel' and 'Nickelodeon' dedicated to their age group.*

The advantages of TV include:

❏ *Impact*: sight, sound and motion combine to appeal to our senses and emotions.

❏ *Reach*: 'reach' is a measure of how many people in the target market are exposed to a particular advertisement in a specific period. If a promotional objective is to achieve a 'high reach' of a national market, TV is often the most effective answer.

❏ *Attention*: when we watch TV we tend to be a captive audience absorbing whatever is shown as there are few distractions.

TV advertising is restricted to under one third of UK media expenditure because it does have some significant disadvantages:

❏ *High total costs*: although it can be a cost-effective media for high turnover products, the costs of production and airtime are prohibitive for products with a more limited appeal. The risks involved if the advertising does not work are also greater.

❑ *'Clutter'*: television programmes are increasingly 'cluttered' by advertising. The average number of ads shown by the commercial stations continues to rise and viewers are becoming more immune to promotional messages because of the overload. Remote-control units and video recorders can remove the advertising content of viewing time.

❑ *Impermanence*: advertisements on TV last 30 seconds or less and are rarely stored. This does not make it a good medium for the communication of detailed or complex messages.

However expenditure on TV continues to grow quickly for both media and production. Figure 11.3 shows its progress between 1985 and 1996.

	1985 £m	1990 £m	1996 £m
Transmission charges	1,188	2,004	2,827
Production costs	188	321	506
Total	**1,376**	**2,325**	**3,333**

Figure 11.3: *UK advertising expenditure on television*
(Source: *Advertising Statistics Year Book, 1997*)

Radio

The BBC monopoly on broadcasting made commercial radio a relative latecomer in the UK. Although Radio Luxembourg and the offshore 'pirate' stations pioneered the way in the 1960s, it was not until 1973 that the first commercial stations broadcast from the UK mainland. In other countries, especially the USA, the explosion of popular music in the 1950s and '60s helped establish the radio as an effective advertising medium to the fast growing youth market. Today commercial radio broadcasts on a regional and local basis to an audience that has expanded to include motorists, housewives, senior citizens, factory operatives and other subgroups.

The popularity of 'Classic FM' which attracted 4.5 million listeners a week after its launch in 1992 and 'Jazz FM', a popular addition to London's radio stations, proved that commercial radio could have a more varied musical diet and helped to attract a wider listening audience.

The advantages of radio as an advertising medium include:

❑ *Low cost*: radio advertising is still relatively cheap in terms of the costs per listener.

❑ *Selectivity*: radio can provide advertisers with access to specific groups at specific times, such as car owners whilst driving, housewives whilst working in the home, teenagers whilst listening to music.

❑ *Geographic segmentation*: although radio can provide mass coverage, it can be restricted to a geographic area for local businesses.

Radio has disadvantages, including:

❑ *Single sense*: as it works only through our hearing, radio's creative and impact possibilities are limited.

❑ *Attention*: the radio is frequently played in the background with low attention given to content.

❑ *Impermanence*: like TV ads, we are only fleetingly exposed to a radio commercial which has only a few seconds to make its impression or be forgotten.

Cinema

Although the popularity of television and videos has greatly restricted cinema audiences, there has been an increase in the number of cinema-goers since the 1980s. In 1985, there were 70 million admissions to cinemas and by 1996 this had grown to 123 million. Over 70 per cent of the UK population over seven years old now visit the cinema, and 16 per cent go more than once a month (*Advertising Statistics Year Book, 1999*). The success of films made especially for the big screen, and improvements to cinema facilities and standards of comfort have made it more worthwhile to leave the convenience of home entertainment in favour of a visit to the cinema. Audiences are predominantly young, with 70 per cent aged between 15 and 34 years old. This was an obvious attraction to an advertiser like Levi's who first launched their 501s campaign in cinemas.

Other advantages of cinema advertising include:

❑ *Impact*: the size, colour, movement and stereophonic sound from the big screen combine to make its potential impact second to none.

❑ *Control*: unlike TV, the advertiser has the controls over such variables as sound volume and colour quality and the viewer cannot turn off the ads.

Disadvantages include:

❑ *Audience size*: whilst not quite the 'dying-breed' they were once feared to be, cinema-goers are still limited in total numbers and regularity of visits.

❑ *Youth-bias*: on average only 30 per cent of cinema audiences are over 35 years old.

Posters

Posters were the chosen medium for one of the most famous advertising campaigns. In the 1930s, Guinness used simple statements of benefit – 'Guinness for strength' or 'Guinness is good for you' – accompanied by tongue-in cheek illustrations, such as a workman carrying a metal girder obviously too heavy for normal mortals. The campaign made an Irish stout an everyday part of English life and gave Guinness an entry into almost every pub in the land.

More recently, another beer, Skol lager, was promoted on posters to halt the decline in its sales. Again the creative interpretation was humorous, depicting a head replacing the 'O' in the word 'Skol'; one of them was a garden gnome with the caption above: 'It's got more taste than the bloke who bought me'. The campaign cost £500,000 for posters on 500 sites in 31 towns and ran for three months. It achieved its objective and slowed the decline in Skol consumption.

Posters have been used intensively by tobacco companies following their ban from advertising on television. The relatively low cost and blanket coverage of posters also makes them popular for advertising political parties.

Advantages of poster advertising include:

❑ *Repeat exposure*: as we are creatures of habit, we tend to pass the same hoardings more than once and see buses carrying poster advertising on the same routes. This means we are exposed to the same message several times.

❑ *Low cost*: multiple poster sites spread across a town or city can be rented relatively inexpensively and production costs can be kept low with simple copy and graphics.

❑ *Low competition*: sites are usually well separated from other poster sites so that there is little confusion of messages.

❑ *Supportive*: poster advertising is often used to support other media which takes the bulk of the spending. The government's offering of shares during the privatisation of industries such as gas and electricity was advertised in this way with posters highlighting the theme of the main campaign on TV and in the press.

Disadvantages of poster advertising include:

❑ *Creative limitations*: little detail is possible on posters which minimises the creative opportunities.

❑ *Unselective*: posters tend to be seen by a wide variety of people and can be differentiated only by geographic market segments.

❑ *Access*: the tobacco and drinks industries have built up substantial portfolios of poster sites rented on a long-term basis which has compounded a general shortage of well-positioned sites. Other advertisers can have difficulties gaining access to good sites, although legislation to restrict tobacco advertising further will change this situation.

Direct mail

Direct mail is advertising by post. It became increasingly popular with advertisers in the 1970s and had grown to over a billion items mailed by the 1980s. Computerisation has helped the direct mail industry to develop even more strongly since then and total expenditure now exceeds £1.5 billion on over 3 billion items mailed. This is divided between consumer and business mailing as shown in Figure 11.4.

	1986 Million items	1996 Million items
Consumers	976	2,436
Business	425	737
Total	1,401	3,173

Figure 11.4: *Direct mail volumes and destinations*
(Source: *Advertising Statistics Year Book, 1997*)

Direct mail is frequently used in business-to-business marketing applications. Its ability to target buyers more precisely than other media make it a particularly appropriate selling aid in industrial markets where careful use of the direct mail 'rifle' beats a more random 'shotgun' approach. Sales people use direct mail to introduce themselves to potential customers that they have identified, or as a follow-up to demonstrations they have made.

However, the largest growth has been in the area of consumer rather than business mailings. The private sector has realised the value of advertising services such as insurance and DIY through direct mail, and the lessons from the success of companies like Readers Digest who have long been experts at selling through the post are now being learned by others. But it is non-profit making organisations that have lead the way in an increasingly sophisticated use of direct mail.

- *Charities are one of the biggest users of direct mail, representing about 10 per cent of consumer mailings. Oxfam first wrote to its supporters asking for money in the 1950s, and appeals by post are now an integral part of charitable fund-raising. Direct mail can be targeted at known supporters, and it produces immediate returns in the form of donations without the need for further follow-up. It is also an 'invisible' form of marketing with a cost-effective image, important to charitable organisations which do not wish to be seen spending funds on more ostentatious promotions. As the volume of mail arriving in our homes has increased, charities have become more creative in commanding our attention. Mailshots regularly inform donors about how their money is being spent. Recognising the benefits which information technology offer to direct mail marketing, charities such as Oxfam have developed profiles of supporters on their lists so that they can appeal to their specific interests. The immediacy of direct mail allows charities to reach their supporters within days of disasters or emergencies for which special appeals are required.*

Other advantages of direct mail include:

❑ *Measurable*: the results from direct mail are measurable directly as the receiver is invariably asked to respond in some way. The cost per response can be calculated to judge the campaign's cost effectiveness.

- *The costs of a particular mail shot including postage were £500 per thousand mailed. For every thousand sent, 50 replies were received, a response rate of 2.5 per cent. The cost of each reply was therefore £10 (£500 divided by 50). The sender of the mail shot could now estimate if it was worth spending £10 for each response.*

❑ *Testable*: mailings, particularly larger ones, can be tested before the complete list is mailed. A sample is mailed and evaluated to arrive at a cost per response before the mail shot is 'rolled out' to the full list, or aborted.

❑ *Targeted*: the list to which a mail shot is sent is crucial to its success; an out-of-date or inappropriate list can ruin the effectiveness of the best-designed mail shot. If an organisation does not possess an adequate list from its own records, these can be purchased from mailing houses who offer ranges of specialised lists, from the names of process engineers to purchasers of gardening tools.

Disadvantages of direct mail include:

❑ *Image*: the image of 'junk mail' is not helped by the quantity of unsolicited material received by the modern household and office. This has been swelled by the door-to-door delivery of leaflets, samples and coupons in order to reduce mailing costs.

❑ *Waste*: a high proportion of mail shots are not read or acted on. Non-response rates of 99 per cent or more from a mailing are common. (However, with the right offer, even mailings with a response of 1 per cent or less can work.)

❑ *List quality*: lists rapidly become out of date as people move or change jobs and keeping them up to date is a constant and costly operation. Organisations can damage their image by sending several copies of the same mail shot to one address but duplications of names are notoriously difficult to eradicate.

The Internet

The Internet has become an important advertising medium, generating much activity in recent years as organisations have competed for attention on the world wide web. The Internet offers a number of new ways of promoting products and services:

❑ *Websites*: websites are the key to advertising on the Internet and most established businesses now have their own site carrying information about their products and services. A website is a specific location on the world wide web managed by an individual or an organisation, usually consisting of several web pages, introduced by a home page of contents. Website files are housed and maintained by 'hosts' or 'servers', of which there are over 70 million world-wide and nearly 2 million in the UK (Keynote, 2000a). Websites carry marketing communications about the host organisation for potential customers, employees, investors and other stakeholders including product information, news and events, and job vacancies. They are also a source of market information as they can be programmed to identify the number and geographic origin of site visitors. 'Cookies', or small files inserted by website servers into visitors' computers, provide more detailed information on visitors' behaviour (e.g. which web pages were opened, time spent on the site, number of repeat visits, and purchases made). This data can then be used to personalise messages and information for visitors when they revisit a site. For example, visitors to the Tesco Direct website can review their previous purchases or favourite items placed in their electronic 'shopping carts'.

❑ *Portals*: portals are websites which form a gateway into the Internet by offering the user a starting point from which to navigate around the complex myriad of sites and services on the world wide web. Some (such as Yahoo! and Altavista) are essentially 'search engines' which help to locate any type of information on the web. Others are more specialised and targeted at particular interest groups (e.g. Business Answers UK at www.businessanswers.co.uk is a portal for business-related issues). If successful, such portals attract many visitors so that they can sell advertising on their sites.

❑ *Banner advertising*: 'ad. banners' are the most common form of advertising on the web, so-called because they form a banner across the top of web pages, carrying promotional messages and links to the advertiser's website. The success rate of the advertisement is measured by the number of 'click-throughs' to the advertiser. They may be paid for like more traditional forms of advertising (from small sums for relatively unknown sites, up to £10,000 per month for popular sites). Banners are also exchanged through reciprocal arrangements under which two or more organisations agree to link their sites to increase traffic to each other.

❏ *Pop-ups*: marketing communications may also appear in smaller windows once a site is opened. These 'pop-ups' are often used to advertise specific promotional offers such as free software downloads or competitions. They often contain cookies to gain information about the user.

❏ *Rich media advertisements*: advertising on the Internet can attract attention through interactivity, animation and sound. For example, a building society's site can ask potential customers to type in the amount and term of the mortgage they want and give an immediate quotation. Many websites offer downloads containing 'rich media' software of high specification graphics and sound, that makes possible highly creative and interesting communications. However many web users do not have sufficient PC capacity to access these rich media sites or become frustrated because of the long download times.

Advertising on the Internet has several advantages:

❏ it can be relatively inexpensive to set up;

❏ visitors to websites can be tracked to provide market information;

❏ it has the potential to reach audiences world-wide immediately; and

❏ it can be very creative and interactive.

The significant disadvantage is that it is very difficult for an advertiser to be noticed by their target market in a relatively disorganised, unstructured system of millions of websites. 'Visibility' of a website is as least as important as its design. For this reason search engines such as Askjeeves.com and Alltheweb.com have become very important. These search the text of web pages on the instructions of a user who asks for sites containing certain keywords or phrases. As search engines rank the sites found according to their relevance to the user's search, advertisers need to ensure their site is ranked as near to the top as possible because users rarely bother to look beyond the first ten names. This entails constant vigilance and management to ensure that websites are configured to the search engines' criteria for listing results ('hits') of keyword searches. As each engine uses different criteria to search millions of web pages, managing the visibility of a website has become a skilled job.

Organisations now use a variety of offline promotional methods to increase traffic to websites because of the difficulties in raising and maintaining visibility online. These include main media advertising through television, radio and direct mail, as well as general publicity by including website addresses on letterheads and marketing literature.

All of these factors mean that advertising on the Internet may not be as cost effective as it may at first appear. Whilst sites can be designed and hosted relatively cheaply, maintaining sites and promoting their visibility can become expensive.

Advertising on the Internet is still in its infancy. It has grown rapidly to an expenditure level of approximately £100 million in the UK (Keynote, 2000b), but this is still very small compared to the £12 billion spent on advertising through traditional media.

Evaluating the results

The evaluation of an advertising campaign involves measuring how well it communicated its message, and what effect it had on sales or other tangible objectives of the organisation.

Effectiveness of communication

Advertisers want to know how well their campaign communicates a message to its target audience. This can be done by:

❑ *Pre-testing*: before an ad is launched it can be tested by showing it to a selected audience.

❑ *Post-campaign recall*: research is carried out to determine which advertisements the target audience saw. This research uses *spontaneous* recall ('Thinking back over the past week, which commercials can you remember seeing or hearing?'). It also uses *prompted* recall ('Which of the following advertisements do you remember seeing or hearing recently?') in order to judge the attention achieved by an advertisement.

❑ *Tracking*: in order to fully test the effectiveness of promotions, some organisations set up customer panels to permanently track their awareness and attitudes to products.

Effect on organisational objectives

The ultimate justification for advertising is not just that it communicates well but that it helps an organisation meet its objectives. For example, tracking research may indicate that brand awareness has been improved through advertising, that the communication objectives were met. But how does this translate into sales? Unfortunately this is never easy to answer as it is difficult to isolate advertising as a single variable. A straightforward comparison of sales or income generated with advertising expenditure does not take account of other factors such as competitive activity or economic trends. More thorough research can attempt to isolate other variables by comparing results in similar geographic areas with and without advertising. Evaluation of advertising remains an inexact science, justifying perhaps the complaint of one chief executive who said that fifty per cent of his company's advertising didn't work, but he didn't know which half!

The five aspects involved in planning and implementing an advertising campaign are summarised in Figure 11.5.

3. SALES PROMOTIONS: PUSHING AND PULLING BELOW THE LINE

'Above and below the line' advertising

Sales promotions are sometimes referred to as 'below the line' advertising compared to media advertising which is 'above the line'. The 'line' was originally drawn by advertising agencies to distinguish between advertising activities for

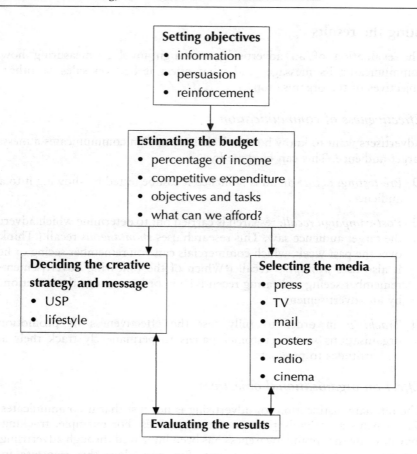

Figure 11.5: *Planning and implementing an advertising campaign*

which they were paid a commission on media purchased ('above'), and other activities for which their involvement was charged directly to the client as no commission was applicable ('below'). In practice the line is a grey one as many sales promotion activities rely on media advertising to promote them, and special offers and incentives are an integral part of a promotional campaign.

- *Both British Airways and Virgin Atlantic have used sales promotions as part of their overall advertising strategy to woo the business traveller. BA's 'Air Miles' and Virgin's 'Freeway' offer the possibility of free air travel to frequent travellers who collect enough points to qualify. Research has indicated that business and first class passengers rate such schemes more highly than the cheapest available fare. Most airlines therefore offer a frequent traveller incentive scheme as an integral part of their marketing effort which is featured in media advertising and other sales efforts.*

Sales promotions can be defined as *inducements or incentives outside of the normal terms of trade to encourage sales within a specific time period.* Their popularity has increased to the point where expenditure below the line in the UK runs at over £3 billion a year.

Sales promotions are not just targeted at final consumers. They can be used to 'push' products through the distribution system by incentives to the trade or to salespeople, as well as to 'pull' products through to end users.

'Push' promotions

Trade promotions

Some promotions attempt to push more products through the distribution chain. These may offer distributors inducements to stock certain products or to display them in a certain way and include the following types of promotions:

❑ *Profit incentives*: increased discounts for products purchased in a given period; bonuses or retrospective additional discounts for purchases above a certain level; one-off additional discounts for stocking a product range for the first time.

❑ *Credit incentives*: 'sale or return' facilities, or extended credit for a limited period; delayed invoicing to dealers for certain products.

❑ *Staff promotions*: dealer staff training; a competition for dealer sales teams; participation in events such as golf tournaments.

❑ *Joint promotions*: free in-store display materials; exhibitions; shared mailings to customers; contributions to promotional expenses.

Many organisations operate a combination of promotions to ensure their products are well represented through the channels of distribution.

- *Letraset sold their graphic art products through a network of specialist dealers and retailers. As the cost of stocking Letraset was high, a special additional discount was offered to new dealers who bought a comprehensive range. Retrospective additional discounts if turnover exceeded certain trigger points encouraged dealers to sell Letraset rather than competitive products. Towards the end of their financial year, Letraset sometimes offered special financial and other incentives to dealers to ensure that sales targets were met. They also offered dealers facilities to exchange slow moving stock for faster selling items. Sales training was offered to all dealer staff with competitions featuring free holidays to encourage them to sell Letraset products.*

Sales force incentives

Sales promotions to an organisation's salesforce reward particular achievements with prizes and awards. They can be used for several objectives including:

❑ Improving the overall sales performance of the organisation by offering prizes and special bonuses to those that sell most.

❑ Targeting the sales of specific products by making them the subject of special incentives on a short-term basis.

❑ Improving the teamwork and motivation of the salesforce by using incentives as the focus for regular news bulletins, meetings and other communications which keep salespeople informed about what is happening elsewhere.

- *One insurance company motivates its salesforce through a combination of annual and monthly competitions backed up by newsletters and meetings. There is a top annual prize of a £5000 holiday and awards for the next best 15 performers. Monthly incentives of vouchers to spend at Currys and Dixons are used to reward those who meet varying targets which are regularly changed – sales of a particular policy, or opening the most new accounts, for example. A newsletter announces winners and new incentives, wall charts display individual performances, and monthly meetings are held to review progress.*

'Pull' promotions

As consumers we are offered an increasing variety of incentives to buy products. These include discounts, samples, coupons, competitions, sponsorship, multiple packs, point-of-sale displays and credit facilities.

Both manufacturers and retailers use sales promotions.

Manufacturers' promotions

Promotions by manufacturers include incentives to consumers which are 'redeemed' either directly or through the retailer.

- *Coupons have become a popular promotional device with over 5 billion circulated each year in the UK. These are often distributed through mailings or inserts in newspapers and offer the consumer free products or discounts on presentation of the coupon. This form of incentive has been boosted recently by the publication of several new 'free standing inserts' (FSI). 'Shoppers Friend' and 'Money Savers' are two such publications which follow the style of successful 'coupon magazines' in the USA. Packed with coupon offers ranging from 10p off toilet tissues to free admission to theme parks, they are distributed as an additional section in many newspapers.*

Retail promotions

Retailers also run their own promotions with loyalty cards and special offers of their own. Supermarkets now offer a host of promotions including money off, holiday promotions, gifts, bulk purchase discounts and demonstrations. For example, in one year alone, Tesco gave 13,000 educational items to 8000 schools in return for coupons collected by parents shopping in their stores.

Sales promotions on the line

Sales promotions have had a chequered history and are still regarded by some as the least acceptable form of advertising. Some incentives seem to encourage consumers to buy what they do not need and others are accompanied by high pressure selling techniques. For example, criticisms have been made about the use of incentives to induce people to see 'hard sell' presentations of time-share holidays and other products. Even well known brand names have received adverse publicity over the less ethical aspects of sales promotions.

- *One promotion threatened to discredit the whole industry. In 1992, Hoover offered consumers two free return flights to Europe or America if they purchased any of its washing machines or household appliances worth more than £100. The company expected that its very generous promotion would attract buyers who would be put off taking up the offer by the small print which laid down strict conditions about how and when the flights could be taken. In the event, a large numbers of consumers bought cheap appliances at around £120 and claimed their airtickets worth £500, Hoover ran into difficulty honouring the offer, leading to scepticism over the value of such promotions.*

4. PUBLIC RELATIONS: PROMOTING AN ORGANISATION TO ITS PUBLICS

Who are the 'public' in public relations?

The Institute of Public Relations define PR as: 'the deliberate, planned and sustained effort to establish and maintain mutual understanding between an organisation and its publics'.

An organisation's public relations activities attempt to maximise the benefits of favourable publicity and minimise the damage done by adverse communications. PR is used to present positive aspects of an organisation whilst attempting to exercise some influence over the less controllable communications which impact on an organisation's image.

- *Virgin Airways and British Airways issued a series of press releases with their versions of events over the allegations of a 'dirty tricks' campaign. Amongst other claims, Virgin accused BA of planting 'hostile and discreditable stories' in the press, including an attempt to destabilise Virgin by falsely claiming that they were no longer able to get credit to pay for fuel. The public feuding was part of an attempt by both airlines to influence politicians and aviation authorities over access to flying routes and airports. Virgin were pressing for more competition on some of BA's most lucrative flying routes and wider access to take-off and landing slots at Heathrow airport.*

This dispute illustrates the importance of 'publics' other than customers to an organisation. American and European aviation authorities, the ministry of transport and members of parliament were all involved in decisions which would have a significant impact on both Virgin and BA. In Chapter 3, we examined the environment of the marketing process, looking at the influence of internal forces (such as organisational objectives and priorities) and external constraints (such as the political and socio-economic factors). PR can attempt to influence all these environmental forces. Whereas other types of marketing communications are focused mainly on customers and consumers, PR is aimed at a wider range of targets.

The 'publics' important to an organisation might include:

❑ *The workforce*: the most important PR is often accomplished internally by involving employees in the goals and achievements of an organisation. A mutual understanding of what goes on and a sense of belonging can be encouraged by internal communications such as newsletters and activities from social outings to service awards. An active social involvement is often an indicator of a well-motivated workforce.

❏ *Suppliers and distributors*: other organisations involved in the supply chain of the industry are also important contacts with whom to communicate on a regular basis. Suppliers and distributors benefit from information about organisations with whom they do business. Rumours among 'the trade' can have an important influence, for example on the credit-worthiness of a company. PR can help manage these informal communications amongst professional and industry contacts.

❏ *The local community*: organisations, like private citizens, are members of a local community such as a town or a district. Good relations and understanding with that community and its representatives can benefit all parties. It may help resolve planning problems or issues over trading hours, for example. PR activities such as sponsorship of local causes and participation in community events can help integrate an organisation into its local community and foster a sense of mutual support.

❏ *The financial community*: the cash resources made available to an organisation are controlled by an internal and external financial community including boards of directors, public fundholders, banks, investing institutions, financial analysts and city commentators. PR can influence which way the funds flow. For example, publicly-quoted companies try to build relationships with financial institutions, pension funds and other important investors to enhance their share price. Public services such as education and transport use PR to sell the value of their services to central and local government decision-makers in order to maximise their share of the allocation of tax receipts to the various public services.

❏ *Policy-makers*: many bodies including the European and UK parliaments, local councils, trade associations and regulatory bodies make policies, laws and regulations which have direct and indirect effects on the success of an organisation. Pressure groups and individual petitions, often supported by PR in the form of press releases and public statements, can influence the formulation of policy. We have already described how one influential pressure group, the breweries, persuaded the government to modify the original proposals by the Monopoly and Mergers Commission for the supply of beer to changes more acceptable to the industry (see Chapter 3, section 5). Many local issues involve the use of PR, including proposals to build roads or to close schools.

❏ *Customers and consumers*: indirect marketing communications form an important input into the image of an organisation formed by customers and consumers. PR can attempt to influence these less controllable communications such as stories in the press and word-of-mouth comments by ensuring that the organisation's viewpoint is at least represented.

Organisations develop and maintain relationships with these and other stake-holders who are important to its long-term success. PR is often used to help mutual understanding and is particularly needed in times of change.

- *A state secondary school was going to be run by a private company. Following declining pupil numbers and poor inspection reports, the education authority had decided to hand over the management of the school to a company who would change the school into a technology college, specialising in science and IT subjects. This move had been hotly debated among parents, staff and governors, with accusations and counter-accusations between the supporters and opponents of the change. A new headteacher began a PR campaign to heal some of the wounds once the decision had been taken. This involved communicating with many groups with an interest in the future success of the school. Meetings with teachers and parents reassured them that the very survival of their school depended on making it more specialised and outlining the benefits to pupils of planned investment in new facilities. Information sheets explained the changes to pupils so that any feelings of insecurity about the future of the school were minimised. Governors met to discuss the implications and briefed members of the local community about the benefits. Meetings were held with representatives of the local education authority and the central department for education to work out arrangements for the transition. Relationships were developed with local suppliers who were asked to quote for contracts for administrative services. At the end of a very hectic period the school emerged with an image enhanced not only by the extra resources under its direct control but also by the way in which it appeared to manage them. This positive image soon spread by word of mouth among parents and the school received more applications to take pupils as a result.*

PR activities

A variety of methods are used to communicate with the various publics important to an organisation.

Media

Relationships with the press and other media are important means to the end of communicating with an organisation's publics. Larger organisations try to develop long-term relationships with key journalists so that when issues arise they can ensure that their viewpoint is heard. Smaller organisations may benefit from the free publicity that can be obtained from stories in the local or trade press.

Developing media relations is a key part of a PR strategy. It involves:

❑ *Setting PR objectives* which are consistent with the overall marketing strategy and can be integrated into the marketing mix. This implies considering what image an organisation wishes to project in line with its market position and the audiences it wishes to communicate with in line with its target market segments.

❑ *Identification of the relevant media* – that is, media which is directed at the pertinent audience and conveys the appropriate marketing message. 'Down-market' publications cannot be used to project 'up-market' images.

❑ *Preparation and development of newsworthy stories.* The press and TV are interested in news – good or bad – and not information which says nothing new, however interesting it may seem to the organisation publishing it. The media publish stories about the launch of new products but not about the benefits of existing ones. We read headlines such as, 'school goes private' or 'local firm opens new factory', rather than 'school teaches 11 to 16 year olds' or 'firm continues to employ 200 people'. Organisations have limited windows of opportunity to ensure that their newsworthy stories are published; an active PR strategy seeks these out and communicates them to the media.

❑ *Media contact.* The standard means of communication is by a press release, sometimes supported by press conferences if the occasion is important enough. These can be supported by informal meetings and phone calls with journalists to develop an ongoing relationship.

Information

Organisations generate many types of information about themselves that form part of their corporate image. This information is not restricted to leaflets and promotional literature but includes statutory documents (such as annual reports and accounts), reference material (such as prospectuses and catalogues), and internal publications (such as company newsletters). Some organisations give out information through video films, training courses, visits to their premises and open days.

The design and delivery of all types of information, no matter how specialised, helps create impressions of an organisation which contribute to its corporate image. PR's role is to ensure that these impressions are consistent with each other and with the marketing strategy of the organisation.

Lobbying

If an organisation wishes to influence decisions that could affect its future, it needs to make its point of view known amongst decision-makers. The cultivation and lobbying of key decision-makers is part of the PR function. It can be done in a relatively formal way by membership of trade pressure groups or the employment of consultants specialising in political lobbying. It is also done informally by getting to know people in influential positions. At a local level this might include borough councillors, chambers of commerce members or leaders of amenity groups and residents' associations.

'Good causes'

Some organisations try to project an image of responsibility and care for their community and environment by linking their name to 'good causes'. This may involve sponsorship of charities, sporting events, fund-raising activities or shows. Organisations that may be perceived as environmentally 'unfriendly' try to improve their image in this way; the tobacco companies were leading sponsors of professional sport (until prevented by legislation), and energy corporations sponsor many 'green' causes. Organisations can enhance their image with their local community by supporting shows and festivals.

Crisis management

When an organisation becomes embroiled in a crisis, PR can help manage the situation and limit the damage done to their image. British Airways have tried to minimise damage to their reputation over the Virgin Airways dirty tricks affair by differentiating carefully between the way the whole organisation is trained to treat passengers and the way a few individuals mistakenly tried to deal with competitors like Virgin. By developing clear viewpoints on controversial issues and making them known internally and externally, an organisation may hope to ride a particular storm. Avoidance of difficult issues is not always a guarantee that they will go away, however.

- *British Petroleum decided to take a low key attitude in response to the huge oil spillage from the tanker 'Braer' off the Shetland Islands. Although the incident highlighted the international problems of oil transportation and the potential harm to wildlife and the environment from spillage, the company's PR department decided that this was not a good time to be drawn into a public debate on tanker safety. Neither the tanker nor the oil belonged to BP and the company did not wish to be implicated in a disaster in which they had no direct involvement. The environmental pressure group, Greenpeace had other ideas. Thanks to a leaked BP internal memo advising executives to 'keep their heads down on this one', Greenpeace drew public attention to what they considered to be the complacency of the major oil companies. Advertisements headlined 'oil leak' quoted the memo in full and demanded more environmental action rather than fine sounding rhetoric from the oil corporations. BP spends large sums of money in order to convince the public that it is a responsible, environmentally aware multinational. Ironically, its green record came under attack due to an incident outside of its control.*

The BP example illustrates the need for surefooted PR strategies to cope with the possibility of publicity – positive and negative – from any direction. In its early days as a profession, public relations may have been regarded as little more than a method to get free advertising. It has now become an integral part of marketing communications which organisations can rarely afford to overlook.

5. KEY POINTS

- ❑ *Advertising* campaigns can be planned and implemented in five stages:
  - ❑ *Setting objectives* of informing, persuading and/or reinforcing.
  - ❑ *Estimating the budget* by considering expenditure as a percentage of income, competitive expenditure, objectives and tasks, and/or what is affordable.
  - ❑ *Deciding the creative strategy and message*, for example USP or lifestyle.
  - ❑ *Selecting the media* from press, TV, radio, cinema, posters, direct mail and the Internet.
  - ❑ *Evaluating the results.*

❏ *Sales promotions*, or 'below the line' advertising, can be:

   ❏ *'push'* promotions, such as trade promotions and salesforce incentives; or

   ❏ *'pull'* promotions to consumers, such as discounts, samples, coupons, competitions, sponsorship, point-of-sale display and credit facilities.

❏ *Public relations* are the efforts to establish and maintain understanding between an organisation and its publics.

❏ *'Publics'* important to an organisation include the workforce, suppliers, intermediaries, customers, local community, financial community and policy-makers.

❏ Methods used to communicate with publics include media relations, published information, lobbying, support for 'good causes' and crisis management.

6. | DEVELOPING MARKETING SKILLS

Exercises

1. Consider an advertising campaign you have seen recently on TV or in the press.

   (i) Do you think the objectives are to inform, persuade or reinforce, or a combination of these? Why do you think these objectives were chosen?

   (ii) What is the creative strategy and message – USP, lifestyle or a different strategy?

   (iii) Why do you suppose the chosen media was selected?

2. Evaluate a sales promotion campaign you have been exposed to as a consumer. What were its objectives and how effective do you think it was?

3. Suppose you have been asked by your local district council to improve their image through a PR campaign. To whom would you direct your message and what activities would you recommend?

Developing a marketing plan

Activity 11 An advertising, sales promotion and PR strategy

Complete your promotional plan by establishing advertising, sales promotion, and PR strategies:

❏ What will be your objectives?

❏ How much do you plan to spend?

❏ What media will you use and what types of sales promotions will you consider?

❏ What will be the creative strategy?

❏ How will you evaluate the results?

❏ What PR activities do you intend to undertake?

FURTHER READING AND REFERENCES

General

Fitzgerald, M. and Arnott, D. (1999) *Marketing Communication Classics*, Thomson Learning. (This includes a selection of seminal articles in the area.)

Monye, S.O. (editor) (2000) *The Handbook of International Marketing Communications*, Blackwell.

A number of practitioner journals contain examples and cases of promotional campaigns and topics including: *Advertising Age; Campaign; Grocer; and Marketing Week*.

Advertising

Advertising Statistics Year Book, The Advertising Association, NTC Publications Ltd. (For detailed statistical coverage of the UK's advertising and media markets.)

Butterfield, L. (editor) (1999) *Excellence in Advertising*, Butterworth Heinemann.

Jay, R. (1998) *Profitable Direct Marketing*, Thomson Learning.

National Statistics (2001) *Annual Abstract of Statistics*, Office for National Statistics (for statistics of population demographics).

Ogilvy, D. (1995) *Ogilvy on Advertising*, Prion Books.

Packard, V. (1963) *The Hidden Persuaders*, Cardinal.

Internet advertising and new media

Barwise, P. and Hammond, K. (1998) *Media*, Phoenix. (A concise summary of what family life may be like in 2010, thanks to the digital revolution.)

Chaffey, D., Mayer, R., Johnston, K. and Ellis-Chadwick, F. (2000) *Internet Marketing*, Pearson Education, chapters 8 and 9.

Hardaker, G. and Graham, G. (2001) *Wired Marketing*, John Wiley & Sons, chapter 4.

Keynote report (2000a) *Internet Usage in Business*, 4th edition.

Keynote report (2000b) *New Media Marketing*, 2nd edition.

Yuill, V. (1999) *Successful Internet Marketing*, David Grant Publishing.

Sales promotions

Blythe, J. (2000) *Marketing Communications*, Financial Times/Prentice Hall, chapter 10.

Davies, M. (1992) Sales promotion as a competitive strategy, *Management Decision*, **30**(7), pages 5–10.

Public relations

Dolphin, R. (1998) *The Fundamentals of Corporate Communications*, Butterworth Heinemann.

Harrison, S. (2000) *Public Relations: an Introduction*, Thomson Learning.

CHAPTER 12

Place: Marketing Channels

This chapter looks at how products and services are 'placed' into the market – a further important ingredient in the marketing mix. We examine the choices of distribution channels available and strategies for managing them. Marketing channels have changed significantly in recent years and developments in retailing and franchising are discussed.

1. CASE STUDY: FABIO FABRIK – DISTRIBUTING VISION

Antonio Sollicor knew that he had a serious conflict of interest to resolve. His meetings with representatives from the ophthalmic trade had made it quite clear that selecting and managing channels of distribution in the UK for his company's products was not going to be an easy matter. He was the international marketing manager of Fabio Fabrik, Italian manufacturers of spectacle frames, lenses and ready-made reading glasses. Their range of upmarket 'designer' optical products were expensive, but many customers in Italy, France, Germany and other continental European countries were prepared to pay the price for good design and the desirable 'Luce' brand name on their spectacle frames. As he was responsible for all sales outside of Italy, Sollicor was particularly keen to make progress in the UK, a market in which his company sold comparatively little but which had been opened up by deregulation.

In the past, British customers were reluctant to buy anything other than utilitarian frames and few indulged in the continental habit of owning several sets of spectacles to suit the occasion or the wearer's clothes. The NHS voucher scheme, which provided financial assistance to those who qualified, still accounted for over 40 per cent of dispensed spectacles and tended to depress the average price of a pair of glasses. (The average spend on a pair of NHS voucher spectacles was £60 compared to £90 for privately dispensed spectacles.) Luce frames alone without lenses were priced from £85 to £225, but they had begun to sell through a select number of opticians since the 1990s. The 1988 Health and Medicines Act deregulated the ophthalmic market, ending the registered opticians' monopoly position. It abolished free sight tests for all and encouraged more competition in the supply of optical products. Frame design began to gain a higher profile among customers, tentatively encouraged by a profession which began to realise the importance of offering higher quality branded products in a competitive market-place. Consumers had begun to show an increasing interest in designer label frames.

Sollicor had found it difficult to establish effective distribution channels for Fabio Fabrik in a fragmented UK optical trade. Many of the 7000 optical retailers were independents with an estimated 50 per cent share of the market. However this had fallen substantially since deregulation as a number of major retail chains had expanded through organic growth and acquisition. Four market leaders, Specsavers, Boots, Dolland and Aitchison and Vision Express, and a growing number of smaller chains, had emerged since the legislative changes. Specsavers had expanded rapidly by setting up joint venture franchises with professional opticians; it had over 350 outlets in the UK, and recently launched its own brand, 'Ayesha' for women. Boots' 300 outlets were divided almost equally between free-standing and in-store outlets; it particularly concentrated on own-label and exclusive frames which accounted for two thirds of sales. Dollond and Aitchison was the oldest established chain with over 450 branches in the UK; it had recently launched an innovative Internet service allowing customers to scan in a photograph of themselves for a 'virtual fitting' of different frames. Vision Express, had already grown to over 130 outlets since its formation in 1988 and was one of the trade's most prolific spenders on advertising; in 1997 it was acquired by a French group specialising in optical and photographic development stores. Total advertising expenditure by opticians had increased rapidly from just over £1 million at deregulation in 1988 to nearly £50 million ten years later.

Initially Luce branded products were available to any optical retailer who wished to stock them, but Sollicor was considering changing his strategy. He had been approached by 'Horatio's', an ambitious new group which operated on a franchise basis emphasising elegant style and design in their themed outlets. They were asking for more exclusive rights to the Luce range which they claimed would give them the confidence to emphasise it in their promotional campaigns and would enhance the exclusive image of the products. 'Each of our retail outlets is owned by the franchisee manager', Horatio's founder, Juliette Nelson, had told Sollicor, 'which gives them the motivation to increase the average value of each sale by explaining the benefits of high quality, well designed frames to customers.'

Sollicor also had to find effective distribution channels for his company's range of ready-made reading glasses. The 1988 Act made it possible to buy ready-mades over the counter from any shop without a sight test. A market which did not exist before 1989 grew rapidly to sales of over 2 million pairs of reading glasses in a few years. Fabio Fabrik made an attractive range of ready-made glasses under the Luce label and although they would retail above the common price range of £15–£20 per pair, they would still be well below the £80 average price of glasses dispensed through an optician. However Sollicor had spoken to opticians who were far from persuaded by arguments that ready-mades were targeted at consumers who did not need specialist advice in spectacle selection because their eyes were not defective, just weakened with age. Some of his customers told him of their outright opposition to the sale of ready-mades: 'Each person's eyes require individual treatment – sometimes they differ from each other so there is no guarantee that the purchaser will find the right lenses without expert help. And ready-mades mean fewer eye tests to spot more serious problems in good time.' He knew that other distribution channels were more enthusiastic as chemists, department stores and even garages sold ready-mades.

Although ready-mades were still a small part of the total £1.2 billion UK market for spectacles, Sollicor acknowledged that his company could enter this fast growing segment relatively easily as it already produced a suitable range. His problem was how to win support for Luce products from opticians, the key distributors of frames and lenses, whilst establishing effective distribution for

305

ready-mades whose introduction had been opposed by the profession.

'If we see Luce ready-mades in all the chemists and garages of the land, it will undermine the value of the brand and not encourage us to recommend the same company for high quality bespoke frames,' one of his biggest accounts had told him.

Points to consider

1. What different aspects of 'placing' his product in the marketplace does Sollicor need to consider? Which major decision areas does the place element of the marketing mix cover?

See section 2.

2. Consider the types of distribution channels that are illustrated in this case. What are the advantages and disadvantages of using these intermediaries for a company such as Fabio Fabrik?

See section 3.

3. Which distribution channels should Sollicor select for the different lines in the Luce range? How should he manage these?

See section 4.

4. What trends in the general distributive and retail sector are illustrated in this case? What future developments do you think could be particularly important for the distribution of optical products?

See sections 5 and 6.

2.	PLACING PRODUCTS: LOCATION, LOGISTICS, AND CHANNELS

As one of the 4 Ps in the marketing mix, 'place' refers to how goods and services are made available to customers in the marketplace. The concept of 'place' refers not only to the location in which products are offered, but also the channels of distribution through which products move from producer or supplier to the final user and the physical methods that are used to achieve this. The Internet has added further possibilities to how products and services are transferred to customers.

Location

Access to customers

Physical location is a key ingredient in the success of many types of business, particularly retail and business services that rely on customers visiting them. It has been said that the three most important factors in the success or failure of retail outlets and hotels are location, location and location. Retailers in sectors such as food, clothing and household goods need easy access to appropriately sized populations to survive as most people still do a majority of this type of shopping within a few miles of where they live. Customers choose hotels on the basis of where they are situated before considering other factors.

Location is also a major factor in the delivery of many public services in areas such as local government, education and healthcare. As public services have become more focused on service users, location has become an important issue. For some services it is a key influence, but outside of the direct control of local managers. For example, most parents choose to send their children to the primary school that is nearest to them, so that the viability of a school depends crucially on the size of the population in their immediate catchment area – a factor over which headteachers and governors have no control. For other public services, cost restrictions limit the choice of location. For example, local councils might prefer to locate their various services in decentralised sites near to centres of population, but normally they are forced to adopt the less expensive option of centralising all departments in one, less accessible building. The National Health Service has tended to concentrate its resources in large regional hospitals which are more efficient but often less convenient than smaller community units which have been closed.

Access to resources

The location of some types of business is less dependent on proximity to a customer base. Manufacturers may produce for regional, national or international markets as they do not need to be geographically near to customers. Developments in communications technology means that many intangible products can be made available anywhere by telephone, email or over the Internet.

- *Banks and building societies originally evolved on a geographic basis as customers needed to visit their local branch to negotiate loans and mortgages or deposit and withdraw money. The names of many of the institutions reflect their geographic origins – for example the Midland Bank (now HSBC – the former Hong Kong and Shanghai Banking Corporation), the Bank of Scotland, and the Halifax, Woolwich, Bradford and Bingley, and Chelsea Building Societies). Financial transactions can now take place remotely using post, telephone or the Internet. This has allowed newcomers such as Egg and Virgin One to emerge that have no natural geographic base. Traditional banks and societies have changed the way they operate substantially in order to compete in the new environment. Marketing strategies are now less reliant on location of branches and more dependent on the provision of a wider range of competitive services. A spate of mergers and take-overs has reduced the number of branch outlets in the high street as online and telephone banking services have become increasingly popular.*

In these circumstances, location may still be an important consideration in the cost base and service levels provided by the company. Access to resources, such as appropriately skilled employees or suitable premises, is dependent on location. For a manufacturer, the location of suitable premises near to a skilled labour force may be crucial to their ability to deliver competitively priced products on time. The key resource for service industries such as banks and building societies is people. Customer services have been concentrated in call centres located in areas of relatively high unemployment to ensure access to a good supply of employees.

Physical distribution, or logistics

The methods by which goods and services are transferred from supplier to consumer requires careful consideration. Sometimes referred to as 'logistics', physical distribution can represent a significant proportion of the final cost of a product. It includes order processing, warehousing, storage, transportation and handling, all of which can add considerably to the manufacture costs of a product. Modern developments have changed physical handling systems dramatically.

❏ *Containerisation*, or putting goods into large containers or trailers, allows products to be moved easily between two or more different transportation methods. Containers can be transferred quickly and efficiently from ship to lorry, to rail or to plane, making it possible to select the most effective mode of transport for each leg of the journey.

❏ *Computerisation* has improved many stock control and order processing systems, reducing costs to the organisation and achieving higher service levels to the customer – once the inevitable bugs are removed from the system. 'Just-In-Time' (JIT) systems are designed to provide the customer with components for manufacturing as they are needed. This reduces the need to carry large stocks of items, and therefore reduces the cost of manufacturing.

- *Michael Dell began to assemble and sell computers whilst still at university and went on to revolutionise computer making. His business model was relatively simple: he supplied computers direct to end-users according to their own specification. It meant that customers got the computer they wanted at lower prices. The model worked for the customers and it also worked for Dell Computers which became the number one PC supplier. A key factor in Dell's success was his ability to reduce component stocks to well below the industry norm. PCs are made mainly from standard parts. By delivering direct according to a customer's specification, Dell reduced the stocks he had to hold to a minimum. In practice the number of options available to customise a computer are limited mainly to the speed of the processor and size of the memory. This made it possible for Dell to offer made-to-order PCs whilst keeping stock levels down. As computer technology changes so quickly, it is particularly important to avoid having obsolete stocks. Lower stock levels than his competitors made Dell's company more profitable, with more money to invest in marketing to build an even larger share of the market.*

❏ *Online products* have eliminated the need for physical distribution altogether. Some product categories can be digitised and transferred from one computer to another over the Internet. This has the potential to completely change the way in which some sectors, such as the music, publishing and information industries, distribute their products. But it is taking longer for this to happen than some analysts predicted.

- *Music can be distributed directly over the Internet because musical content itself can be digitised and downloaded onto computers. However, this has yet to be turned into a profitable business model. 'Napster' developed a huge following by offering free downloads, but this violated copyright laws.*

David Bowie's 'Hours' album was offered as a download only version two weeks before it was released in hard copy form through standard distribution channels. However it made only 800 Internet sales at the cost of alienating traditional retailers. Although the Internet has become an important medium for promoting and ordering CDs and tapes, it has still to realise its potential for direct delivery of music. This may develop more rapidly as the major companies are beginning to enter the field. For example, EMI recently made over 100 albums and 40 singles available for digital download, and BMG has re-launched Napster as a legitimate paid-for service.

Channels of distribution

Most products often move through various distribution channels such as agents, wholesalers or retailers which act as intermediaries between producer and final customer. These intermediaries usually take title to the goods; that is they buy them from the previous link in the chain before selling them on to the next.

- *Producers of cola such as Coke and Pepsi sell their products through a variety of channels. One route is through franchised bottling companies around the world who purchase syrup and the rights to sell on the final branded consumer product to wholesalers and retailers of soft drinks. The cola producers also sell their syrup direct to large retailers who bottle it under their own label. Agents buy cola syrup from the producers and sell it to restaurants and bars with the necessary equipment and supplies to provide the final product on tap. A drink purchased in a dispensing machine, shop or bar has passed through multiple channels of distribution before reaching the final consumer.*

Decisions on marketing channels sometimes do not receive the same level of attention as other marketing decisions. Yet distribution channels crucially influence the other elements of the marketing mix:

❑ *Products* are often developed or acquired because they complement existing distribution channels.

- *Over-capacity amongst Europe's car producers has lead to a number of take-overs and rationalisation of ranges. Some have proved more successful than others. In 1994 the German car manufacturer BMW acquired the Rover group from British Aerospace for £800 million. Rover's special relationship with the Japanese group Honda which had given the British car company access to much needed technical and production expertise was broken by the deal. Rover's management remained convinced that they would benefit more as part of BMW because it gained them access to a distribution network which they claimed could give them an extra 100,000 car sales from day one. BMW's strong distribution networks, particularly in Germany and the USA, could boost sales in the short term of Land Rover and smaller cars like the Metro and the Mini which complemented BMW's executive range. In the event, the strategy worked for only part of the range. Land Rover and a new generation Mini proved complementary to*

309

the BMW ranges and benefited from new investment and strengthened distribution. But Rover Cars continued to lose market share whilst BMW's own brands gained ground. In 2000, BMW sold this part of the business through a management buy-out as the ranges had proved too close to fully differentiate in an increasingly competitive market.

❑ *Pricing* has to take account of the traditional margins which wholesalers and retailers expect in the particular trade or industry.

- *A wine producer in France knew that a bottle of wine sold by their vineyard for 10 francs (or approximately £1) would retail in the UK for over £3 by the time that not only had taxes been added but the various intermediaries such as the importer, wholesalers and retailers had added their appropriate mark-ups. This was an important influence on their pricing decisions as the UK was a key export market.*

❑ *Promotions*, however persuasive, are not effective if the product is not readily available in the appropriate place in the market.

- *A publisher decided to launch a new magazine and drew up plans for a launch campaign of promotional activities to the target market. They had to drastically modify their plans however when initial meetings with key wholesalers and retailers indicated they would not be prepared to stock the product as they believed that sales would not justify the shelf space.*

The types and roles of distribution channels are explored more fully in section 3 below.

3. MARKETING CHANNELS

Channel levels

A manufacturer is usually faced with the choice of selling products through a number of channel levels, or distributing direct to the customer. Some of the choices available through traditional distribution channels are illustrated in Figure 12.1.

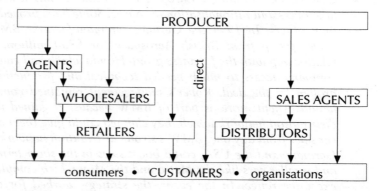

Figure 12.1: *Distribution channel levels*

This shows different channel levels, or layers of intermediaries, which can become involved in the distribution process, each one adding to the length of the distribution chain. Although definitions vary from industry to industry, some commonly used terms are as follows:

❑ *Agents* are independent intermediaries who represent producers or suppliers, often with particular responsibility for a geographic territory. For example, they may import a range of goods from one or more overseas manufacturers into their home country. In turn, they supply wholesalers, retailers or sell direct to end users.

❑ *Sales agents* are also intermediaries who represent producers and suppliers, but they usually do not take title to the goods as they act in a marketing and sales administration capacity only. For example, smaller publishers of greetings cards often use independent sales agents or *agents-on-commission* as they cannot individually justify the costs of personal selling to fragmented stationery and gift retailers. Brokers sell insurance direct to the final customer in return for a commission from the insurance company who write the policy. Office equipment manufacturers appoint sales agents to distribute their products directly to organisations or through distributors and dealers.

❑ *Wholesalers* are organisations which buy a range of stock from producers or their agents, which they then resell to the retail trade. A full service wholesaler provides a range of facilities including selling, order processing, and delivery. For example, newspaper and magazine wholesalers receive print runs in bulk from the publishers which they break down into smaller quantities for onward transmission to the many retail outlets around the country.

❑ *Retailers* sell goods or services direct to the final consumer. Retailing outlets vary from hypermarkets to village stores and an increasing variety of non-store methods such as mail order catalogues, telemarketing and electronic shopping. The different types of retailer and trends in the sector are discussed in section 5 below.

❑ *Distributors and dealers* also sell goods direct to the end user but in this case the customer is often a business or an organisation. For example, educational books and other teaching products are often sold to schools through independent distributors. Dealers sell office products such as furniture and stationery to small businesses. Distributors representing specialist manufacturers provide restaurant owners with the equipment they need. Even though a majority of their sales are business-to-business, some dealers also have a retail outlet open to all as the distinctions between wholesalers, distributors and retailers become increasingly blurred. For example, dealers originally set up to sell PCs and software to the local business community found their services increasingly required by individual customers as the computer revolution spread from the office to the home.

Producers employ the channel options that they consider appropriate to their organisation, its products and the market.

• *Letraset, the manufacturer of transfer products, developed distribution networks around the world to suit the circumstances of the market and the*

311

resources of the company. In the UK, the 'instant lettering' product was sold to the graphic art user via retail outlets. Some very large, specialised accounts, such as government departments, were supplied direct. In each overseas market an exclusive agent was set up to manage the local distribution system. In large markets such as the USA these agents also sold through wholesalers to the smaller retailers. As Letraset grew it began to establish its own subsidiary companies in major markets in Europe, North America and Australasia. These subsidiaries took on the role previously played by the importing agent. Letraset also sold a range of transfers for children often offered as promotions for other products such as breakfast cereals. These sold through sales promotion agencies who were the specialised distributors for this type of product to organisations such as cereal producers. In international markets sales agents were appointed to co-ordinate the efforts of these distributors.

Advantages of intermediaries

As they usually do little to change the actual product, what roles do intermediaries play to justify their place in the chain to the ultimate consumer?

❑ *Reduced investment*: by shifting the responsibility for stockholding further down the chain, a manufacturer can reduce the amount of their own funds tied up in stocks. They can also minimise their investment in premises, transport, systems and other aspects of the distribution infrastructure.

❑ *Local knowledge*: an intermediary such as an agent or a wholesaler usually operates in a geographic area where they understand the business environment and have good local contacts. If an organisation wishes to expand into areas where they have little experience, they may need the knowledge and networks of a local intermediary, at least for a while.

   • *As we have described above, Letraset set up distribution agents in countries around the world. As their products were protected initially by patents the company wanted to take full advantage of this limited window of opportunity. By penetrating international markets whilst competition was limited, they put themselves in a strong market position for the tougher times when the patents expired. They could only do this by using the resources and knowledge of national agents who were able to sell products quickly into their local distribution networks. Later, Letraset wished to profit more from its strong market position, using its increased resources to cut out some of the channel levels to keep a larger share of the financial pie in the company. Many agents were replaced by directly controlled subsidiaries who were able to build on the work of the agent by focusing solely on Letraset products.*

❑ *Economies of scale*: a distributor or retailer selling more than one manufacturer's products spreads the distribution costs which should achieve some economies of scale.

❑ *Transactional efficiency*: by consolidating a number of producers' products in one place, an intermediary cuts down the number of transactions required to give customers what they need.

- *Robin Hood and his Merry Men were concerned at the increasing risks of buying their bows and arrows in Nottingham. Four of them took it in turn to visit local artisans who supplied bows, strings, arrow heads and shafts. This required sixteen transactions to secure what they needed, a time consuming and risky process not only for the wanted men but also for the artisans if they were caught supplying the outlaws. Happily, a middleman set himself up in Nottingham market selling the goods of the four artisans, thereby halving to eight the number of the risky transactions needed to supply Hood and his men.*

A: Direct contacts

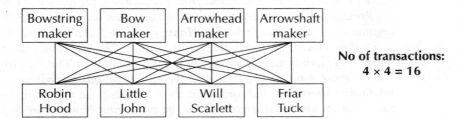

No of transactions:
4 × 4 = 16

B: Transactions through an intermediary

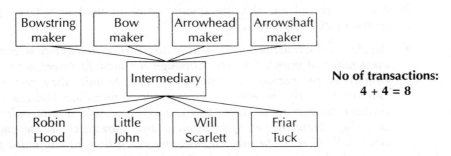

No of transactions:
4 + 4 = 8

Figure 12.2: *Transactional efficiency*

❑ *Breaking bulk*: sometimes intermediaries take a large consignment of goods and break it down into more manageable units for the next distributor or customer in the chain. This process of 'breaking bulk' takes place, for example, when an economic shipment quantity, such as a full container of electronic goods, arrives at an importing wholesalers and is divided up into the smaller quantities required by retail outlets.

Disadvantages of intermediaries

Some manufacturers still opt to sell direct to the final consumer; so what are the disadvantages of using intermediaries?

❑ *Loss of contact with the marketplace*: organisations which rely on intermediaries for their distribution and selling are one or more steps removed from the consumers they are trying to serve. They can become reliant on

313

intermediaries for information about developments in the marketplace, so that the distribution channels become more influential over product developments than the producers.

- *The channels of distribution for food have become increasingly controlled by the large retailers. In the UK three groups, Sainsbury, Tesco, and Asda, control 50 per cent of retail food sales. Farmers have become increasingly remote from the public they serve, powerless to influence the type of products that are made available to the consumer in these large retail outlets. One of the largest land owners in England is trying to change this trend by shortening the lines of communication between producer and user. Keen to make more organic food available from his estates in the Duchy of Cornwall, the Prince of Wales decided to launch his own branded food products. Using organic wheat and oats from 'The Home Farm' in Tetbury, Gloucestershire, and other Duchy of Cornwall farms, Prince Charles commissioned the design and manufacture of a range of biscuits branded as 'Dutchy Originals'. Unlike most food products where the origin of the ingredients remains relatively unknown to the consumer, these biscuits proclaim the name of the farm and its agricultural policies on the packaging in an effort to put the farmer back in touch with the consumers of their produce.*

❑ *Less control over marketing methods and effort*: if intermediaries present the product to the final consumer, they have considerable influence not only over how it is marketed but also the amount of effort used to sell one product compared to its competitors.

- *An electrical retailer provides in-store information and advice to consumers on a range of branded goods. Although the manufacturers have invested heavily in promotions in support of their brands, they rely on staff employed by the retailer to present the appropriate benefits of their products to customers. The retailer is also responsible for after-sales service and the administration of guarantees and warranties. These and other potentially major influences on customer perceptions of a branded product are in the hands of a third party. The retailer's management and staff also exercise choice over which products receive most effort in terms of display, promotional effort and selling time.*

❑ *Less revenue per item sold*: intermediaries cost money as margin is taken at every level of the distribution channel. Although this is not a fixed amount but varies with the level of sales, the potential loss of revenue to a manufacturer can be substantial. Retailers commonly keep between one and two thirds of the final consumer price of most products. If agents' and wholesalers' margins are added, the producer can receive as little as 25 per cent of the final retail price.

- *A suit was for sale in a fashionable boutique for £150 plus VAT. As it was a fashion item which would date rapidly, the retailer needed a 60 per cent margin to justify the stock risk. This meant they had bought the item for £60 from the wholesaler who was making a 20 per cent margin on the garment, having purchased it from the importer for £48. The importer also made a 20 per cent margin having paid the garment manufacturer just over £38 for the suit, or 26 per cent of its final selling price (without VAT).*

4. CHANNEL STRATEGY: SELECTION AND MANAGEMENT

Strategic decisions on channels of distribution cover the *selection* of the appropriate distribution system and the *management* of that system so that it meets organisational goals. These two topics of channel selection and management are discussed in the following sections followed by a summary of the influences that determine channel strategy.

Channel selection

The selection of distribution channels involves consideration of the existing market situation to decide on the *direction* of the channel in relation to competitive products and an assessment of the *intensity* of the distribution required.

Channel direction

In today's competitive markets, new products have to earn their place in a distribution system. Limited shelf space in retailing outlets is hard fought over as the numbers of products have proliferated. Electronic point of sale devices (EPOS) now monitor the movement of goods from retailers' shelves so that poor performing products can be replaced or repositioned in the store. Faced with the need to compete for exposure to customers in the marketplace, producers can select from two basic alternatives:

❑ A *frontal strategy* of using the same channels as existing products. This may be appropriate if:

  ❑ the new product has clear advantages over competitive products;

  ❑ there is evidence of consumer demand because the product appeals to a new market segment or it has a track record of success through other channels; or

  ❑ the distribution channels are likely to favour the new product because it offers them better profits or because of their past relationship with the producer.

❑ A *bypass strategy* of going around the competition by using alternative arrangements. When the distribution channels are full or hostile to new additions this may be the only alternative. The Internet has opened up opportunities to bypass existing channels and sell direct to consumers, and reduce costs at the same time. For example, the travel industry is becoming less reliant on travel agents as a method of distribution as most operators offer on-line booking services. Some now encourage customers to book on the Internet by offering discounts. Potential distribution bottlenecks in other markets can also be side-stepped.

  • *The publisher whose plans to launch a new magazine were blocked after exploratory talks with the major wholesalers and retailers, decided that the only option was to distribute direct to the reader. The powerful wholesaling and retailing operations of WH Smith and John Menzies accounted for over two thirds of the market and their co-operation was vital to the success of any new publication sold through newsagents. As they were not convinced of the viability of the publication, the publisher redesigned the product and sold it as a newsletter-style magazine on an annual subscription basis downloaded over the Internet or by direct mail. The success of this approach allowed the publisher to return at a later date to the distributive trade and persuade them that the product would sell if given the necessary space in the major retailers.*

Distribution intensity

The number of customers reached by a distribution strategy is a function of how intensively the potential channels are used. Where wide coverage is required an intensive strategy sells products through as many outlets as possible. Narrower market penetration indicates the need for more selective distribution. Distribution intensity can be typified as a continuum as shown in Figure 12.3.

◄◄◄ **Exclusive** ◄◄◄◄◄◄◄ **Selective** ►►►►►►► **Intensive** ►►►

Dutchy	Letraset	Coca Cola
Originals	Ford cars	Mars bars
Rolls-Royce		

Figure 12.3: *The continuum of distribution intensity*

❑ *Exclusive distribution* implies that the producer wishes to maintain high service levels to a select number of customers. A small number of intermediaries distribute the product because the producer wants to keep control of the channels or has limited production capacity.

  • *'Dutchy Originals Oaten Biscuits' (see previous reference in section 'Disadvantages of intermediaries' above) are available in a limited number of outlets. They are available in some wholefood shops and upmarket stores such as Fortnum and Mason. This is in line with the exclusive image of the product as well as its limited production capacity.*

❑ *Selective distribution* covers the principal areas for a product without extending beyond its main target markets.

  • *Letraset's early distribution strategy was to cover international markets as rapidly as possible, as we have described. However within each geographic market, the distribution was restricted to graphic art dealers with sufficient resources to offer rapid service to their customers from a well stocked range. In this way Letraset hoped to make their product readily available to their prime target customers without over-extending themselves in the marketplace.*

❑ *Intensive distribution* seeks to provide as many customer purchase points as possible. It is the norm for impulse consumer products, particularly those in the mature phase of their product life cycle, which need as much exposure as possible to maximise sales.

- *Cola drinks are distributed intensively and are to be found in a wide variety of sales outlets including supermarkets, small corner shops, garages, newsagents, restaurants, bars, hotels, trains, planes, motorway cafes and dispensing machines in public places. Geographically, the distribution of the leading brand Coca Cola is so intensive that it covers almost every country on earth and has made 'coke' a universally understood word.*

Channel management

Distribution channels made up of largely independent operators sometimes work efficiently and co-operatively, but often they do not. To resolve some of the conflicts that arise, members attempt to manage the channel through co-operation and coercion.

Channel conflict

There are many opportunities for the participants in a particular distribution channel to come into conflict with the other members.

❑ *Horizontal conflict* arises when distributors on the same channel level disagree. For example, one dealer may complain that another is 'poaching' their business, or neighbouring retailers start a price war by discounting the same product. This may happen when there is unclear specification on the rights and responsibilities between channel members.

❑ *Vertical conflict* arises between different levels of the channel. Producers may come into conflict with the retail or wholesale sector over trading terms and pricing policies. Conflicts of interest arise as channel members seek to enlarge their share of the same cake by changing discount structures, improving payment terms or reducing their stock holding requirements at the expense of the next member of the distribution chain.

- *Nashua, an American office equipment supplier established a subsidiary in the UK to distribute their range of office copiers. To maximise sales whilst keeping the investment and risk at reasonable levels, the UK manager set up offices with a direct salesforce in Greater London, Birmingham and Manchester only and sold through a network of distributors and dealers in the rest of the country. Problems were not long in surfacing. The first issue was how to deal with large multi-site customers. Should they be serviced by Nashua's salesforce or the dealer in whose territory the central buying office was located, even if machines were then sent to locations in other agent's territories? Complaints from dealers who discovered that equipment had been sold into their territory without their participation and disputes over 'customer ownership' became common. The next issue was over profit margins. Some dealers were single line – that is they stocked only Nashua's products. They demanded higher discounts as reward for their loyalty which, they claimed, resulted in higher sales penetration than that achieved by the multi-line dealers who could pick and chose over which supplier to recommend.*

Conventional distribution systems such as the one described can become inefficient and problematic as independent members try to meet their own objectives without regard for the health of the system as a whole.

Vertical marketing systems

Vertical marketing systems (VMS) have developed as a way of managing and controlling distribution channels to resolve some of these issues. In a VMS, the channel members – producers, wholesalers, retailers or dealers – operate as a unified system. This is achieved by combinations of coercion and co-operation. Some channels are controlled effectively by one very powerful member. Others are either owned by one organisation or bound by strong contractual links between all the parties.

Corporate vertical marketing system

A corporate VMS unifies successive stages of manufacture and distribution under a single owner. A producer may decide to achieve control of the distribution channels by *forward integration*, that is buying into or setting up their own wholesaling and retailing operations. Or retailers may decide to own their own suppliers by a process of *backward integration*.

- *In the UK, the major footwear manufacturers are also the largest retailers. The British Shoe Corporation was the market leader with 20 per cent of the market both as a producer and retailer of shoes, until its demise in the 1990s. This large conglomerate of over 2000 outlets trading as Freeman Hardy and Willis, Saxone, Dolcis, Trueform, Shoe City, Curtess, and Cable and Manfield, was broken up into smaller groups. The largest of these is Stylo Barratt which owns Barratt shoes and Saxone. The largest UK footwear group is now C&J Clark, a family-owned manufacturer and retailer trading through 600 outlets as Clarks Shoes, Peter Lord, Ravel and K shoes.*

Although a corporate VMS exercises a great degree of control through ownership, there are disadvantages:

❑ *Resource intensive*: owning and managing a complete distribution chain absorbs such large amounts of financial and management resources that it may lead to neglect of other areas such as product development and customer service.

❑ *Expertise*: it is arguable whether one organisation can excel at both manufacturing and retailing. Retailers such as Marks and Spencer have deliberately avoided ownership of production and concentrated on retailing, their traditional area of expertise. The Burton Group moved away from their manufacturing base in the 1970s in order to concentrate on a targeted retailing approach.

❑ *Conflict*: vertical integration does not eliminate the possibility of conflict. In some cases it exacerbates it.

- *Letraset developed their distribution internationally, first through agents and then subsidiary companies distributing through the local dealer network (see 'Channel selection' above). As the market for 'instant lettering' matured, the company embarked on a strategy of forward integration to secure growth by taking a share of the dealers' business. Retail operations were bought or set up in Canada and Australia to test the concept. The reaction from the independent dealers was universally hostile. They felt threatened by a major supplier operating on the same channel level as themselves and many looked for alternative sources of supply for the first time. The company was still dependent on the dealer network for a large percentage of sales and when their own retailing operations did not match their profit expectations they abandoned the strategy.*

Contractual vertical marketing systems

A contractual VMS co-ordinates the distribution system not by ownership but by contracts between the participants. These contractual arrangements include:

❑ *Co-operatives* between producers, wholesalers or retailers who agree to join together to gain economies of scale or increase their purchasing power.

- *Smaller vineyard owners set up co-operatives to wholesale their wines and undertake production activities such as bottling to spread the fixed costs and minimise individual investment. In the UK, several wholesale buying groups have emerged in the food sector to service independent retailers under pressure from the power of the grocery multiples. So-called 'symbol group convenience stores' such as Spar, Londis, VG, and Mace are independently owned outlets which compete not only by offering late night shopping but also low prices through the buying power of their symbol group.*

❑ *Franchises* legally define the rights and responsibilities of the parties involved in a distribution system. Franchising is a business arrangement in which one party (the franchisor) allows others (the franchisees) to use a business name, or sell products in such a way that the franchisee can still operate as a legally separate business. It can mean as little as an agreement to sell a company's products in a specific territory or as much as a complete business package specified by the franchisors. It is this latter type of so-called 'business format franchising' which has today become common in some industries such as fast food (Kentucky Fried Chicken, Burger King, Pizza Hut, McDonald's) and instant print (KallKwik, Prontaprint). Although franchising does not eliminate conflict, it does result in a set of mutually dependent operators whose interests all lie in making the system work. As it has become such an important force in distribution networks, franchising is considered in more detail in section 6.

Administered vertical marketing system

An administered VMS is one in which the buying or supplying power of one the members ensures the co-operation of the rest of the channel. The concentration of retail outlets in some sectors has given the multiple chains such buying power that they can effectively tell the manufacturers what to do.

- *The UK clothing industry has been increasingly dominated by large multiple retailers. The largest groups, including the Arcadia Group (Burtons), Sears*

(Fosters, Hornes, Miss Selfridge), Marks & Spencer, Next, Matalan, GPS (Gap), Debenhams and BHS control over half of the sales of clothing and footwear in the UK giving them enormous buying power over producers. They have added to their buying muscle by their marketing strategy of selling mainly their own brands which gives them complete control over product specification and quality standards.

In other industries, the power of the producer unifies the distribution channel.

- *Letraset's share of the graphic art lettering market was so high in the UK that it became the generic term for rub-down lettering. Sales of Letraset became a significant proportion of the total business of many of the dealers, some of whom were either ex-Letraset employees or trained and advised by the company in how to make a graphic art dealership work. Regular seminars and sales conferences promoted the unity of the dealer network which Letraset dominated until their product was made obsolete by the introduction of computer graphics.*

The types of vertical marketing systems are summarised in Figure 12.4.

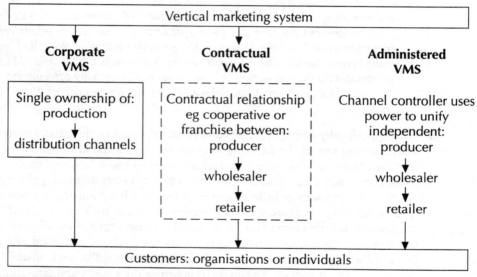

Figure 12.4: *vertical marketing systems (VMS)*

Horizontal marketing systems

Horizontal marketing systems involve two or more organisations on the same channel level who co-operate to pursue a marketing opportunity.

- *Two car producers, Honda and Austin Rover co-operated to help each other in their respective areas of strength. The arrangements through which Rover gained access to Honda engineering expertise and Honda gained penetration of European markets through Rover's existing networks, ended when the German car maker BMW acquired Rover from its parent company British Aerospace.*

This did not produce the expected synergy and in 2000 BMW sold most of the Rover business back to a management consortium.

- *Food retailers have been looking to increase their turnover by widening their distribution horizontally. Out-of-town superstores have added petrol filling stations on some of their sites to service the car-borne shopper. Tesco, Asda and Sainsbury are becoming major petrol retailers with filling stations at their superstores. They are also expanding their in-store facilities. Tesco have in-store pharmacies throughout the UK, run by independent pharmacists dispensing NHS prescriptions. Other facilities include post offices and banks.*

Influences on channel strategies

Channel strategies – the selection and management of distribution channels – are influenced by a number of factors as illustrated in Figure 12.5.

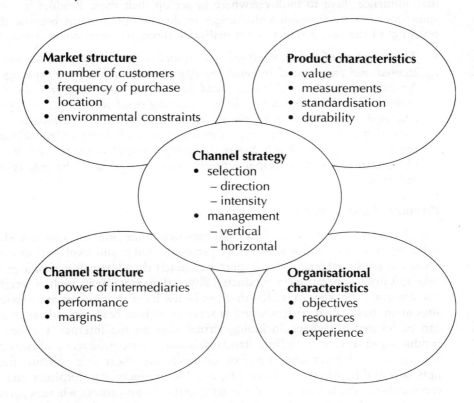

Figure 12.5: *Influences on channel strategies*

Market structure

The numbers of customers, their frequency of purchase and location is a key influence on channel length and width. If a product has many potential customers who buy relatively often in geographically dispersed locations, it requires intensive distribution and greater numbers of channel levels to reach the market. For this reason, low value consumer products such as confectionery items are sold through a variety of wholesale and retail outlets, whilst high value industrial products such as aeroplanes have a selective distribution restricted to few or no intermediaries between producer and buyer.

Constraints in the business environment also shape the distribution system. The Monopolies and Mergers Commission report on the distribution of beer in the UK, which recommended the loosening of ties between licensed outlets and the big breweries, lead to a radical change in the number and type of public houses in the UK.

Channel structure

The power and performance of the existing channels of distribution are an important selection consideration. A well-organised distribution structure offering adequate margins is attractive to producers. A fragmented, disorganised system may influence them to look elsewhere or set up their own. Product innovations sometimes initiate fundamental changes to distribution systems because the full potential of the new product is not realisable through conventional channels.

- *The inventors of the plain paper copier found the existing print trade too short-sighted and fragmented to seize the opportunity of this break-through. The Xerox corporation decided to build their own marketing and distribution system in the USA by renting the new copying equipment direct to customers. Although they did not have the resources to expand internationally on their own, they still preferred to bypass existing channels when selling overseas. In the UK they set up Rank Xerox, a jointly owned company with the Rank Organisation whose principal activities until then were in the entertainments industry.*

Product characteristics

The characteristics of the product itself help determine how it is distributed. High value or complex products requiring personal selling and explanation (such as houses or pensions) tend to have shorter channels than low value, simple products (like soft drinks or stationery products). Physical measurements such as weight and size constrain the types of outlets that can be used: car showrooms are restricted to sites away from town centres whereas services such as banking and estate agency can be located anywhere, including virtual sites on the Internet. Custom made products and services with little standardisation require producer and customer to communicate directly and therefore channels are short (e.g. picture framing, opticians and hairdressers). Long life, durable products (e.g. furniture and tools) can survive in the warehouses of a lengthy distribution process whereas perishable items (e.g. milk and bread) need shorter, more immediate channels.

Organisational characteristics

The objectives, resources and experience of the organisations involved influence not only the channels used but also how they can be managed. A small business with the limited objective of making a comfortable living for its owner follows different distribution strategies to more ambitious organisations that are seeking to become market leaders. In many sectors there is a trade-off between the costs of distribution and the degree of control that can be exerted over the channel members This is illustrated in Figure 12.6.

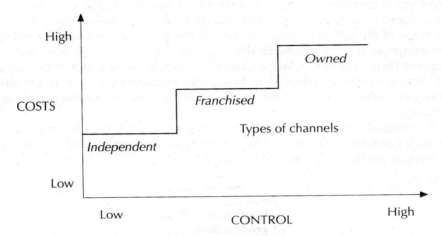

Figure 12.6: *Costs versus control in channel options*

An organisation's distribution strategy often evolves in line with its resources and experience to take account of this trade-off.

- *The Body Shop developed rapidly because it managed the relationship between distribution control and costs in various phases of growth. Anita Roddick was so encouraged by the success of her first Body Shop in Brighton in 1976 that after only six months' trading she decided to open another one in Chichester. The costs of this second outlet were high: to raise the necessary £4000 finance she sold half the shares of her fledgling company to an outside investor. However, the ownership of her own outlets helped her to develop an innovative range of body care products marketed in a radically different way to traditional cosmetics. Once they had proved that their ideas were commercially sound in their own shops, Anita and her husband Gordon Roddick realised that fast growth for the new concepts could not be achieved through company-owned outlets because of their very limited resources. The next phase of growth came from selling their body care products in the distinctive plastic bottles to other independent retailers. Initially, the Roddicks made only loose arrangements with the new group of Body Shops that emerged, reflecting their emphasis on growth at minimal cost during that time. This evolved later into a tightly controlled franchise operation as the resources and experience of the company grew. The Body Shop now carefully selects its franchisees and controls and monitors their activities on a regular basis.*

Categories of retailer

Retailing is sometimes thought of in the narrow sense of selling products in stores and shops. In fact, retailing is the general term for a wide variety of activities involved in the selling of goods or services directly to the end user for individual consumption. It covers the marketing of goods through outlets of many sizes from supermarkets to kiosks. It may include the consumption of goods or the provision of services on the premises as in hotels and restaurants, or it may not involve premises open to the customer at all, as in the case of mail order or on-line retailing.

Retailing can be grouped into various categories according to the emphasis given to such variables as the product line or the types of premises used, if at all. These categories are illustrated in Figure 12.7.

Figure 12.7: *Categories of retailing*

Depth and width of product lines

As customers we tend to think of retailers according to the products they sell, so that the depth and width of the product lines on offer is an important distinguishing feature.

☐ *Speciality outlets* carry a narrow product line in some depth. Most high streets are dominated by these types of retailers specialising in products and services from shoes (Clarks) and confectionery (Thorntons), to property and financial services (estate agents, banks and building societies).

☐ *Departmental stores* offer a wide range of products divided into various category areas, or departments, under one roof. Although many stores have had to carefully reposition themselves to survive the twin threat of supermarkets and speciality shops, they contain some of the flagship names in British retailing such as Harrods, Debenhams, House of Fraser and the John Lewis Partnership.

☐ *Variety chains* offer a limited number of product ranges in depth. Marks and Spencer specialise in clothes, footwear and food; WH Smith offer stationery, magazines, books and music. Other variety chains include Boots and Woolworths.

☐ *Supermarkets* carry a wide range of food and household products in large, self-service outlets at low prices. Their development in the UK was lead by the grocery chains such as Sainsbury, Tesco and Asda but their success has encouraged other sectors from toys to car parts.

☐ *Superstores and hypermarkets* are giant supermarkets located in out of town centres. Whereas a typical supermarket might offer 10,000 product lines from 20,000 square feet of floor space, a superstore occupies at least 25,000 square feet and sells 20,000 items. Hypermarkets range from 50,000 to 150,000 square feet of selling area, displaying enormous volumes of products.

Customer service levels

Levels of service in retailing vary according to the needs of the product and the emphasis placed on service in the marketing mix.

☐ *Personal service* has diminished as an essential part of retailing as goods have become standardised and pre-packaged. However it is still needed if products are tailor-made to customer requirements (e.g. picture framing) or for services such as travel agencies or insurance brokers. It is also a featured by retailers who differentiate themselves from competitors by emphasising higher service levels, for example some department stores and restaurants.

☐ *Limited service* has become the norm in many speciality stores and variety chains. Goods can be self-selected but staff are available for help and advice.

☐ *Self-service* keeps contact with staff to a minimum, usually restricting it to paying at centralised cashpoints. It is now the familiar shopping experience not only in supermarkets but also in other retail environments, from online shopping and catalogue showrooms to banking and petrol stations.

Price position

Competitive prices are an important element in most retailers' marketing strategies. There is however a relationship between other factors, such as convenience and customer service levels, and price. Some retailers offer more service or convenience for higher prices: department stores offer higher levels of personal attention, whilst convenience stores stay open for longer hours. Both tend to be more expensive as a result. Some retailers sacrifice service levels and concentrate on low prices.

❑ *Discount stores* have become familiar in the household goods sector including electrical specialists (Dixons, Currys and Comet), and furniture retailers (MFI).

❑ *Cash and carry or warehouse retailers* emphasise the price advantage for consumers to buy in bulk. For example, Majestic Wine Warehouses sell wine by the case in no-frills outlets away from the high street offering more variety than supermarket wine departments and lower prices than off-licences and traditional wine merchants.

❑ *'Category killers'* are so-called because they take the strategy of 'piling it high and selling it cheap' to such an extreme that other retailers find it hard to compete. They are superstores which specialise in a clearly defined product category at discount prices. Examples include the furniture retailer IKEA, and Toys R Us, both currently expanding rapidly in Europe and the USA. This type of retail operation has succeeded by bringing economies of scale and buying power into sectors where the fragmentation of the existing retail structure made it relatively inefficient.

Ownership

Conforming to the trends in North America and Western Europe, the UK retail trade is becoming more concentrated in terms of ownership and sales through the larger groups.

❑ *Small retail businesses* are defined as independents with one outlet and smaller multiples with a turnover below £4.5 million. These are still the most numerous category of retailer, but their numbers are falling and they take a diminishing percentage of total retail sales. In 1997, the sales of these outlets represented only 23.9 per cent of total UK retail sales of £178.2 billion (see Figure 12.8).

❑ *Large retail businesses* outperform other retailers in key measures such as turnover per outlet and stock turnover, and these efficiency advantages have helped them take an increasing share of retail business. They now account for over three quarters of the UK retail trade through less than 20 per cent of the total number of outlets. Although their prices are generally lower, they operate on similar gross margins to independents and small multiples because of their buying power and other economies generated from their higher turnovers.

Figure 12.8 illustrates this breakdown of retail business, showing the sales of large (sales over £4.5m) and small (sales under £4.5m) retail businesses.

❑ *Co-operatives* began as self-help movements in the eighteenth and nineteenth centuries and continue in the retailing sector today as co-operative societies such as the Co-operative Wholesale Society (CWS) which operates department

Sales of large and small retail businesses at current prices (£s bn)

	1990	1997	% change
Large businesses	86.6	135.6	+56.6
% of total	*67.7*	*76.1*	
Small businesses	41.4	42.6	+2.9
% of total	*32.3*	*23.9*	
Total	128.0	178.2	39.2

A 'large retail business' is defined as having sales of more than £4.5 million

Figure 12.8: *The concentration of UK retailing* (Source: *Keynote, 1998*)

stores, supermarkets and convenience stores. Although they have steadily lost market share, the 85 UK retail societies still accounted for nearly £4 billion of retail sales in 1991.

❏ *Franchises* have become the fastest growing form of contractual VMS which attempt to gain the efficiencies of a well-organised, controlled marketing channel whilst retaining the independence of individual members. (Franchising is described more fully in section 6.)

Location

Location is a key factor – in some cases *the* key factor – which distinguishes one retailer from another.

❏ *High street* locations have the highest costs but customer traffic still attracts speciality retailers, variety chains and department stores.

❏ *Out-of-town* shopping has grown substantially since the 1980s. Lead by furniture and DIY multiples such as MFI, B&Q, Homebase and Do It All, out-of-town superstores took advantage of increased car ownership by developing in more spacious, lower cost retail parks away from congested high streets. The leading food groups such as Tesco and Sainsbury soon followed although they have preferred to develop on sites devoted solely to their use.

❏ *Neighbourhood or convenience stores* have stepped into some of the gaps left by the withdrawal of major chains from town centres. Food retailers, confectioners, and newsagents, sell a limited range of goods priced above superstores in recognition of their longer opening hours and ease of access by local populations. Most are independent, although a majority operate within a 'symbol' or buying group, such as Spar. Others are owned by convenience store companies such as Cullens, and an increasing number are oil-company owned as they have become popular within petrol stations.

❏ *Shopping centres* have become another feature of modern retailing. These are large scale developments, usually over 100,000 square feet, which provide a cluster of retail outlets under one roof. Many are in town centres such as the large, 350,000 square feet, Charles Darwin Centre in Shrewsbury. Regional shopping centres, including Brent Cross in North West London and the MetroCentre in Gateshead, are even bigger, servicing large population groups from lower cost, out-of-town sites on good access routes.

Non-store retailing

Non-store retailing has had considerable publicity in recent years with the development of online shopping. In fact 'home shopping' has a long history and takes a variety of forms.

❑ *Mail order* traditionally covered orders taken and delivered by post from the large catalogues distributed by companies such as Littlewoods and Grattans. Although the full range of catalogues still exists, technology and targeting have changed the industry. Today most orders are taken by phone or online and paid for by credit card. Smaller catalogues target specific market segments with tailored products. The 'Innovations' catalogue offers products with a high-tech image, whilst Readers Digest targets consumers with information on specific subjects ranging from astronomy to gardening.

❑ *Direct mail* is even more targeted, with offers from bank loans to bedspreads sent using selected mailing lists.

❑ *Teleshopping* is used increasingly to achieve the same ends as mail order – direct contact with a customer who is offered the possibility of buying without leaving home. Although some companies sell direct over the telephone only, most offer the alternative of ordering online

❑ *Online shopping* over the Internet is a relatively recent phenomenon. There were earlier attempts to introduce forms of electronic retailing (or 'e-tailing'). As with Internet shopping, customers could use computer terminals at home to search for the product they wanted, enquire about features, pricing and delivery terms, place orders and arrange payment. Although services were tried in the USA and Europe, they failed to develop because too few customers subscribed to the system and invested in the necessary special equipment. The growth of the Internet made special systems and equipment unnecessary, and online shopping is now forecast to develop quickly. However, it represents a small sector of retailing at present. Although over half of shoppers have now purchased online, the value of consumer purchases was estimated at £2 billion in the UK in 2000, just over 1 per cent of total retail purchases (Keynote, 2000a). Penetration is higher in some categories such as books, music, software, videos, and consumer electronics. It is also expected to grow strongly in the travel, apparel and toy markets (Ernst and Young, 2001). Online retailers are a mixture of newcomers and traditional companies. The most popular UK online retailer is Amazon, who welcomed their two millionth customer in 2000. Established airlines (e.g. British Airways) and travel companies (e.g. Eurotunnel) offer tickets online. Existing food retailers have extended their services by offering home deliveries ordered over the Internet (e.g. Tesco).

❑ *Network or multi-level marketing* is the latest in many forms of door-to-door selling which have emerged over the years. A network of sales agents promote a manufacturer's products not just to consumers but also to other agents. As agents receive commission on everything that is sold either by themselves or the other agents they have introduced or 'sponsored', they can earn a substantial income, although most people in a network are part-timers supplementing their income. Some American organisations (e.g. Amway and National Safety Associates (NSA)) have developed extensive networks of self-employed agents using these systems selling household cleaners and personal care and diet items.

Whilst the industry still makes exaggerated claims about the earning capacity of its agents, it has moved on from the discredited days of 'pyramid selling'. Regulations now exist in Europe and North America to prevent some of the unscrupulous operations which developed. In these pyramid schemes, distributors paid an entrance fee and bought stocks of product which they then attempted to sell on at a profit to other agents or consumers. There were no fixed prices and stocks were often passed on to agents at prices above their real consumer value. UK regulations now limit the entry fee into a network and insist on formal contracts between the supplying company and the independent distributor. Above all, schemes have to demonstrate that their products have genuine end-users.

'Party plans' are another style of network in which agents organise household gatherings to demonstrate products including plastic containers (Tupperware) and cosmetics (Avon).

The new channel 'captains'

Channel 'captains' or 'controllers' use their influence to resolve issues such as the levels of service given to customers, the financial deal available at each channel level and demarcation disputes between members. As the examples given (in section 4) have shown, channel captains can be an independant producer (Letraset), wholesaler (Spar), or retailer (Marks and Spencer); they can be franchisors (The Body Shop) or vertically integrated corporations (Clarks). Recently, trends in consumer marketing have shifted control from the producers of branded goods to the large retailers. The development of branded products earlier this century gave their producers considerable muscle in the marketplace. Brand leaders such as Kelloggs, Mars, Heinz and Kodak could dictate terms to the wholesalers and retailers who had to stock their products or lose sales. The producers effectively controlled how their goods were marketed from setting the recommended retail price to determining how they should be displayed and promoted in-store. Today, the development of retailing giants in key sectors such as food and clothing has shifted the balance of power further down the distribution channel as the retailer now calls the marketing tune and sets quality and service standards.

- *Sainsbury challenged the world's leading brand Coca Cola in what were called the 'the cola wars'. Sainsbury replaced its own-label brand of cola which accounted for about 24 per cent of its sales with 'Classic Cola' an exclusive Sainsbury product purchased from a Canadian supplier. Coca Cola, which made up 62 per cent of Sainsbury's cola sales prior to the launch, threatened legal action on the grounds that the new product closely resembled the name and packaging of its own famous brand. Their protests were intensified by initial reports that sales of the new 'Classic' made up 70 per cent of Sainsbury's sales in the first few weeks whilst 'the real thing' fell to 27 per cent of purchases within the supermarket's outlets.*

329

Own-branding

The launch of an exclusive branded cola product by Sainsbury is a recent development in a longer-term move towards 'own-branding' by the major multiples. Some retailers only sell their own branded products (e.g. Mothercare). Others sell a high percentage of own-branded products (Sainsbury 60 per cent, Tesco 55 per cent). Many are still keen to sell manufacturers' branded products, knowing that a large investment has been made to build the brand reputation. For example, electrical retailers still sell a high percentage of branded products (e.g. Dixons and Currys sell less than 20 per cent own-brands). However the growth of own-brands to about 25 per cent of all UK retail sales has shifted the balance of power towards the large retailer and put a question mark against the long-term value of manufacturers' branded products.

6. | FRANCHISING

Franchising was defined (in section 4, 'Channel management') as an arrangement in which one party (the franchisor) allows others (the franchisees) to use a business name or sell products in such a way that the franchisee can operate their own legally separate business. Today there is a major distinction between two forms of franchising: product/trademark franchising and business format franchising.

Product and trademark agreements

By making agreements to distribute their products through licensed dealers, manufacturers created an early form of franchising. Breweries were probably the first franchisors when they introduced the system which 'tied' otherwise independent publicans to one producer of beer. Car manufacturers and oil companies developed the distribution of their products through various licensing arrangements under which a local dealer or distributor took responsibility for sales in a certain territory in return for some element of profit. The producers developed their products and the goodwill associated with the trademarks; the local distributor contributed local knowledge, contacts, effort, and usually some investment. Such distribution arrangements are still common, for example, in the soft drinks industry.

Manufacturing processes are also distributed in this way. If the inventor of a patented process wishes to exploit their innovation on a wider basis than their resources allow, they may permit other manufacturers to use the process under licence in return for a royalty.

- *Alistaire Pilkington's invention of 'float glass' enabled his company to manufacture a distortion-free glass at low cost to replace cheap but optically imperfect 'sheet' glass or expensive, hand polished 'plate' glass. The size and fragility of the product favour local manufacture, and as Pilkington did not wish to set up manufacturing plants all around the world, he 'distributed' the concept by licensing other manufacturers to use the new system.*

Intangible assets such as well-known names and celebrities are also franchised to reach a wider public. Products are endorsed by fictional characters or real people under licensing agreements specifying how the name or image may be used and what royalties are payable for the privilege.

Business format franchising

Franchisor and franchisee may enter a more comprehensive relationship than a simple trademark or licensing arrangement. *Business format franchising* goes beyond the supply of products and trade names to cover many more aspects of how a business is run.

Franchisors offer a complete package allowing the franchisee to use a format which has been developed and proven commercially whilst retaining legal independence. The business format offered by the franchisor may cover many aspects including:

- ❑ trade name, business style, logo, house colours;
- ❑ detailed product or service specification;
- ❑ training and help to set up and ongoing advice on running the business;
- ❑ national and local marketing;
- ❑ centralised purchasing or supply of products;
- ❑ management control and operating systems; and
- ❑ research and development of new products and processes.

In return the franchisee pays the franchisor agreed sums of money which usually include:

- ❑ An initial franchise fee as a one-off payment to the franchisor to cover the goodwill of the name and training. This can vary from £1000 (e.g. for a Unigate Dairies milk round) to £25,000 or more (e.g. a Burger King franchise).
- ❑ The costs of setting up and running the business as specified by the franchisor. These include the costs of buying equipment, fitting out premises, stock, promotional literature and stationery. The minimum start up investment for franchises varies enormously depending on the value of the name and the nature of the business (e.g. £4500 for Unigate Dairies and £700,000 for Burger King).
- ❑ Annual charges or fees. An ongoing service fee is charged, often as a percentage of sales (typically 5 to 15 per cent of invoiced sales value). Other levies on the franchisee include contributions to national advertising and training for staff.

A franchise agreement sets out the obligations of both parties including how the franchisee is to run the business, what payments they make and what the franchisor will provide in return.

The franchising market

Franchising has developed strongly in the USA where it now accounts for over one third of all retail sales. Entrepreneurs such as Colonel Sanders and Ray Kroc pioneered the concepts from the 1950s. Sanders travelled around America persuading people to cook chicken his way as Kentucky Fried Chicken franchisees. Ray Kroc modelled his franchise on the standardised burger production techniques of the McDonald brothers. Today US franchisors have spread their concepts internationally with globally recognised brands such as Domino's Pizza and McDonald's.

In the UK, franchising is less significant but it is a fast growing sector. The annual turnover of franchised companies was nearly £9 billion in 1999, representing around 5 per cent of total retail sales, made through 30,000 franchised outlets operated by over 600 franchisors (Keynote, 2000b). These can be divided by market sector as shown in Figure 12.9. Although fast food outlets are the most visible franchises in the high street, business services have grown rapidly to become the most numerous sector.

Sector	% of total franchised units	Examples
Business services	25	KallKwik, Interlink Express
Catering	21	Perfect Pizza, KFC, Wimpy
Personal services	16	Stagecoach Theatre, Wedding Guide
Store retailing	14	Body Shop, Tie Rack
Property services	13	Dyno-Rod, Apollo Window Blinds
Transport services	11	Kwik-Fit, Green Flag, Autoglass

Figure 12.9: *Franchised outlets by sector* (Source: Keynote, 2000b)

The advantages and disadvantages to franchisors

Factors which attract organisations to franchising as a distribution method include:

❑ The ability to extend the distribution of products or concepts quickly. As expansion is funded mainly by the franchisees, less capital is required from the franchisor.

❑ The recruitment and retention of committed managers who as franchisees have the additional motivation of business ownership.

❑ More control over outlets than totally independent distribution channels.

However, disadvantages for franchisors include:

❑ Less control over franchisees than fully owned outlets.

❑ The continued obligations of the franchise agreement to provide central support services, even if the franchisor wishes to exit from the business.

7. KEY POINTS

❑ *The place element* of the marketing mix involves decisions about the location in which goods and services can be purchased, the distribution channels through which they pass from producer to final user, and the physical distribution methods used.

❑ *The Internet* represents both a threat and an opportunity to distribution methods as it can both replace and complement existing channels.

❑ *Intermediaries* between producers and consumers operate on a number of different channel levels. They include agents, wholesalers, distributors, dealers and retailers.

❑ *Advantages of intermediaries* include reduced investment, local knowledge, economies of scale, transactional efficiency and breaking bulk.

❑ *Disadvantages of intermediaries* include less control over marketing methods and effort and less revenue per item sold.

❑ *Channel strategies* cover the selection and management of distribution systems:

    ❑ *Selection* involves decisions on the direction and intensity of distribution.

    ❑ *Channel management* decisions attempt to overcome conflict and create efficiencies through vertical or horizontal marketing systems.

❑ *Vertical marketing systems (VMS)* can be corporate, contractual or administered.

❑ *Horizontal marketing systems* operate on the same channel level.

❑ Factors which influence channel strategies include market structure, channel structure, product characteristics, and organisational characteristics.

❑ *Retailing* can be categorised and evaluated by trends in the depth and width of product lines offered, customer service levels, price position, ownership, location and non-store retailing such as online shopping. The large multiples have become channel 'captains' in some sectors because of the concentration of retail sales in their outlets.

❑ *Franchising* is a fast developing channel system which can be sub-divided into trademark and licensing agreements, and business format franchising.

8.   DEVELOPING MARKETING SKILLS

Exercises

1. Imagine you have developed a new ice cream which you manufacture on a dairy farm. What marketing channels would you consider and which would you select? What distribution problems would you foresee?

2. Create a retail 'map' of an area you know well and use personally.

    (i) Draw an outline street map and place the principle types of retailers on it. Categorise them by ownership types (e.g. large multiples, franchises, independents) and other important classifications.

    (ii) Describe the main changes you have witnessed in the area. If possible talk to someone from an older generation to obtain a longer-term perspective. What developments do you foresee in the future?

(iii) Consider which shops you use and the patterns of shopping within your family and amongst your friends. How have these changed in recent years?

Developing a marketing plan

Activity 12 The distribution strategy

How will you place your product or service into the market? Consider issues of location and marketing channels. Define your channel strategy in terms of:

❑ selection (direction and intensity); and

❑ management (creating efficiencies and overcoming conflict).

FURTHER READING AND REFERENCES

General texts

Brassington, F. and Pettit, S. (2000) *Principles of Marketing*, 2nd edition, Financial Times/Prentice Hall, chapters 12 and 13.

Dibb, S., Simkin, L., Pride, W.M. and Ferrell, O.C. (2001) *Marketing Concepts and Strategies*, Houghton Mufflin, chapters 12, 13 and 14.

Channel management

Christopher, M. (1998) *Logistics and Supply Chain Management*, 2nd edition, Financial Times/Prentice Hall.

Saunders, M. (1997) *Strategic Purchasing and Supply Chain Management*, 2nd edition, Financial Times/Prentice Hall.

Retailing

Keynote Report (1998) *Retailing in the UK*, 3rd edition.

Mintel (2000) *Department and Variety Store Retailing*, December.

Sullivan, M. and Adcock, D. (2001) *Retail Marketing*, Thomson Learning.

E-commerce

Ernst & Young (2001) *Global Online Retaining Report*, Cap Gemini, Ernst & Young.

Keynote Report (2000a) *Internet Usage in Business*, 4th edition.

Mintel (1999) *Online Shopping*, July.

Franchising

Felstead, A. (1993) *The Corporate Paradox: Power and Control in the Business Franchise*, Routledge.

Keynote Report (2000b) *Franchising*, 7th edition.

Hoy, F. (1994) The dark side of franchising or appreciating flaws in an imperfect world, *International Small Business Journal*, 12(2).

CHAPTER 13

The Application of Marketing – Concepts in Context

This chapter summarises the use of marketing in different situations, reviewing some of the concepts discussed in earlier chapters in specific marketing contexts. Modern marketing concepts are applied in a wide variety of circumstances and contexts. These include industrial and consumer markets, intangible and tangible products, small and large firms, international and local markets, and public and private sector organisations. A premise of this book is that basic marketing principles apply in all of these situations, but strategies and tactics have to adapt to the context. The practical examples used in the text have been drawn deliberately from a wide range of contexts to emphasise this assumption. Although they may be based on the same principles, marketing strategies and activities need to be tailored to the circumstances. The philosophy of customer orientation may apply throughout, but *how* it is applied through the marketing mix will vary A small firm selling an industrial service in a localised area would not expect to use the same marketing programmes as a large international producer of consumer goods, even though they shared the same philosophical approach. This chapter draws together some of these variations in the application of marketing. It examines how product, market, organisational and environmental considerations shape the application of marketing strategies and tactics. Many of these circumstances are discussed elsewhere in the text but are summarised here for further discussion and ease of reference. The four longer case studies in Chapter 14 are designed to complement this chapter by illustrating more complex marketing situations in different contexts.

1. CASE STUDY: MIXED MARKETING

Max Barton had recently joined the marketing agency, BFG, and had been assigned to work with Jane Allen on her accounts. He was rather surprised when he read the lists of clients.

'This looks an interesting mixture,' he said, looking at the list she handed him.

'But how do you cope with the diversity? Surely they will all need very different marketing approaches and different marketing mixes?'

Points to consider

❑ Consider the marketing environment of each of the following clients. What additional factors would you expect to see at work in each case, and how might this influence the marketing mix in the case of:

Organisation	Activities
Metropol Zoological Park	Service organisation providing entertainment for visitors and conservation for wildlife.
Robotic Research Corporation	Designer and manufacturer of robotic products for industrial markets.
LinkLine Electronics	Small business selling electronic products.
Fabio Fabrik Internatinal	International marketer of spectacles and frames.
KidKare	Charity for Childrens' hospital.

❑ Metropol Zoological Park

See section 1.

❑ Robotic Research Corporation

See section 2.

❑ LinkLine Electronics

See section 3.

❑ Fabio Fabrik International

See section 4.

❑ KidKare

See section 5.

(See also the four longer case studies in Chapter 14 which can be used in conjunction with each of the sections as referenced below.)

2. | SERVICES

(See case studies 1, 'Food, females and family', and 4, 'Hit or miss?', in Chapter 14.)

Services are products which are primarily intangible. They have grown to account for around two thirds of business activity in the UK so that services marketing concerns an increasing number of managers.

Characteristics of services

Services have the following characteristics which distinguish them from more tangible products and affect the application of the marketing mix (see Chapter 8, section 2 'What is a product?'):

❑ *Intangibility*. We cannot normally touch, hold, see or even smell a service. This intangibility makes them difficult to demonstrate or sample. Because prior evaluation is impossible we rely on the experience of others to guide our choice of services. The reputation of the provider of a service becomes a crucial ingredient in the buying decision, and word of mouth a powerful advertising force. Professional services offered by accountants, solicitors, medical practices, schools and universities are often selected by personal recommendation.

❑ *Inseparability*. Services are difficult to separate from those who provide them. As they depend so crucially on the people that provide them, services are often personified by the provider. Hairdressers, dentists, advertising directors and consultants often take their clients with them when they change from one firm or practice to another.

❑ *Perishability*. Services cannot be stored. They cannot be produced in advance and held in stock until required. An empty seat on a train or an aeroplane is a lost sale for ever. Unfilled appointment times at a hairdresser or dentist cannot be replaced.

❑ *Heterogeneity*. Services are non-uniform and difficult to standardise, as they are usually tailor-made for the customer. The product may be a unique solution to a customer's requirements, such as a consultant's report, a dental filling or a haircut. At other times the choice is limited to a 'menu' of services on offer, for example a house mortgage, a car service or office cleaning. Even so there is likely to be considerable personalisation of the service to meet an individual customer's requirements: the amount, term and interest rates of a mortgage vary from customer to customer within the overall guidelines of the building society, for example. This lack of standardisation of the final delivered product makes personal contact between the supplier of a service and the customer desirable and often inevitable.

❑ *Ownership*. Although purchased, services may not be 'owned' in the conventional sense. Services are sold on the basis of access to facilities, information and expertise (e.g. hotels, libraries, legal advice) or the use or rental of items (e.g. passenger transport by train, video hire, bank loans).

Impact on the marketing mix

These characteristics of services have lead some commentators to add three more 'Ps' to the commonly used four of the marketing mix:

❑ *Physical evidence*. Most services have a tangible aspect to them which can provide some physical evidence to the potential buyer about the service on offer. The waiting or reception area at a dentist's, solicitor's or accountant's gives an initial impression of the quality of the service provided. Perceptions formed by these physical attributes are particularly important because they are often the only evidence that the customer can easily gain about the service.

- *For example, parents visiting a primary school to assess its suitability for their children find it difficult to judge the quality of teaching as they walk round and rely heavily on tangible aspects such as the children's work on display and the condition of the buildings. Marketing activities need to pay particular attention to the impressions formed by any physical evidence of a service. Banking services use the design of cheque books and the colour of credit cards to enhance the image of their services. The importance of letter-headings, visiting cards and the layout of reports is recognised by consultants and professional advisers in the selling of their services.*

❑ *People.* If people are inseparable from the service they provide then they become very important aspects of the marketing of that service. We make decisions about which service to choose not only on our experience of the quality of what is provided but also on our perceptions of the person providing it. The confidence and trust built up by a hairdresser, dentist or solicitor is a crucial factor in how their services are perceived. Restaurants are selected not just on the basis of the food served but also on the people that serve it. Staff selection, training and motivation become significant ingredients in the marketing mix as a result.

❑ *Process.* Customers are often involved in the process of delivering a service because they are present when the service is produced and an integral part of it. As customers visit the premises of service deliverers such as hairdressers, dentists, teachers and restaurant owners, the process itself takes on a marketing significance. A happy experience matters as much as the quality of the service in forming the perceptions and future choices of the customer. The way the service is delivered can become as important as the end result. Mistakes and conflicts are difficult to conceal and relationships with a customer may never recover from just one processing error.

This is not the case with tangible products as the manufacturing process is usually hidden from the eye of the consumer. We do not form impressions of a tin of beans from an involvement in the production process or a knowledge of the number of rejects in the system (or if we do it often has lasting effects!). Visibility of the process can be used as a positive marketing tool. For example, fast food restaurants often deliberately make the food production area visible to customers to add to the image of efficiency and hygiene which they wish to portray. Some restaurants are themed around the concept of involving customers in the cooking of ingredients selected by them.

Automation and standardisation of some services can become important marketing tools to overcome the problems of variability of service provision. Automatic cash dispensing machines have improved banking services. Hotel groups and car rental companies have built world-wide chains based on the standardisation of services so that the customer knows what to expect no matter the geographic location.

3. INDUSTRIAL MARKETS

(See case study 2, 'On the carpet', in Chapter 14.)

Industrial marketing has been developed as a specialised subject area because of generalised differences that exist between industrial and consumer markets.

Characteristics of industrial markets

These differences (as discussed in Chapter 4, section 6 'Organisational and consumer markets') include:

❑ Products used by manufacturers, business and public services are usually more complex than those sold in consumer markets. These products can be classified as:

  ❑ installations, capital and accessory equipment, such as factory buildings, machinery, trucks and computers;

  ❑ raw materials and component parts, such as iron ore, cloth, wire, yarn, circuit boards and buttons;

  ❑ supplies and services, such as lubricants, computer disks, cleaning and accounting.

❑ Demand in industrial markets is derived from other customers in the chain and ultimately the end user. Changes in consumption patterns further down the chain eventually effect those higher up.

❑ Purchasing patterns are usually different. Industrial customers tend to be relatively small in number, purchasing in larger amounts, sometimes on an infrequent or contractual basis. Consumers tend to buy a large number of relatively small value products on a frequent basis. Consumer markets therefore tend to be made up of large numbers of customers spending small amounts reasonably often.

❑ The decision-making process is often different. Customers in consumer markets tend to make individual decisions with only the most important purchases referred to more than one person (e.g. buying a house). Organisations frequently involve more than one person in a buying decision of any importance. A decision making unit (DMU), consisting of a number of individuals who influence the buying process, can be involved particularly in 'new task' purchasing decisions. (See Chapter 5, section 5 'Organisational buyer behaviour'.)

There are exceptions to these generalisations. Some consumer markets involve infrequent purchases of complex, high value products by a few customers (luxury cars, second homes). There are 3.7 million businesses in the UK alone so products which are used by most of them (stationery, office furniture) are sold into relatively large markets. Most decisions made in many small businesses involve only one person – the owner manager.

Impact on the marketing mix

In industrial markets these generalised differences have an impact on each element of the marketing mix:

❑ *Products* tend to be more customised and less standardised. Some industrial products are completely made to order (for example, an electronic circuit for a mobile telephone, designed and manufactured by a sub-contractor). Others are partly standardised with options available depending on the customer's specification (e.g. a fleet of passenger aircraft ordered by an airline).

❑ *Prices* tend to be quoted for individual orders and therefore less uniform. Customised products need separate prices, and an organisation's purchasing power for more standardised products influences pricing levels.

❑ *Promotions* rely more on personal contact and less on advertising. In general, personal methods of promoting such as personal selling and exhibitions are more suited to communicating in industrial markets. Conversely, impersonal methods of communicating such as advertising are more appropriate to promoting to the large number of relatively small buyers typical of consumer markets. (See also Chapter 10, section 4 'Promotion mix decisions'.)

❑ The order of preference of promotional methods changes therefore between industrial and consumer markets:

  ❑ In industrial markets, personal selling is the most used method followed, in order of preference, by sales promotions, advertising and public relations.

  ❑ In consumer markets, advertising and sales promotions are most used, followed by personal selling and public relations.

❑ *Placing* products into industrial markets is more likely to involve a shorter chain of intermediaries or no intermediaries at all. A producer needs to keep direct control of marketing channels if customised products are personally sold and individually priced. Where the elements of the marketing mix can be more standardised, distributors and dealers are used (for example, in the distribution of office equipment such as copiers and furniture). In these circumstances, producers have to consider a 'pull through', as well as a 'push', strategy to ensure the flow of products into the next link in the chain.

4. SMALL ENTERPRISES

(See case study 3, 'Back to school', in Chapter 14.)

Small businesses have become more numerous and economically significant in western economies. In the UK, the great majority of businesses are small and medium-sized enterprises (SMEs); 99 per cent of all businesses employ less than 50 people, and 95 per cent employ less than 10. Whilst larger organisations have tended to shed jobs, the small business sector has created new employment and increased its share of economic activity. SMEs now account for more than half of total UK employment and business turnover (DTI, 2000).

However the owner-managers of small businesses often do not follow what textbooks might regard as best marketing practice. They seem to have a paradoxical attitude to marketing. On the one hand, they may regard marketing campaigns as 'something for the larger companies'. The resources of small firms do not usually run to specialist marketing departments and responsibility for marketing is often taken by owner-managers, who may have little knowledge or experience of specialised aspects. On the other hand, the same owner-managers adopt marketing-oriented practices because the small size of the business allows them to stay close to the customer. Whereas the manager in a larger firm can become remote from the marketplace and slow to respond to changes in it, the small business manager can adapt quickly to shifts in customer needs (see Chapter 3, section 3 'Organisational resources').

This environment tends to give marketing in the small firm a distinctive style with a number of characteristics:

❑ *Informal marketing strategies*: marketing in small firms often lacks formalised planning, tending to be ad-hoc and reactive to competitive activity or a down-turn in sales.

❑ *Restricted scope*: small firms cannot afford the same pro-rata level of marketing expenditure as larger companies. They have less to spend on marketing as other fixed costs such as salaries and rent tend to account for a higher proportion of income than in larger companies.

❑ *Simplistic and haphazard*: small businesses rely more on random, basic marketing efforts than sophisticated, integrated campaigns.

❑ *Evolutionary*: marketing practices in new ventures tend to evolve with the business. An initial phase of pro-active marketing activity when the business is first set up is superseded by a more reactive approach in which marketing efforts respond to customer enquiries or competitive threats. More positive marketing approaches may be adopted as the firm grows, leading to the planned, integrated campaigns of larger companies.

Whilst a small firm may adopt a customer-oriented strategy, resources and other constraints restrict their use of the tactics and techniques of marketing.

Impact on the marketing mix

These factors mean that small business marketing does differ in practice from that of larger organisations.

❑ *Product* considerations highlight the small firm's dilemma. Without new products, small companies do not last long in competitive markets, yet the costs and risks of new product development can stretch their limited resources to unacceptable levels. Despite these constraints, small businesses can be more innovative relative to many of their larger counterparts because of their entrepreneurial management style and shorter internal lines of communication. But many small companies become too dependent on a narrow product line and underuse other variables in the marketing mix, especially promotions and distribution.

❑ *Pricing* often represents a small firm's competitive advantage. In some markets this is a sustainable competitive advantage. For example, personalised services are not usually susceptible to economies of scale so that the lower overheads of smaller businesses allow them to provide good quality services at lower prices. However, larger firms in industries which offer more standardised products and services can use their buying power or production economies to undercut smaller operators who have to seek competitive advantages elsewhere or go out of business. This has been the trend, for example, in many retail markets in which the small shop can compete on the basis of convenience and personal service, but not on price. There is evidence that small business owners do tend

341

to under-price their products and services through over-reliance on price as a competitive weapon. It is common practice to use cost-plus pricing methods and neglect to research other factors such as what the customer is prepared to pay.

❑ *Place* is a restricted element in most small firm's marketing mix. Although some distribute products nationally, most small businesses do not make use of intensive distribution systems. With over 90 per cent in the service sector, small firms are restricted mainly to serving their local market. Distribution in international markets is particularly uncommon as most small firms do not export at all.

❑ *Promotional methods* in small firms tend to rely on interactive marketing communications, especially word-of-mouth recommendations and personal selling rather than advertising and sales promotions. The role of word-of-mouth marketing is considered in more detail in the section below.

Entrepreneurial marketing

'Entrepreneurial marketing' describes marketing as practised in entrepreneurial contexts, recognising that marketing as practised by entrepreneurs is somehow different. Research indicates that entrepreneurs tend to act in an informal, unplanned way, relying on individual intuition and energy to make things happen (e.g. Chell *et al.*, 1991). A typical marketing manager, on the other hand, takes action based on a deliberate, planned process involving a careful identification of customer needs and manipulation of the marketing mix through formal market research. These contrasting behavioural patterns of the archetypal entrepreneur and marketer make it easier to understand why small business owners (who are especially, but not exclusively, associated with entrepreneurship) should have particular problems with marketing according to the textbook.

Entrepreneurs also have a limited view of what marketing is. They tend to define marketing in terms of selling and promotions to attract new business, whilst ignoring other aspects such as product development, pricing and distribution. However this does not necessarily mean that they overlook these other areas of marketing, only that they are unaware of the terminology. Indeed, the business owners' narrow view of marketing is not always borne out by what they actually do. For example, entrepreneurs rate recommendations from customers as the number one way of attracting new customers. However, this does not mean that they put little effort into marketing as such recommendations are often hard won. To an outside observer, it is all too easy to accept a business owner's comment that they 'do not have the time or resources for marketing', when those same owners devote many hours building relationships with satisfied customers who then recommend the business to others.

Interactive marketing

Entrepreneurs usually spend a considerable part of their working day in contact with customers and practising forms of interactive marketing. This involves a high level of interactions with their customer base which managers in larger firms struggle to match, even with the latest technological advances. Entrepreneurs specialise in interactions with their target markets because they have strong preferences for personal contact with customers rather than impersonal marketing through mass promotions. They seek conversational relationships in which they can listen to, and respond to, the voice of the customer, rather than undertake formal market research to understand the marketplace. In many smaller firms, the ability of the owner-manager to have meaningful dialogues with customers is often the unique selling point of the business. Interactive marketing for small firms implies responsiveness – the ability to communicate and respond rapidly to individual customers. Entrepreneurs interact with individual customers through personal selling and relationship building approaches, which not only secure orders but generate recommendations to potential customers as well.

The influence of word-of-mouth marketing

Entrepreneurial marketing relies heavily on word-of-mouth marketing to develop the customer base through recommendations. Research studies inevitably cite recommendations as the number one source of new customers for small firms (e.g. Stokes *et al.*, 1997). Such recommendations may come from customers, suppliers or other referral groups.

For smaller firms with limited resources, reliance on recommendations has advantages:

- ❏ Referrals incur few, if any, additional direct costs.

- ❏ Most owner-managers prefer the slow build up of new business which word-of-mouth marketing brings because they would be unable to cope with large increases in demand for their services.

Word-of-mouth marketing has disadvantages:

- ❏ It is self-limiting: reliance on networks of informal communications restricts organisational growth to the limits of those networks. If a small business is dependent on recommendations for new customers, its growth is limited to those market areas in which its sources of recommendations operate.

- ❏ It is non-controllable: owners cannot control word-of-mouth communications about their firms. As a result, some perceive there to be few opportunities to influence recommendations other than providing the best possible service.

In practice, successful entrepreneurs find ways of encouraging referrals by more pro-active methods. Direct incentives can help but often it is the customers' feeling of involvement or participation with a small business that is most linked to their recommending behaviour. Parents who become more involved with their children's school, through helping in class or fund-raising activities, are more likely to become strong advocates of the school. Similarly in the private sector, successful owners encourage involvement of some sort with the business, so that customers feel an added sense of commitment to it, and in turn this improves word-of-mouth communications.

- *An entrepreneur bought a health and fitness club where sales had been stagnant for many years. He soon found out why. The membership was dominated by body-builders primarily interested in increasing muscle bulk through demand-*

ing routines of lifting heavy weights. These members represented a small section of the total health market, and were resistant to recommending the club to new members who were primarily interested in general fitness rather than body-building. In order to enlarge this limited network for recommendations, the owner encouraged fitness instructors to use his gym for aerobic and other classes. Only then was he able to introduce a new type of member more interested in fitness and health rather than perfect pectorals. This type of member gradually increased in numbers through word-of-mouth communications. He stimulated these recommendations by offering a different class of 'premier membership' to those who introduced a new member. This operated like a 'club within the club', encouraging greater involvement of members by more frequent access to facilities and incentives such as free holidays.

Networking

Formal market research plays an important part in each stage of the traditional marketing process. Market orientation relies on research to determine customer needs. Strategic segmentation and targeting is determined by market research. The success of adjustments to the marketing mix is tracked by consumer research. Successful entrepreneurs shy away from such formal research methods. They prefer more informal methods of gathering market information, usually through networks of contacts involved in the industry or trade. Successful entrepreneurs maintain an external focus to their activities which alerts them to opportunities and threats in their environment. Their informal information gathering techniques allow them to monitor their own performance in relation to competitors and react to competitive threats. They are also open to new ideas and opportunities through a network of personal and inter-organisational contacts. This process restarts the marketing cycle by forming the basis for further innovative adjustments to the activities of the enterprise.

5. | INTERNATIONAL MARKETING

(See case studies 2, 'On the carpet', and 4, 'Hit or miss?' in Chapter 14.)

International marketing – or marketing across national boundaries – has increased dramatically in recent decades. Developments in the European Community, Eastern Europe and elsewhere indicate that it will become an even more significant factor in the future, spurred on by advances in communications, transfers of finance, and transportation.

However, the size of many businesses restricts their trading to regional or national boundaries because they do not have the appropriate products, resources or motivation to extend themselves internationally. Organisations involved in international marketing tend to be either:

❑ *Global corporations* such as Shell, Ford and Unilever which regard the world as one market and carry out manufacturing, R and D, finance, marketing and other activities in the most suitable place irrespective of national boundaries. Such organisations now tend to call themselves 'global', rather than 'multinational', corporations because the later term has become associated with concern over the potential abuse of the substantial power and resources which these large corporations command with little accountability to the societies in which they operate.

❏ *Smaller organisations* which have to consider international markets because of the restricted scope or competitive pressure of the home market. This might apply particularly to companies involved in specialised technologies and products, such as scientific instruments and computer software, which readily cross national borders.

Impact on marketing activities

The problems of marketing in countries with differing cultural, political and economic structures and conditions are considerable and have defeated many organisations that have attempted it. Marketing techniques and approaches have to take account of local requirements.

❏ *Research* is obviously essential to understand the conditions, regulations and peculiarities of national markets. Although there are many sources of information, difficulties may exist in the interpretation and comparability of data.

❏ *Products* can be sold internationally in three basic ways:

  ❏ as the same product in all countries through a strategy of market extension; this is appropriate in some industries (e.g. soft drinks and clothes) but not in others (e.g. magazines and newspapers);

  ❏ as a modified product adapted to local conditions (e.g. right hand drive cars in the UK); or

  ❏ as a new product developed in response to the unmet needs of individual nations (e.g. training courses for Eastern European industrialists with limited experience of managing in a market economy).

❏ *Pricing* has to take account of new influences such as tariffs, local taxes, exchange rates and potentially higher distribution costs. The use of barter or 'countertrade' in which payment is made in goods rather than money can also become a factor.

❏ *Promotions* are most likely to require local adaptation if only because of language differences. The high creative costs of television advertising has pushed many global corporations towards using 'umbrella' campaigns in which the visual and music content of an advertisement are standardised whilst the verbal message is localised.

❏ *Place* considerations depend on the initial approach to international markets. Options include:

  ❏ exporting, or producing goods in one country and sending them to another;

  ❏ licensing in which a local operator is given the right to produce or sell within a given market;

❑ joint venture between a foreign company and a national organisation who come together to form a new business;

❑ direct ownership of a foreign subsidiary to manufacture or sell products in their local market.

International marketing strategies

These choices which face organisations considering marketing on an international scale can be categorised into different strategic approaches:

❑ *Globalisation*, which standardises products to generate the maximum economies of scale, on the assumption that they are meeting universal needs which exist regardless of national differences.

❑ *Localisation*, which treats every national market as different, tailoring all aspects of the marketing mix to local conditions because of significant variations between countries.

❑ *'Glocalisation'*, which is a mixture of the first two approaches in that products and marketing activities are standarised wherever possible, but adapted where necessary within a uniform format to take account of significant local needs.

Impact of the Internet

The Internet has the capability to create marketplaces without boundaries. Bill Gates (1995), and others, presented visions of how information technology will transform global commerce following the advent of the world wide web in the mid-1990s. But despite its mass-market potential, the Internet has not transformed markets for most consumers. There are still constraints imposed by the technical, financial and cultural development of particular regions. Even in the USA and Europe, e-commerce is still in its infancy in terms of share of consumer spending; by 2000 online retailing had reached £2 billion in the UK, or just over one per cent of total retail sales. However, most Internet communications and transactions are business-to-business, rather than business-to-consumer. If e-commerce has yet to make a major impact, 'e-business' is already transforming the ways in which global trade is conducted because of three principal benefits:

❑ *Improved communications between customers and suppliers*. The Internet facilitates fast, cost effective and convenient communications internationally. It is inexpensive to use and overcomes some of the problems of operating across different time zones. Quotes, product information, documentation and reports can be circulated faster and more easily at any time of day, to any country of the world.

❑ *Lower costs of international transactions*. According to Bill Gates (1995, p. 158): 'the information highway will extend the electronic marketplace and make it the ultimate go-between, the universal middleman'. Unlike the human middleman, the Internet does not expect a cut of the proceeds. Transaction costs are becoming lower as buyers and suppliers make direct contact for the first time. This is sometimes in conjunction with other companies through a 'virtual marketplace' such as the WorldWide Retail Exchange, or 'reverse auctions' in which buyers communicate their purchase requirements and suppliers bid for the order, successively lowering the price. More commonly, it is the individual, direct contact between a buyer seeking goods and services finding an international supplier through the Internet.

❑ *Easier access to relevant information*. Finding out about market conditions such as customer preferences and competitive activity is always more difficult at a distance. Networks and databases accessible via the Internet help to provide appropriate information quickly and cheaply. It is now possible to research important information for entry into an overseas market such as potential distributors and competitors' products, pricing and advertising without leaving the office.

6. THE NON-PROFIT SECTOR

(See case study 3, 'Back to school', in Chapter 14.)

In the opening pages of this book, we noted that the UK Institute of Marketing define marketing as 'the management process responsible for identifying and satisfying customer requirements profitably' (Chapter 1, section 2, 'The marketing concept'). Does the inclusion of the profit objective exclude all non-profit making organisations from marketing activities? In fact, public services and charities have become increasingly involved in marketing decisions as the many examples given in other parts of this book illustrate.

Types of non-profit organisations

Although the sector does not have a tradition of overt marketing practices, non-profit organisations have shifted towards customer-oriented strategies because of changes in the methods of funding and increased competition. This general trend has taken on several specific forms. At one extreme, some organisations have joined the private sector and adopted profit objectives. At the other extreme functional departments have become cost centres responsible for providing specific services to internal purchasers.

❑ Several public sector organisations have moved totally or partially into the private sector. In the UK, the privatisation of public utilities such as gas, electricity and water exposed major organisations to competitive forces for the first time. Public corporations in telecommunications, airports, air travel, and steel production are now answerable to shareholders rather than taxpayers.

❑ Public services in education, health and local government have been divided into more autonomous units responsible for providing a specific service for an allocated budget. As the budget allocation depends in many cases on the number of 'customers' served, individual units have an incentive to compete between themselves to maximise their income. For example, the money given to a school depends mainly on the number of pupils in attendance, which encourages each school to market its services to attract the maximum possible number of students.

❑ Non-profit institutions such as theatres, orchestras, museums and research bodies now compete more openly for public and private funds. Cut backs to the amounts of public funds made available has forced them to market themselves more aggressively not only to those who pay money to benefit from their service (such as the visitors to a museum) but also to the private sector for sponsorship and to government agencies for allocations of public funds.

❑ Charities such as Oxfam, the National Trust, the Salvation Army, RSPCA and Greenpeace use marketing strategies in two separate directions. First they need to persuade people to give them money as they rely on charitable donations from individuals and corporations and other fund-raising activities. Secondly they use a variety of marketing activities from personal selling to PR in their role as a pressure group in support of a chosen cause. Funding in particular has become more competitive as the numbers of causes have increased faster than the levels of charitable giving.

❑ Numerous other non-profit organisations, from political parties and religious movements to sports and social clubs, are dependent on the support of their membership. Many use marketing campaigns to increase membership or promote their beliefs.

The non-profit marketing environment

Although many non-profit organisations have adopted marketing strategies, their specific environment does influence their ability to fully adopt marketing concepts, (see also Chapter 3, section 3, 'Organisational objectives'). For example, there are many influences which potentially inhibit public services from becoming fully customer-oriented:

❑ *Restricted markets*: public services exist in markets subject to ongoing regulation and direction from one or more source. Some services have simply been divided into two parts, labelled the 'purchaser' and the 'provider', with neither additional choice for the users nor competition for the providers. For example, the 1990 Community Care Act gave local authorities the responsibility for determining local needs for social care and purchasing services to meet them. But this did not necessarily produce competitive market conditions because in some areas only a single provider existed and the purchaser/provider split remained shallow. Some public services are restrained from competing with the private sector on the grounds of preventing 'nationalisation by the backdoor'. For example, community care legislation prevents residential homes controlled by local authorities competing on equal terms with private sector providers. This led one commentator to describe the market conditions produced by some of the changes to the UK public sector as 'playing at shops' (Common *et al.*, 1992 p. 15).

❑ *Confusion over who is the customer*: more than one group of people can lay claim to being the 'customer' of public services because of the separation between those that pay for the service, those that choose it, and those that use it. In education there is a clear split between those that ultimately pay for the service (taxpayers), agencies that control the purse-strings (local education authority), people who decide what is on offer (inspectors, teachers and governors), those who decide which particular institution to attend (parents and pupils) and those that directly receive the service (pupils). The users of a service may not be the most obvious target of marketing campaigns. It may be a misnomer to consider some users as 'customers' at all (e.g. inmates in prison), or inappropriate to consider their demands on a par with other stakeholders (e.g. the desire of pupils for longer playtime and no homework).

❏ *Open access*: most public services are available to all and have to take account of the needs of a very diverse range of people. The opportunities to target services on segments of users with similar needs may be limited: health authorities have a responsibility to provide services ranging from emergency admissions to maternity care; the police and fire services have a duty to protect all citizens irrespective of location and socio-economic group. Evidence of the deliberate targeting of a public service through rationing of some groups for the benefit of others has been greeted with public outcry and political intervention.

❏ *Public service ethos*: the need for public services has been explained in terms of the need to atone for the failure of market forces to safeguard the public good by providing welfare to those disadvantaged by the interactions of the marketplace (Isaac-Henry *et al.*, 1993). This notion that a benevolent public realm is needed to compensate for the excesses of the private domain does not sit easily with the encouragement of private sector practices within the public sector. Some public sector managers have resisted business approaches on the basis that they represent concepts that are alien to the ethos of their service. To some, the very language of commerce represents a threat, so that the culture of marketing is seen to be unacceptable.

❏ *Public accountability and scrutiny*: because they are intended for the general good, public services are accountable to a wide audience. All activities can be scrutinised by the public or their political representatives in a way that does not exist in the commercial world, especially for small enterprises such as private family businesses. An important factor in the management environment of schools is the legal requirement to appoint at least eight governors, in contrast to equivalent-sized private sector enterprises which are controlled typically by one owner-manager. Ultimate responsibility for public services rests with politicians who may be more cautious because of their exposure to public criticism than innovative entrepreneurs answerable only to themselves.

❏ *Objectives may be multiple and contradictory*: unlike the private sector where the profit objective tends to be the rule, public sector organisations have multiple and often contradictory objectives. The requirement on many public services to cut costs and improve services simultaneously may not be realistic unless they restrict public access to their services. For example, the NHS faces the choice in some aspects of its health care provision of providing a higher standard of care for a selective group of patients or offering a lower quality service available to everyone.

Impact on the marketing mix

The contexts which we have discussed already in this chapter involve non-profit as well as private sector organisations:

❑ Most non-profit organisations are *services* and subject to the additional influences of people, processes and physical evidence in their marketing mix.

❑ Some are involved primarily in *industrial marketing* because they sell their services only to other organisations, not individual consumers. For example, the Defence Research Agency is a public body which provides research and development facilities and expertise to the armed forces. The emphasis of their marketing mix is not unlike other industrial marketing companies, relying heavily on personal contact and selling of complex products to decision-making units.

❑ Many non-profit organisations are *small enterprises*. The devolution of responsibility and authority has created many small semi-autonomous units in some public services. For example, a typical primary school employs less than 20 people and controls funds of around £500,000, a similar size to many small businesses. There are over 150,000 registered charities in the UK, most of which are small. They share small business management issues of lack of resources and expertise in considering their marketing programmes.

❑ Some charities such as Oxfam are *international* organisations facing many of the cultural, political and economic environmental considerations of the international marketer in other sectors.

Non-profit objectives may influence the application of the marketing mix more specifically:

❑ *Product* or service strategies typically take most emphasis. In the education and health services, for example, the delivery of the curriculum or health care 'product' rightly takes precedence over other marketing issues such as advertising or pricing.

❑ *Price* issues often translate into the more general aims of providing 'value-for-money' services or the maximisation of revenues rather than the pricing of specific items practised in the private sector.

❑ *Promotional* campaigns are limited as most non-profit organisations rely on word-of-mouth communications to promote their cause.

❑ *Place* is often an issue of location. For some public services it is an important marketing influence, but outside of direct management control. For example, the recruitment of pupils to a school depends crucially on one factor over which headteachers and governors have no control – where it is located. Where there is some choice, location is often determined by historic factors and cost considerations rather than customer convenience. For example, the main offices of Surrey County Council are not even in Surrey as its headquarters building was caught on the wrong side of a boundary change and it is too expensive to move.

7.	KEY POINTS

Although marketing principles can be applied in many different circumstances, the choice of strategy and the emphasis placed on the elements of the marketing mix vary according to the context.

❑ *Services* are characterised by intangibility, inseparability, perishability, heterogeneity and ownership. This adds a possible further 3 Ps to the marketing mix because of the increased importance of the *physical evidence* of a service, and the *people* and *processes* that deliver it.

❑ In *industrial markets*, products tend to be more complex and demand is derived from customers further down the chain. Purchasing patterns normally involve less frequent purchases of relatively expensive products compared to consumer markets and the buying process may involve a decision-making unit (DMU). These differences influence the marketing mix as products and prices tend to be more customised and less standardised, promotions rely more on personal methods such as selling and less on impersonal activities such as advertising and PR, and distribution channels are often shorter than in consumer markets.

❑ *Small enterprises* often follow the marketing concept of orienting their organisation around customer needs but may not have the resources, skills or motivation to use more sophisticated marketing techniques. Marketing strategies tend to be informal, restricted in scope, simplistic, and evolutionary. Although small firms can be very innovative, many rely on narrow product ranges. Pricing is a key competitive weapon where economies of scale are not available, although many small firms under-price their products and services. Distribution is restricted, with few small enterprises exporting. Promotions tend to rely on word-of-mouth and personal selling. 'Entrepreneurial marketing', or marketing in entrepreneurial contexts, can be as successful as more traditional marketing, however. It tends to rely on interactive marketing methods with more direct customer contact. Two particular features are the use of pro-active word-of-mouth strategies which attempt to stimulate recommendations, and the use of networks to provide market intelligence and business opportunities.

❑ *International marketing* is marketing across national boundaries. Research into the cultural, political, economic and other local conditions is essential. Products can be sold into international markets in unmodified form to benefit from scale economies, modified to take account of local conditions, or developed as new to meet unfulfilled local needs. Approaches to international markets include exporting, licensing, joint ventures, and direct ownership. The options for marketing strategies are globalisation, localisation or 'glocalisation'. The Internet is having a particular impact on international marketing as it provides opportunities for better world-wide communications, lower transaction and distribution costs, and rapid access to market intelligence in other countries.

❑ *The non-profit sector*, including public corporations, public services, institutions, charities and social clubs, has increasingly adopted marketing strategies in the UK because of more competition and changes to methods of funding. However there are inhibitors on customer-orientation, including restricted markets, confusion over who is the customer, multiple objectives, open access to all, public scrutiny and a public sector ethos. Non-profit organisations are subject to many of the contextual constraints of private sector companies. In addition, their non-profit objectives influence the marketing mix, often placing most emphasis on product considerations and limiting promotional activities.

8. DEVELOPING MARKETING SKILLS

Exercises

1. You are a self-employed business consultant serving industrial clients. How would you go about marketing your services to obtain new business? What would be the important features of your marketing mix?

2. You are the marketing director of a large international charity, raising funds across Europe and providing resources for your cause in many countries of the world. List the main marketing activities you would expect to be involved in:

   (i) to raise funds; and

   (ii) to increase awareness of your cause.

Developing a marketing plan

Activity 13 Forecasting and Controlling

The final section of the marketing plan is to evaluate the likely cost implications and to specify how the activities will be controlled and monitored:

❑ What is the budget required for the marketing activities and how can this be justified?

❑ What is the timetable for specific activities?

❑ How will the results be monitored and evaluated?

❑ What are the contingency plans if results are different to expectations?

REFERENCES AND FURTHER READING

Marketing contexts

Chaston, I. (1999) *New Marketing Strategies: Evolving Flexible Processes to Fit Market Circumstances*, Sage Publications.

Kotler, P. and Levy, S. (1969) Broadening the concept of marketing, *Journal of Marketing*, 33, January.

Services marketing

Berry, L. and Parasuraman, A. (1991) *Marketing Services through Quality*, The Free Press.

Christopher, M., Payne, A. and Ballantyne, D. (1994) *Relationship Marketing*, Butterworth-Heinemann.

Cowell, D. (1993) *The Marketing of Services*, Butterworth-Heinemann.

Gabbott, M. and Hogg, G. (1997) *Contemporary Services Management: a Reader*, Thomson Learning, part 1: 'The classics' (includes seminal articles such as Shostack, L., 'Breaking free from product marketing').

Gronroos, C. (1994) From marketing mix to relationship marketing: towards a paradigm shift in marketing, *Management Decision*, **32**(2), pages 4–20.

Gummesson, E. (1987) The new marketing – developing long term interactive relationships, *Long Range Planning*, **20**(4), pages 10–20.

Payne, A., Christopher, M., Clark, M., and Peck, H. (1995) *Relationship Marketing for Competitive Advantage: Winning and Keeping Customers*, Oxford, Butterworth-Heinemann.

Zeithaml, V., Parasuraman, A. and Berry, L. (1985) Problems and strategies in services marketing, *Journal of Marketing*, **49** (Spring), pages 33–46.

Industrial/business-to-business marketing

Chisnall, P. (1995) *Strategic Business Marketing*, Prentice Hall.

Collin, S. (2000) *Business-to-Business Bible*, John Wiley & Sons.

Doyle, P. (1998) *Marketing Management and Strategy*, 2nd edition, Prentice-Hall.

Hakansson, H. (1987) *Industrial Technological Development: a Network Approach*, London: Croom Helm.

Trimmers, P. (1999) *Electronic Commerce: Strategies and Models for Business-to-Business Trading*, John Wiley & Sons, chapters 3, 5 and 6.

Turnbull, P. (1999) Business-to-business marketing, in Baker M.J. (ed.) *The Marketing Book*, 4th edition, Butterworth-Heinemann.

Wilson, D. (1999) *Organizational Marketing*, Thomson Learning.

Small enterprise and entrepreneurial marketing (including word-of-mouth strategies)

Arndt, J. (1967) Word-of-mouth advertising and informal communication, in Cox, D. (ed.) *Risk Taking and Information Handling in Consumer Behaviour*, Boston, Havard University.

Bayus, B.L. (1985) Word of mouth: the indirect effects of marketing efforts, *Journal of Advertising Research*, **25**(3), pages 31–39.

Carson, D. (1985) The evolution of marketing in small firms, *European Journal of Marketing*, **19**(5), pages 7–16.

Carson, D., Cromie, S., McGowan, P. and Hill, J. (1995) *Marketing and Entrepreneurship in SMEs*, London, Prentice Hall.

Chell, E., Haworth, J. and Brearley, S. (1991) *The Entrepreneurial Personality: Concepts, Cases and Categories*, London, Routledge.

DTI, (2000) *SME Statistics for the United Kingdom*, SME Statistics Unit, Department of Trade and Industry.

File, K.M., Judd, B.B. and Prince, R.A. (1992) Interactive marketing: the influence of participation on positive word-of-mouth and referrals, *Journal of Services Marketing*, 6(4), Fall, pages 5–14.

Hall, G. (1995) *Surviving and Prospering in the Small Firm Sector*, London, Routledge.

Hisrich, R. and Peters, M. (1995) *Entrepreneurship*, New York: Irwin.

Hulbert, B., Day, J. and Shaw, E. (eds) (1999) *Proceedings of the Academy of Marketing Symposia on the Marketing and Entrepreneurship Interface 1996–1998*, Northampton, Nene University College.

Shaw, E. (1997) The real networks of small business, in Deakins *et al.* (eds) *Small Firms and Entrepreneurship in the Nineties*, London, Paul Chapman Publishing.

Shaw, E. and Carson, D. (1995) The emergence of entrepreneurial marketing: a new paradigm?, *Proceedings of the Marketing Education Group Annual Conference*, 2 (July), pages 713–723, University of Bradford.

Stokes, D.R. (2002) *Small Business Management*, 4th edition, chapter 12, London, Continuum.

Stokes, D.R., Fitchew, S. and Blackburn, R. (1997) Marketing in small firms: a conceptual approach, *Report to the Royal Mail*, Small Business Research Centre, Kingston University.

International marketing

Chaffey, D., Mayer, R., Johnston, K. and Ellis-Chadwick, F. (2000) *Internet Marketing*, Pearson Education, chapter 1.

. Chaston, I. (2001) *E-Marketing Strategy*, McGraw Hill, chapter 1.

Ernst & Young (2001) *Global Online Retaining Report*, Cap Gemini, Ernst & Young.

Gates, W.H. (1995) *The Road Ahead*, Viking, Penguin Books.

Harris, G. (1994) International advertising standardisation: what do multinationals actually standardise?, *Journal of International Marketing*, 2(4), pages 13–30.

Keynote Report (2000) *Internet Usage in Business*, 4th edition.

Kumar, V. (2000) *International Market Research*, Prentice Hall.

Levitt, T. (1983) The globalisation of markets, *Harvard Business Review*, May–June, pages 92–102.

Wheatley, M. (2000) Supplies on de-mand, *Supply Management*, 21 (September), pages 11–12.

Public sector marketing

Barnes, C. (1993) *Practical Marketing for Schools*, Oxford, Blackwell.

Common, R., Flynn, N. and Mellon, E. (1992) *Managing Public Services: Competition and Decentralisation*, Oxford, Butterworth-Heinnemann.

Gewirtz, S., Ball, S.J., and Bowe, R. (1995) *Markets Choice and Equity in Education*, Buckingham, Open University Press.

Hannagan, T. (1992) *Marketing for the Non-profit Sector*, Macmillan Press.

Isaac-Henry, K., Painter, C. and Barnes, C. (eds) (1993) *Management in the Public Sector*, London, Chapman and Hall.

Stokes, D.R. (1997) A lesson in entrepreneurial marketing from the public sector, *Marketing Education Review*, 7(3), Fall, pages 47–55.

Walsh, K. (1994) Marketing and public sector management, *European Journal of Marketing*, 28(3), pages 63–71.

CHAPTER 14

Further Case Studies

This chapter contains four case studies. These are longer than the cases in other chapters as they are intended to integrate the principles of marketing into one context. Case study 1 illustrates some of the issues of a fast growing company in consumer marketing with a strong service content. Case study 2 is about a manufacturing company operating in international, industrial markets. Case study 3 is about a small, non-profit enterprise trying to pull out of a downward spiral. Case study 4 is about a music company facing up to the opportunities and threats posed by the distribution of music over the Internet.

❑ The principal organisations and characters featured in these cases studies are fictional and no likeness to real people is intended. However the cases are based in realistic contexts and summarise the realities of the relevant marketplace.

❑ Each case needs to be considered at a strategic level (e.g. determining target markets, positioning and competitive strategy) and at a tactical level (e.g. recommending specific marketing activities). This can be done by developing an outline marketing plan in each case, using the four principal planning stages of:

- analysis

- objectives

- methods

- evaluation (see Chapter 2, 'Planning for marketing').

A quicker exercise is to consider each case in terms of:

- a marketing strategy (objectives and target markets); and

- key elements of the marketing mix.

❑ Specific contextual guidance for each case in Chapter 13 'The application of marketing' is as follows:

- case study 1, Food, females and family (see Chapter 13, section 2 'Services');

- case study 2, On the carpet (see Chapter 13, section 3 'Industrial markets' and section 5 'International marketing');

- case study 3, Back to school (see Chapter 13, section 4 'Small enterprises' and section 6 'The non-profit sector');

- case study 4, 'Hit or miss?' (see Chapter 13, section 5 'International marketing').

CASE STUDY 1. FOOD, FEMALES AND FAMILY

Introduction

David and Susan O'Brien were discussing their future after ten, eventful years as business partners. When they had purchased their first free-house pub in 1987, they had not foreseen that it would expand into the present, fast-growing chain of 20 outlets. The expansion had been born partly of the need to survive in a market which had seen considerable change in a decade. From the traditional male-dominated drinking venues, pubs had been forced to adapt into more family-oriented centres in which food and females played an increasingly important part. The growth of in-house entertainment, demographic change and government deregulation had not only shaken up the industry but also given the O'Briens opportunities to grow their business. They had turned their pubs which served some food, into restaurants which reflected their pub origins but focused primarily on serving interesting food in a themed environment. Now they had a crucial decision to make. What should be the furture theme of their outlets and how could they attract people into them on a consistent basis?

The industry

The supply of beer orders

Government intervention aimed at breaking down the monopoly of the large breweries had given the O'Briens the major break they needed to expand their business. The Monopolies and Mergers Commission's investigation into the brewing trade, and the ensuing 'Supply of Beer Orders' in 1989, had forced the major brewers to release half their public houses, over a 2000 minimum, from a tie to the brewery. The objective of the government's intervention was to decrease the domination of the retail beer trade by the major brewers. It certainly had the effect of giving the sector a major shake-up, although in some areas it had actually decreased competition as an estimated 500 pubs per year had closed in the 1990s, many in sparsely populated areas. Since the orders came into force more than 14,000 pubs had been sold, increasing the numbers owned by the independent sector.

The industry was hit badly by the twin forces of demographics and the recession. Demographics had been a problem for publicans for some time as the population aged and the peak, beer-consuming group of young males had declined in numbers. The recession had been a particular problem for the independent pub sector because it had affected the value of the properties on which the business was based. Many publicans who bought their business when property prices were high, could not survive the effects of high interest rates and a downturn in demand, coupled with a decline in the value of their property asset, the main collateral for loans on the business. By 1991, it was estimated that one third of free-house pub sales were forced on the owner. David and Susan O'Brien were able to benefit from the misfortune of others.

The pub-restaurant

At times, they had wondered if they were going to survive themselves. Competition for alcohol sales became fiercer as sales declined and the remaining pubs fought for survival. By 1996, the total number of pubs had declined to an estimated 65,000 compared to nearly 68,000 at the end of 1989. By contrast other sectors of the catering industry were faring better. During the 1980s, the numbers of restaurants and snack bars had increased by over 40 per cent. Although the recession had halted the expansion, the second half of the 1990s saw continued growth in the restaurant sector. The conclusions for publicans were inescapable: diversify into food or risk failure. The product-mix in public house sales already reflected this thinking by the early 1990s: by the mid-1990s food consumption had risen to an estimated 33 per cent of pub sales compared to under 15 per cent in the early 1980s.

This average sales figure hid some important differences as pubs became increasingly targeted. Some, such as the Firkin chain, retained the focus on drink by aiming at the youth and student market. Others concentrated on food sales which became the dominant product of the outlet. Chains owned by the major brewing groups such as Whitbread's 'Beefeater' and Bass's 'Harvester' aimed at value-for-money, family eating. Other outlets, such as the 'All Bar One' chain, targeted younger, professional women by providing low-fat foods in smoke-free, clean environments. Whitbread was one of the most successful groups at implementing a strategy of targeting pubs at segments of the market, following their 'three F's' policy which emphasised 'Food, Females and Family'.

The business

Susan O'Brien's background in the hotel and catering industry made it even more obvious to her that they should diversify away from reliance on 'wet' sales when they purchased their first pub. She began by offering a select menu, specialising in seafood, ordered from the bar and served in a separated seating area. This had proven popular enough to survive the recession and given them the confidence to look around for opportunities to grow. Because they had access to finance from a small group of private investors, they were able to buy free houses and other pubs at bargain prices for a few years. Their single pub in 1987 had expanded to a chain of 15 by 1998 and they had added a further five since then to bring the total to 20. They were constantly looking for more, not to run as traditional pubs serving food, but as the new brand of outlet – the themed pub-restaurant.

The Jolly-Boat Inn

They had developed two distinct themes in their chain. Some of the earlier acquisitions were in large, coastal towns where Susan's original seafood concept seemed a natural theme for this new chain of 'Jolly-Boat Inns'. The essential character of the traditional pub was evident, with decor reflecting the seafaring name. Outside, play boats and pirate activity areas provided safe but noisy playgrounds for children. But the profits came from a seafood menu chalked on a large board with daily specials from the local catch. The average price was £12 per head, although lower-priced mini-meals such as mussels and chips were also popular. By 2001 they had opened 12 of these, mainly along the south coast and in the West Country.

❑ Although they were very popular, this part of the chain suffered from consistency problems. It was difficult to reduce the cooking of seafood to a formula, which meant the quality of the food and service varied – as the O'Briens knew from some complaints they had received. Seasonal factors did not help either as some of the pubs became overcrowded at popular holiday times, making it uncomfortable for diners wanting a serious meal. Because of the variable cost of seafood, margins were also less predictable; the average gross margin of 65 per cent on food could show wide variations according to the outlet and time of year. However, a Jolly-Boat Inn developed loyal customers, particularly amongst middle-aged men, who liked eating there for lunch, or families on a day out in the summer.

Tai-P'Inn

Their fastest growing concept was 'Tai-P'Inn', a hybrid which David O'Brien had developed from the time when he had lived in Hong Kong. It aimed to combine the sociability of the English pub, the service concept of the American bar-diner and the growing popularity of Oriental cuisine. The name was adapted from James Clavell's well known novel, 'Tai-Pan' (Chinese for 'ruler') set in the historical context of English trade and rule in Hong Kong. The bars reflected this background with lavish decorations along the theme of 'where east meets west'. Framed sayings of Confucius competed with British imperial memorabilia, model Chinese sampans with naval frigates. The menu borrowed heavily from Thai cuisine, but O'Brien had not been afraid to dilute it with other popular, eastern dishes. The average spend per head on a meal was around £15, but he also emphasised value-for-money with set menus and special offers for off-peak dining.

Business performance

Sales turnover		£'000s		
	1998		2001	
Jolly-Boat Inn	4,800	(12)*	5,400	(12)
Tai-P'Inn	1,500	(3)	3,500	(8)
Total sales	6,300	(15)	8,900	(20)
Net profit	870		1,400	
* (Number of outlets in brackets)				

The turnover of the two chains and overall group profitability is shown below.

The first Tai-P'Inns had proved very popular in their largely cosmopolitan catchment areas in larger towns and cities. After the first year, David O'Brien thought he had found the formula on which to base the rest of their expansion. But Susan pointed out one worrying trend from their marketing information. Customers were not as loyal to this type of outlet as they were to the Jolly-Boat. Despite their problems, each Jolly-Boat Inn had built up a following who regularly returned for their fresh seafood. Tai-P'Inns attracted many curious customers, some who returned but often after a relatively long gap.

Market information

In order to understand their business better, the O'Briens invested in some research. First, they studied some secondary sources of market information and found that population changes were still having a significant impact on the pub-restaurant market.

	'000's				% change 1990–2000	
	1990		2000			
Age range	Male	Female	Male	Female	Male	Female
15–24	4,368	3,444	3,718	3,518	-15	-16
25–34	4,497	4,371	4,403	4,205	-2	-4
35–44	3,962	3,946	4,486	4,387	+13	+11
45–54	3,235	3,240	3,890	3,903	+20	+20
55–64	2,847	2,992	3,009	3,100	+6	+4
65+	3,597	5,435	3,881	5,473	+8	+1

Source: Mintel   *UK population by age group and gender, 1990–2000*

The consumer

Drinking in pubs used to be the preserve of younger, single men and older, working men. The population profile above, which shows significant growth in the middle age bands, and the increasing importance of females in the older population, helps explain why pubs have to make a broader appeal to survive. Now, women are just as likely to eat in a pub as men, with the habit most popular in the over 25 age ranges.

Pub-food eaters	
Age range	% of age range, 1996
15–19	62
20–24	69
25–34	76
35–44	73
45–54	68
55–64	68
65+	51

Source: Mintel

Children in pubs

Legislation concerning the admission of children into pubs was relaxed through the introduction of Childrens' Certificates in 1995. A pub with a certificate can admit chidren of all ages into the bar area if accompanied by an adult.

Tourism

Tourism can have a major impact on pubs as tourists are more likely than the normal consumer to need food as well as drink. UK families taking holidays in the

UK steadily increased in the 1990s and, with it, the demand for pub food and also lodgings.

Primary research

The O'Briens tried to find out how their own customer base compared to the national picture by commissioning both quantitative and qualitative research.

❑ A demographic profile was taken of a sample of 500 customers in both chains of restaurants. The results are shown in Appendix 1.

Qualitative research

Secondly, they undertook qualitative research in the form of discussion groups in order to find out more about the attitudes of customers and non-customers. The findings are documented in the Appendix below.

The problem

The problem for the O'Briens was to decide the marketing strategy for their future expansion. If they were to capitalise on the current wave of interest in eating out, they knew they had to act quickly and expand fast. The shareholders had agreed to fund an ambitious plan to open a further 50 outlets in three years. They needed a marketing formula for these outlets which they could replicate consistently around the country, confident that it would work without constant supervision. David O'Brien had told the Board of Directors:

> 'We need to take the consistency of McDonald's into pub-restauranting. When you eat in one of our outlets you know what to expect whether it's in the north of Scotland or the south of England. We need economies of scale in our marketing efforts by using national campaigns for a recognised brand that we know will work for every outlet.'

❑ The O'Brien's immediate task was to decide the specifics of a marketing plan for the business. They not only had to decide the strategy in terms of target market and type of pub-restaurant, but also how to market these outlets to existing and potential customers to maximise sales and profits on a consistent basis.

Appendix 1: Demographic profile of customers

	Jolly-Boat	Tai-P'Inn
	% of customers	
Age range		
15–24	10	19
25–34	13	23
35–44	22	21
45–54	30	20
55–64	14	10
65+	11	6
Social group		
AB	24	19
C1	32	28

C2	19	24
D	14	20
E	11	9
Lifestyle		
Pre family	16	42
Full Nest I (young children)	25	13
Full Nest II (older children)	17	21
Empty Nest	34	18
Solitary survivors	8	6
Gender		
Male	56	47
Female	44	53

Appendix 2: Qualitative research results

Aims

The aim of the research was to investigate people's attitudes to eating in pub-restaurants. In particular the O'Briens wanted to know how the linkage between pub and restaurant was perceived. They also wanted to obtain views on themes and menus of pub-restaurants and compare the attitudes of male and female customers.

Methods

In total, ten groups of six people each were organised. Four of the groups were made up of people who had not been customers of either Jolly-Boat Inns or Tai-P'Inns. The rest were divided equally between Jolly-Boat and Tai-P'Inn customers. Five of the groups were all male and five all female.

The findings

Most of the participants claimed that they eat out at least once a month, although everyone stressed that this did vary and 'averages' were hard to estimate. The main reason for choosing pub-restaurants rather than other restaurants was their perceived informality and good value for money. For a number, convenience in terms of access (parking, near to home or work) was also a feature. Reservations about pub-restaurants included the atmosphere which was perceived to be more noisy and smokey than in restaurants, a concern particularly expressed by the women's groups. There was also a feeling that the food, whilst likely to be acceptable, was unlikely to be excellent, except in rare circumstances.

Typical comments included:

'It's not the sort of place you would go for a gourmet supper.'

'Good for families, when you're paying the bill for four or five people but not the place you would go for a romantic evening or to impress an important visitor.'

'If you get a table away from the bar, OK. Otherwise be prepared to have smoked everything and not much conversation.'

Pub-restaurants were also seen as good places for lunchtime eating, away from the office.

'I usually eat in one at lunchtime, as it's quick, not too expensive and they have draught beer – but the lunch menu is a bit restricted if you don't like ploughmans or sandwiches.'

The women's groups particularly mentioned the need for more vegetarian food and facilities for children.

'I always seem to be choosing from only one or two vegetarian dishes.'

'My daughter is vegetarian so we have to be careful there is enough choice for her. I don't like to eat red meat either if I haven't bought and cooked it myself – it's not worth the risk these days.'

'We went to a pub which had a play area for the kids. As soon as they had eaten, they were gone; my friend and I could relax and talk to each other without worrying about whether they were eating properly or quarrelling.'

Concerning Jolly-Boat Inns specifically, the customers liked the freshness and variability of the food. Some did comment negatively on the service; others enjoyed its idiosyncracies.

'There's always something special on the menu even if you eat there more than once a week.'

'I had to wait over an hour for my food but what do you expect when they have to go out and catch it!'

"I complained once that my fish was undercooked because it had red streaks in it. The chef came out personally and told me that red mullet always looked a bit bloody – the 'Woodcock of the sea' he called it. He certainly knew what he was talking about – I thought he was going to throw me out for questioning his cooking!'

Tai-P'Inn customers enjoyed the experience and the service although the food was seen as rather specialised. These outlets seemed particularly popular among women and older families.

'The atmosphere is great with all that memorabilia from different places. It kept the kids interested for ages. Definitely worth a visit.'

'The food is very interesting. Too spicy for my kids some of it but they need to taste something different now and again.'

'I always get my husband to take me there for our anniversary treat.'

'They cater for women. The loos are clean, and the bar stools low, so we don't mind sitting down on either of them.'

CASE STUDY 2. ON THE CARPET

Introduction

'You have twelve months to improve sales or we will have to consider closing down the UK operation.'

Christopher Davidson repeated the words of his managing director over to himself as he drove away from the company headquarters in Rotterdam. It had not been an easy meeting. The UK subsidiary which he managed was performing well below other European markets and the patience of the directors of Novalis, the Anglo-Dutch holding company, was running out. Novalis International was one of the leading manufacturers of artificial playing surfaces, selling their branded 'Noval-Sport', synthetic grass carpets and other sports surfaces around the world. In the UK, as in most European markets, a fully owned subsidiary was responsible for the local marketing of the product range. Davidson had only just taken over as general manager in the UK and now he knew why his predecessor had departed in some haste. Sales had stagnated over the last three years, at a time when they showed substantial growth in all other European markets.

'The marketing in the UK is all wrong. I know you can't change it overnight but unless we see an improvement soon, we have to consider reverting to agents rather than continuing the expense of our own subsidiary.'

The meaning of the managing director's words could not have been clearer. Davidson had to act quickly to save his own job.

Background

Participation levels in sports and leisure activities had been expanding considerably for several years. Adults had become more aware of the need to keep healthy and fit, whilst having more free time in which to do so. The demands of academic subjects may have kept down the time devoted to sport in schools, but there was increasing recognition of the importance healthy exercise played in the development of younger people. In the UK, 'home' of many traditional sports such as football, rugby, bowls, cricket and tennis, newer activities such as ice hockey, basketball, rollerblading and tenpin bowling had been imported on an increasing scale, partly stimulated by the interest of younger generations demanding more variety in their diet of sporting activities.

Facilities for most sports had improved considerably in the last decade but the authorities responsible had found it diffcult to keep pace with the demand for the specialised provision of many different types. A noticeable trend had been the concentration of sports facilities in one area of intensive use. The acres of grassed playing fields and open air facilities, which can only be used in good weather and daylight, were giving way to sports halls, leisure centres and artificial grass pitches, used intensively from early morning to late at night irrrespective of the weather conditions.

The development of artificial surfaces for sports from tennis and hockey to bowling and baseball had been part of this trend. From the original, abrasive nylon, astroturf pitches, these had developed into more user-friendly, all-weather

363

playing surfaces. Overhead floodlighting, multi-use pitch marking and easily-movable equipment meant that a range of sports could be played intensively on one surface, rather than needing large areas of land dedicated to one type of sport.

The product

The surface of an all-weather pitch was usually constructed of a porous, polypropylene carpet infilled with sand. This provided a true and durable surface which could be used in most weather conditions for many types of sport. Noval-Sport, a leading brand of these polypropylene sports carpets, was manufactured in rolls and then laid and joined in situ on a specially prepared surface. It came in four qualities depending on the depth of pile and playing characteristics required. Novalis's confidence in its quality was shown by the minimum ten year guarantee offered with each surface laid by an approved sub-contractor, an unusually long warranty in the industry.

Davidson knew, however, that the carpet was only the tip of the iceberg as far as an artificial pitch was concerned. Underneath, several other layers were all crucial to the durability and life of the pitch. Immediately underneath the carpet was a shockpad, usually made of rubber, which provided cushioning to the hard play surface. The specification of the shockpad had to be carefully matched to the requirements of the pitch as it affected the bounce of balls on the playing surface. Beneath the shockpad was a base made of various levels of foundation material such as stone and macadam. The composition of this base and the accuracy with which it was laid, was crucial to the trueness and longevity of the pitch. Foundations susceptible to frost, for example, could cause damage to the pitch through the expansion of frozen water in the base.

A key part of Davidson's job, and those of the small team of sales engineers that worked for him, was to make sure that the construction of the whole pitch, and not just the surface carpet, was correctly specified and built.

The distribution

Davidson's predecessor had appointed a small number of approved agents – building companies whose expertise in design and quality in construction could be totally relied on. The problem was that they were very few in number – one in England, one in Scotland, and one in Northern Ireland. Only by contracting with these agents did the Noval-Sport long life guarantee apply.

All-weather pitches were sold and laid by construction companies who bought the artificial carpet and shockpad from companies such as Novalis. In the UK, only a small number of contractors specialised in building artificial pitches with the expertise to take a wide range of customer requirements through the various stages of design to the final, completed pitch. Davidson needed to be sure an approved agent not only understood construction matters but also the specific technology of artificial pitches, not to mention the extras that often go with them, such as fencing and floodlighting. A larger number of contractors offered a less complete service. Some builders could handle only smaller contracts such as tennis courts. Others offered a design consultancy or a project management service. All were potential customers for Novalis, as integral parts of the decision-making process which could specify a Noval-Sport, or a competitive, product. Inevitably, Davidson and his team were often called in to advise at various stages of this process, particularly the design and tendering stage.

The market

The market for artificial play surfaces had taken off in the 1980s. The pressure on the use of open spaces combined with the advantages of synthetic surfaces in terms of durability, trueness of surface, and usage in all weathers and at all hours, made them increasingly popular for many sports including football, tennis, bowling, hockey and golf driving ranges. Hockey in particular was now played on this type of surface for all serious competitions because the trueness of the surface allowed for more precise ball control. The extra wear characteristics made it a popular alternative for tennis as it was more like grass than standard asphalt courts. Evening training for football and other sports was also popular on these surfaces under floodlights. Densely populated areas of Europe in Holland, Belgium and Germany were the front-runners in the laying of artificial pitches. In the UK, their installation increased in the late 1980s and early 1990s and was given a real boost by the availability of Lottery money, through the Sports Council, for the improvement of sports facilities.

The customer

Customer segmentation

The buying of artificial pitches was a complex process, often involving many organisations in the installation of one pitch. Davidson segmented the market into a number of different types, involving substantial and smaller buyers and private and public sectors. Private clubs, part of large, private sector businesses, were involved in the provision of leisure facilities, such as indoor tennis courts, which use artificial carpets. Some were commercial operations in their own right, others were provided by large companies for the benefit of their employees. Contracts for this business, often multi-million pound sales, were fiercely contested by the trade. In the public sector, local councils, still a major provider of sports facilities, were often involved in large projects, sometimes in partnership with private companies. Education establishments from schools to universities represented another segment involving public sector finance. The remainder of the market tended to be very fragmented, made up of a variety of smaller clubs, some with charitable status, a few privately owned. Customer requirements ranged from a small artificial green for the local bowls club to the provision of multiple tennis courts and hockey/football pitches for a regional sports centre.

The decision making unit

One of Davidson's key problems was to find out who made the decision to specify the surface. Usually a number of people and organisations had an input. These included:

- The end-users, often represented by a committee of a sports club or representatives of a board of governors of a school or university. Sales presentations to the end-users were sometimes made by Novalis, sometimes by a contractor making a bid for the business, or both.

- The fund providers, such as the Sports Council, the Department for Education, the local authority or a private company. These organisations were increasingly acting jointly to provide money for a specific project. For example, Lottery money was normally allocated on the basis of a percentage of the total costs, with the rest coming from other sponsors.

- The advisors involved in the design and management of the project – architects, surveyors, project managers, consulting engineers, sports consultants or a combination of these.

- Building and construction companies bidding for part, or all, of a project involving artificial surfaces. These ranged from specialised sports surface companies to more general contractors.

Pricing

Often, contractors were appointed to projects by a tendering system in which they specified the type and price of surface they recommended. A typical price for one football-sized pitch, or three tennis courts, including the preparation of the site, laying of the base, shockpad and carpet and the provision of fencing and floodlights was £250,000 to £500,000 plus VAT. The price of the Noval-Sport carpet and shockpad was a relatively small part of the total cost, representing 15–25 per cent of the price of the contract. The building industry was generally price sensitive, with competitive quotations obtained for projects of this size.

The replacement costs for just the artificial carpet, which had a lifespan of 7 to 20 years depending on use and quality, was up to £100,000.

Noval-Sport had two main qualities which were reflected in price. The lower quality was priced favourably compared to the competition, but Novalis sales advisors tried to always recommend the higher quality carpet. Although this was priced some 20 per cent above competitors, it had a guaranteed life of ten years and normally lasted twenty years or more, which made it less expensive in the long run.

The marketing problem

The turnover of Novalis UK had stagnated at a time when the market was growing strongly. Although it was still regarded by many in the trade as the best quality, Noval-Sport carpets had lost its position as market leader, overtaken by more aggressive manufacturers who had invested heavily in sales and promotion campaigns. A French company 'Surface Sportive' were particularly active in hospitality and publicity campaigns surrounding contracts at high profile venues such as the All England Lawn Tennis Club.

Davidson had two main marketing problems. Although his brand was well known, his small sales support team of three people including himself, were so busy following up enquiries and troubleshooting that they had little time to develop new contacts in a very fragmented marketplace. For new business they relied heavily on the approved agents who were proving a bottleneck because of capacity problems.

'You have to give me time to sort out our sales strategy,' Davidson had argued at the meeting with the Novalis directors. 'We haven't seen the full benefit of the Lottery money now being invested in pitches because our agents are working to capacity and turning down work. If I allow others to lay our carpets, quality becomes an issue as some of them are definitely not up to our standards. Do you want me to make sales at the cost of potential problems in a few years time when surfaces laid by inexperienced contractors start to deteriorate?'

A second problem was that their products were perceived as more expensive. 'I know it lasts longer, and we guarantee that, but often our contractors are bidding mainly on price because that's how they are trained. The users may find we are cheaper in the long run, and the funding bodies are also interested in the longer term. But the building trade still likes to compete on price because they believe that the lowest bidder usually wins. It's hard to sell on the basis of savings in ten years time or more.'

Davidson had promised to return to the following Novalis board meeting with a presentation of his marketing strategy and plans for the future. He knew that this was something he could not sweep under the carpet.

CASE STUDY 3. BACK TO SCHOOL

Introduction

'Marketing may seem an alien concept in education, but we have no choice but to use it more, if we wish to keep our school open.' Felicity Cox, the headteacher of Abbotsfield Primary School, looked at the solemn faces of the six teachers facing her as she spoke. She knew that one of them would have to lose their job at the end of term, and others the following term, unless recruitment of pupils into their school improved. Numbers at the inner-city school for 5 to 11 year olds had been falling for some time and the budget could no longer sustain the present staffing levels. 'We need to market our school, but in a different way to the methods we have already tried, and I need your ideas,' she said, hoping that her staff could come up with something she had so far failed to find – a successful way of marketing their primary school.

The situation

Her predecessor as headteacher had described the area around the school as 'a leafy ghetto' when Felicity Cox first arrived two years ago. Across the road from Abbotsfield were tree-lined roads of relatively affluent housing, but behind the school was a 1960's tower block estate – 'the result of a social experiment which went wrong', the retiring headteacher had described it. The children at Abbotsfield School came mainly from that estate. A geo-demographic analysis of the school's parents profiled them as predominantly 'multi-cultural, low income and single parents, with high levels of unemployment and crime'. The surrounding area was densely populated, served by several other primary schools. Two were within easy walking distance and parents from the Victorian and Edwardian houses across the road, mainly from B, C1 and C2 socio-economic groups, sent their children to these middle-class schools.

Changes in the policies of the local council meant that the numbers of children living in the tower blocks were gradually falling, and Abbotsfield's traditional catchment area was drying up. The school had a physical capacity to take 245 children in its seven classrooms, with a further 45 part-time places at the attatched nursery school. Although the nursery school was full, 30 per cent of places in the main school were empty, with one classroom unused. The numbers of pupils recruited for each of the last four years had shown a decrease.

Abbotsfield School was part of Lampdale Education Authority, which was responsible for a total of 19 primary schools in an inner-city area. These schools together had a total of 5300 places, but, with 4350 pupils attending them, there was surplus capacity and the Authority was anxious to save money by closing one or two of their less popular schools.

Market forces

Changes to the way schools are managed had introduced market forces into primary and secondary education during the 1980s. Culminating in the 1988 Education Reform Act, legislation had forced schools to become more competitive towards each other. Each school's budget was now largely determined by how many pupils attended there – the more pupils a school attracted, the more money it was allocated. At the same time, parents now had an open choice of which school to send their children, providing it had spare places. In those schools that were full, places were allocated primarily on the basis of who lived nearest. Less popular schools could be caught in a downward spiral: as many costs were relatively fixed, less money meant that there was less to spend per pupil, which in turn affected education standards and facilities. This influenced parents against sending their child to the school, so there was even less money to spend, and so on until the school became unviable and was forced to close.

The consumer

Abbotsfield was caught in just this downward spiral. Appendix 1 below summarises its financial resources. Felicity Cox recognised the problem when she became headteacher. But she assumed that she could turn the school round by improving its reputation amongst local parents. She knew that parents selected primary schools mainly on the basis of two factors – location and reputation. Location was a key factor not only because of the convenience of closeness to home but also for social and security reasons, such as the attendance of friends and the safety of the journey to school. Although this was largely an uncontrollable factor as far as Abbotsfield was concerned, the school was in a densely populated area, with plenty of school-aged children in close proximity to the school.

'This means that if we can improve the reputation of our school, we will attract more parents,' Felicity had explained to one of the early Governing Body meetings at which she outlined her first plans. 'A recent report on school choice emphasises that parents choose on the basis of reputation if location factors are equal'. She had gone on to explain how she intended to improve their reputation. 'What influences parents to believe a school has a "good" reputation is not totally clear. They rely heavily on word-of-mouth recommendations from other parents and friends in forming their impressions of a school. But we do know what they mean by a "bad" reputation. It means poor discipline, badly behaved pupils and a poor academic record. This is what we need to improve if we are to change our reputation from bad to good.'

Standards of education

The new headteacher had zealously set about implementing her plans to improve the school when she arrived. First, she tackled the question of discipline by agreeing expected codes of behaviour with staff and enforcing them. A strict school uniform policy was introduced to symbolise the new order and, after a few teething problems and misunderstandings, the school became a well ordered and disciplined place.

Academic standards were also improved. Abbotsfield was helped by one of the few advantages of unpopular schools: at a time when crowded primary school classrooms of 35 children or more had become a major political issue, it always had relatively small classes of under 30 pupils. Several members of staff left when they realised that the new head expected them to work well beyond normal school hours to prepare classes for the next day. The new staff were handpicked by Felicity Cox to ensure they could deliver the highest possible standards. And they did. By the end of the second year, a school inspection concluded that:

> 'The quality of education is good. Although standards of achievement are below those expected nationally by children of the same age, they are above standards expected in relation to children's abilities. The emphasis given by the school to the teaching of the basic skills is successful and children's competencies in literacy and numeracy are sound. Standards in all subjects of the National Curriculum are sound or above. The standard of work in French is particularly good throughout the school. Technology, especially in the provision of computer equipment, and the teaching of physical education require improvement.' (Abbotsfield Ofsted Inspection Report, 1999)

Initial marketing activities

Felicity Cox saw the endorsement by the inspectors of the good educational standards as the right moment to try to change people's perceptions of the school. Her marketing activities concentrated initially on PR, advertising and sponsorship. An extensive PR campaign targeted the local press with news about the school. Their achievements in the teaching of French was used as one particular theme. For example, a school journey to Lampdale's twinned town in France attracted considerable attention, with several photographs of the children and their French counterparts in the local press. A sponsorship deal with a nearby McDonald's also created considerable publicity. The school brochure was upgraded from the original duplicated sheets to a glossy production including colour photographs of school life. It was circulated directly to prospective new parents who enquired at the school, and also, via estate agents, to families moving into the area. Open days for new parents were extensively advertised in the papers to try and improve attendance at the event itself and also raise awareness of the school.

Felicity Cox was bitterly disappointed when all her efforts went unrewarded. For all the activity, recruitment to the school that year did not improve. Moreover, the marketing activities themselves were becoming more difficult to sustain. The local press was at first keen to print reports of school events but after the first year this tailed off and the conversion of press releases to printed stories became low. Potential new parents showed a lack of enthusiasm for looking round the school or attending open days. The new brochures stayed largely on the shelf.

Market research

Bemused by the lack of response to her efforts, the headteacher decided to find out what people felt about the school. As she could not get access to sufficient numbers of prospective new parents, she decided to conduct research amongst existing parents and teachers to find out their perceptions about Abbotsfield. Students from a nearby Business School designed and administered a questionnaire, sent to all parents, teachers and governors. Over 55 per cent of parents responded, and some of the results are shown in Appendix 2. Felicity Cox was particularly disturbed when she read the following analysis provided by the students:

'Many parents believe they are not involved in the life of the school. When asked to rate their overall involvement, 65 per cent said they felt "not at all" or "a little" involved. Only a small minority (7 per cent) felt "involved a lot". Parents are at odds with the views of the school inspectors as they feel the teaching of many of the core subjects is not good. Mathematics is perceived to be a particular problem with over half of parents rating it as poor or very poor. Even the teaching of French, which has a high profile at the school, is seen to be poor or worse by almost a third of parents. Other areas where the school has made deliberate efforts to improve performance such as discipline and communications are not rated highly by many parents.

These findings are consistently at odds with the views of teachers and governors who rate standards and achievements more highly, although they broadly agree that the levels of parental involvement at the school are low.' (Market Research Report, 2000)

Could do better?

The headteacher realised that if she were to be awarded marks for her marketing efforts to date, they would be very low indeed. But, with the limited resources at her disposal, how could she do better?

Appendix 1 Abbotsfield School – Financial Information

£000's	1997/8	1998/9
Income		
(including carry forward)	505	486
Lettings and money raised	2	3
Total income	507	489
Expenditure		
Teaching and other staff	384	372
Educational resources	34	29
Premises costs	48	47
Other expenditure (including marketing)	37	38
Carry forward	4	3

Appendix 2 Abbotsfield School – Market Research

Sample questions and results from the school survey of parents. (Results are shown as the percentage response for each case.)

1. *Please rate your involvement in aspects of the school listed below on a scale of 1 to 4, where 1 is 'not at all involved', 2 is 'involved a little', 3 is 'involved occasionally' and 4 is 'involved a lot'.*

	1	2	3	4
Helping in the classroom	39%	34%	20%	7%
Fund-raising events	15%	36%	29%	20%
School functions (e.g. Xmas play)	13%	38%	27%	22%
Parents' evenings	17%	34%	29%	20%
PTA social events	35%	38%	18%	9%
Marketing the school to other parents	37%	36%	21%	6%
Overall involvement in the life of the school	27%	38%	28%	7%

2. *Please rate the teaching of the subjects listed below on a scale of 1 to 4 where 1 is 'very poor', 2 is 'poor', 3 is 'good', 4 is 'excellent'.*

	1	2	3	4
Reading	9%	34%	38%	19%
Mathematics	8%	43%	29%	20%
Science	9%	32%	39%	20%
Art	0%	4%	63%	33%
French	6%	26%	52%	14%

3. *Please rate the school's performance in the areas listed below on a scale of 1 to 4 where 1 is 'very poor', 2 is 'poor', 3 is 'good' and 4 is 'excellent'.*

	1	2	3	4
Discipline in school	11%	23%	28%	38%
Keeping parents informed	19%	23%	42%	16%
Answering your queries in person	15%	27%	39%	19%
Answering your queries on the telephone	21%	25%	39%	15%

CASE STUDY 4. HIT OR MISS?

Introduction

At a board meeting of the Revelation Music Company, the directors were faced with a difficult decision. The Internet had promised much for their company, but had so far delivered little. Now they had to decide whether to continue with the expensive development route they had initiated or return to more traditional marketing methods.

The Revelation Music Company had had a chequered history. Founded by Johnny Revels towards the end of his performing career, it had traded very close to the brink of liquidation in its early years. Although the company signed up some successful bands and acquired the rights to some popular music, the managers had not been able to turn these assets into regular profits and positive cash flow. Part of the problem lay in the nature of the music industry. Producing and promoting music required considerable up front expenditure in terms of advances to the artists and marketing costs. Income in the form of record sales and royalties from the music rights took longer to arrive through a complicated chain of intermediaries and collection agencies. It took Revels a few years to build up a catalogue of established music with an ongoing revenue stream. Although he never fully mastered the details of running a business in this complex industry, he did have the good sense to recruit some managers who did. Whilst he fulfilled the A&R (artist and repertoire) role, acting as the 'ears' of the company listening out for new bands and musical talent, his two senior mangers Paula Wilson and Dan Bright ran the business. Although they experienced near misses of bankruptcy proceedings, they also had some hits along the way. Groups under contract to them, such as the cult band, 'Devil's Coachmen', sold sufficient records to eventually provide the cash flow to keep the business going. However, their most dependable revenues came from royalties from the performance and broadcasting rights of music. For example, they were fortunate to have signed up Sam Spir who wrote a stream of hits for his own band, 'Helite', as well as for other musicians.

A sound performance

By the late 1990s the company had become one of the largest independent music companies outside of the major corporations such as EMI and Sony. The revenues from its back catalogue of recordings and published music had gradually increased to a size where the company was cash positive and looked set for long term survival. It had recording contracts with several well known bands in niche markets; it published the music not only of its own bands but also of a growing number of other writers who liked the company's informal style but international coverage. It had developed a specific marketing strategy for promoting its artists and their music that seemed particularly cost effective. Because it did not have the funds to compete with the promotional campaigns of the major record companies, it had adopted a very targeted approach. By attracting artists from narrow musical genres (e.g. ska punk), it could develop relationships with the promoters of that music to ensure their artists achieved the airtime they needed. Instead of using expensive mass media, it promoted to the end-users through appropriate specialised clubs and media. The Revelation Music Company seemed set for a long and prosperous future.

The digital revolution

Then the Internet began to destabilise the entire industry. Traditional music products such as CDs and tapes proved to be amongst the most popular selling items for new 'etailers' such as Amazon. But the new digital technology also meant that musical content could be distributed directly over the Internet. Digital recordings of music can be encoded on the Internet using the MP3 format, compressed and distributed across computer networks. Music could be copied and quickly distributed anywhere in the world. Whilst the big five music companies tried to ignore the new technology, Revelation's managers saw it as a major opportunity. Marketing Director Paula Wilson explained the vision when launching their website www.disconline.com to investors:

'The digital revolution in music has the potential to finally level the playing field in the production and distribution of music. Until now the majors have held all the cards – they have the advantage of economies of scale in the manufacture of records; they can monopolise the distribution channels as many of the chains will only stock the top selling hits; and they can afford to promote through mass marketing media. Digital sales over the Internet mean they lose their competitive advantage in each area: we can compete on manufacturing costs because customers can simply download their music; we can bypass the traditional distribution channels, and we can have direct contact with customers, so we don't need to pay for costly advertising in mass media.'

Disconline.com acted as a portal to sell recordings or musical scores of particular artists and songwriters direct to the public. It offered a free download of one track per band, then the option of paying for the rest. This generated revenues through sales of music direct to the end-user. But it also created market intelligence on the artists and their followers as downloads, click-throughs and other website activity was closely monitored. This market research could then be sold to promoters and agents on the basis that it made spotting new talent more of a science than the guesswork it had hitherto been.

At least that was the theory. In practice the number of paid-for downloads was very disappointing. Although site traffic was reasonably high, it was achieved at a cost, as traditional advertising was needed to drive visitors to the site. The main problem was the unwillingness of consumers to pay for anything they found on the Internet. Although by 2001 nearly a million people in the UK were downloading music, not many were paying for it. The 'Napster' phenomenon was part of the problem. Founded in September 1999 to allow users to swap music files amongst themselves, Napster quickly developed a huge following of 70 million users worldwide. Although Napster's operation was declared illegal in 2001 as it violated copyright laws, the damage had been done in terms of devaluing musical content provided over the Internet.

Another problem was 'artist power'. One of Revelation's bands set up their own website to sell records, which made other artists reluctant to sign up to the company website in case it proved more profitable to do it themselves.

Technologically, Revelation's directors had chosen to exploit downloading musical content onto existing hard format such as CDs and tapes via computer networks. But many in the industry believed the future for music distribution would be 'streaming' – instant access to any music via pocket computers and advances in telephony so that the user did not need to store anything.

Summing up the score

The directors of Revelation had to make some marketing decisions that would be fundamental to the strategic direction of the business. Dan Bright presented the key issues to the Board meeting:

'It has become clear that online orders are not going to replace sales through our traditional wholesale and retail channels as quickly as we first thought, if in fact they ever do. Disconline.com is still losing money and burning cash at the rate of around £1 million per annum which means it will eat through our current cash reserves in approximately 18 months. This leaves us with a number of issues to resolve. First, do we continue to support digital distribution and hope it can become profitable within 18 months? If we do, we will have minimal financial resources to promote bands through traditional media. Some of our artists are already restless at how much emphasis we have put on Internet sales, so we could have difficulties in signing up new talent. Secondly, if we do move away from downloading, do we continue to sell traditional products over the Internet, or rely on specialist retailers such as Amazon to do this for us? And, as I've said, we already have complaints from managers of bands who say we are not doing enough to promote them, so exactly where do we put our promotional effort in future?'

Summary financial data

	£s million	
	Revelation Group	Disconline.com
Sales	17.5	1.2
Gross profit	12.7	0.9
Overheads	9.2	1.9
Pre-tax profit	3.5	(1.0)
Cash reserves	1.7	

APPENDIX

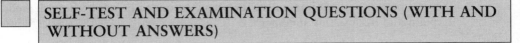

SELF-TEST AND EXAMINATION QUESTIONS (WITH AND WITHOUT ANSWERS)

This appendix reviews each chapter by asking:

❑ self-test questions on specific sections of the text; and

❑ typical examination questions relating to the subject of the chapter.

There are outline answers at the end of this appendix to some of the examination questions.

Chapter 1 What is Marketing?

Self-test questions

1. How would you define marketing? Why do you think the marketing concept is sometimes misunderstood or defined too narrowly?

See section 2

2. What three basic ideas are fundamental to the marketing concept? How would you describe each one?

See section 3

3. Organisations can adopt alternative orientations to the marketing concept. Can you name and describe three of these?

See section 4

4. Marketing has been practised since trade began but it has only been formalised into a taught discipline in relatively recent times. What were some of the factors that made this necessary? Can you trace the adoption of more formal marketing practices in the UK economy since the end of the Second World War?

See section 5

5. It has been suggested that in some circumstances the marketing concept is an inappropriate management approach. Describe some of these circumstances. Do you agree that marketing has less to offer in these cases?

See section 6

6. The adoption of the marketing concept by many sectors of our economy has lead to a variety of undesirable social effects. What are these undesirable social effects and do you agree that they can be directly linked to marketing?

See section 6

Examination questions

A. Define the 'marketing concept'. Discuss its relationship to other business orientations. (*answer on page 389*)

B. 'Several factors make it imperative for organisations to be marketing oriented.' Explain and discuss this statement.

C. There is some debate about whether or not the marketing concept helps organisations of all sizes in all sectors improve their performance. Using examples with which you are familiar state your views.

Chapter 2 Planning for Marketing

Self-test questions

1. What processes are required to implement the marketing concept of customer-orientation?

See section 2

2. What are the four basic stages involved in a marketing planning process?

See section 2

3. What categories of information would normally be considered in the analysis stage of a marketing plan?

See section 3

4. What areas would you expect corporate objectives to cover?

See section 3

5. What information is considered in internal and external marketing audits?

See section 3

6. What is the purpose of a SWOT analysis?

See section 3

7. What is distinctive about marketing objectives?

See section 4

8. What categories would you expect to see covered in the methods and evaluation sections of a marketing plan?

See sections 5 and 6

9. What are the benefits of marketing planning?

See section 8

10. What are the potential problems in marketing planning?

See section 9

Examination questions

A. You work for a marketing consultancy and since your old school/college has become a client, you have been given responsibility for the account. You decide that the first step is to produce a marketing plan which takes into account the limitations in funding of educational establishments. What are the main stages in the marketing planning process that you would undertake and what are some of the issues you would expect to have to deal with in each stage? (*answer on page 390*)

B. There is 'widespread ignorance about strategic marketing planning and confusion about the difference between strategic marketing planning and sales forecasting and budgeting, which encourages business people to perpetuate an essentially parochial and short-term view of business' (McDonald). Explain why this is so and what benefits can be had from marketing planning.

Chapter 3 The Marketing Context

Self-test questions

1. The marketing environment can be classified under the three headings of internal, micro- and macro-environments. What factors could be included under each of these headings?

See section 2

2. Organisational objectives differ between the public and private sectors. How do objectives affect marketing decisions in the public sector?

See section 3

3. What is meant by the term 'stakeholder'?

See section 3

4. How does the lack of resources in small firms influence their marketing approaches?

See section 3

5. How does organisational culture and structure influence marketing decisions?

See section 3

6. Give some examples of how the micro-environment can have a key impact on the marketing success of organisations.

See section 4

7. Explain how each of the main forces in the macro-environment can affect marketing decisions.

See section 5

8. In what ways can an organisation manage or influence its environment?

See section 6

Examination questions

A. For your local leisure centre:

    (i) conduct an environmental (external) audit;

    (ii) carry out a SWOT analysis; and

    (iii) develop a short-term marketing strategy.

B. Discuss some typical uncontrollable factors in the marketing environment, giving some examples of their effects on controllable marketing decisions. (*answer on page 391*)

Chapter 4 Customers and Competition

Self-test questions

1. What is the difference between customer needs and wants? How did Maslow classify our needs?

See section 2

2. Give some examples of 'marketing myopia'.

See section 3

3. Describe a feature of a product and the corresponding benefit to a customer.

See section 4

4. What is the difference between customer and consumer? Give some examples of customers who are not consumers.

See section 5

5. How can marketing be directed at 'internal customers'. Give some examples.

See section 5

6. Compare some commonly found characteristics of mature and immature markets.

See section 6

7. What types of 'organisational markets' are there and in what ways do they often differ from consumer markets?

See section 6

8. What five forces affect the competitive structure of a market?

See section 8

9. Describe the barriers to entry that may deter a new entrant into the car manufacturing industry. Which substitute products could be said to compete with cars?

See section 8

10. What are the factors which can affect the balance of power between buyers and suppliers?

See section 8

Examination questions

A. 'Short-sighted managements often fail to recognise that in fact there is no such thing as a growth industry' (Levitt). Discuss this statement. (*answer on page 392*)

B. Carry out a competitive analysis of an industry of your choice using Porter's 'Five Forces' model.

Chapter 5 Customer Behaviour

Self-test questions

1. What is meant by the 'black box' in a model of customer buying behaviour?

See section 2

2. What are the inputs into the black box in the form of uncontrollable and controllable stimuli?

See section 2

3. List the types of social factors that exert influence on consumer buying decisions.

See section 3

4. List the types of individual, psychological factors that exert influence on consumer buying decisions.

See section 3

5. What is meant by 'pyschographics'?

See section 3

6. Give some examples in which consumers have

   (i) a high involvement,

   (ii) a low involvement

   in the buying decision-making process.

See section 4

7. Describe five possible stages in a consumer buying process.

See section 4

8. Describe three main types of buying decisions in organisations.

See section 5

9. Describe eight possible stages in an organisational buying process.

See section 5

10. What different roles might be played by individuals in an organisational decision making unit (DMU)?

See section 5

Examination questions

A. If marketing management wish to change consumer attitudes towards a product or service, what behavioural factors should they take into account?

B. Why is it important to understand family roles and decision-making processes for products and services that are consumed by the household as a unit?

C. An individual is buying a computer for their own use at home. An organisation is buying the same product for use in the office. What differences would you expect to find in the buying behaviour of the individual and the organisation in making their decision? (*answer on page 393*)

Chapter 6 Marketing Research

Self-test questions

1. What is meant by a 'marketing intelligence system'?

See section 2

2. Give an example of the application of marketing research in one non-profit and one private sector organisation.

See section 2

3. Marketing research can be divided into five major areas based on the type of questions it seeks to answer. What are these five areas?

See section 3

4. What are the main steps in the marketing research process?

See section 4

5. What is the difference between quantitative and qualitative research?

See section 5

6. List three advantages and three disadvantages for both primary and secondary research.

See section 5

7. What are the main sources of secondary data?

See section 6

8. Name four different approaches to the collection of primary data.

See section 7

9. What happens in a group discussion?

See section 7

10. How would you rate telephone interviewing in terms of quantity of data, control of the sample, speed and response rate compared to other research contact methods?

See section 7

11. Give examples of open, closed and multiple-choice questions.

See section 7

12. What is meant by 'funnelling' in structuring a research questionnaire?

See section 7

13. What is the difference between a random probability sample and a quota sample?

See section 7

14. What is an 'omnibus survey'?

See section 7

Examination questions

A. An office equipment dealer has approached you with a view to carrying out some market research on their image, product range and staff morale. Outline the marketing research plan that you would recommend with justifications for your recommendations.

B. You are considering setting up a take-away pizza business. What market research would you require before you make a decision? Present your answer as a market research plan. (*answer on page 394*)

C. What are the main steps in carrying out a market research exercise? Give examples of the problems you might expect at each stage.

Chapter 7 Marketing Strategy

Self-test questions

1. What is the difference between a strategic and a tactical decision? Give an example of a strategic marketing decision and the tactical activities which might result from it.

See section 2

2. What is a market segment and a market niche?

See section 3

3. Give four advantages of market segmentation strategies with an example of each.

See section 3

4. 'Benefit segmentation looks for the major benefits that are given priority by a significant number of customers and then seeks to identify with that group through consistent marketing efforts.' Can you name some of the benefits that are used by organisations in this way and examples of their use?

See section 3

5. In what other ways can markets be segmented?

See section 3

6. Following an analysis of possible customer segments, three basic strategies can be considered to direct marketing efforts. What are they? Give some possible advantages and disadvantages of each alternative?

See section 4

7. Name four criteria which influence the viability of targeting a particular market segment.

See section 4

8. Give an example of how

   (i) an industrial marketing company, and

   (ii) a public service organisation

   might segment their customer groups.

See section 4

9. What is meant by 'positioning'? Can you position some of the restaurants in your local area on a 'positioning map' using price and quality as the parameters?

See section 5

10. What impact has the Internet made on marketing strategy?

See section 6

11. 'Effective strategies harmonise the elements of the marketing mix into a consistent approach to the target markets.' What are these 'elements' and why do they need to be harmonised?

See section 7

Examination questions

A. You have been asked to advise an entrepreneur who wishes to start up a restaurant on his marketing strategy, with particular reference to the segmentation, targeting and positioning process. How would you advise him to segment his market, select a target segment and position his business?

B. 'Positioning is in the mind of the consumer.' Critically evaluate this statement. (*answer on page 395*)

C. Which do you think is the most important element in the 4 Ps of the marketing mix?

Chapter 8 Product Strategies

Self-test questions

1. How would you define a product?

See section 2

2. Give some examples of tangible and intangible products.

See section 2

3. Name three ways in which products are classified.

See section 3

4. What general distinctions can be made between the marketing of intangible and tangible goods?

See section 3

5. Name some of the terms used to aggregate, or collect together, individual products.

See section 3

6. What is meant by the term 'augmented product' and what are the implications of this concept for marketing strategies?

See section 4

7. What is branding and why is it important?

See section 5

8. Describe two commonly used branding strategies with examples.

See section 5

9. What are the stages of the product life cycle?

See section 6

10. What typifies the use of the 4 Ps of the marketing mix in each stage of the product life cycle?

See section 6

11. What are the resourcing and competitive implications of the stages of the product life cycle?

See section 7

12. Draw the Boston Consulting Group's growth-share matrix. Name and describe each quadrant.

See section 7

13. Describe the General Electric multifactor portfolio model. What different product strategies does it suggest?

See section 7

14. What are the four basic product strategies suggested by Ansoff's matrix?

See section 7

Examination questions

A. Marketing activities should change as a product progresses through its life cycle, according to product life cycle theory. Describe the main stages of the Product Life Cycle and illustrate how and why you would expect marketing activities to change, using a product of your choice to illustrate your answer.

B. (i) Why are people willing to pay more for branded rather than unbranded products? Explain how, using examples where relevant, the brand name is used to add value to the product.

   (ii) Show how the positioning of brands varies in a market of your choice.

C. Product portfolio analysis helps an organisation to plan its product strategies. What are the benefits of this? Describe one model that can be used in the process. (*answer on page 395*)

Chapter 9 Pricing

Self-test questions

1. Why is pricing becoming a more important function in public services which traditionally have not charged for their services?

See section 2

2. Summarise the main influences in the pricing process.

See section 3

3. With examples describe how marketing strategies influence pricing decisions.

See section 4

4. 'Pricing possibilities are constrained by the financial structure and financial objectives of an organisation.' Explain and illustrate this statement.

See section 4

5. What is meant by 'elasticity of demand'? How does it affect pricing policies?

See section 5

6. Competitors and environmental factors are important determinants of prices. In what way?

See section 5

7. Describe the two generic pricing strategies giving examples that favour the adoption of each strategy.

See section 6

8. Describe cost-based, competition-based and customer-based pricing methods. How can all three be used in practice to set the optimum price?

See section 7

Examination questions

A. The physiotherapy department of an NHS hospital has been told to price its services both internally and to private patients. What influences would you expect to be taken into account? What general and particular advice would you give to the superintendent of the department regarding pricing?

B. Price is the only element of the marketing mix to produce revenue, all the others add costs. What are the major pricing strategies? When should each be used? Illustrate your answer with relevant examples. (*answer on page 396*)

C. Compare and contrast cost-based and demand-based pricing.

Chapter 10 Promotions I: Marketing Communications and Selling

Self-test questions

1. Why should both marketing managers and sociologists alike be concerned at the levels of promotional communication?

See section 2

2. Describe the process in which messages travel from the sender to the receiver.

See section 3

3. Using the AIDA model of marketing communications, describe and explain how the objectives of marketing communications change.

See section 3

4. Explain how the diffusion process operates in some markets.

See section 3

5. 'Organisations communicate with their publics and consumers through many forms of marketing communications. Some they control directly themselves; others are less controllable.' Summarise the main types of communication of each category.

See section 4

6. How can 'uncontrollable' communications be more controlled?

See section 4

7. How does the product life cycle impact on the promotional mix?

See section 4

8. Why does the sales profession sometimes suffer from a bad image? What factors are helping to improve it?

See sections 5, pages 230–232

9. Customer experience and product complexity change the nature of the required selling role. Describe four different selling roles which illustrate this point.

See section 5

10. What are the roles of sales management?

See section 5

11. What types of selling activities are undertaken by an office copier salesperson other than making sales presentations?

See section 6

12. Describe the stages of making a sale using the AIDA model. What are the key factors that ensure progression from one stage to the next?

See section 6

Examination questions

A. In what ways does an organisation communicate with its marketplace? How can it ensure that the messages received are positive ones?

B. What are the advantages and disadvantages of personal selling compared to other elements in the promotional mix? (*answer on page 398*)

C. Assess the changing role of selling as an element in the marketing mix.

D. You are demonstrating a new product to a customer with the objective of taking an order from them at the end of your meeting. Describe and explain how you would attempt to progress from the stage of introducing yourself to the point where you could take an order from the customer.

Chapter 11 Promotions II: Advertising, Sales Promotions, and Public Relations

Self-test questions

1. What are the five steps in planning an advertising campaign?

See section 2

2. 'Advertising can achieve one or more of three main types of objective.' What are these? Give examples of the use of each type.

See section 2

3. Compare the merits of the various ways of arriving at an advertising budget.

See section 2

4. Describe two basic types of creative strategies, with examples.

See section 2

5. Discuss the types of media available to an advertiser with an analysis of the advantages and disadvantages of each type.

See section 2

6. How can the results of advertising be evaluated?

See section 2

7. What is the difference between above and below the line advertising?

See section 3

8. Give examples of sales promotions which 'push' and those which 'pull' products towards the buyers.

See section 3

9. Describe, and give some examples of, some of the ethical issues in sales promotions.

See section 3

10. What is public relations? Who does 'public' refer to?

See section 4

11. Describe with examples the principle PR activities.

See section 4

Examination questions

A. Your local amateur dramatic society is suffering from falling attendances. Draw up a promotional plan to help them address this problem.

B. What factors influence the use of the media available in an advertising campaign? Discuss some general advantages and disadvantages of the types of advertising media in relation to these factors.

C. You are the head of a sales promotion agency. You are making a presentation to a new client on the effective use and pitfalls of sales promotion activities. Outline the contents of your presentation.

D. The board of governors of a local secondary school has asked you to advise them on the types of PR activities they might undertake to promote the standing of the school within the community with the ultimate aim of increasing student recruitment. What advice would you give them?

Chapter 12 Place: Marketing Channels

Self-test questions

1. What does the role of 'place' include as one of the 4 Ps in the marketing mix?

See section 2

2. What is meant by 'channels of distribution'? What types of channel are there?

See section 3

3. What are the advantages of using intermediaries to help distribute goods from producer to user? What are the disadvantages?

See sections 3

4. Discuss some of the strategic choices in channel selection.

See section 4

5. What is a Vertical Marketing System (VMS)? Explain, with examples, the differences between a corporate, contractual and administered VMS.

See section 4

6. What are the main influences on the choice of channel strategy?

See section 4

7. Retailing can be grouped into various categories according to emphasis on a number of variables such as product line or price position. Describe up to six such classifications.

See section 5

8. Why are retailers being described as the 'new channel captains'?

See section 5

9. What is a product or trademark agreement?

See section 6

10. What is 'business format franchising' and what are the advantages to the franchisor?

See section 6

Examination questions

A. A European soft drinks manufacturer is preparing to launch its range of non-alcoholic health drinks into the UK. Advise them on the different channels of distribution that they may use, making a recommendation to them with justifications for your proposals.

B. You are the marketing manager of a medium-sized manufacturing company. In a meeting with a large retail group, their chief buyer tells you: 'Don't worry about distribution and promotion of the product. We will take care of that. Concentrate on manufacturing the quality and quantity we need.' Draft a memo to your own managing director addressing what you think are the main issues raised by this statement and outlining some alternative courses of action open to you.

C. What is franchising? How might a producer benefit by using it as a method of distribution? (*answer on page 400*)

Chapter 13 The application of marketing

Self-test questions

1. Which characteristics of services have particular implications for marketing strategies? How do they influence the marketing mix?

See section 2

2. 'In industrial markets, personal selling is the most used method.' Why is this so?

See section 3

3. Discuss and explain the apparent paradoxical attitude to marketing of small business owners who adopt a customer-oriented strategy but only adopt

restricted and haphazard marketing activities.

See section 4

4. Outline three different strategic approaches to international marketing.

See section 5

5. Explain, with examples, why marketing activities are increasingly used in non-profit organisations.

See section 6

Examination questions

A. What is the difference between international marketing and exporting?

B. A small charity is suffering from falling income because of the increase in charitable causes asking for donations. How would you advise them to increase their share of the charitable donations cake?

Outline answers to some examination questions

Suggested answers given here are in outline, or note form, only. The level of detail and analysis required depends on the type of examination taken. Answers usually benefit from appropriate examples taken from your own experience or from sources such as this book.

Chapter 1

Question A

Define the 'marketing concept'. Discuss its relationship to other business orientations.

Key Points

The marketing concept: a business philosophy or strategy which orientates an organisation around the needs of customers. Can be confused with marketing as a tactical function which involves activities such as advertising, selling, pricing, product development and market research.

Three ideas fundamental to the marketing concept:

1. Customer orientation – the most crucial of all marketing principles as embodied in the UK Institute of Marketing's definition of marketing: 'the management process responsible for identifying, anticipating and satisfying customer requirements profitably.' Easy to pay lip-service to customer needs whilst organisation is in fact driven by other priorities such as production or selling needs.

2. Organisational integration – concept of customer orientation has to involve whole organisation and everyone in it; the marketing concept is not just the responsibility of the marketing department.

3. Mutually profitable exchange – customer may be 'king' but not a tyrant as long-term organisational needs of the supplier have to be met as well. In the private sector this is expressed as profits or return on investment; not-for-profit organisations have other objectives such as measures of funds raised, or patients treated. The marketing concept implies a balancing act between needs of customers and needs of the organisation so that both benefit in the long term from the exchange process.

Alternative business orientations include the production, product, service and sales concepts.

The production concept assumes that production efficiencies and economies of scale will ultimately benefit the customer in lower prices. Although this logic was behind many of advances of the industrial revolution, the insistence on standardisation wherever possible ignores individual preferences and is inappropriate in modern markets where supply generally exceeds demand.

The product concept focuses on developing 'better' products. This can drive organisations to supply what is technologically possible rather than what the customer wants.

Service oriented organisations assume that their professional skills are so specialised that customers do not have the necessary knowledge to choose for themselves. This may lead to misinterpretations of customer demand in some aspects of the service provided as the professional is blinded to customer needs by their in-depth knowledge.

The sales concept uses marketing techniques to promote products and services without adopting the overall marketing concept of matching what is sold to customer needs. The focus is on how to sell existing products and services rather than to find out what might meet customer needs more fully.

Chapter 2
Question A

You work for a marketing consultancy and since your old school/college has become a client, you have been given responsibility for the account. You decide that the first step is to produce a marketing plan which takes into account the limitations in funding of educational establishments. What are the main stages in the marketing planning process that you would undertake and what are some of the issues you would expect to have to deal with in each stage?

Key Points

Main stages of the marketing planning process are analysis of the existing situation, setting objectives for the future, deciding methods of how to achieve them, and evaluation of progress.

Analysis includes clarifying 'corporate' objectives, conducting internal and external audits, noting assumptions and summarising through a SWOT analysis.

Issues for a state school: Difficulties in internal audit due to lack of past marketing records and a need to use information not produced for marketing purposes. External environment fast changing and difficult to predict as dependent particularly on political influences.

Objectives include specifying measurable results for identified products in target markets.

Issues for a state school: Objectives set at various levels, i.e. state, local education authority and school. Some of these may be contradictory, e.g. school's need to maximise its revenues by attracting as many pupils as possible versus the educational need to keep classes small.

Methods involve strategies and programmes for the 4 Ps of the marketing mix.

Issues for a school: Definition and control of some of the 'Ps' difficult. The curriculum as the 'product' of a school is more controlled by central government. 'Price' is not a factor for most 'customers' (parents and pupils) in state education. 'Place' is beyond local management control as headteachers cannot decide to move their school to a more desirable location. 'Promotion' restricted by lack of finance to mainly word-of-mouth recommendations.

Evaluation involves controls on marketing activities and feedback from them.

Issues for a school: Unaccustomed to 'tracking' results of marketing campaigns. Lack of resources for follow up.

Chapter 3

Question B

Discuss some typical uncontrollable factors in the marketing environment giving some examples of their effects on controllable marketing decisions.

Key Points

Uncontrollable factors in the marketing environment include:

1. Internal factors – organisational objectives, resources, culture and structure.

    Example – *a library may restrict its marketing activities aimed at finding new customers because it does not have the resources or structure to deal with more borrowers. Its objectives to keep within a tightly defined budget restrict the role of marketing to improving the service to the existing number of borrowers.*

2. Micro-environmental factors – impact of suppliers, intermediaries, customers and competitors.

    Example – *intermediaries between manufacturers and the final consumer have increased their power over the marketing decisions on many products. Major retailers of food, clothes and household goods give manufacturers strong guidelines covering many marketing decisions such as packaging, display, pricing and promotions.*

3. Macro-environment – socio-cultural, technological, economic and political factors.

    Example – *new technology in form of electronic point of sale (EPOS) data capture has given retailers an important new marketing tool. For the first time major retailers can monitor the purchases of individual customers through loyalty card schemes and use this information as the basis of marketing campaigns to attract them back to the store.*

Chapter 4
Question A

'Shortsighted managements often fail to recognise that in fact there is no such thing as a growth industry' (Levitt). Discuss this statement.

Key Points

Levitt's concept of 'marketing myopia' behind this quote. In looking for customer 'needs', some organisations mistakenly concentrate only on customer 'wants'.

Needs are something necessary for the maintenance of life at a basic or more evolved level – see Maslow's hierarchy of needs for survival, security, socialisation, success and self-actualisation.

Wants are choices of how that need is to be fulfiled.

Marketing myopia is mistaking wants for needs. Levitt gives example of drill bits which are wanted only until a better way of fulfilling the need for making holes is found.

Although needs are relatively constant, wants are influenced by the environment and individual background. Developments in the technological, socio-cultural, economic and political environment change what is 'wanted' to fulfil a particular 'need'. As these changes happen all the time, today's growth industry is tomorrow's industry in decline.

Levitt's example of the North American railroad which was once an all-powerful industry filling the need for transport and communication until superseded by other industries which developed more convenient, flexible methods of meeting the same need and so became 'wanted' instead.

Criticisms of Levitt such as 'nice theory, which offers no solutions'. What can marketing managers do about industrial cycles largely outside their control? Concern over long-term future of industry can lead to unwise diversification and distraction which hastens decline.

However three principles from the concept of marketing myopia:

1. Customers loyal to capabilities of products to fulfil needs not to products themselves. As they buy benefits not features of a product, marketing campaigns should emphasise key benefits over competitors.

2. Products have limited lifespan before demand shifts to preferred means to the same benefit. Concept of product life cycle of introduction, growth, maturity and decline stages.

3. Organisations restricting themselves to one product or industry therefore limiting own life expectancy as will not be a growth product or industry for ever.

Chapter 5
Question C

An individual is buying a computer for his/her own use at home. An organisation is buying the same product for use in the office. What differences would you expect to find in the buying behaviour of the individual and the organisation in making their decision?

Key Points

Marketing inputs into the buying process may be the same – uncontrollable factors such as social, technological, economic and political influences; controllable marketing factors such as product, price, promotion and place.

But buying influences tend to differ between an individual and an organisation. See 'black box' models.

Individual buying influences include:

1. Social – culture, sub-culture, social class, reference groups and family.

   Example – *reference groups important in computer purchase as can influence basic system preferred (e.g. PC or Macintosh) and types of software as used by acquaintances. Family influence – systems used by husband/wife at work, children at school.*

2. Individual – motivation, personality, self-image, perception, learning (from past experiences), beliefs and attitudes.

   Example – *personality influence on whether buy compulsively on recommendation or after careful shopping around and detailed information search.*

Organisational buying behaviour influenced by decision making unit and type of buying decision.

Decision making unit (DMU) depends on size and culture of organisation. Roles of players within DMU include 'gatekeeper', 'user', 'influencer' and 'decision-maker'.

Types of buying decision classified as straight re-buy, modified re-buy, or new-task decisions.

   Example – *in large bureaucratic organisation, a replacement of existing computers (re-buy, or modified re-buy) may be prescribed by central purchasing authority in which decisions made by committee. In a smaller entrepreneurial organisation, the owner manager may make the choice of computer alone.*

Buying process likely to be more complicated between individual and organisation. Individual process: need recognition, information search, evaluation of alternatives, purchase choice, post purchase experience.

   Example – *because computers are irregular purchase of relatively high value to individual, buyer involvement likely to be high and all stages of the process completed.*

Organisational process: need recognition, general need description, specification of product, search for suppliers, requests for proposals, selection of supplier, specification of terms, performance review.

   Example – *relatively low value of single computer to organisation probably shortens process, e.g. search for supplier and request for proposals not carried out if straight re-buy decision.*

Chapter 6
Question B

You are considering setting up a take-away pizza business. What market research would you require before you make a decision? Present your answer as a market research plan.

Key points

(Note this is one example only. Other plans are also possible, e.g. research into attitudes of target market to take-away food.)

Objectives of research:

To assess level of demand for a take-away pizza restaurant in location X and to evaluate effectiveness of competitive services in meeting demand.

Market to be investigated:

Prime customer groups assumed to be 15–25 year olds and families of adult(s) and dependent children. Product offered is take-away pizza service (collect only).

Measurements to be made:

Value of overall take away purchases of target group. Suppliers currently used. Satisfaction with existing suppliers. Exposure of target groups to local advertising media.

Methods to be used:

Secondary research – Search for national and regional reports on industry including trends in take-away foods, pizza consumption, new food fashions in Mintel, EIU, Key Note reports, etc.

Location of competitive businesses offering either take-away, pizza or both and collection of literature, menus, etc.

Primary research

(i) Quantitative survey of local residents by postal questionnaire with return incentive. Objective – to assess recent take-away and/or pizza purchases, place of purchase and measure level of satisfaction. Target response 200. Sample from Acorn.

(ii) Qualitative research into attitudes to take-away pizza and quality and level of local provision by group discussions. Four groups of about six people each, two groups from youth and two from family market.

Costs and timing:

Approximate budget and time involved for various stages.

Chapter 7
Question B

'Positioning is in the mind of the consumer.' Critically evaluate this statement.

Key Points

'Positioning' is a broad term with many definitions. Originated in packaged goods marketing where 'product positioning' is used to define tangible attributes such as packaging design and price relative to competition.

Now more commonly used to define not product attributes but consumer perceptions or images of product. Consumers think of products and organisations in a certain simplistic way, e.g. as either 'up-market or down-market', 'exclusive', 'traditional' or 'go-ahead'. Such perceptions describe position of product in consumer's mind in relation to competitive products. In this sense positioning is in mind of consumer as it summarises the general impression given by a product to its target customers.

Positioning can happen by chance – word-of-mouth reputation that develops over the years. But also part of deliberate management process, so that not just left to 'mind of customer'. Process involves three stages of segmentation, targeting and positioning:

Segmentation – dividing a market into distinct groups of buyers who require similar products and marketing mixes.

Targeting – measuring the attractiveness of market segments and selecting a preferred market to enter.

Positioning – adopting an appropriate market position which appeals to the selected segment.

Steps in developing a positioning strategy include:

(i) Deciding positions most relevant to market segment and most likely to influence buying habits.

(ii) Evaluating position which the organisation can deliver effectively.

(iii) Communicating selected position through marketing activities.

This implies positioning is about influencing consumers' minds – not only psychologically as the product has to deliver on its promises. Positioning is not 'just a mind game'.

Positioning maps – use in plotting aggregated customer perceptions of competitive products against key criteria.

Chapter 8

Question C

Product portfolio analysis helps an organisation to plan its product strategies. What are the benefits of this? Describe one model that can be used in the process.

Key Points

Product portfolio analysis linked to concept of product life cycle (PLC).

Organisation offering portfolio of products at different stages of life cycle has to consider implications of various stages which for a 'typical' product might be:

Profits – losses in development and introduction stages of PLC, profits in growth and possibility of profits or losses in maturity and decline stages.

Cash – negative in development, introduction and growth stages; positive in maturity and into decline if well managed.

Other resources – more management time required in introduction and growth stages. 'Economies of experience' in maturity and decline.

Implication is need for balanced portfolio of products which complement each other in terms of demands made on resources of organisation, i.e. balance of higher growth, profitable, but cash and time absorbing, products with low growth, less profitable, less time consuming, but cash positive, products.

Portfolio analysis can highlight contributions made by individual products now and in the future to this balance to assess longer-term prospects of organisation.

Competitive positions change also during PLC:

Introduction – low competition; growth – new competitors; maturity and decline – shake out which often favours those with highest market shares who can benefit from economies of scale, buying power, etc. High share not just growth important to long-run success of product.

Example – The Boston Consulting Group growth share matrix considers market share and market growth:

High growth/high share – 'star' which provides high revenues and profits but absorbs cash.

High growth/low share – 'wildcat' which is growing fast but in relatively weak competitive position especially as markets mature.

Low growth/high share – 'cash cow' exploiting strong position in mature market to generate surplus cash for investment elsewhere.

Low growth/low share – 'dog' draining resources because of poor position in unattractive market.

In more complicated models other criteria are used for market attractiveness (in addition to growth) and competitive position (in addition to share), e.g. the General Electric multifactor portfolio model.

Such analysis assists product investment decisions by highlighting products justifying more investment (high market attractiveness/competitive position), those requiring selective management (medium market attractiveness/competitive position), and those in need of 'harvesting' or divestment (low market attractiveness/competitive position).

Chapter 9

Question B

Price is the only element of the marketing mix to produce revenue, all the others add costs. What are the major pricing strategies? When should each be used? Illustrate your answer with relevant examples.

Key Points

Two generic pricing strategies are:

Skimming – high price strategy to 'skim the cream' off the market; and

Penetration – lower price strategy to penetrate the market as thoroughly as possible.

Skimming

Price skimming aims to develop a market by attracting the least price sensitive segment of customers first and satisfying their demand with high prices until demand begins to fall or further growth is required. Then prices are lowered to attract the next segment of customers who are attracted at slightly cheaper prices. Process can be repeated until all potential markets are satisfied, although competition may hasten the development of sales to new customer groups at lower prices.

> **Example** – first personal computers developed by Apple and later IBM (and more recently Dell) targeted at business applications with prices companies could afford. As the only comparison was with bigger, more expensive computers there was little price resistance among larger companies who were the first to see the potential of PCs. As prices were gradually lowered, smaller businesses also became interested in the benefits versus the costs of the new equipment. New entrants into the market such as Sinclair and Amstrad forced the pace by cutting prices so dramatically that a much wider home computer market was opened up.

Price skimming strategies can be used in following circumstances:

(i) Introduction of new products which have unique advantages (electronic innovations such as PCs). High initial prices may be needed to recover the investment in research and development, and the best time to do this may be when competition is likely to be at a minimum.

(ii) Mature or saturated markets which can be segmented with differentiated products or services. The travel industry is now well developed with distinct pricing strategies for different customer segments such as business and tourist. British Rail also increased their revenues by charging premium prices for Inter-City and peak hour commuter travel.

(iii) Suppliers with limited resources who wish to maximise revenues from the capacity they have. This might apply particularly to smaller organisations with limited resources or desire to expand. Also to publishers of limited edition prints.

(iv) Need for exclusive image from status of higher prices and limited availability, such as designer label clothes.

Penetration

Pricing to achieve market penetration involves keeping prices as low as possible to achieve highest potential level of sales. This may be achieved by taking market share from competitors, or rapidly growing the total market, or a combination of both.

Some new products need to develop rapidly into their marketplace to consolidate their position before competitive products arrive and to achieve economies of scale through larger production volumes. Amstrad regularly use this strategy for their new products such as their combined fax/answering machine.

Also used as a strategy to improve the competitive position of existing products.

Example – Rupert Murdoch, chairman of News International believed that the decline in readership of tabloid newspapers such as their paper the *Sun* was partly in reaction to the cover price of papers which had increased by an average of 11 per cent a year since 1983. The industry had believed hitherto that sales of newspapers were price-inelastic and regularly increased prices above the rate of inflation. However, Murdoch felt that the market had become price sensitive and decided to cut the cover price of the *Sun* from 25p to 20p in an attempt to win back lost readers. The strategy had two aims: to improve circulation figures for the total market and to gain market share from the other tabloids. Murdoch at least proved that newspaper sales are price sensitive: the *Sun* gained daily sales of 200,000 in the first week at its lower price, although his strategy sparked off a price war in the industry.

Circumstances in which market penetration can be used include:

(i)   Markets in which demand is price elastic. There is no point in offering lower prices if demand is unaffected (which was the collective wisdom of the newspaper industry before Murdoch launched his price war).

(ii) Industries which offer economies of scale to the largest producers or suppliers. The large retail chains and supermarkets look for this benefit when offering low prices as they know that they can replace lost margin by spreading their fixed costs over higher volumes of sales.

(iii) Launch of new products where rapid adoption and awareness is a key marketing goal. This may apply, for example, to products expected to enjoy a market advantage for a limited period only.

(iv) In markets dominated by a small number of major suppliers (oligopolies). Price wars are often the trigger to the elimination of weaker suppliers with subsequent gain in market share by the survivors. There were two loss-making titles among the tabloid press, *Today* and *The Star*, both candidates to assist other papers increase their circulation by becoming the casualties in any prolonged price war.

(v) To deter new entrants into the market by making profit margins very slim.

Chapter 10

Question B

What are the advantages and disadvantages of personal selling compared to other elements in the promotional mix?

Key Points

Personal selling has general advantages and disadvantages compared to the other elements of advertising, sales promotion and PR in the promotional mix. It has the advantage of face to face contact with the buyer. This allows for immediate, two-way communications in which the seller can find out the individual circumstances and needs of the buyer and respond to them. Other forms of promotions are impersonal, unable to respond as directly and immediately to customer needs. Personal selling can achieve immediate action as orders can be agreed at the time of a sales presentation. Other promotional activities are likely to experience delays between the promotional communication and order taking. However personal presentation of a product is expensive and time consuming. It is resource intensive and cannot reach as many of the target customer audience as quickly as other methods. It is also less controllable as it relies on the individual expertise and integrity of the salesperson.

Specific advantages and disadvantages are conditioned by the type of purchase, the objective of the communication process and the product life cycle.

Type of purchase

In general, personal methods of promoting such as personal selling and exhibitions are more suited to communicating to markets made up of a relatively small number of large customers. Conversely, impersonal methods of communicating are more appropriate to promoting to a large number of relatively small buyers. A complex, infrequent purchase is more likely to need personal attention than a simple, frequently made one.

This means that the order of preference of promotional methods changes particularly between industrial and consumer markets. In consumer markets, advertising and sales promotions receive most resources followed by personal selling and public relations. In industrial markets, personal selling is the most used method followed by sales promotions, advertising and public relations in that order.

Objective of the communication process

The buying process has a number of stages. In consumer markets these have been classified as: need recognition, information search, evaluation of alternatives, purchase choice and post-purchase experience. During this deliberate or unconscious process that customers go through in making buying decisions, they adopt various attitudes, or they are in various states of mind, in relation to products on offer. It is the job of marketing communications and the promotional mix to influence these attitudes or states of mind so that the customer completes the process in favour of a particular product. As this state of mind changes through the buying stages, so the nature and objectives of promotions change to match. The AIDA model has been advanced to illustrate these changing objectives as the consumer progresses from a position of unawareness of a product to one of willingness to purchase it. Promotions seek first to gain Attention (an awareness of the benefits of a product), secondly to create Interest (by an understanding of those benefits in relation to a personal need), thirdly to arouse Desire (when the benefits are wanted to fulfil a need), and finally to obtain Action (by arranging for the customer to acquire the product). When awareness of a product is low, communications need to gain attention and advertising and public relations are often the most effective at this stage. PR and sales promotions are widely used to generate interest in a product as well as advertising. When awareness and

399

understanding of the benefits on offer is higher, sales promotions and personal selling are the more effective methods to increase desire, whilst some form of personal selling is normally required to complete the necessary action to make a purchase.

Product Life Cycle

The stage a product has reached in its life cycle also influences the relative merits of promotional methods.

In the introduction stage, personal selling is important to introduce the product to the trade even for consumer products. Advertising and public relations are used to generate awareness and understanding of the product. Sales promotions are used to attract the 'early adopters' to try the product. In the growth stage, sales promotions and selling may be less needed as advertising and PR maintain the momentum. In the maturity stage, the product is usually well known so that the level of advertising may be cut back with more reliance on sales promotions to provide a stimulus to sales. In the decline stage, whilst sales promotions may still be used to prop up sales, expenditure on other forms of promotion is usually reduced to a minimum.

> Example – These various influences on the composition of the promotion mix can be seen at work in the launch and subsequent management of new products. For example, a large company launched a new brand of toothpaste. A special conference trained and motivated the company's own salesforce to introduce the product into the toiletries trade so that it received good display and shelf space particularly in the large multiple retailers. A TV advertising campaign attracted the attention and interest of the target buyer groups. Free samples and discount coupons, some given away by company representatives during in-store promotions, introduced customers to the product. Press releases told the story of the new product to the trade and national press. The strong growth and continued national advertising of the toothpaste maintained the retail trade's interest in stocking the product, so the level of selling activity was reduced as the brand achieved its market share targets. When growth slackened to mirror the maturity of the total market, the company cut back on their advertising budget in order to maximise profits from the product. Market research revealed a high level of consumer recognition and acceptance of the brand so, as sales peaked, promotional activity concentrated on coupon offers and competitions to win free holidays as a means of stimulating demand.

Chapter 12

Question C

What is franchising? How might a producer benefit by using it as a method of distribution?

Key Points

Franchising is a business arrangement in which one party (the franchisor) allows others (the franchisees) to use a business name, or sell products in such a way that the franchisee can still operate as a legally separate business. It can mean as little as an agreement to sell a company's products in a specific territory or as much as a complete business package specified by the franchisors. It is this latter type of so-called 'business format franchising' which has today become common in some industries such as fast food (Kentucky Fried Chicken, Burger King, Pizza Hut, McDonald's) and instant print (KallKwik, Prontaprint).

However product and trademark franchise agreements still provide producers with several benefits. By making agreements to distribute their products through licenced dealers, manufacturers created a wider market for their products whilst still controlling the distribution. Breweries were probably the first franchisors when they introduced the system which 'tied' otherwise independent publicans to one producer of beer. Car manufacturers and oil companies developed the distribution of their products through various licensing arrangements under which a local dealer or distributor took responsibility for sales in a certain territory in return for some element of profit. The producers developed their products and the goodwill associated with the trade marks; the local distributor contributed local knowledge, contacts, effort, and usually some investment. Such distribution arrangements are still common, in the soft drinks industry for example.

Manufacturing processes are also distributed in this way. If the inventor of a patented process wishes to exploit their innovation on a wider basis than their resources allow, they may permit other manufacturers to use the process under licence in return for a royalty. Alistaire Pilkington's invention of 'float glass' enabled his company to manufacture a distortion-free glass at low cost to replace cheap but optically imperfect 'sheet' glass or expensive, hand polished 'plate' glass. The size and fragility of the product favour local manufacture, and as Pilkington did not wish to set up manufacturing plants all around the world, he 'distributed' the concept by licensing other manufacturers to use the new system.

Intangible assets such as well-known names and celebrities are also franchised to reach a wider public. Products are endorsed by fictional characters or real people under licencing agreements specifying how the name or image may be used and what royalties are payable for the privilege.

Franchisor and franchisee may enter a more comprehensive relationship than a simple trade mark or licencing arrangement. 'Business format franchising' goes beyond the supply of products and trade names to cover many more aspects of how a business is run. Franchisors offer a complete package allowing the franchisee to use a format which has been developed and proven commercially whilst retaining legal independence. The business format offered by the franchisor may cover many aspects including:

❑ trade name, business style, logo, house colours

❑ detailed product or service specification

❑ training and help to set up and ongoing advice on running the business

❑ national and local marketing

❑ centralised purchasing or supply of products

❑ management control and operating systems

❑ research and development of new products and processes.

In return the franchisee pays the franchisor defined amounts of money which usually include:

(i) An initial franchise fee as a one off payment to the franchisor to cover the goodwill of the name and training. This can vary from £1000 (e.g. for a Unigate Dairies milk round) to £25,000 or more (e.g. a Burger King franchise).

(ii) Annual charges or fees. An ongoing service fee is charged, often as a percentage of sales (typically 5 to 15 per cent of invoiced sales value). Other levies on the franchisee include contributions to national advertising and training for staff.

In addition the franchisee has to meet the normal costs of setting up and running the business including the costs of buying equipment, fitting out premises, stock, promotional literature and stationery, although many of these items are specified by the franchisor. The total minimum start up investment for franchises vary enormously depending on the value of the name and the nature of the business (for example £4500 for Unigate Dairies and £700,000 for Burger King).

A franchise agreement sets out the obligations of both parties including how the franchisee is to run the business, what payments they make and what the franchisor will provide in return.

In the USA format franchising now accounts for one third of all retail sales. In the UK, franchising is less significant but it is a fast growing sector. Sales in 1999 were around £9 billion, or 5 per cent of total retail sales, made through 30,000 franchised outlets operated by over 600 franchisors.

Benefits to producers of using franchising as a distribution method include:

(i) The ability to extend the distribution of products or concepts quickly. As expansion is funded mainly by the franchisees, less capital is required from the franchisor.

(ii) The recruitment and retention of committed managers who as franchisees have the additional motivation of business ownership.

(iii) More control over outlets than totally independent distribution channels.

However, there are disadvantages for franchisors including less control over franchisees than fully owned outlets and the continuous obligation to provide central support services even if the franchisor wishes to exit from the business.

INDEX